The Social Democratic Movement in Prewar Japan

Volume I of

STUDIES ON JAPAN'S SOCIAL DEMOCRATIC PARTIES

New Haven and London, Yale University Press, 1966

GEORGE OAKLEY TOTTEN, III

THE SOCIAL DEMOCRATIC
MOVEMENT
IN PREWAR JAPAN

戦前日本の社会民主主義運動

Copyright © 1966 by Yale University.
Designed by Arthur G. Beckenstein,
set in Baskerville type,
and printed in the United States of America by
the Vail-Ballou Press, Inc., Binghamton, N.Y.
Distributed in Canada by McGill University Press.
All rights reserved. This book may not be
reproduced, in whole or in part, in any form
(except by reviewers for the public press),
without written permission from the publishers.
Library of Congress catalog card number: 66-12515
Published with assistance from the foundation established
in memory of William McKean Brown.

*This book is affectionately dedicated
to my wife, Astrid Maria, who shared all too deeply
in the travail of its creation,*

*To my daughters, Vicken Yuriko and Linnea Catherine,
who grew up in the meantime, unconcerned, and*

*To my deceased father, on the hundredth anniversary of his birth,
who dedicated his* Maya Architecture *to my brother and me.*

Preface

The rise and fall of social democracy in prewar Japan has many of the elements of Greek tragedy. It entered the political stage in the 1920s full of hope and determination. Messages of encouragement came from home and abroad. But already discordant notes of reaction could be heard in the background chorus. The fates seemed to be set against it.

The movement overcame great environmental obstacles in coming into existence. In fact, it achieved its greatest numerical successes in 1936–37 just as foreign and domestic events began to proclaim its doom. It tried to save itself by an anguished denial of its own birthright as a protest movement. Too late did it perceive that national planning and reform, when done in the name of a "holy war" that was fundamentally imperialistic, would hardly produce socialism, much less democracy.

Unlike an individual hero, however, a movement can come back to life again and rise from its own ashes. The socialists did reorganize after the surrender of 1945, rise to quick prominence, decline, and then gradually grow again on a firm base. This time the feeling is that they will inevitably reach power, a goal that has sometimes loomed close at hand only to recede frustratingly into the future again.

New freedoms have come to Japan and new world alignments have formed, but many of the structural factors of the socioeconomy that hindered the movement in pre-World War I days have carried over. Subjectively the movement has been conditioned by its prewar experiences. The very reactions of its veteran leaders are fully understandable only in the light, or should we say the shadows, of the specters of prewar days.

This study attempts to analyze the characteristics of that prewar movement, not simply as a forerunner for understanding the main opposition in Japanese politics today, but also as a movement significant in and of itself. It exhibited behavioral characteristics important for the comparative study of politics, repeating patterns common to similar movements in other countries but with variations peculiarly Japanese. At the same time an understanding of its role is essential in comprehending the process of modernization in Japan.

What is meant by the "social democratic movement" in this study are principally the noncommunist proletarian parties that existed in Japan from 1925 to 1940. But beyond that, it extends to the labor, agrarian, social, national minority, and other movements that supported these parties during and between the local and national elections. Without adhering to an overly pedantic consistency, the term "socialist" has been used broadly to cover the social democratic, communist, anarchist, and even national socialist movements and more particularly the stem movement that began to take form in the mid-1890s and out of which the others proliferated. Alternate terms for "socialist" as used here might be "social" or "proletarian." Communist with a capital "C" is here reserved specifically to denote members of the Japanese Communist Party and those directly under its guidance.

While "social democratic" as employed in this study does not encompass the Comintern-recognized Japanese Communists, it no more excludes "Marxists" than does the term in the interwar German context. In the Japanese case, a clear decision had to be made by proletarian party leaders as to whether they intended to operate within the narrow confines of permitted political liberty—not without continually testing them, of course—or whether they sought to alter the "emperor system" directly, thus subjecting themselves, if caught, to the indictment of lèse-majesté. This study focuses on the legal, reformist parties which sought to champion the interests of the propertyless or proletarian classes, whether labor, agrarian, or other. This whole study in a sense constitutes a definition of social democracy in the prewar Japanese context.

The basic problems are posed in Part I: How did the social democratic movement come into being in Japan? How hospitable was the Japanese economic and sociopolitical environment? What antecedents pointed the way for the growth of social democracy and directed the tradition it was to inherit? What was the process which differentiated the organized Communist movement from what became the various elements of the social democratic—whether Marxist, Fabian, Christian, or other? And, finally, what events and rationalizations pressured the proletarian party leaders to disavow to such an extent many of the tenets of their earlier beliefs?

Part II is devoted to leadership. What kinds of persons came to be leaders of various strands of the noncommunist proletarian movement? Further, how did the various leadership factions differ from one another on the criteria of recruitment, age, education, and other background factors? My research has indicated that the key to understanding the continuity behind the kaleidoscopic changes is factional cohesiveness and persistence.

Building on this, Part III delves into what the social democrats implicitly thought the function of proletarian parties to be. What classes did they intend to represent? What kinds of parliamentary and extraparliamentary struggles did they engage in? What kinds of policies did they propose for domestic reform and for Japanese diplomacy—as well as for their own international contacts? In responding to changing times, what threads of policy continuity were discernible?

Part IV treats the question of electoral and organized support. Previous studies have not given much attention to the large social democratic successes in the elections of 1936 and 1937 nor attempted to account for them, assuming that the revolutionary élan was already dead. Here the intricate skeins of organized support have been untangled in order to lay bare the factional continuity behind the bewildering number of formal organizational transformations. In this connection, attention has also been allocated to the role of women in the social movement and the degrees of involvement in it of the organized minority group of former *Eta* outcastes and of the Korean workers residing in Japan.

In the concluding chapter, the overall characteristics of the social democratic movement and its role in the Japanese milieu are set forth in a manner intended to facilitate comparative use of this knowledge. This has involved interpretations of the roles of the movement as a whole and its various subsections. Since so little of the material on which these interpretations were based had hitherto appeared in English, it was felt that including it here would be helpful to others. The questions specifically dealt with include: To what degree was the social democratic movement a foreign import? From what social elements were leadership and support drawn? And what ideological functions did the social democratic strand perform in the socialist movement as a whole?

This investigation does not claim to be all-inclusive. By intention the cultural arena of proletarian art, literature, and criticism has been considered entirely peripheral. A more detailed study of social democratic ideology has been reserved for later publication. The Communist movement and the national socialists have been dealt with only insofar as necessary to clarify the role and limits of the social democrats. Awareness of the history of modern Japan has been assumed as background. This book has been thought of as a pioneer study that will hopefully open the way to a series of more detailed monographs. With the groundwork laid out, they may fall into place the more easily.

Yet no matter how much needs to be done hereafter, and despite the limitations of this study, the subject opened up here deserves consideration by any serious student of twentieth-century Japan or any scholar concerned with the comparative study of social movements in the process of modernization.

This study was made possible by the generous help of various institutions, foundations, and individuals both in this country and in Japan. Essentially this is the first of a two-volume study of Japanese socialism and as such is one of the fruits of "Studies on Japan's Social Democratic Parties," a project on which I have had two major collaborators, Allan Burnett Cole and Cecil Hideo Uyehara. Volume 2, entitled *Socialist Parties in Postwar Japan,* was coauthored by the three of us, with one chapter contributed by Ronald P. Dore; it is also being published by Yale University Press. The project was sponsored by The Fletcher School of Law and Diplomacy, with the encouragement of Dean Robert Burgess Stewart, and supported by grants from the Ford Foundation under the care of Mr. John Scott Everton and Mr. Cleon Swayzee.

The Japanese-material bibliographical section of the project has already been published as *Left-wing Social Movements in Japan: An*

Annotated Bibliography by Cecil H. Uyehara (Tōkyō, Japan, and Rutland, Vermont, The Charles E. Tuttle Company, 1959). This has obviated the need for appending a special bibliography to the present study, because in that work most of the Japanese materials used are included, except for some more recent secondary materials. These and most of the Western language materials are cited in full in the footnotes to the present volume.

As an aid to those who may wish to use this volume as a reference, I am including, in the index, Romanizations of the Japanese for almost all proletarian organization names, as well as laws and regulations, cited. The Appendices are also designed to help establish names and dates of certain organizations and individuals; but only those people who work with the original materials will fully understand the problems, and in some cases impossibility, of final verifications.

This volume was also made possible by earlier assistance, inasmuch as I utilized part of my doctoral dissertation, largely in condensed form, for certain sections of the present study. Thanks in part to Mr. Elbridge Sibley, an Area Research Training Fellowship from the Social Science Research Council enabled me to spend a year in Japan consulting numerous Japanese scholars and participants in the social movements and working on primary sources available only in Japan.

My most heartfelt thanks go to Professor Chitoshi Yanaga of Yale University for the time he has unstintingly given in both criticism and encouragement. I am grateful to Professor David N. Rowe, also of Yale University, for his prodding and his advice to keep the subject matter within the bounds of manageability. Among those I wish particularly to thank for reading and commenting on the entire manuscript are Professor Masao Maruyama of Tōkyō University, Professor Iwao Ayusawa of International Christian University, Professor Ronald P. Dore of the London School of Economics and Political Science, Professor Robert S. Cohen of Boston University, Professor Albert Craig of Harvard University, and Professor Tamio Kawakami, now of Tōkai University; and for going over sections of the manuscript I am grateful to Professor Kazuo Ōkōchi, now President of Tōkyō University, and Professor Shinkichi Etō, also of Tōkyō University.

Of those associated with our project, I am most indebted to my main collaborators, Allan Cole and Cecil Uyehara, for sharing their knowledge, insights, and accumulated materials and for their thoughtful consideration and generosity throughout the project, and for a shorter period, to Ronald Dore. In addition, I want to express my sincere appreciation here to the three official advisors to our project: Dr. Yanaga, Dr. Masamichi Rōyama, now of International Christian University, and Dr. Edwin O. Reischauer, now American Ambassador to Japan, for their time and effort on my behalf. And finally I want to acknowledge the valuable assistance of Seiichi Izumi, a freelance author, translator, and scholar in Tōkyō, Michio Rōyama, now a director at the International House of Japan, and Masao Yoshida, now at Tōkyō University, all of whom contributed to making the project a real success.

I am grateful to Mr. Tarō Yashima, whose book, *The New Sun* (New York, Henry Holt and Company, 1943), was a kind of distant or original inspiration for my study. I came across it while at Military Intelligence Japanese Language School during the war.

I must also mention the special assistance given me by the librarians at Yale (especially Mr. Tsuneishi), Harvard (Mr. K'ai-Ming Ch'u), Columbia (Miss Kai, Mr. Linton, and Mr. Yampolsky), The Fletcher School, Stanford, the Library of Congress (Mr. Kuroda and Mr. Beal), the Tōkyō and Kyōtō University libraries, the Tōkyō Institute of Municipal Research (especially Mr. Sadayoshi Tanabe), and several others; my thanks to them all.

And finally I would like to thank the very fine people at Yale University Press who have been so helpful: Miss Ruth L. Davis, Mr. David Horne, and Mr. Arthur Beckenstein.

Actually it is impossible in this space to list all the people who have been of help, nor would it be possible for me here to express adequately the depth of my gratitude to them; however, I still must mention the one most important of all, my wife.

No matter what help I have received, however, all responsibility for the acceptance or rejection of "fact," interpretations, or criticisms is entirely my own, and my views as expressed in this book are not necessarily those of any of the other persons or institutions connected with its conception, research, support, or publication.

George O. Totten

Tallringen
Peace Dale, R. I.
August 1965

Contents

ELECTORAL AND ORGANIZED SUPPORT

CONCLUSION

APPENDICES

Environment and History

1: The Inhospitable Environment

That the Japanese social democratic movement was able to send even a half dozen Representatives to the Imperial Diet in the late 1920s was an achievement of no mean proportions considering how inhospitable was the political, economic, and social environment of contemporary Japan. That was the culmination of an uphill fight of three decades in which labor, tenant farmers, and others banded together for collective action in their own behalf. In the light of European experience, it can be argued that this was only a natural concomitant of industrialization. Yet considering the rapidity of Japan's modernization in other respects, the growth of social democracy in presurrender Japan was retarded.

Perhaps a traditional culture undergoing modernization at a forced pace cannot afford to give much consideration to the welfare of the peasants and their brethren who had begun to toil in the burgeoning nonagricultural sectors of the economy. That appeared to be true at least in Japan where the transition of power from the old to the new power elite was effectuated with a remarkable minimum of conflict, where government and business leadership sprang largely from the same samurai stock, and where a fear of possible foreign encroachment heightened feelings of national solidarity.

While bringing power and wealth to the ruling elite, industrialization was hardly an unmixed blessing to those who responded to the lure of city, factory, and mine. The increasing tempo of instability of prices and jobs could not help but suggest the possibility of remedial self-help through collective action and organization. Knowledge of foreign examples stimulated trade union organization and later farmers' groups. Led by intellectuals who were more sensitive to the distinctions among foreign ideas, politically oriented groups coalesced. All these activities in response to the new conditions created by the introduction of capitalism were called "social movements" (*shakai undō*).[1] The social democratic movement was only one; others included the labor, agrarian, student, feminist, and outcast minority movements as well as the politically motivated socialist, anarchist, and eventually communist. They all shared the same roots.

These roots reached into the Meiji Restoration of 1868, led and later consolidated by an elite which differed from the preceding Tokugawa power holders in that it understood the necessity for change. The feudal economic order was replaced by private ownership in land and in other means of production. Legal restrictions barring the accumulation of wealth by the most enterprising were swept away. Gradually new class divisions formed in the countryside, among which were landowners resentful of the high land taxes the government had instituted in order to build its own power and pay for its own initiatives in industrialization. But the danger of discontent among the rapidly growing class of tenant farmers soon convinced them that their interests lay in supporting a strong central government which could put down uprisings and safeguard private property rather than in undermining and limiting the powers of Tōkyō which were increasingly exercised in the name of that mystical embodiment of national authority, the Emperor.

Nourished by the wars of 1894–95, 1904–05, and 1914–18, industrialization enveloped the great cities and ports and spread into the mines, forests, and small shops of the countryside, but it did so in

1. For a good explanation of this term, see Heibonsha, ed., *Dai Hyakka Jiten* (The Great Encyclopedia Dictionary) (Tōkyō, Heibonsha, 1932) *12*, 142–43. For the European origin of this term and its use in English, see Rudolf Heberle, *Social Movements* (New York, Appleton-Century-Crofts, 1951), pp. 4–6. The classical German definition of the term corresponds most closely to present-day Japanese usage, and that has been followed in this study.

spurts and in an uneven fashion. While small enterprises mush-roomed, giant enterprises towered over them without an intervening middle range of business. Cartelization thrived in the higher reaches of the economy, while cutthroat competition characterized small business. This hindered the development of open, horizontal labor markets, thwarting the rise of trade unionism. Recruitment followed vertical lines of personal contact, sustaining traditional familialism. The very backwardness of the agricultural sector rendered it a reser-voir of cheap labor as well as a sponge to absorb the unemployed in times of depression. Because unemployment was thus not actually a matter of life and death to those involved, it could the more easily be disregarded by both government and management. Closely linked with these political and economic conditions, social patterns of feudal behavior persisted, exaggerating both deference and resistance in class relations. All of these aspects of the unfriendly environment left their particular marks on the infant social movements.

POLITICAL RESTRICTIONS

The most obviously restrictive aspect of the environment was the lack of political freedom. Unlike the French Revolution of 1789, the Meiji Restoration was not accompanied by a ringing declaration of the Rights of Man. It is true, however, that within the first decade an incipiently democratic movement did arise which attacked the gov-ernment in the name of "freedom and people's rights." But its ex-samurai leaders soon divided among themselves, compromised with the government, and gave up their militancy in return for the prom-ise of a Constitution to be bestowed upon the people by 1889. The mass basis for middle-class democracy was missing.

The political liberties stipulated in the Meiji Constitution were not really "guaranteed." They could be easily suspended by the gov-ernment through laws and administrative regulations. When the first Japanese industrial workers began to appear in the 1890s, they found themselves in much the same position as their German counterparts decades earlier, in conflict not only with management for better wages and working conditions but also with governmental authori-ties for the rights of free speech, assembly, and organization. No democratic tradition restrained the bureaucracy from forcibly sup-pressing activity that appeared to disrupt the prevailing calm of the obedient populace. The authoritarian attitudes, thus maintained, stunted the growth of the social movements and in fact tended to bring out undemocratic tendencies within them. Extremism was more appealing when there was little chance to work for social change within the narrow context of legality. Factionalism in the various movements promoted personal loyalty and insincere ideological compromises among factions at the expense of vigorous free discussion.

The numerous suppressive laws and regulations prior to 1900 had been largely directed against the "freedom and people's rights" movement, but by 1898 its leaders had attained political respectability as cabinet members and raised no protest against enactment of the Peace Police Law of 1900 whose Article 17 in effect forbade labor organization and strike activity. Still, that law did not ameliorate the conditions which led inexorably to an increasing frequency of strikes and disputes. Workers' mutual aid groups formed, and by the end of World War I many had in fact become trade unions with enough strength to make the law unenforceable in the strict sense. Political campaigns directed toward its repeal were necessarily accompanied by demands that the restrictive franchise be extended to include the working classes. Universal manhood suffrage was granted in 1925 and Article 17 repealed in 1926, but the circumstances at the time did not give much latitude to political and economic liberties.

In the same year that the suffrage was extended, a drastic and vaguely worded antisubversive act went into effect. Called the Peace Preservation Law, it prohibited activities that would change the "system of private property" or alter the "national polity." Purportedly aimed at Communists, its scope was broadened in practice. In addition, other early statutes remained on the books—such as the 1890 Administrative Enforcement Law, the 1908 Ordinance Concerning Punishment of Police Offenses, and certain prefectural police regulations. Numerous other ordinances were enforced in such a way as to control labor activity: for instance, those covering obstruction of administrative affairs, disturbances of the peace, hindrance of traffic, trespassing, calumny, violence, intimidation, and slander against a person's honor or the reputation of a business.

The repeal of Article 17, nevertheless, made it possible in 1926 to pass the Labor Disputes Conciliation Law. Ironically, its seemingly democratic provision for a tripartite conciliation commission was hardly ever invoked, whereas the government and local police continually interfered in disputes in accordance with other provisions of the act.[2] In fact, experience gained by them led to their later role in the Industrial Patriotic Movement (Sampō) through which labor–capital relations were controlled during the Pacific War.

The Japanese government's oppressive legislation against labor, which began at the turn of the century, meant that labor was deprived of legal means for bettering its conditions. If the government had embarked upon a program of paternalistic social legislation to protect labor from excessive abuse and to ameliorate working conditions, it might have been less necessary for labor to try to organize and support a political movement. Bismarck attempted to do just this, but the Japanese government did not. Only in 1911 was the Factory Act—the first important law for the protection of workers—passed.[3] It was not put into force until 1916, and even then was not applicable to the mass of smaller shops and factories.[4] With Japan's increasing military involvement in Manchuria and China in the 1930s, social legislation again became an issue. This was motivated not by concern for the poor working conditions of labor but rather by shock at the discovery of the inferior physical condition of recruits for the Imperial Army. Several slightly ameliorative laws resulted, including one providing social insurance.[5]

Although state oppression of the labor and socialist movements never disappeared in prewar Japan, it was not always of the same degree or kind. While the early ban against labor organization gave

2. Izutarō Suehiro, *Nihon Rōdō Kumiai Undō Shi* (A History of the Japanese Labor Union Movement) (Tōkyō, Kyōdō Tsūshinsha, 1950), p. 69.

3. The Factory Act (*Kōjō Hō*) applied only to workers in factories employing over 15 persons or to those engaged in dangerous tasks. Most of the protective legislation applied only to women and youths. Some provision was also made for maternity protection and factory inspection. For a discussion of the Act, see International Labour Office, *Industrial Labour in Japan,* Studies and Reports, Series A (Industrial Relations), 37 (Geneva, International Labour Office, 1933), p. 138 and passim.

4. The enforcement of this law had been put off because factories did not make the necessary preparations for its enforcement mainly for three reasons: (1) a depression followed by World War I, (2) the rapid change of cabinets, and (3) the fears generated by the Kōtoku Trial of 1910–11. Yasoji Kazahaya, *Nihon Shakai Seisaku Shi* (A History of Japanese Social Policy) (2d ed. Tōkyō, Aoki Shoten, 1952), *1,* 188–90.

5. These remedial laws were intended not only to improve the physical condition of army recruits but also probably to serve as indications to workers and farmers that cooperation with the rising military would more effectively counteract the influence of capitalists and result in reforms than heeding social democratic and other labor and agrarian leaders.

way before the economic facts of life and the rise of liberal ideas after World War I, the greater suppression of labor than of socialist groups had by then already led to an intellectualization of the socialist movement that kept it like a sect isolated from the workers. The conditions of the immediate post-World War I period enabled the labor and socialist causes to amalgamate into a compound movement. The government responded to this situation with a new policy of suppressing the radical and encouraging the reformist elements, thus providing a legal, albeit a narrow, basis for the development of social democracy.

Japan's increased military commitments on the mainland, however, necessitated greater control over labor. This led to governmental suppression of the last of the left wing represented by the non-communist popular front in 1937 and to the awarding of semiofficial posts in the early 1940s to those social democrats who cooperated with the government. There were no such rewards for the mass of workers who constituted the backbone of the home-front war effort. Governmental control reached its peak during the Pacific War with the introduction of compulsory manpower allocations. Agitation in the interests of labor had long since become impossible.

ECONOMIC UNEVENNESS

The lack of political rights alone is nevertheless insufficient to explain the limited growth of the labor and socialist movements in Japan. Roughly similar conditions prevailed in Germany at the end of the last century, yet the growth of German social democracy was phenomenal. The explanation of Japanese backwardness must also be sought in other economic and social factors, perhaps the most outstanding of which was the uneven economic development between agriculture and industry.

The land program of the Meiji Restoration, despite the abolition of feudal rights and duties with regard to agricultural holdings and the recognition of private property in land, imposed a land tax—payable only in money and never varying with crop or market conditions—which soon forced many of the liberated peasants into a condition of partial or complete tenantry on the land they had so recently and briefly owned. Through tireless industry others retained possession of tiny plots, although they, too, could not escape the moneylender. Those who prospered seldom did so by farming alone. The early Meiji government had to rely heavily on land taxes in order to finance political centralization and the construction of key industries. This left little capital available in the countryside for large-scale capitalistic agriculture.

The peasants were never expelled from the land en masse; they were only siphoned off as needed for nonagricultural work. In 1920, for instance, of the gainfully employed population in Japan, 50 per cent were engaged in agriculture, whereas only 19.7 per cent were in industry. Because of the instability of economic conditions and low wages, the workers could not afford to break their ties with the village. In the cities power-driven machines both large and small became prevalent, but on the farms agricultural methods remained unmechanized, dependent on labor-intensive hand tools. To keep from starvation, the farming population was forced either to engage in subsidiary industry in the village, or to send members of the family away to work in the cities, or both.[6]

The size of the stabilized working population remained exceedingly small, and this severely limited the organized support for the labor and socialist movements regardless of how tolerant or hostile the government was. It also meant that in order for a political labor movement to be strong it would have to have the support of votes from the agricultural villages, particularly the tenant farmers, and even in urban areas would have to address itself to those who were laborers only temporarily.

A sharp disproportion in economic development grew up not only between agriculture and industry but also within industry itself, and could be seen in the uneven development between light and heavy industry (such as between textiles and machine tools), between government-managed and private industry, and between the giant monopolies and the innumerable small enterprises. These unbalanced developments deeply affected the character of the Japanese social democratic movement.

The disproportionate development between light and heavy industry can be illustrated by the growth of the textile industry, which,

6. Temporarily working away from home to help supplement the household income is called "dekasegi" in Japanese. Professor Ōkōchi of Tōkyō University argues that it is characteristic of almost all labor in Japan. Kazuo Ōkōchi, Reimeiki no Nihon Rōdō Undō (The Dawn of the Japanese Labor Movement) (Tōkyō, Iwanami Shoten, 1952), pp. 4–7.

soon after the turn of the century, came to be the largest employer of labor in Japan. In 1929 the cotton and silk spinning and weaving industries alone claimed 54.7 per cent of all factory workers. In comparison, the number of workers in the metal and machine tool industries was low. In 1929 their number (281,093) was only 28 per cent of the number of textile workers (997,690).

The extremely small size of most factories was yet another factor that made labor organization difficult. In 1935 the number of workers in establishments employing five or less workers was 1.5 times as great as the number employing more than five.[7] Instead of disappearing in the process of competition with larger, better-run enterprises, these small factories were able to survive through a system of subcontracts, which created a hierarchy of echelons with the zaibatsu on top. Each subordinate level had a lower margin of profit and an inferior bargaining position. The uneven development of industry is also evident in the large public sector of the economy devoted to military and naval work. Militant unions were impossible here.

A peculiar feature of the structure of Japanese labor derived from the singularly high proportion of female workers, attributable to the early rise of the textile industry, equipped with machinery that women could run. With greater diversification their proportion decreased, but even at the outbreak of World War I women constituted some 60 per cent of the work force. The proportion was not reversed until about 1937. Many of the female textile workers were transient in the sense that their fathers would contract them out to work in the mills for two or three years, after which they would return home to marry. Living in dormitories, most were subject to strict management paternalism. Such conditions were hardly conducive to trade union militancy or political involvement.

With primogeniture still practiced widely, the male work force was largely recruited from the younger sons of farming families. Psychologically they felt that "home" remained in the countryside, where they would be received again when industrial depressions occurred or when strikes failed.[8] This did not mean that their goal was to earn enough money to retire in the countryside. They intended to "make a go of it" in the city. But the fact that they could expect help

7. The total number of workers in Japan in 1935 was some 5,900,000. About 95 per cent of them worked in factories employing less than thirty persons!

8. Ōkōchi, *Shakai Seisaku no Keizai Riron* (The Economic Theory of Social Policy) (Tōkyō, Nippyō Shinsha, 1952), pp. 216–17.

from their main family (*honke*) made them somewhat "independent" in relation to such organizations as trade unions which were supposed to protect their livelihood. Union membership melted away in bad times, weakening the foundation for a political labor movement.

The large underemployment existing in the countryside helped maintain what was known as cheap labor, despite comparatively low official unemployment figures. Besides wages being below those in the advanced countries against which Japan was competing, neither the form nor the content of Japanese working conditions was rationalized. Wages paid were as a rule not sufficient to provide for the family; all able-bodied members of the household had to work to ensure a subsistence for the family as a whole.[9] While this enabled Japan to compete successfully overseas, it also delayed the introduction of new machinery and the possible consequent improvement in labor conditions.

Cheap labor heightened the need for a political labor movement, but poor conditions militated against its realization. Poverty kept union coffers low; fatigue made meetings difficult to conduct or even hold; the lack of open labor markets transformed unemployment into a more frightening specter. The desperation of the workers encouraged communist and anarchist tactics, whereas their insecurity sometimes gave the advantage to the more conservative of the social democrats and ultrapatriotic groups. Thus, the miserable working conditions helped to bring about the characteristic polarization of the socialist movement in Japan.

In the countryside cheap labor had its counterpart in the excessively high rents large sections of the tenantry paid with somewhat similar feelings of insecurity and extremism. Although the tenants, as part of the village communities, were essentially traditional and conservative, they could be goaded by severe conditions to desperately radical action.

9. Ōkōchi argues that in Japan wages did not have the traditional meaning defined by Adam Smith, namely the amount of money sufficient to supply the worker's family with the necessities of life. Rather, wages in Japan have by and large amounted to nothing more than a meager cash supplement to the impoverished farming family's income. See Ōkōchi, "Rōdō" (Labor) in Tadao Yanaihara, ed., *Gendai Nihon Shōshi* (A Short History of Contemporary Japan) (2 vols. Tōkyō, Mizusu Shobō, 1952), *1*, 130. For Ōkōchi's definition of cheap labor see his *Reimeiki no Nihon Rōdō Undō*, pp. 10–11, and his *Rōdō Mondai* (The Labor Question), Keizaigaku Zenshū (Complete Series on Economics), 11 (Tōkyō, Kōbundō, 1955), p. 40.

TRADITIONAL SOCIAL RELATIONSHIPS

In addition to this economic insecurity, surviving feudalistic social relationships adversely affected the development of the labor and socialist movements in Japan. Although industrialization usually creates the opportunity for freer and more democratic interpersonal relations, in Japan the rural submissiveness to authority was brought fresh from the village into the urban factory. Feudalistic ties of obligation (*on* and *giri*) were carried by the workers into new conditions, kept alive by festivals, visits, presents, terms of respect, and appropriate behavior with regard to family events, such as births, deaths, and marriage registrations.

Village connections and family contacts served as a basis for the vertical recruitment of labor. Through jobbers, subcontractors, or go-betweens, businesses could bypass employment agencies and deal directly with specific rural regions. Recruited in this fashion, workers would more easily fall into hierarchical patterns both within and outside the factory, rendering it difficult for a union to organize and, if formed, to spread beyond the particular enterprise. Craft and industrial unions were thus severely restricted. Enterprise unions, organizing one specific plant, bypassed the intermediate steps of organization and affiliated directly with national federations.[10] Not familiar with local conditions, and not accepted by management, the federations ignored negotiations over working conditions and concentrated more on political issues, making declarations as though they represented the whole working class, when in fact they gathered loosely together a motley array of single-enterprise unions of various sizes and strengths.

Enterprise (rather than class) identification found support in feudalistic concepts of paternalism. Even the educational system preached that the "friendly ties of master and retainer" (*shūjū no jōgi*) should be maintained, as though the enterprise were a family (*jigyō ikka*). The employer, who was often only a generation or two removed from his samurai progenitors, would try to patronize his

10. For a succinct explanation in English of this enterprise unionism see Solomon B. Levine, "The Labor Movement and Economic Development in Japan," Reprint Series No. 36, Institute of Labor and Industrial Relations, *University of Illinois Bulletin, 53* (September 1955), 7–12, and *Industrial Relations in Postwar Japan* (Urbana, University of Illinois Press, 1958), pp. 101–07 and passim.

workers like a father but would be shocked and indignant when they showed "lack of respect" (complained) or "conspired" (took collective action) against him. When they did so, the workers often felt both guilt and desperation; consequently, any collective bargaining in a businesslike manner suffered under severe handicaps.

Employers took advantage of this feudal psychology. The small boss utilized his "father-status" (as *oyabun*) to control both the economic and social life of his "children-status" employees (*kobun*), even to arranging their marriages. Large factories, by contrast, emphasized the more martial elements of tradition—setting up factory hierarchies and in some cases giving the employees insignia of rank to wear on their collars.[11] "Face" was manipulated by awarding honors and demerits.

Apart from the private efforts of management in this respect, not to mention those of the landlords with regard to their tenant farmers, the state itself took an active part in molding attitudes that weakened social and political movements. The schools, the state subsidized shrines and temples, and other means of mass communication hammered on the theme of unquestioning obedience to governmental authority capped by the Emperor. The overall effect of compulsory education on the worker was not only to give him the basic skills needed for industrial society but also to make him feel how little he knew and how useless it was to fight against things as they were. Universal military conscription reinforced this kind of indoctrination.

The lack of egalitarianism deeply affected Japanese social movements. Labor and agrarian disputes took on the character of revolts or mutinies. Quick changes of loyalty produced great instability in union and party leadership. Leaders could easily become isolated because of a sudden retreat or an unexpected militancy on the part of the rank and file. Heroic, self-sacrificing leaders would sometimes emerge, but more often labor bosses (who were also politicians)

11. Many examples of an army-like hierarchy of workers in military, naval, and civilian factories are found in Moritarō Yamada, *Nihon Shihonshugi Bunseki* (An Analysis of Japanese Capitalism) (Tōkyō, Iwanami Shoten, 1934), pp. 135–59. It is interesting that a workman, no matter how intelligent or industrious, could seldom rise beyond a foremanship. University graduates came in at the lowest staff rank and monopolized opportunities for advancement in management. This meant that dissatisfied foremen were logically potential labor leaders, but they were usually restrained by fear of losing the job and rank it had taken them so long to achieve.

built dictatorial control on the submissiveness of the workers. The more cautious leaders split away from the leftist enthusiasts whose appeal was often limited to the minority of politically conscious workers. The vast majority of labor was not even touched by the labor movement. In fact, the percentage of the organized among eligible workers never exceeded 7.9 (1931); the actual number never went beyond 420,589 (1936) in the prewar Japan.

Yet what there was of a labor movement was driven by the inhospitability of the environment into various degrees of political protest. Labor needed friends and allies. The proletarian parties responded to these needs. They sought to join the tenant farmers' protest to that of labor and then to add the discontented city masses and whatever other alienated elements they could, such as the former social outcaste minority and even the Koreans.

Whether such a social democratic movement, ranging from three to ten per cent of the popular vote and presumably representing the freely expressed will of the same proportion of the total population, was great or small, early in developing or late, depends on what it is compared with. The popularity of Marxism made England the model of comparison for most of the Japanese left. Japanese industrialization still lagged far behind England's, and so did the size of the labor movement and the socialist parties in Japan. The more impatient Leninists went on to point out that Russia, in many ways more politically and economically backward than Japan, had nevertheless experienced a socialist revolution. The bureaucrats and progovernment academicians of the "social policy school" pointed to German history and hoped a Bismarckian policy might forestall a revolution. The American model appeared irrelevant to Japan. The United States had no feudal past, its capitalism grew off the fat of the land, and its generous political freedoms did not force labor into developing a political movement of its own—it could simply reward its friends and punish its foes among the middle-class politicians.

In comparison with China and the colonial world, however, Japanese industrialization was a miracle, but it was not characteristic even of the Japanese left to take satisfaction in such comparisons. It did not occur to them that something about the nature of social change could be learned from studying the later developing societies. There was no one on the left in prewar Japan to suggest that the survival of feudal social discipline may have made possible Japan's rapid industrialization, a fact instinctively realized and acted upon by management. Japan was the only Asian country where a social democratic movement could grow. In other areas where rudimentary parliamentary institutions had been established—as in India, Burma, and the Philippines—a foreign power ruled, infusing all protest with the seeds of nationalism. In China, parliamentary government did not exist and no movement could thrive without its own military forces.

In terms of such comparisons the social movements in Japan were truly advanced, though not yet revolutionary. They were the products of an industrialization encouraged by a strong, legitimate, and indigenous government that had never groaned under a foreign yoke, one that was willing to innovate and knew the value of educating as well as indoctrinating the people. It also valued order and stability and was sophisticated enough in the use of the instruments of power to maintain its full authority in the face of change.

By the mid-1920s, however, the original leaders of Meiji Japan had died, leaving their divided successors in control of the various institutions that had been created—the rival ministries of the government, the political parties, the military branches, and the zaibatsu interests. In this environment, mutually competitive socialist leaders made their bid for power. They were up against giants. Although their bid was made possible, if not inevitable, by the process of industrialization and Japan's being caught in the swirl of world events, the immediate struggle seemed to them, on balance, an unequal one and the environment inhospitable.

2: Antecedents of Social Democracy:
1870s - 1922

The birth of the social democratic movement in the 1920s can be fully understood only on the basis of its recent historical antecedents. These need be traced back no farther than the "liberal" movement of the 1870s, because modern socialist thought in Japan does not claim to have roots in the indigenous tradition. While the liberal movement began as a power struggle by the samurai "outs" against the "ins," it gained inspiration from foreign sources, mainly French and English. That it petered out so soon betrayed how shallow were its leaders' liberal convictions. But it nevertheless helped bring into being a parliamentary *form* of government, whose content could be supplied in time, as the franchise was extended and as representation was focused in political parties.

Another importation in the 1890s gave form to the grievances of the men who had been drawn into work at the newly created metal, machines, and railroad industries, namely, trade unionism from the United States. Consciousness of the social problems resulting from increasing industrialization sent some intellectuals in search of Western theories of socialism as prescriptions for dealing with them. The labor and socialist movements, it turned out, were premature. The workers were not yet ready for widespread trade unionism and the socialists dabbled with anarchism. They were thus snuffed out by the hostile governmental authorities. A trade union base had to await the patient development of a mutual welfare society and the industrial boom of the First World War. In the wake of labor organization, tenant farmers began to organize in the early 1920s. Supplying theoretical orientations for the labor and tenant farmers, the socialists argued among themselves as to which was the true remedy. Three main themes emerged: anarchism, communism, and varieties of social democracy. Thus, the amorphous socialist movement split even before mass-based social democratic political parties could form and send representatives to the Imperial Diet and there join the bourgeois parties which also ironically traced their lineages back to the old liberal movement.

The agitation for constitutional practices was the first antigovernment campaign to have definite democratic overtones. Rejecting the more traditional form of revolt, it was touched off in 1874 by Taisuke Itagaki's memorial calling for the establishment of an "elective assembly." While this began as an elitist protest, it gained a measure of mass support by representing the peasant discontent over the government's heavy-handed collection of the burdensome land tax. It became known as the "movement for liberty and popular rights." [1] To give it direction, Itagaki of the former Tosa clan organized the Liberal Party (Jiyūtō) in 1881, the progenitor of a succession of parties down to the present. Also wishing to profit from the possible future benefits of this protest movement, Shigenobu Ōkuma, the disgruntled statesman from Hizen who had just been eased out of the government, organized a more moderate group the following year under the name of the Progressive Party (Kaishintō) to which the

1. "*Jiyū minken undō*," or "freedom and people's rights movement." In English this is frequently shortened to the "liberal" or "democratic" movement. For a series of interpretations of it and the results it achieved, see George O. Totten, ed., *Democracy in Prewar Japan: Groundwork or Façade?* (Boston, D. C. Heath and Company, 1965). This contains a bibliography of works in English, the most relevant items of which for this movement are the following: Nobutaka Ike, *The Beginnings of Political Democracy in Japan* (Baltimore, Johns Hopkins University Press, 1950); E. Herbert Norman, *Japan's Emergence as a Modern State: Political and Economic Problems of the Meiji Period* (New York, Institute of Pacific Relations, 1940); Robert A. Scalapino, *Democracy and the Party Movement in Prewar Japan* (Berkeley, University of California Press, 1953); and George M. Beckmann, *The Making of the Meiji Constitution: The Oligarchs and the Constitutional Development of Japan, 1868–1891* (Lawrence, University of Kansas Press, 1957). Hugh Borton calls it simply "the movement for people's rights," *Japan's Modern Century* (New York, Ronald Press, 1955), p. 103.

chief rival parties over the next half century could trace their source.[2] The Tosa and Hizen clansmen as a whole resented the monopolization of the new government by the Satsuma and Chōshu clans in the light of the fact that the Restoration had been made possible by the cooperation of all four clans. Ex-samurai, rich merchants, and the more well-to-do farmers led the movement locally. Peasant farmers and the small groups of artisans and wage laborers supplied mass support. The rationale of the movement, verbalized by such men as Emori Ueki and Tokusuke (pen name, Chōmin) Nakae, derived particularly from the French revolutionary theories of the rights of man and the Rousseauian concept of the social contract.[3]

This potentially democratic movement was brought to a standstill by a combination of internal and external circumstances. From 1881 to 1885 the country was gripped by a serious economic crisis, produced by a combination of currency deflation, falling prices, and continued high taxation.[4] This resulted in large-scale peasant dispossession of land which subsequently became concentrated in the hands of the landlords who were often simultaneously moneylenders and small entrepreneurs.[5] It was unavoidable that an economic crisis which gave to one element of the liberal movement and took from the other should tend to split it in two. Under the influence of a few of the more militant leaders the poor peasants formed local political groups with such names as Debtors' Party, Tenants' Party, Poor People's Party, and even Oriental Socialist Party. Such peasant activities aroused the fears of the wealthier leaders concerning their

2. See Joyce C. Lebra, "Ōkuma Shigenobu and the 1881 Political Crisis," *Journal of Asian Studies 18* (August 1959), 475–87. For a detailed study of his rival, see C. B. Cody, "A Study of the Career of Itagaki Taisuke (1837–1919), A Leader of the Democratic Movement in Meiji Japan" (Ph.D. dissertation, University of Washington, 1955; University Microfilms No. 14,245).

3. Ike has done an interesting study of the ideology of these two men, bringing them to light again after a period of neglect. Ike, pp. 124–37.

4. It has also been argued that this crisis marked the transition from a predominance of mercantilism to one of industrial capitalism. Yamada, *Nihon Shihonshugi Bunseki,* pp. 5–6.

5. The number of persons who through nonpayment of the land tax or of the "local taxes and Ku and village expenses levied on land" were forcibly dispossessed of their land (by public sale or confiscation by government or local authorities) reached 367,744 during the period from 1883 to 1890. Of these, 263,965 persons, that is, 77 per cent, had to be classified even by government statistics as unable to pay because of poverty. Yoshitarō Hirano, *Nihon Shihonshugi Shakai no Kikō* (The Structure of Japanese Capitalist Society) (Tōkyō, Iwanami Shoten, 1934), p. 388.

privileges as landlords. To them the advantages of free conditions for economic activity began to appear less desirable than police protection of property and governmental suppression of assemblies which were so bold as to discuss proposals for a moratorium on interest payments and rent.

The deteriorating economic situation was thus causing a rift in the liberal movement, driving the peasants to more radical, desperate action and simultaneously drawing the semicapitalist landlords closer to the side of established law and order. The Meiji government leaders were capable enough to take advantage of the situation in order to widen the split. They employed a double tactic: suppression and promises. With the Press Regulations of 1875 and the Regulations on Assembly of 1880 as legal bases, they mobilized the constabulary and a network of spies for suppressing small gatherings and the new conscript army for the bigger disturbances. The most important promise was made in 1881 when the Emperor proclaimed that in eight years he would grant the nation a constitution and, in the year following that, a parliament or diet. The government also employed such behind-the-scenes political tactics as inducing Itagaki to go abroad and leave his movement leaderless during its most restless period.[6]

These tactics were successful; the peasants were suppressed and the liberal leaders placated by the promise of a Diet, while illiberal, feudalistic attitudes remained dominant in Japanese political and social life. The supreme authority of the Emperor had been retained and the independence of the bureaucracy, especially the army, had been assured. The *octroyé* (*kintei*) Meiji Constitution of 1889 recognized few of the rights the liberal movement had sought, and the Diet which opened in 1890 was so powerless as to be more of a parliament in name than in fact.

Within this political and social milieu a new era began in the development of the Japanese economy. By 1890 the policy of selling government-built industry was completed and concentration of capital in the hands of the zaibatsu had begun. Only a few years before, in 1882, the Bank of Japan had been set up and the currency unified. Prospects for the healthy development of industrial capitalism with-

6. Ike presents a plausible account of the government's diabolically successful plot to get Itagaki to travel abroad, after failing to get rid of him by assassination. Ike, pp. 151–53.

out its hitherto heavy reliance on government subsidy seemed bright, when in 1890 the first depression caused by overproduction relative to purchasing power occurred in Japan.

The poverty of the huge peasant sector of the economy, brought about in part by the costs of building the new industrialism, now limited the expansion of the home market and created the need for foreign outlets. In 1893 Japan sent abroad her first shipment of goods produced on the machines she had imported: 11,000 bales of cotton yarn and cloth to markets in Korea and China.[7] The import duties and restrictions imposed on Japanese goods by those two countries just as export was becoming vital to the Japanese economy added to Japan's determination to demonstrate her strength vis-à-vis China and thereby serve notice to the rest of the world that she wished to be regarded as a Great Power.

The increase in Japanese productive capacity can be counted as one indirect cause of the Sino-Japanese War of 1894–95, and further, it was a decisive factor in Japan's defeat of China. Victory benefited the Japanese economy by the injection of new capital derived from the two hundred million taels of silver received from China as war indemnity, a sum which enabled the Japanese government to repay the large war debts it had incurred. Furthermore, Japan was able to go onto the gold standard, begin investments in her new colony of Taiwan, and extend her foothold in the China market.

THE PIONEER LABOR AND SOCIALIST MOVEMENTS

The expansion of Japan's industrial plant, however, also brought with it new problems connected with the increase of wage labor. The number of workers in the new industries totaled only 294,425 in 1892 but by 1897 had jumped to 439,549. Of these, the silk industry employed 23.4 per cent (68,793). Already a machine tool industry—that true harbinger of industrialism—had come into existence, although it as yet accounted for only 0.4 per cent (1,041) of the work force.[8] The war also brought increased taxes and inflation. Consequently a number of wage disputes occurred. In just the latter half of 1897 some 32 strikes broke out involving 3,517 persons, and

7. Yanaihara, ed., *Gendai Nihon Shōshi, 1,* 181.

8. These figures are from a table in Eitarō Kishimoto, *Nihon Rōdō Undō Shi* (A History of the Japanese Labor Movement) (Tōkyō, Kōbundō, 1950), p. 12. The follow-

in the following year 43 strikes involved 6,293 persons.[9] Contemporary observers were becoming increasingly aware of the problems posed by these developments. For instance, in the late 1890s an outstanding journalist, Gennosuke Yokoyama, made a study of the changes taking place among the "lower strata," and reported, "I believe that the Sino-Japanese War was responsible for the new epoch of labor problems. I do not mean that the war was directly related to the labor question, but that, as a result of the war, mechanized industry was given the boost that gave rise to the labor question." [10]

The Japanese labor movement began as an attempt to bring order into this spontaneous activity on the part of the workers. Various trade union attempts were made, but the most important occurred in Tōkyō in April 1897, when Hannosuke Sawada, a tailor, Tsunetarō Jō, a shoemaker, and Fusatarō Takano, a journalist, who had all learned the techniques of labor organization in the United States, held a meeting attended by another returnee, Sen Katayama, who subsequently devoted his life to the labor and socialist movements.[11] Together they formed the Knights of Labor (Shokkō Giyūkai),[12]

ing historical summary of the labor and agrarian movements to the early 1920s by the present author has already appeared in somewhat similar form in his "Labor and Agrarian Disputes in Japan Following World War I," *Economic Development and Cultural Change: City and Village in Japan, 9* (October 1960), 187–212.

9. In 1899, the trend was definitely down: 15 strikes involved 4,284 persons. Kishimoto, p. 38.

10. Gennosuke Yokoyama, *Nihon no Kasō Shakai* (The Lower Strata of Society in Japan) (Tōkyō, Iwanami Shoten, 1953), p. 304. Yokoyama's book was first published in 1899.

11. The best biography of Katayama is by Hyman Kublin, *Asian Revolutionary: The Life of Sen Katayama* (Princeton, Princeton University Press, 1964). This period is dealt with on pp. 105–28.

12. Interestingly enough the study group originated in the United States in 1890. Jō, Takano, Sawada, Hirano, Mutō, Kinoshita, and others who were working in San Francisco at the time formed this organization to prepare to tackle the labor problem in Japan. They had carefully studied the problem as it had developed in the more industrially advanced nations of the West. See Sen Katayama, *Nihon no Rōdō Undō* (The Japanese Labor Movement) (Tōkyō, Iwanami Shoten, 1952), p. 18. The section of the book referred to here was written by Katayama in 1901 in collaboration with Kōjirō Nishikawa. For substantiation that the Shokkō Giyūkai was probably a Japanese translation of Knights of Labor, see Hyman Kublin, *Meiji Rōdō Undō Shi no Issetsu: Takano Fusatarō no Shōgai to Shisō* (One Act in the History of the Labor Movement During the Meiji Period: The Life and Thought of Fusatarō Takano) (Tōkyō, Yūhikaku, 1959), p. 54. Shortly after the Shokkō Giyūkai was formed, the American Federation of Labor eclipsed the Knights of Labor in strength and influence. As a result, when writing from Japan to Samuel Gompers and other members of the A.F.L. in the United States, Takano translated Shokkō Giyūkai as "Friends of Labor."

which became the Association for the Formation of Labor Unions (Rōdō Kumiai Kiseikai) in July 1897. On December 1 of the same year the Association succeeded in organizing the Iron Workers' Union with over a thousand members who were mainly metal workers and machinists at combined military arsenals and iron factories in the Tōkyō–Yokohama area. This was the first labor union in Japan whose constitution and by-laws were modeled on those of American unions. The union members elected Katayama as their secretary and under his editorship published the *Labor World* (*Rōdō Sekai*), in effect the sole organ of the labor movement of that time.[13]

In February of the next year the Japan Railway Company engineers and firemen won their demands for better treatment by threatening a full-scale strike and forming the Society to Correct Abuses (Kyōseikai). At about the same time, after several unsuccessful attempts, over a hundred workers at the Fukagawa Printing Company formed a union. By 1900 it boasted over 2,000 members. Through the efforts of Katayama and others, labor organizations developed in a rather orderly fashion. By 1900 the Iron Workers' Union had over 5,400 members.[14]

A great blow to the development of the labor movement proved to be the promulgation of the earlier mentioned [Public] Peace Police Law of March 1900.[15] Before this time, there prevailed greater optimism concerning the bright future of the movement than pessimism at the difficulties in its path. In fact, the emerging labor leaders were surprised at the capitalists' lack of resistance to labor demands. Some of them thought that the more paternalistic attitudes of Japanese

13. See Sen Katayama, *The Labor Movement in Japan* (Chicago, Charles H. Kerr and Co., 1918), p. 38.

14. Kazuo Ōkōchi, *Reimeiki no Nihon Rōdō Undō*, p. 70. Incidentally, the mistake of giving this figure as 54,000 was made by an earlier labor historian noted above, Suehiro, p. 26.

15. It has often been said that the history of the Japanese labor movement is one long tale of suppression. In the Peace Police Law (*Chian Keisatsu Hō*), Article 17 was specifically aimed at suppressing organized labor activity. It is instructive to compare this with the British Combination Act, which treated organized action on the part of the workers as interference in the process of bargaining between the employer and each employee. In contrast, the Japanese law treated similar action as a disturbance of the public peace. The Peace Preservation Law (*Chian Iji Hō*) and the Disputes Arbitration Law (*Sōgi Chōtei Hō*), which were later enacted, were based on this same principle. See Masajirō Ujihara, et al., *Kyōiku* (Education), Nihon no Mondai (Problems of Japan) 2 (Tōkyō, Iwanami Shoten, 1952), p. 218.

management might enable the Japanese working class to avoid some of the agonies of capitalism experienced in the more advanced industrial West. From the very beginning, however, they had been worried by the degree of police surveillance.[16] Now this new law gave the authorities added power to suppress labor unrest.

But even before the law's enforcement, attempts to organize and unify the labor movement were running into real difficulties. The more modern workers who had acquired new skills, such as railroad engineers, refused to join with the dirty, unskilled laborers recruited from the peasantry. Then those who worked in the various crafts, such as sawyers, held on to exclusive guild traditions, while the mass of women and children in textiles hardly constituted much of a base for building trade unionism. An immense gap existed between the foreign-oriented intellectuals and the squalid laborers who by and large accepted their miserable lot in life and were loath to part with the few sen for union dues, all too often rightly suspecting that the funds would be squandered by union leaders instead of bringing them the promised welfare. A host of factors other than the reactions of the capitalists, some of whom were actually sympathetic with early trade unionism,[17] were holding back the movement before the severe attitude of the government brought it to a standstill. The union organizers, who were having so much difficulty communicating with the workers anyway, now became more convinced than ever that the capitalist system itself was at fault and that the workers could not be "saved" by merely trying to remedy surface ills. They also became convinced that, since the legal obstacles were the most immediate, labor must turn to politics.

The attempted formation of the Social Democratic Party on May 22, 1901, by Katayama and a group of socialist intellectuals with labor union support, especially from the railroad engineers' Society to Correct Abuses, might be considered the point from which the political socialist movement could be dated. The so-called "proletarian parties" that were formed after the franchise was greatly extended in

16. The labor leaders' attitudes toward the capitalists and the police are clearly exhibited in reports and letters Takano sent back to the United States. For English versions, see Kublin, *Meiji Rōdō Undō*, pp. 3–114.

17. Such was Teiichi Sakuma who owned a printing shop and because he tried to establish ideal conditions for his own workers was often called "the Robert Owen of Japan."

1925 trace their lineages back to this party, called in Japanese the Shakai Minshutō.[18] As a matter of fact, the men who formed that party later came to represent the major trends in Japanese socialist activity: Denjirō Kōtoku became an anarchist; Sen Katayama a Communist; and Isoo Abe a social democrat.

These socialist intellectuals and their comrades, supported briefly by the infant labor movement, were already the products of several diverse influences that had evolved over the preceding two decades. Some of the more radical participants in the people's rights movement had begun to read and help in the translation of Western works that dealt with socialism in one way or another. The transliteration of the term "socialism" as *"soshiaruisume"* by Hiroyuki Katō, an early radical who later became conservative, first appeared in a book of his in 1870.[19] The translation of this term as *"shakai-shugi"* first appeared in print in 1878 when the press reported the attempted assassination of Kaiser Wilhelm I by the Socialists (giving fuel to police suspicions). But the popularization (among a limited audience to be sure) of the word took place in 1887 when the first number of *Nation's Friend* (*Kokumin no Tomo*) started a serialized translation of one of the writings of Henry George in which he made frequent reference to "socialism." [20] This journal became for a time the mouthpiece of the left wing of the Liberal Party, which still car-

18. To be sure, some "parties" that might be considered forerunners of the socialist political movement appeared earlier, such as the previously mentioned Oriental Socialist Party (Tōyō Shakaitō), which was formed by Tōkichi Tarui in 1882 and disbanded a month later. Thus, Isoo Abe claims Tarui to be a pioneer socialist in Shigenobu Ōkuma, ed., *Fifty Years of New Japan* (Kaikoku Gojū Nen Shi), English version ed. by Marcus B. Huish (2d ed. London, Smith, Elder, 1909–10), 2, 505. Actually he represented peasant unrest that formed part of the basis for the liberal movement. A much more convincing case is made by Kublin for considering that the founding of the immediate forerunner of the Social Democratic Party signaled the birth of the socialist movement in Japan. Hyman Kublin, "The Origins of Japanese Socialist Tradition," *Journal of Politics*, *14* (May 1952), 261, n. 13. He is referring to the Society for the Study of Socialism, mentioned below.

19. His 1870 book was called *Shinsei Taii* (Principles of True Government). See Sōgorō Tanaka, *Nihon Shakai Undō Shi* (A History of Japanese Social Movements) (3 vols. Tōkyō, Sekai Shoin, 1947–48), *1*, 50.

20. The translation *Nation's Friend* for *Kokumin no Tomo* is used because the name was inspired by the American magazine, *Nation*. The translator of Henry George's articles was Tsunetarō Jō, mentioned earlier as an organizer of the Knights of Labor (Shokkō Giyūkai). For copies of the *Kokumin no Tomo* containing these articles, see Ōhara Shakai Mondai Kenkyūjo (The Ōhara Institute of Social Research), comp., *Nihon Shakai-shugi Bunken* (Japanese Socialist Source Materials) (Ōsaka, Dōjinsha Shoten, 1929), pp. 110 ff.

ried on the tradition of the "freedom and people's rights movement" and espoused the principles of the French Revolution. It carried articles by students studying in France or Germany or who had just returned from abroad.

Being now in possession not only of foreign books and articles but also firsthand reports, a number of small groups met to discuss the "advanced" thought of the West regarding various aspects of the "social question" with a view to discovering what might be applicable to Japan. Most of these groups were ephemeral, but one that became permanent was the Social Policy Academic Association (Shakai Seisaku Gakkai) formed on April 2, 1896. Drawn to a study of the contemporary German *Sozialpolitik* school, this group rejected "socialism" and laissez faire but urged the state to work out welfare policies. Composed of government people and professors at Tōkyō Imperial University, it was to become a continuing antagonist to the French-English-American-inspired humanists, on the one hand, and the later class-conscious Marxists, on the other.

Another influence that had been at work to swell the ranks of socialists was Christianity, which had reentered the country after Japan's long period of isolation. It brought with it this time a sense of social consciousness and concern for the physical as well as spiritual well-being of others, of which the recent Protestant uplift movements were a manifestation. Some Japanese who were impressed with this element of Christianity but repelled by the doctrinal differences among the various Protestant sects welcomed the Unitarians who appeared to them most tolerant. But again the very tolerance of the Unitarians led some eventually to abandon Christianity altogether in favor of various socialist doctrines.

In the midst of this process, which had been hastened by a spate of translations of Western socialist authors, a group of Christian socialists began to meet together with members of the left wing of the Liberal Party in the hall of the Unitarian Society in Tōkyō. They formed the Society for the Study of Socialism (Shakaishugi Kenkyū-kai) in the fall of 1898 and began a somewhat systematic discussion of such writers as Saint-Simon, Proudhon, Fourier, and Marx, with a view to applying socialist theory in Japan.[21] After two years, some of

21. A copy of the original prospectus stating this purpose may be found in Kyokuzan Ishikawa and Shūsui Kōtoku, "Nihon Shakaishugi Shi" (A History of Japanese Socialism), *Meiji Bunka Zenshū* (Collected Works on Meiji Culture), ed. by Sakuzō Yoshino (Tōkyō, Nihon Hyōronsha, 1929), *21*, 363.

the members became impatient for action. This caused those who
were lukewarm to the idea to drop out and the group was reorganized into the Socialist Society (Shakaishugi Kyōkai) in 1900. While
the forty or so members left were too few to do much by themselves,
they supplied the nucleus of the attempt to rally a broader group and
win labor support for the formation of the Social Democratic Party.
Five of the six initiators were Christians at the time.[22]

The fact that this party had obtained enough backing to be
launched at all was viewed so seriously by the cabinet of Hirobumi
Itō (the supposedly more liberal of the oligarchs) that the Home
Ministry ordered its immediate dissolution. In any case, it is doubtful
that the party could have had much success at the polls, since only a
well-off minority of the propertied class was allowed to vote. The
leaders of the party, such as Katayama, Abe, and Kōtoku, could have
avoided the government's order to disband if they had compromised
the party's platform in certain respects, but this they refused to do
lest such a precedent cripple the socialist movement from its birth.

In retrospect, the Social Democratic Party's platform appears
moderate indeed, and most of its immediate aims were democratic
rather than socialist in nature.[23] The party declared that it did not
champion the interests of the poor only, nor was it hostile to the
rich, but desired to work for the prosperity of the nation as a whole.
Its goals were not socialist, but rather either democratic—popular
referendum and abolition of the House of Peers—or pacifist—an
end to military expenditures. The fact that these demands were
attacked as "seditious" by government-party politicians, some of
whom were formerly leaders in the people's rights movement, shows

22. These were Isoo Abe, Sen Katayama, Kiyoshi Kawakami, Naoe Kinoshita, and
Kōjirō Nishikawa. Denjirō (Shūsui) Kōtoku was the exception. Among others motivated
by Christian humanitarianism who were actively interested in the early labor and socialist movements were Tomoyoshi Murai and Kanzō Uchimura. Humanitarianism, especially emphasized by the Unitarians at the time, made the recent Japanese converts see
their environment in a new light; feeling shocked at the inhuman labor conditions in
Japan they took an interest in labor problems and the socialist theories for their solution. See Ōkōchi, *Reimeiki no Nihon Rōdō Undō*, p. 89.

23. A copy of the platform of the Social Democratic Party may be found in Sōgorō
Tanaka, *Shiryō Nihon Shakai Undō Shi* (A Documentary History of the Japanese Social
Movement) (Tōkyō, Tōzai Shuppansha, 1947), *1*, 328–40. An English translation appears
in Karl Kiyoshi Kawakami, *The Political Ideas of Modern Japan* (Iowa City, 1903), pp.
564–65. Radicalism is, of course, a relative thing, and although the platform was in
part inspired by the Communist Manifesto, even the latter had lost much of its impact
in the light of social progress since 1848.

to what extent the Japanese liberals had abandoned their former demands for political liberties and universal suffrage.[24]

In the decade after 1900 the authoritarian attitude of the government and the weakness of labor inevitably inclined the socialist movement toward intellectualism rather than activism. The Peace Police Law crushed the incipient labor union movement, and the order to disband the Social Democratic Party left no room for even moderate political reformist activities. The socialist movement after 1901, therefore, was confined to educational and propaganda activities. With the divorce of the socialist and the labor movements, socialist leadership fell from the hands of the then more moderate and organizationally minded Sen Katayama and was taken up by the more anarchistic and intellectually inclined Denjirō Kōtoku and his close disciple, Toshihiko Sakai. The resultant tendency toward radical theorizing rather than practical activity became a marked characteristic of the Japanese socialist movement.

If the social movement is thought of in the singular, it contained in the years 1899 to 1902 two aspects: labor and socialist. In 1899 the handful of socialists were discussing and studying the abstract theories of socialism, while the infant labor movement and its leaders were negotiating about concrete working conditions and actually carrying on strikes. By 1901 the socialists who were eager for political activity found the incipient trade unionists receptive to the message that political reforms were a necessary concomitant to purely economic demands if labor's condition were really to be bettered. But by 1902 the trade union movement had been struck down and had collapsed, and the socialists were left no alternative but to confine themselves to education and propaganda.[25]

Despite the severity of its measures against the unions and labor activity, the government continued to tolerate the existence of the Socialist Society. Socialist thought even became a limited intellectual fad around 1902–03 among the avant-garde, but at the same time the socialists themselves had lost contact with the very working classes whose interests they were supposedly championing.

With the danger of an outbreak of hostilities with Imperial

24. The "old liberals" had by this time regrouped into the Kenseitō, a party supporting the Itō government.

25. An example of drastic action by the government was the dispatch of troops to quell the Kure Navy Arsenal strike of about 5,000 workers in July 1902.

Russia, however, the socialist movement again came to grips with a
vital problem: would war benefit or burden the poorer classes in
Japan? Traditional socialist thought seemed to brand war as evil.
Around this conviction the socialists created an antiwar movement,
led by Kōtoku and Sakai who together founded the Commoners' Society (Heiminsha) and began publishing the *Commoners' Newspaper* (*Heimin Shimbun*) on November 15, 1903.[26] This journal carried many antiwar articles, the main theses of which were as follows:
(1) war is contrary to the way of human love and subverts the just
principles of society; (2) war benefits the bourgeoisie but sacrifices
the common people; (3) the House of Representatives which approved the war represents the landowners and the capitalists, not the
common people; therefore we are against war and the very existence
of our army.

The socialist movement now began to encounter sterner restrictions by the government, especially after the outbreak of the Russo–
Japanese War in 1904. These they resisted for over a year, carrying
on their peace campaign by writing, making speeches, and holding
meetings. On January 29, 1905, however, the 64th issue of the *Commoners' Newspaper* was suppressed and the Commoners' Society ordered disbanded on October 9, 1905. This antiwar movement, supported by the Christian pacifists and Christian socialists, who had
combined forces with secular socialists, put up a brave fight but their
influence reached little beyond a limited circle of intellectuals and
did not penetrate the ranks of labor.[27]

When the more liberal Saionji first succeeded Katsura as Prime
Minister, the socialists immediately formed the Japan Socialist Party
(Nihon Shakaitō) and, on January 28, 1906, received permission to
be a legal party inasmuch as they advocated "socialism within the
limits of the Constitution." The "materialists" published a journal

26. The Commoners' Society then became the headquarters of the socialist movement
because Katayama, at whose home activities had centered up to now, went abroad to
attend the Convention of the Second International in Amsterdam in 1904. Kanson
Arahata, *Nihon Shakaishugi Undō Shi* (A History of the Japanese Socialist Movement)
(Tōkyō, Mainichi Shimbunsha, 1948), p. 56.

27. Katayama pointed out that Kōtoku, Sakai, and others were well versed in Japanese
literature and had a fair command of English; thus, they tended to present socialism
in such a way as to attract the interest and support of only the student classes. Katayama, *The Labor Movement in Japan*, p. 102. For a vivid description of the whole
antiwar campaign, see Hyman Kublin, "The Japanese Socialists and the Russo–Japanese
War," *Journal of Modern History*, 22 (December 1950), 322–39.

called *Light* (*Hikari*) while the Christian socialists put out *New Century* (*Shinkigen*). Then in 1907 the two groups united for a time and revived the *Commoners' Newspaper,* this time as a daily. Although they broadened their activities, they never succeeded in doing more than defeating a fare raise on the Tōkyō municipal trolley system. They were, in effect, the direct successors of the Socialist Society, engaging mainly in education and propaganda while the labor unions had become almost entirely defunct.

Deteriorating labor conditions, however, were having an effect on the workers. The Russo-Japanese War had reduced the low living standard of labor still further and had brought about a great deal of suffering which resulted in a series of spontaneous strikes, numbering 107 between 1903 and 1907 and involving 20,789 workers. The frustration of constant defeat gave rise to anarcho-syndicalism within the ranks of labor.

EARLY ANARCHO-SYNDICALIST TRENDS

This radical development was reflected in the socialist movement by the complete conversion of Kōtoku in 1906. Until November 1905, he had been in prison for his antiwar activities during the Russo-Japanese War. When released, he traveled for nearly a year in the United States where he was impressed with the anarcho-syndicalism of the International Workers of the World (IWW). The antiparliamentary bent of anarcho-syndicalism and its emphasis on direct action seemed attuned to the situation in Japan at the time—the postwar poverty, the social unrest, the severe suppression of socialist thought.

Kōtoku's new turn of thought convinced a number of the intellectuals who made up the small socialist movement.[28] On June 28, 1906, at a Socialist Party meeting to welcome him back to Japan, Kōtoku made a speech on "The Tide of the World Revolutionary Movement." [29] In it he rejected parliamentarianism because he found that the victories of the British Independent Labor Party and the German Social Democratic Party did not immediately usher in the

28. For a study of the larger effects of Kōtoku's change of thought on his return from America, see Shōbei Shioda, "Kōtoku Shūsui no Shisōteki Tenka" ([Denjirō] Shūsui Kōtoku's Change of Thought), *Shakai Kagaku Kenkyū, 1* (April 1948), 52–75.

29. "Sekai Kakumei Undō no Chōryū," see Hisao Itoya, *Kōtoku Shūsui Den* (A Biography of [Denjirō] Shūsui Kōtoku) (Kyōto, Sanichi Shobō, 1950), pp. 168–69.

new world of the proletariat. He rejected not only reformism, but also the contemporary "orthodox" Marxism of Bebel and Kautsky. Instead, he called for direct negotiation with employers and the use of the strike if necessary, and argued against involvement in political issues on the grounds that that would divert the energy of labor from its real fight against the capitalists.

At the Socialist Party Conference of February 1907, Kōtoku, excited by the current Ashio Copper Mine disturbance, gave a one-hour speech advocating what he called "direct action." As a result of this, the Saionji Cabinet ordered the immediate disbanding of the Socialist Party. The movement then split into two main factions: the believers in parliamentary means (Sen Katayama, Tetsuji Tazoe, and Kōjirō Nishikawa) and the believers in "direct action" (Kōtoku, Sakai, and their younger followers, Sakae Ōsugi and Hitoshi Yamakawa.)

Kōtoku's brand of anarcho-syndicalism was peculiarly Japanese. European syndicalism was born mainly out of a feeling that the social democratic parties had become compromising and ineffective within the national legislatures, that politics was a set of tricks by which the bourgeoisie distracted the working class, and that, consequently, direct action by well-organized and synchronized labor unions was the only thing that would get results. In contrast to this, Japanese syndicalism expressed the feelings of frustration that arose from the inability to get even a voice in the Diet, the prompt police suppression of any kind of labor activity, the all-pervading ideology of the "emperor system" that restricted any fundamental criticism of the state, and finally, the prevalence of scattered, spontaneous strikes that resembled small-scale uprisings more than modern organized action.

At that time Sen Katayama and other socialists criticized this kind of syndicalism, branding it a dangerous tendency.[30] They advocated organizing the workers peacefully without provoking the ruling classes. Nevertheless, the syndicalist trend became more pronounced and brought in its wake first the Red Flag incident in 1908 and finally the High Treason Trial of 1910–11 in which Kōtoku and eleven other socialists were condemned to death for allegedly plotting

30. Katsuzō (pen name, Kanson) Arahata, one of the other contemporary socialists, pointed out that to be effective the general strike tactic had to be carried out by a large, well-organized federation of unions, which simply did not exist in Japan at the time. To advocate a general strike without such strong backing was tantamount to inviting extinction. Arahata, pp. 199–200.

against the life of the Emperor. This trial now appears to have been a conscious frame-up by the Katsura government.[31]

After the trial, police suppression of the socialist movement intensified. No distinction was made between syndicalists such as Sakae Ōsugi and orthodox socialists such as Sen Katayama, who at that time supported the Second International. Katayama led a strike of workers in the Tōkyō municipal trolley system, but that was his last activity in Japan. In complete frustration, he finally left his homeland in 1914, never to return.[32] The socialist movement was at a standstill.

THE NEW LABOR AND AGRARIAN MOVEMENTS

Subjected to continuous suppression, labor remained almost completely unorganized until the time of the First World War. The one important exception was the Friendly Society (Yūaikai), headed by Bunji Suzuki. The Society was organized by well-wishers on the outside as a mutual aid society for workers, and had no pretensions of being a trade union federation until shortly after the close of the First World War.

The war itself was a turning point, for it gave tremendous impetus to the development of the Japanese economy. Investment capital in enterprise had expanded 16-fold over 1914. Factory workers more than doubled in number from 853,964 in 1914 to 1,777,177 by 1919.[33] Heavy industry grew and the movement of workers into large factories increased in tempo. The percentage of workers in metal, machines, and chemical industries jumped from 13.6 in 1909 to 24.2 in 1919. In the same period, the percentage of workers in factories employing over a hundred workers rose from 43.5 to 55.6. The number of urban workers available for permanent employment increased greatly in comparison with the traditional type of transient

31. See, for instance, Kiyome (Seima) Sakamoto, "Gyakuto to Iwarete: Zaigoku Nijūgo Nen: Kōtoku Jiken no Shinsō" (Being Called a Traitor: The Truth about the Kōtoku Incident for which I Was in Prison for Twenty-five Years), *Chūō Kōron, 10* (September 1952), 120–27.

32. Katayama subsequently became a Communist and eventually a member of the Comintern in Moscow. The process of this transformation was the subject of an article by Hyman Kublin, "Katayama Sen: The Birth of a Bolshevik," *Shakai Kagaku Tokyū, 1* (June 1956), 1–30 (or 389–369, the Japanese pagination being in reverse order); also *Asian Revolutionary*, pp. 261–87.

33. For these and the figures in the paragraph below, see Kishimoto, pp. 122–25.

laborers. Their growth created a basic prerequisite for the development of a social democratic mass movement.

The war-produced spiral in prices, the work speedups, and the influence of the Russian Revolution drove labor to greater activity and self-awareness. The Rice Riots of 1918 dramatically revealed deep and widespread unrest, and in this setting labor's demands for higher wages increased rapidly; in 1918, 417 disputes occurred in which 66,457 workers were involved; in 1919, 497 disputes involved 63,137 workers. Though still technically illegal, labor unions increased from a scant 40 in 1911 to 107 in 1918, to 187 in 1919, and to 273 in 1920.[34] In 1919 the Friendly Society, which had started out in 1912 as a moderate welfare association based on the principle of harmony between capital and labor, transformed itself openly into a trade union federation dedicated to the fight against capital in the interests of labor. It soon adopted a name more in accord with its new outlook: the Friendly Society Greater Japan General Federation of Labor. Two years later it dropped the first three words from its (English) title.

In terms of numbers the Friendly Society had grown rapidly until it reached a plateau in 1917, hovering around 30,000 workers. In 1920 it began to grow again. Even before the change in name its goal had become industrial unionism, but since the majority of members were employed in small industry, mixed or general locals were most common. Regionalism also characterized the General Federation. A brisk rivalry developed between the Kantō and Kansai area federations; within these geographical groupings and elsewhere subregional localism prevailed over industrial or craft ties. Activities included welfare, recreation, education, savings, employment exchanges, and organizing consumers' unions, as well as negotiating or disputing with management when warranted.

At this time the movement for universal suffrage was gaining more support than ever and by 1919 labor was taking part in it on a national scale. However, when the government dissolved the Diet rather than allow a vote on the suffrage bill presented in February 1920, labor's interest cooled. The postwar depression had set in, weakening labor's bargaining power and forcing its strategy to change from offense to defense. After May 1920, with the defeat of labor's campaign to obtain the right to organize, revolutionary syn-

34. Kyōchōkai (The Harmonization Society), eds., *Saikin no Shakai Undō* (Recent Social Movements) (Tōkyō, Kyōchōkai, 1929), p. 255.

dicalism, most successfully advocated by Ōsugi, pervaded the labor movement and reached its peak in the period 1921–23.

Although this postwar syndicalism was not essentially different from the principles of direct action advocated by Kōtoku after the Russo-Japanese War, it was more influential in the labor movement. Some anarcho-syndicalists were actually leading strikes against management and struggles against police interference. The general disillusionment with the Diet and the inability to secure recognition of the right to organize were conducive to radicalism.

In these circumstances socialists again began to organize. The fact that the labor movement had become more active could not help but stimulate the surviving socialists, who again began to make contact with one another through articles in magazines and through meetings. In December 1920 they formed the Japan Socialist Federation (Nihon Shakaishugi Dōmei), composed of all sorts of socialists, ranging from anarchists to "Bolsheviks" and from parliamentarians to state socialists. It included the old socialists and the new ones whose experience had begun in the World War period. As a result, it led a stormy life, before being dissolved by the government in May 1921.

The Federation had nevertheless served to bring the veteran socialists into close touch with the labor movement. The dominant controversy between anarcho-syndicalism and Bolshevism took on a new importance. The former meant the use of nonpolitical, economic direct action by way of spontaneous strikes, building up eventually to the "general strike" which would achieve workers' control over production. It deemphasized organization in favor of courageous action by leaders even in the face of violence. In opposition to this, what was known as Bolshevism in the Japanese labor movement at that time meant an emphasis on building strong labor organizations, uniting them with close ties, appealing for public support in labor disputes, and linking up labor demands with political issues. The Japan General Federation of Labor (the former Friendly Society) championed this type of Bolshevism since it was in line with the General Federation's aspiration to rally all the other unions to its ranks.

The conflict between anarcho-syndicalism and Bolshevism came to a head on September 30, 1922, when the syndicalists failed in their attempt to organize a loose general alliance of all the important unions on the basis of independent union autonomy. The failure was due to the opposition of the General Federation which held out for its alternative proposal for a strong federation of disciplined unions operating under centralized direction. After that the tide of anarcho-syndicalism began to recede rapidly.

It had been a grave blunder for the anarchists to adopt tactics of the offensive during a period of recession when the workers were at a disadvantage. Many syndicalist unions had thus been utterly wiped out and workers had turned away from them. The police hounded and harassed the anarchist leaders to such an extent, because of their involvement with violence, that their effectiveness was greatly impared. Abroad, especially in Italy where it had been an important force, anarchism had met serious setbacks, convincing Japanese anarchists that they were on the wrong track. In the meanwhile, the Russian Bolsheviks appeared to be successfully defending their revolution in the largest nation on earth.

The new popularity of Bolshevism in Japan again directed the attention of labor leaders to the possibilities of political action and thus helped create the climate of opinion favoring the formation of political parties based on organized laborers and farmers. It had become clear to socialist and labor leaders alike that without the support of at least a section of the agricultural population, they could not hope to be politically effective in the future.

Industrialization was indirectly responsible for the rise of the agrarian movement, which developed in an even more unorganized, spontaneous, and erratic fashion than did labor. Certainly peasant uprisings had been frequent from time to time throughout the Tokugawa regime and in the early Meiji period, but these preindustrial riots were on the whole simply explosions of hopeless wrath demanding the restoration of some traditional right. What characterized the few attempts at tenant-farmer organization that began to appear around the turn of the century was a more conscious response to the unequal distribution of wealth, to the growth of a money economy, and to the economic fluctuations that reflected a national market more and more dependent on the interrelationship between Japan and foreign industrialized economies.

While the labor movement was getting a start under Katayama, Takano, and others, a man named Kentarō Ōi was attempting to bring some organization to the increasing number of peasant disturbances. In 1899 he organized the League for the Establishment of

Tenancy Regulations (Kosaku Jōkai Kisei Dōmeikai) in Ōsaka. Ōi had already had a good deal of experience, since he had been primarily responsible for the formation of the abortive Oriental Liberal Party (Tōyō Jiyūtō) in 1892. But he was not able to accomplish much with his League other than for a short time collecting information concerning tenancy and tendering advice when disputes arose.[35]

Actually it was not until after the Rice Riots of 1918 that any large-scale organizational attempts by tenant farmers were made. The war produced differential benefits that tore at the social fabric in the countryside. Among other things it caused inflationary trends in both manufactured commodities and agricultural produce. Although the price of rice rose, the costs of agricultural implements, work animals, and fertilizer rose even more. Soaring rice prices benefited the landowners, as land values went up and afforded greater opportunities for profitable speculation. The increased rate of land turnover, in turn, increased absentee landlordism. With more cash on hand the landlords were able to lend more money at usurious rates of interest to their tenant farmers who usually had to supply their own tools and fertilizers at the higher costs.

While the war had thus been an economic boon to the landlords, it was the reverse for the small independent and tenant farmers. Many small landowners were forced to become tenants through mortgage foreclosures. During the war the number of middle-sized farms decreased, while the number of both the smallest and largest rose. The tenant farmers were forced to pay higher rents in kind. After meeting their obligations many did not even have enough rice left for their own families, much less any to sell. They were faced with the predicament of having to buy rice at the spiraling market prices. The economic gap between the village landlords, rice merchants, and

35. See Ronald P. Dore, *Land Reform in Japan* (London, Oxford University Press, 1959), p. 68. Ōi was also involved in labor activities; the Oriental Liberal Party, according to Yanaga, was "the first political party to work for the protection of the working class." Chitoshi Yanaga, *Japan Since Perry* (New York, McGraw-Hill, 1949), p. 232. Actually, however, Ōi's concern was to gradually build up the strength of the people so that an aggressive foreign policy could be followed. The platform is reproduced in Tanaka, *Shiryō . . . , 1,* 227–28. His ideas along this line were set forth in his *Jiji Yoron* (Opinions of the Times), published in 1886 and reprinted in Yoshitarō Hirano, *Bajō Ōi Kentarō Den* (A Biography of Kentarō Ōi on a White Charger) (Tōkyō, 1938), pp. 379 ff. Ōi did represent a trend in labor and agrarian concern but one that early veered toward a strong foreign policy and overseas expansion.

usurers, on the one hand, and the poorer farmers and tenants, on the other, grew wider. As conditions worsened, actual starvation among the agricultural population became one of the causes for the great Rice Riots in 1918 which spread to more than thirty prefectures and lasted for 42 days. Although the price of rice was immediately cut in half, this uprising left a profound impression and lingering tensions within the villages up and down the land. The temporary relief which resulted was not to last, since in another two years the international postwar depression hit Japanese agriculture.

Thereafter, tenant farmer distress was increasingly translated into action. The number of disputes, centering mainly on the demand for rent reduction, climbed from 408 incidents in 1920 to 2,751 in 1925. Looking at the number of people involved gives a clearer picture of the extent of these disputes. In 1920, 5,236 landlords had disputes with 34,605 tenant farmers, and by 1925 these figures had risen to 35,705 versus 151,061, respectively. In general, each tenant represented a family, whereas the landlord was often duplicated in these figures, since he might have had disputes with various tenants on different occasions. Therefore, tenant-farmer activity constituted more of a mass movement than these figures at first sight indicate.[36]

Many influences besides those relating to agriculture accounted for this rise in the incidence of struggle among the farmers and for the more organized character the disputes began to take. Of importance was the increase of labor strikes and union organization. It was typical that the younger brother who had gone to the city to work would tell about this when visiting home in the village. Sometimes he would use his experience to advantage in a tenant–landlord dispute. Stories of how the peasants burned the landlord's house in the Russian Revolution and claimed the land they had tilled came to Japanese villages by word of mouth or through the mushrooming mass media.[37]

36. These figures are from tables based on the Nōrin Daijin Kambō Tōkeika (Statistical Section of the Secretariat of the Minister of Agriculture and Forestry), *Nōrinshō Tōkei Hyō* (Statistical Tables of the Ministry of Agriculture and Forestry) (Tōkyō, 1936 and 1940), *13* and *14*, found in Takeo Ono, *Kindai Nihon Nōson Hattatsu Shiron* (A Historical Treatise on Modern Japanese Rural Development) (Tōkyō, Hodoka Shobō, 1950), pp. 64–66.

37. Sometimes a younger son, returned from Japan's Siberian adventure, would take some action prompted by his interest in the revolution he had been sent to quell. One example was a farmer's son in Gifu Prefecture who had been a corporal in the Japanese troops sent to Siberia. His experience there aroused his curiosity about socialism and

On the national level the League of Nations' International Labor Organization (ILO) had a direct influence. While it primarily affected labor policy, it also stimulated the agrarian movement since it proclaimed the right of tenant farmers to organize in their own interest—an act which had been considered illegal in Japan but which the Japanese government, as a member of the ILO, found it increasingly difficult to deny. And finally, there were the Christian, socialist, and democratic ideas that Japanese intellectuals were advocating upon their return from travel and study abroad.

Tenantry disputes gradually spread throughout Japan, beginning in the early part of the war and increasing almost steadily to the mid-1930s.[38] They did at first give a certain amount of relief to the tenant farmers. By 1920 about half of them ended to the advantage of the tenants, but by 1922 the trend had turned the other way. Thereafter disputes lasted longer and became more confounded in litigation. An increasing number of tenant farmers became convinced of the need for political action when they learned how often court verdicts, which were based on existing laws, went against them.[39]

In such conditions, the first tenant-farmer organization of national proportions was born. The Japan Farmers' Union (Nihon Nōmin Kumiai) was founded on April 9, 1922, by moderate socialists, several of whom, such as Toyohiko Kagawa, were Christians. Some of its leaders, including Kagawa, had already gained experience

upon returning home he began to read what he could find on it. Not long afterward he led the village tenant farmers in their first organized action in a dispute with the landlord. They handed back their fields to the landlord and demanded a reduction in rent before they would agree to till the land again. Keiichirō Aoki, *Nihon Nōmin Undō Shi* (A History of the Japanese Agrarian Movement) (Tōkyō, Minshu Hyōronsha, 1947), p. 13.

38. On the spread of tenantry disputes, see ibid., pp. 17–19 and Ono, pp. 66–68. More detailed breakdowns may be found in Kyōchōkai, p. 384 ff. Farmer disputes broken down by prefecture may be found in Naikaku Tōkeikyoku (Cabinet Statistical Bureau), comp., *Rōdō Tōkei Yōran* (Labor Statistics Survey) (Tōkyō, 1932), pp. 256–57. Also see Totten, "Labor and Agrarian Disputes . . ." pp. 194–95.

39. By this is meant that disputes were taken to the courts more frequently. In the absence of any legislation to the contrary, the judges considered the tenantry contract in the same light as any other contract and would enforce it regardless of the social implications. The judgments, based on the terms of the contract and on the provisions of the existing general law regarding contracts, necessarily went against the tenants. For this reason, an increasing number of tenant farmers became convinced of the need for political action as the only way to ameliorate the disadvantageous legal situation. See Takeyoshi Kawashima, *Kindai Shakai to Hō* (Modern Society and Law) (Tōkyō, Iwanami Shoten, 1959), pp. 59–70, 158.

leading labor disputes. The Farmers' Union called for better educational opportunities for tenant farmers, modernization of agricultural techniques, uplifting of moral standards, and raising the cultural level of the rural village. Its appeal was directed toward the tenant farmer and, therefore, it demanded legislation to correct the abuses of tenancy and to provide for arbitration of tenant–landlord disputes. Four years after its founding it reached its prewar peak membership of 67,876.[40]

By 1922 the labor and agrarian movements had begun to take on mass proportions which meant that they were actually growing in the Japanese environment. The inspiration for the early liberal people's rights movement, as well as the pioneer socialist and labor movements at the turn of the century, and even the ideological impetus for the anarcho-syndicalists until the time of Kōtoku's trial in 1911, all came as transplantations from abroad but by the early 1920s the movements themselves had taken root in Japanese soil. With the collapse of anarcho-syndicalism, the question of the political orientation of these social movements became more pressing. The victory of the vaguely understood concept called "Bolshevism" by the Japanese at the time, which called for political involvement, paved the way for the more systematic and sophisticated importation of Leninist and later Stalinist Communist thought and the organizational techniques and tactics of the Comintern. It was as a reaction against this that social democracy began to take form in the Japanese setting. A struggle first developed in organized labor and then among the agrarian unions, resulting in a permanent schism in the Japanese socialist movement.

40. Kyōchōkai, p. 434.

3: Separating the Social Democrats from the Communists: 1922-1932

Almost every month throughout 1922 saw the outbreak of an important strike, and in almost every instance it ended in failure and the destruction of the union that undertook it. The postwar depression was in full swing. This together with the program of arms reduction undertaken by the Japanese government resulted in a sharp increase in unemployment. Only a year earlier the campaign for universal suffrage, which had given labor hope for reform through the ballot box, ended in seeming failure due to Premier Hara's stubborn opposition. Also the government's arbitrary choice of "labor delegates" to the International Labor Conference perturbed the organized union leaders.

Abroad, the world economic recession appeared to support the communist claim that the "inherent contradictions" of world capitalism had caused the expected crisis, while the formation of the Third International in March 1919 gave promise of early success for the world revolutionary movement. With communist appeal at a high pitch abroad and trade union efforts largely frustrated at home, it is not surprising that the attack by Japan's leading labor organization, the Japan General Federation of Labor (Nihon Rōdō Sōdōmei), against syndicalism at its convention in 1922 would be interpreted as

a tacit endorsement of Bolshevism. On August 20, 1922, its Central
Committee denounced the International Labor Conference and revised its original platform in a more radical direction, adding the following items:

> (1) Utilizing the threat of collective action and organization for
> mutual aid, we shall press for increases in economic benefits and
> the spread of enlightenment. (2) With decisive courage and
> effective tactics, we shall fight to the end against the oppressive
> persecution of the capitalist class. (3) We believe that the
> worker and capitalist classes cannot coexist. Through the
> strength of trade unions we shall press for the complete eman-
> cipation of the working class and the construction of a new soci-
> ety of liberty and equality.[1]

This statement from the leading labor organization in Japan gives an
indication of the revolutionary atmosphere in which the Japanese
Communist movement was born.

COMMUNIST PRECEDENCE

The Communist parties of Europe and America grew out of the
compliance of a section of the socialist or social democratic parties
with the twenty-one conditions laid down by V. I. Lenin at the Second Congress of the Communist International in 1920. This, in almost every case, meant a split from the mainstream of the existing
movements by those left-wing elements who supported Lenin's tactics in Russia.

In Japan there was as yet no socialist party at all and consequently
no labor representatives in parliament. Organized labor had become
a mass movement only in the previous five years. It was not a question of living down the opportunities of the past or of setting out on
a new departure by tightening up organization and reestablishing
ideological clarity as was the case in Germany or France, where a
Marxist tradition was already established; rather, it was a question of
starting an organization from scratch and inscribing a program on a
tabula rasa. In this respect the Japanese Communists were in the
same situation as those in the various colonial areas of Asia. But un-

1. Quoted in Katsumaro Akamatsu, *Nihon Shakai Undō Shi* (A History of the Japanese Social Movement) (Tōkyō, Tsūshin Kyōiku Shinkōkai, 1949), p. 221.

like any other Asian country, Japan herself was an imperialist power with a modern army and navy of her own. This combination of circumstances presented the Japanese Communists with very special problems.

The Communist Party in Japan came to life as a small faction—actually as several factions at first, all greatly influenced by anarcho-syndicalism. In fact, the Comintern agents (some of whom interestingly enough were Korean) considered the Japanese anarchists as natural recruiting targets. When converted, Japanese Communists had to organize in an illegal manner and thereafter relied heavily on the Comintern for leadership, training, and funds. After several attempts, the "official" founding of the Japanese Communist Party dates from July 15, 1922, when it secretly held its first "convention" in Tōkyō.

Although the founding members had no choice about whether to organize legally or not, illegality in a sense gave them greater freedom than any socialist organization in Japan had previously enjoyed. Some of the founding members, such as Yamakawa, Sakai, and Arahata, had had almost two decades of experience with organizing socialist "parties," clubs, and publishing houses, but this was the first time they did not seek permission from the authorities. The precedent was thus set not only for all subsequent reorganizations of the Communist Party until Japan's surrender but also for the illegal labor organizations that carried on after open "front" organizations had been disbanded. Being illegal, they did not have to compromise or delete anything from their program. For the first time since early in the Meiji period, here was a group that called for the abolition of the monarchy or emperor system. They tacitly agreed among themselves, however, to handle this one item with the greatest discretion so as not to endanger the lives of party members unnecessarily.

An examination of biographical data on the founders reveals that they were almost all intellectuals.[2] This fact was probably both a re-

2. "Seldom has a political party—Marxist or otherwise—counted among its founders a larger share of intellectuals." Rodger Swearingen and Paul Langer, *Red Flag in Japan: International Communism in Action 1919–1951* (Cambridge, Harvard University Press, 1952), p. 17. For a list of 45 main figures in this so-called first Communist Party and the organizations they were affiliated with, see Katsunosuke Yamamoto and Mitsuho Arita, *Nihon Kyōsanshugi Undō Shi* (A History of the Japanese Communist Movement) (Tōkyō, Seiki Shobō, 1950), pp. 49–50. Out of the 28 whose affiliations are listed, 19 belonged to political or propagandistic groups, 7 to labor unions, and one to an agrarian organization.

flection of, and a further cause for, the successes the Communists made among Western-oriented scholars, publicists, artists, lawyers, and among students rather than the masses. These intellectuals were leaders drawn from the most important radical associations of the day; they thus carried into this "vanguard" party much of the sectarianism and factionalism that had characterized the whole socialist movement so far. Not to be overlooked among the party founders, however, were those who were not intellectuals in the formal sense but men of working class background with little formal schooling, such as Masanosuke Watanabe and Sadachika Nabeyama. Although the party had some key men in the mass labor organizations at the start, it did not have deep roots or influence in the labor movement.

It is also worth noting that a number of these men eventually became social democrats. Once having been identified as among the founders of the Communist Party of Japan they spent much of the rest of their lives clarifying what distinguished them from those who supported the Comintern-recognized body.[3] One of them, Hitoshi Yamakawa, became the leader of the still small band of Communists at the time. He was a veteran socialist, a disciple of Toshihiko Sakai from the days of the *Commoners' Newspaper.* His influence was already widespread. When organizing the clandestine Communist Party he probably became more aware than ever of the necessity for reaching the masses, and in this vein he wrote an article which hastened the eventual appearance of the proletarian and social democratic political parties. Entitled "A Change of Direction for the Proletariat," this article appeared in the July–August 1922 issue of the radical journal *Vanguard (Zenei).*[4]

Yamakawa elaborated on the slogan of the 1921 Third Comintern Congress, "to the masses," which implicitly called for utilizing all the bourgeois freedoms and institutions, however limited they might be, in order to reach the masses. What Yamakawa said to his Japanese audience, in effect, was that up to now the Japanese proletarian

3. Over a third of those 45 listed in ibid. became active social democrats of one brand or another. Others became professional anticommunists, closer to the national socialist or fascist persuasion. Only four retained their original convictions and became well known Communist leaders: Sanzō Nozaka, Kyūichi Tokuda, Kenzō Yamamoto, and, until his early, agonized death in 1928, Masanosuke Watanabe.

4. Hitoshi Yamakawa, "Musan Kaikyū no Hōkō Tenkan," *Zenei* (July–August 1922), pp. 16–25. The title of this article has often been mistranslated as "A Change of Direction for the Proletarian Movement." A microfilm of the original text is in my possession. At the time, the journal was edited by Yamakawa and his wife, Kikue.

movement had been characterized by a small group of "advanced" activists who spent their efforts defining their goals and refining their theories but in so doing had left the main contingents of the working class behind. The time had now come for the minority of socialists to return to the masses armed with their advanced theoretical formulations. Only if the movement discovered what the immediate demands of the masses were and helped to secure them could it hope to win their strong support. "We must represent the present interests of the masses, improve their livelihood, and proceed with partial victories," urged Yamakawa. "The boycotting of politics is a negative tactic, while resistance through the political process is a positive one."

Although the Communists at this time remained a small group, unable to implement the slogan, the appeal was well timed for it verbalized what many in the socialist movement were already thinking. Despite official censorship, this "change of direction" statement became widely known and had far-reaching repercussions.

Behind it lay the extremism that had characterized the various social movements during the preceding three years. The growing number of strikes in 1918 and 1919 were generally mildly successful, especially the "ca'canny" (go-slow) strikes at the Kawasaki and Ōsaka Ironworks, but they gradually became more and more defensive in 1920 and 1921. Perhaps the most symbolic was the tense dispute at the Kawasaki Dockyards in Kōbe, led by Toyohiko Kagawa from June to August 1921. Kagawa worked out a plan for workers' control of the yards based on the idea that it was a shame and a waste to stop production when a strike occurred. But the more radical elements saw this as a step toward abolition of the capitalist system and felt that the revolution in Japan was at hand. Alarmed, the government called in troops to break the system of workers' control. The strike ended in a crushing defeat for the workers with Kagawa and other leaders under arrest. (It also ended Kagawa's leadership in the labor movement; he turned to organizing the tenant farmers.)

The government's stepping in portended both a change in the government's tactics from a somewhat neutralist position with regard to strikes to an aggressive policy for crushing the leftists. The strong action by the government also raised doubts in the minds of those who believed the revolution would soon occur. The failure of this strike helped to convince many that direct action alone was ineffective and that political means must also be adopted. Liberals had long been pressing for universal suffrage but now those who had come to think of themselves as Marxists took the lead in calling for the creation of a centralized, unified, political movement to press for and take advantage of the vote.

Before the newly formed Communist Party could make itself known within the labor and agrarian movements on its own terms, most of its leaders were rounded up in a surprise mass arrest of about a hundred people on June 5, 1923. Since the authorities gave out little information regarding the background of the action, some newspapers played up sensational stories alleging that the Special Higher Police had stumbled upon a plot to assassinate the whole Japanese government and set up a Communist dictatorship by coup d'état. It is difficult to know what was the precise effect on the public of this sudden exposure of the fact that a Communist Party had been formed. But the lack of details given out by the authorities probably induced both the sympathetic and the horrified to exaggerate the strength of the newly organized Communist movement. The long-range results were both a tightening of police surveillance and an increase in the number of people who came forward to dedicate themselves to the direct or indirect service of the Communist movement, as evidenced in its rapid subsequent growth.[5]

The immediate results of the arrests of the Communists in May and the ensuing newspaper publicity given to radical activities were the terroristic attacks against radicals and minority groups in the confusion and disorder following the disastrous earthquake of September 1, 1923, which wrought havoc in the industrial centers of Tōkyō and Kanagawa Prefectures. Amid the smoke, fire, and ruin, hysterical mobs, incensed with racial hatred and whipped up by the recent newspaper campaigns against "subversion," massacred possibly as many as several thousand Koreans and hundreds of Chinese.

5. In several respects the Communist Party differed from all similar groups that had preceded it in Japan. One of the most important was that it inherited the mantle of a well-known and worldwide movement that had already been successful in seizing power in the geographically largest nation in the world. Other socialists (and anarchists) had the burden of convincing would-be supporters of the possibility of success; they also had greater difficulty getting publicity. In the early 1920s in Japan, the Communists' international connections were probably more of an asset than a liability as far as general approbation, especially among the intellectuals, was concerned, because during the decade or so following the First World War articulate Japanese were still reacting against war-inspired nationalism and supporting internationalist hopes for permanent world peace. This atmosphere was to change completely in the next ten years.

Scores of socialists, anarchists, Communists, and radical labor leaders were locked up by the police "as a security measure." Some were tortured, some expelled from the Tōkyō area which had been placed under martial law. At the Kamedo Police Station eight alleged Communist leaders of the Nankatsu Labor Union and one from another union were shot to death, while in another police cell in Tōkyō the anarcho-syndicalist leader, Sakae Ōsugi, his wife, Noe Itō, who was a well-known advocate of women's rights, and his seven-year-old nephew were all strangled to death by Captain Amakasu of the Gendarmerie.

The earthquake and fires that raged in its wake destroyed about 80 to 90 per cent of the industrial area of Tōkyō and Kanagawa, leaving over two thousand workers dead, and some 68,000 jobless. Thus, the labor problem came to the forefront in the gigantic task of reconstruction in the Kantō area.

THE GOVERNMENT'S CHANGE IN SOCIAL POLICY

After countenancing extreme terrorist activities by the police and superpatriotic organizations in the first few days of September immediately following the earthquake, the government for the first time extended a measure of cooperation to organized labor. An office of Emergency Earthquake Relief was hurriedly set up under the Home Ministry. At the same time the General Federation had organized its own Disaster Relief Committee, headed by Bunji Suzuki. Amidst the confusion following the earthquake, Count Shimpei Gotō, the Home Minister of the new Yamamoto Cabinet that had been formed on September 2, called Suzuki to his office and told him he was willing to provide relief work unloading cargoes at the Shibaura reclaimed land area, if Suzuki could muster a thousand workers immediately. Later it was arranged that government money would be granted to the General Federation for managing housing for workers bereft of homes in the earthquake and certain unions would aid in the operation of employment offices to help laborers find work in reconstruction.

Gotō's calling in Suzuki and inviting the General Federation to play a part in relief work indicated that a change in governmental social policy was taking place. The beginning of this change may be traced back to the time of the Rice Riots in 1918 when the ruling

group as well as the radical socialists had become acutely aware that
the possibility of a revolution in Japan could not easily be dismissed.
Shortly afterward, the Home Ministry recommended allowing the
labor movement to "grow naturally" and actually proposed rescind-
ing that section of the Peace Police Law (Article 17, Paragraph 1,
Number 2) which had, as we have noted, prohibited the development of trade unions on an unambiguously legal basis. The establishment in December 1919 of the Harmonization Society (Kyōchōkai) to promote "harmony" between labor and capital, which had
been partly planned and promoted by Takejirō Tokonami, the
Home Minister in Premier Hara's Cabinet, had been yet another
development in this process. Gradually the Home Ministry became
aware that not all elements in the social movement were "dangerous"
but that there existed "sober" leaders who could be helpful. Earlier
Gotō, when he was Home Minister in the Terauchi Cabinet (1916–
18), and then Tokonami had private talks with Bunji Suzuki to
secure information about the labor and socialist movements.[6]

The unrest following the earthquake helped the astute politician
Tsuyoshi Inukai to persuade the conservative Premier, Admiral
Gombei Yamamoto, to promise publicly to push through a bill for
universal manhood suffrage. Coming as it did on the heels of the post-
earthquake terrorism, this move was well timed. In fact it represented such a popular demand that, even when the short-lived Yamamoto Cabinet fell before carrying it out, the public believed that an
extension of the suffrage could not be far off.

Besides the promise to extend the franchise, the government made
another concession to the labor movement. It revised the method of
selecting the labor delegates to the International Labor Conferences
in Geneva. The fifth such conference was held in the summer of
1924, and this time the government allowed each labor organization
with over a thousand members to constitute a voting unit for the
election of a labor delegate to be accredited by the government to the
Conference. Suzuki won the election. The significance of the move
lay not only in the fact that it encouraged the moderates but that,
although no labor law had yet been enacted, the Japanese government had in effect given tacit recognition to organized labor.[7]

6. Bunji Suzuki tells about these talks in his autobiography, *Rōdō Undō Nijū Nen*
(Twenty Years of the Labor Movement) (Tōkyō, Ichigensha, 1931), pp. 340–44.

7. In order to insure that the new method of selecting delegates to the International
Labor Conference would not lead to radicals being elected, the government immediately
allowed "labor unions" to be organized in the navy and army arsenals and in trans-

Furthermore, in harmony with this new departure, the government began appointing trade union officials to the Employment Exchange Committees (Shokugyō Shōkaijo Iinkai) and to the Imperial Economic Congress (Teikoku Keizai Kaigi) set up by the Kiyoura Cabinet in 1924. Finally, in the following year under the Katō Cabinet, Articles 17 and 30 of the Peace Police Law were abrogated, lifting in effect the ban of illegality on the right to strike.

The clearest shift in the government's attitude, however, dates, as we have seen, from the time of the 1923 earthquake. Up to this time the Home Ministry and the police tended to treat labor disturbances as pure disruptions of the peace in which, even if all the laborers were not rebellious ruffians, at least innocent workers were being stirred into rebellion by dangerous criminals. The government realized that a more sophisticated social policy was needed. The tacit recognition of labor organization and activity and the extension of the vote to the propertyless classes imparted a measure of respectability, however slight, to the labor and proletarian political movements. Such a change on the government's part could not but affect the mutual relationships among the rival leaders of the various social movements.

LABOR'S CHANGE OF DIRECTION

The prospect of an opportunity to achieve respectability for trade union activity was appealing to many labor leaders, particularly because of the importance of status in the Japanese cultural environment. It was considered a great honor to be sent abroad as a labor delegate or as an advisor to the International Labor Conference, and the possibility of eventually becoming a member of the Imperial Diet with its attendant prestige certainly had an allure to those who could not otherwise entertain such an aspiration.

At the same time, the exposure and arrest of Communists who held high positions within the General Federation was not a little disconcerting to the other labor leaders, both because of their discovery that a secret caucus was at work in the organization and also because of their realization that police suspicion might be directed

portation. Their main purpose was to obtain eligibility to vote for a labor delegate. Many of these unions died out in a short time, although some developed independently. The bait of obtaining a vote for a labor delegate was a strong factor in almost doubling the number of workers organized in 1923 from some 126,000 to 228,000. Kyōchōkai, *Saikin no Shakai Undō*, pp. 221–24.

against them as well, even to the point where the General Federation might possibly be disbanded by the government.

Summing up the immediate post-earthquake situation, Bunji Suzuki wrote:

> The first lesson for the labor movement from the great earthquake is above all that spouting theories is useless for trade unions. They must have funds and mutual benefit facilities, without which they can be crushed in any crisis. An unctuous, self-righteous movement cannot in the end build up any kind of a social force. The officials of the Nankatsu Labor Union and the Genuine Workers' Union were . . . [murdered] . . . by the Military Police. If these men had generated a stronger social force, they would probably not have met such a terrible fate. This is the on-the-spot lesson that has been dinned into the heads of the labor leaders. With actions rather than words, practice rather than theory, reality rather than idealism, the workers' outlook will become more sobered. That is the proper path.[8]

Opposing the top moderate or right-wing leadership were the leftists to whom Suzuki refers in his remarks about "spouting theories" and being so "unctuous." Although they were presumably heartened by news that a Communist Party had been formed, despite the fact that this news came about through the exposure and arrest of many of its leaders, the leftists were certainly appalled at the lack of organized resistance to these arrests and to the terrorism that attended the earthquake panic. They, too, were ready for a more "realistic" approach: namely, less reliance on heroic tactics and more on reformist measures in order to mobilize the masses.

On the surface both the right and the left wings thus appeared united in desiring a more "realistic" approach—at the time also called a "liberalization" of the labor movement. This agreement took form at the Thirteenth Annual Convention of the General Federation in February 1924 in what was called "A Declaration on

---

8. Suzuki, p. 344. The word "murdered" had been deleted by the censor prior to publication and replaced with Xs. This was typical censoring procedure in presurrender Japan. In any slightly leftist book many words were apt to be deleted, but one could often tell what they were by the context. Only when whole sentences or paragraphs were replaced by a series of Xs or Os or dots, or left blank, did it become impossible to tell what was meant.

the Change of Direction." [9] According to this, a temporary change in tactics was needed to meet the altered social conditions. The impression the statement gives is that it did not propose a fundamental change in policies. It emphasized that parliamentary means should be utilized only for the purpose of gaining certain political advantages and to awaken the masses politically, but did not hold that the parliamentary path opened the way to gaining power by legal means. Both the leftists and the right-wingers put their own interpretation on it and counted it as a turning point in the political development of the General Federation.

The differing interpretations arose basically from conflicting evaluations of the conditions necessitating a change in tactics. The right-wing leaders in the General Federation held that a change was necessary simply because of lack of success so far, whereas the leftists, as Marxists, saw the setbacks as inevitable accompaniments of the "abnormal" development of capitalism in Japan. In other words, the right-wing leaders believed that the defeats of the past were caused by labor's being so extremist as to incite the ruling class into taking drastic measures. They urged labor to moderate its tactics and take advantage of the concessions made by the government, such as international labor representation and the proposal to extend the franchise. The left-wing anti-leadership (anti-Central Committee) faction held that "objective" conditions had been responsible for setbacks along the way and that the "revolutionary" spirit built up over the last few years with such difficulty should not be lost but rather that the struggle must be broadened to include participation in parliamentary elections. Although both factions were agreed on taking a more active part in politics and attempting to reach the masses, the signs of an impending split were already visible in the arguments about the interpretation of this policy declaration.

THE SPLIT IN LABOR

This divergence within the labor movement, which was to lend support on the one hand to the Communist movement and on the

9. "Hōkō Tenkan Sengen." See Ōhara Shakai Mondai Kenkyūjo (The Ōhara Institute of Social Research), comp., Nihon Rōdō Nenkan (The Japan Labor Yearbook) (Ōsaka and Tōkyō), II (1925), 301. For the complete English translation of the Declaration on the Change of Direction, see Theodore Cohen, "The Japenese Labor Movement Since the World War" (M.A. essay, Department of History, Columbia University, New York, 1949), Appendix.

other to the multifarious social democratic movement—this early division into left and right wings—had by 1923 superseded the former conflict between the "anarchists" and "Bolsheviks." Its repercussions spread throughout the various related social movements, but its most open manifestation appeared in the so-called "first split" in the General Federation in 1925.

While the left wing, spearheaded by the newly organized Communists, began to coalesce into a definite faction within the General Federation, other leftist unions were being formed outside it. Several were admitted into the General Federation at its 1924 annual convention, strengthening the leftist forces. The initial assault of the left on the right-wing leadership took place at the April 1924 convention of the Kantō Ironworkers Union (Kantō Tekkō Kumiai) where the leftists succeeded in ousting the old officers and putting in their own candidates. This sudden success of the leftists, concentrating as it did on a naked struggle for positions, almost at once turned the contest into one of persons rather than issues.

Finding themselves disparaged as the "right wing" and by other epithets, General Federation headquarters leaders began closing ranks and determined not to let the leftists have any leeway at all. At the fall convention of the Kantō Federation (Kantō Dōmeikai) which opened on October 5, 1924, Komakichi Matsuoka led the attack. With the chairmanship of the convention firmly in the hands of the rightists, who held the majority of the union offices, and with the leftists silenced on every occasion, Masanosuke Watanabe, who was leader of the Eastern Tōkyō Amalgamated Labor Union [10] and out on bail as one of the 29 arrested in the Communist roundup of 1923, rose, made a statement, and walked out of the hall followed by 28 delegates. This left the convention in the hands of the right-wingers who thereupon proceeded formally to expel Watanabe and four (later five) other top leftist leaders from the Federation.

The expulsions were reviewed later by the Central Committee which repealed them because they were carried out in violation of the Federation's rules. Although the Central Committee was concerned about the rise of the leftists and would have liked to accept

10. This union, the Tōkyō Tōbu Gōdō Rōdō Kumiai, was an expanded reorganization of the Nankatsu Labor Union, some of whose leaders were murdered by the police during the 1923 earthquake. Instead of breaking Communist influence, the police had created martyrs.

the expulsions, it could hardly countenance such a clear violation of union sovereignty as expulsions of individual leaders. The leftists found the violation effective ammunition for their attacks against the entrenched bureaucratic leadership. The struggle was causing such a stir that something had to be done.

A temporary solution was reached by a leftist retreat: the expelled members would resign voluntarily and the left-wing unions would withdraw from the Kantō Federation and instead organize a Kantō Area Council of the Japan General Federation of Labor (Nihon Rōdō Sōdōmei Kantō Chihō Hyōgikai) affiliated directly with the headquarters of the General Federation. This was not a real solution to the problem, which arose from a fundamental difference of philosophy with regard to the role and function of organized labor in Japan and was compounded by the struggle between the entrenched leaders who wished to keep their positions and the rising leftist leaders who sought positions of power in order to carry out the reforms they thought necessary. Setting up the Council only meant that the leftists were now separately organized within the General Federation. The breach between the factions within the General Federation was beginning to assume organized form.

The idea for this solution, albeit temporary, was said to have come from Suehiro Nishio, one of the entrenched leaders and the "boss" of the Kansai Federation. That Federation, which had not yet been torn by factional strife between right and left, opposed the illegal expulsions proposed by Matsuoka and the other right-wing leaders of the Kantō Federation. Nishio, who was also a member of the Central Committee and a close friend of Matsuoka, approached two of the top Kansai leftists, Sadachika Nabeyama (one of the Communist Party founders) and Yoshiaki Nakamura and convinced them to persuade Watanabe and the other four Kantō leftists to resign; in return the leftists could have their own unions attached directly to the General Federation headquarters on a basis of equality with the Kantō Federation. They were granted the further concession of permission to establish their own newspaper, the *Labor News* (*Rōdō Shimbun*) (which began publication in January 1925). The Kantō Area Council was the first federation of unions in Japan under Communist influence.[11]

11. Zentarō Taniguchi, *Nihon Rōdō Kumiai Hyōgikai Shi* (A History of the Council of Japanese Labor Unions) (2d ed. 2 vols. Kyōto, Kōtō Shoin, 1948), *1*, 67.

In an atmosphere that was tense with factional strife, the 1925 General Federation's annual convention opened on March 15 in Ōsaka. The leftist leaders rose one by one to score the right wing's policies and actions. It was expected that the right wing would introduce its motion to expel the leftist leaders and unions. By the third day, the meeting was in an uproar and it was obvious such a motion could not be passed. Taking advantage of the confusion, however, the right wing cleverly introduced and carried through several revisions in the convention rules, one of which in effect transferred from the convention to the Central Committee the power to expel individual members and unions and another revised the system of elections to the Central Committee in favor of the right wing. The Central Committee met in Ōsaka on March 27 and considered the problem, but even there the necessary two thirds needed to approve the expulsions could not be obtained. After a recess, however, the Central Committee did agree on a demand that the Kantō Area Council dissolve itself as a separate organization with the implication that, if it did not do so, it would automatically be expelled for noncompliance with Central Committee directives.

This not only caught the left-wingers completely off guard but it constituted a greater blow than the expulsion of the leaders would have been. The leftists immediately took countermeasures. They approached the other member unions of the General Federation, urging them to oppose the resolution of the Central Committee, and they started a campaign to "clean out" the "degenerate" top officials of the General Federation. In a petition addressed to the Central Committee they asked for (a) a reconsideration of the change in rules which gave the Central Committee, instead of the convention, power of expulsion, (b) a review of the decision to dissolve the Council, (c) a change in the revised electoral districts of the Central Committee members (which the Central Committee had put through to strengthen right-wing representation), and (d) a no-confidence motion on the handling of this incident. So widespread was the anti-leadership sentiment that the leftists obtained 25 union signatures on this petition.[12]

Greatly alarmed, the right-wing leaders reacted by stiffening their stand. They preferred to have only loyal unions in the General Federation even if they constituted but a minority. On April 12, 1925,

12. Kyōchōkai, p. 228.

they refused all the demands in the petition. Four days later Matsuoka ordered the expulsion of the Kantō Area Council, and the
Central Committee supported this action by refusing a last-ditch attempt at mediation on the 25th. The leftists and other interested
General Federation leaders had come to Tōkyō by the 12th to hear
what the Central Committee decision would be, and when they
learned there was no hope of their remaining within the General
Federation with their present organization, they proceeded to set up
a new, more broadly based organization within the General Federation, called the Rally for the Renovation of the Japan General
Federation of Labor (Nihon Rōdō Sōdōmei Kakushin Dōmei).
Within a month's time this Rally had become sizable and the Central
Committee on May 16, 1925, decided to expel all unions supporting
it. Dissatisfaction with the conservative leadership was widespread
even among those who had supported the Central Committee's decision to expel the leftists in May 1925, for a year later the General
Federation split again when the communist issue as such was not involved.

The left wing, in any case, was forced to take countermeasures.
The Renovation Rally held a big meeting in Kōbe, beginning on
May 24, 1925; half way through the Rally was suddenly transformed
into the founding convention of the Council of Japanese Labor
Unions (Nihon Rōdō Kumiai Hyōgikai), which soon became
known simply as the Council (Hyōgikai). All sources agree that the
Council took 32 unions from the General Federation and left the latter with only 35, but there was a wide range of estimates as to the
number of members these unions contained: a right-wing source
states that the General Federation had 19,460 as against the Council's
10,778, while a left-wing source gives the respective figures as 13,110
to 12,505.[13]

With the formation of the Council as a rival to the General Federation, the dynamic center of the labor movement was cleft into the
almost irreconcilable elements under Communist and social democratic influence respectively. As both factions had an eye on the
changing political outlook, this schism in the labor movement soon
led to a split in the campaign to secure universal suffrage and create
"proletarian" political parties.

Inspired by the Allied "victory for democracy" in 1918, the labor

13. The right-wing source is ibid., p. 231 and the left-wing is Taniguchi, *1*, 93.

movement in Japan had campaigned for two years for the right to vote. The Kansai Federation of the General Federation had been especially active. The Christian socialist Kagawa had led the movement there and the veteran liberal statesman Yukio Ozaki had been among those asked to speak in January 1920. But with Premier Hara's decision against enfranchising the masses in 1920 and the rise of syndicalism in the labor movement, the General Federation had turned away from politics, dropping its demand for popular suffrage and rejecting parliamentarianism in January 1923. After the earthquake and Prime Minister Yamamoto's statement promising manhood suffrage, however, the Central Committee set up a Diet Policy Committee in October 1923 which was soon changed into the Political Section of the General Federation, headed, incidentally, by Katsumaro Akamatsu, who had by then moved far to the right from his position of only two years earlier when he had taken part in founding the Communist Party. This action was ratified at the General Federation's convention in February 1924 simultaneously with the "change of direction" statement calling for greater use of political tactics.

DIVISION AMONG THE PROLETARIAN PARTIES

The increasing interest in the possibilities of political action, as evidenced in the creation of the Political Section of the General Federation, was not confined to organized labor. Leftist intellectuals founded the Society for the Study of Political Problems (Seiji Mondai Kenkyūkai) in Tōkyō on December 18, 1923, to consider what should be done in the light of the approaching possibility of universal suffrage. The early leaders included Yūzō Shimanaka, Suekichi Aono, Mosaburō Suzuki, Kamekichi Takahashi, and Katsumaro Akamatsu. They were soon convinced that they should proceed beyond mere study and discussion and actually prepare to organize a political party to represent the propertyless masses that might soon be enfranchised.

Feeling the need for a more formal body, they elected an organizing committee headed by Isoo Abe to draft a constitution and a prospectus. Dropping the word "Problems" from the original name, the new Society for the Study of Politics (Seiji Kenkyūkai) was officially inaugurated on June 28, 1924. It was clearly led by intellectuals. The spellbinder Toyohiko Kagawa made the opening remarks, Tatsuji Fuse, a lawyer, became the chairman, and the energetic and ambitious Yūzō Shimanaka gave the main report. Congratulations were received from various organizations including the General Federation and the Japan Farmer's Union. A headquarters was set up in Tōkyō which among other things inaugurated a journal, *Political Studies (Seiji Kenkyū).* The purpose of the organization was to study the problems involved in creating a political party to represent the nonpropertied masses and to bring together the various labor and tenant farmers' organizations necessary to provide the organized support for such a party.

From the outset, organized labor was cool toward the Society. While the General Federation proclaimed itself in favor of the Society's goal, it was reluctant to have its members join a group that it suspected of harboring aspirations to turn itself into a new political party. The General Federation wanted to have more control over the creation of a proletarian party than it could exercise through its individual members in the Society.

But the Society did grow and by April 1925 had some 4,000 members in 53 branches throughout the country, made up of farmers and laborers not yet organized in unions, small business people, salaried white-collar employees, students, and professionals. The name of the organ was changed in April 1925 to *Democratic Politics (Minshū Seiji)* and the Society embarked on a series of meetings to educate the people concerning what it called "class politics." Its second convention met on April 19, 1925, and decided among other matters that the Society should (1) prepare a draft program for the proletarian party to be, (2) speed the organization of such a party, (3) campaign for the abolition of the newly passed Peace Preservation Law, and (4) demand that women be given the right to participate in politics. Open to all, the Society encompassed persons of a wide variety of political tendencies.

Ever since the Universal Manhood Suffrage Bill made its appearance on the floor of the Diet on February 21, 1925, the labor and socialist movements had been greatly excited by the prospects. Activities connected with the creation of a possible proletarian party were correspondingly accelerated. The conservative parties were aware and wary of this activity, but on the whole appeared confident of holding their own. Prime Minister Takaaki Katō, who had been championing manhood suffrage since the end of the First World War, managed to push through the bill even though he had to extend the period of the Diet session three times. The implacable opposition expected from the House of Peers, which had killed such a bill as early as 1911, failed to materialize in the face of overwhelming popular support for the suffrage, and the bill was promulgated on May 5, 1925. By removing the tax qualification the electorate was immediately quadrupled from three to almost fourteen millions.

This appeared to be the great opportunity for those who wished to exploit the labor vote, although a number of restrictions still remained and some were even augmented. Women were still completely disenfranchised and actually prohibited from taking part in political movements. Eligibility to vote was restricted to those twenty-five years of age or older, and candidacy for office to males at least thirty years old, with the additional qualification that each candidate had to post a ¥2,000 bond. Although these restrictions were not relaxed until two decades later and although other factors were to offset the democratic gain provided by manhood suffrage, at the time it appeared that a new dawn was breaking for Japanese political development.

The importance of trying to exploit the virgin territory of new voters was not lost on the Communists and leaders of the Council of Japanese Labor Unions when it was formed later in the month. The Council, therefore, took an active interest in the Society for the Study of Politics and urged its members to join the Society as individuals. Another organization under incipient Communist influence, the Student Social Science Federation (Gakusei Shakai Kagaku Rengōkai), which held its first national convention on September 14, 1924, also urged its membership to join the Society. With the infiltration of large numbers of leftists from these organizations, the Society as a whole tended to become more radical. The controversy between the "liberals" and the "Bolsheviks" or the "social democrats" and "Communists" became more intense.

As the first step toward forming a proletarian political party to take advantage of the broadened franchise, the Japan Farmers' Union urged cooperation between organized labor and the tenant farmers. On June 21, 1925, it issued a formal invitation to all interested groups to form a Preparatory Committee for the Organization of a Proletarian Party. The Society for the Study of Politics drafted two programs as a basis of discussion and as guides for the coming proletarian party's platform. Both drafts, however, were distasteful to the Council of Japanese Labor Unions. Branding them as "bourgeois," the Council drew up one of its own.

An emergency meeting of the Society was called on October 7, 1925, at which Mosaburō Suzuki defended the Central Committee's drafts while Shōichi Ichikawa (later the author of the official Communist Party history) spoke on behalf of the Council's draft. After much discussion the latter became the basis of the Society's officially proposed program for the new proletarian party.[14] New elections to the Central Committee were held, and some right-wing leaders, including Yūzō Shimanaka, who had helped found the Society, Jusō Miwa, and Kamekichi Takahashi resigned. Mosaburō Suzuki and Tatsuji Fuse remained on the Central Committee, but new leftist members elected to it included Ikuo Ōyama, a professor, and Hisao Kuroda, a specialist in the problems of farm tenancy. By this time the Society, claiming over 80 branches with some 6,000 members, had moved considerably to the left and had become a formidable antagonist to the General Federation which it now attacked vehemently.

In the latter part of September, the General Federation counterattacked by proposing that the Society be expelled from the Preparatory Committee for the Organization of a Proletarian Party, because the Society had become no more than a mouthpiece for the Council of Japanese Labor Unions and in effect gave the Council double representation in the Preparatory Committee.

At the meeting of the Preparatory Committee on September 17–18, 47 items of the program for the new party were agreed upon, but the leftists opposed 13 points proposed by the right-wingers. At the

14. It is interesting to note that the political section of this proposed program for the new proletarian party called for the abolition of the body of Elder Statesmen (Genrō), the Privy Council, the House of Peers, the General Staff, the Military Headquarters, the Military Police (Kempeitai) and the military courts, the nobility, and other institutions that were all finally done away with by the American Occupation twenty years later! (Abolition of the Privy Council was the only recommendation not finally adopted as part of the Farmer Labor Party platform.) It is equally interesting that almost none of the economic demands, as contrasted with the political ones, had been realized more than a decade after Japan's surrender. A number of demands concerning greater equality for women—demands later pushed by the American Occupation—were also inserted in the proposed platform just before it was adopted, on the basis of proposals from the Women's Section of the Society. Kyōchōkai, pp. 551–52.

October 18–21 meeting the leftists retreated, adopting most of the points demanded by the General Federation supporters, but the latter's attitude further hardened to the point of seeking to expel not only the Society but also a radical organization of a social minority in Japan (formerly termed Eta) called the Leveling Society Proletarian Federation. It was alleged that this group also gave extra representation to the Council of Japanese Labor Unions.[15]

The Japan Farmers' Union in vain assumed the role of mediator in this intense rivalry between the social democratic General Federation and the Communist-influenced Council. When the day arrived for the actual founding of the new proletarian party, to be called the Farmer Labor Party (Nōmin Rōdōtō), the General Federation, represented by Hisashi Asō, announced that its Central Committee had met that very morning and had decided to disaffiliate the General Federation from further participation in the Preparatory Committee and its efforts to form a proletarian political party. It branded the Council of Japanese Labor Unions and the Leveling Society Proletarian Federation "Communist-inspired." The Preparatory Committee immediately went into recess so the constituent organizations could confer on the new development.

The withdrawal of the most important labor federation was a tremendous blow to the whole campaign for the formation of a proletarian party and several of the affiliated organizations proposed dissolving the Preparatory Committee then and there. The leftists were alarmed; the Council proposed its own withdrawal from the Preparatory Committee; and the Society promised to dissolve itself as soon as the creation of the new proletarian party was achieved.

Inasmuch as all the preparations for the new party had been carried out, these leftist concessions were accepted and the Farmer Labor Party's official inauguration ceremony began at 5:30 P.M. on December 1, 1925, at the Young Men's Christian Association building in Kanda, Tōkyō, amid strict surveillance by the police. Motojirō Sugiyama was elected Chairman of the Executive Committee and Inejirō Asanuma, Secretary-General. Both men were officers of the Japan Farmers' Union. Sugiyama was a Christian socialist; Asanuma

15. For the history of the Leveling Society and the political development of the social minority of former outcastes, see below, Chap. 15, "Organized Women and Minority Groups," pp. 366–73.

was one of the early members of the Communist Party but soon moved to a more moderate political position.

At 7 P.M., thirty minutes after the ceremony ended, the new party officers were called to the Metropolitan Police Board and were informed that the party was ordered to disband under Article 8, paragraph 2, of the Peace Police Law. The government charged Communist influence and objectives, branding as "Communist" such planks as government housing for proletarians to be administered by themselves, and tillers' control over the production and distribution of fertilizer and agricultural tools. Communism, it was stated, was incompatible with the "national polity" of Japan. One of the reasons enumerated (thus becoming a hindrance to subsequent party organization) was that the party recognized collective union memberhip; since many of the unions included in their ranks women and minors who were forbidden by law to engage in political activity, the party was violating Article 5, paragraphs 5 and 6, of the Peace Police Law.[16] Japanese proletarian parties were thereafter theoretically based on individual membership but in actuality received collective support respectively from the unions or federations whose leaders were also officers in the particular parties.

The day following the inauguration and the police ban of the Farmer Labor Party, the Japan Farmers' Union Central Committee met in Tōkyō and sadly announced the demise of the first proletarian party in Japan. At the same time, however, the committee voiced its determination to make another attempt to form a single party to represent on a national scale the so-called "proletarian masses."

Acutely aware of the widespread desire for the creation of such a party, and also conscious of the government's firm stand against the allegedly Communist elements, Takeo Yamagami of the Japan Farmers' Union and Yasutarō Kawamura of the General Federation of Labor in Government Enterprises took the lead in a campaign for the rebirth of a proletarian party without the participation of the four leftist groups: the Council of Japanese Labor Unions, the Society for the Study of Politics, the All-Japan Proletarian Youth Federa-

16. Kyōchōkai, pp. 566–67 and 645. The relevant texts of the law are quoted in ibid., p. 742. The Peace Police Law, which had been issued in 1900 and revised in 1922 and 1926, continued in force despite the promulgation of the Peace Preservation Law in April 1925.

tion, and the Leveling Society Proletarian Federation. They held the first round-table discussion on this problem on January 13, 1926, in Ōsaka. The new Labor Farmer Party (Rōdō Nōmintō—reversing the order of the former name) was duly inaugurated on March 5, 1926, in Ōsaka—with policies, platform, and manifesto all moderate in tone. Motojirō Sugiyama of the Farmers' Union was elected Chairman of the Central Executive Committee, while Jusō Miwa of the General Federation became Secretary-General. The other members of the Central Committee were elected from the various labor unions and the Farmers' Union. Abe and Kagawa were chosen as the party's Advisors (*Komon*).

With the exclusion of the Communists and all Communist-influenced organizations, it would appear that this was the first really social democratic party in Japan founded on a mass basis. At that time, however, the general atmosphere within the labor movement was still too radical or revolutionary (using the term advisedly) for the only proletarian party to remain so moderate. The problem of the continued exclusion of the Communists came up as soon as the party's legal existence was assured. The debate over whether to have an "open door" policy or an exclusionist one disrupted the Central Executive Committee meetings; on October 24, 1926, several of the important constituent unions, stating they were tired of this conflict between the right and left wings, announced their withdrawal.

Thereupon the strongest representative of the right-wing position, the General Federation, finding itself in such sharp disagreement with the Japan Farmers' Union which advocated the open door, announced through Suehiro Nishio that it was withdrawing. Simultaneously the Advisors and the Secretary General resigned. Actually the only important supporting organizations remaining were the Japan Farmers' Union and the Ceramics Federation (Seitō Dōmei). The Central Executive Committee, nevertheless, decided to rebuild the constituent elements of the party and move forward. Kanemitsu Hososako was elected Secretary-General to succeed Jusō Miwa, and the first national convention was planned for December 12, 1926, at the Kyōchō Kaikan in Tōkyō. There Ikuo Ōyama was unanimously elected Chairman of the Central Committee to succeed Sugiyama who had resigned. Membership in the party was opened to all, which in the context of the existing situation meant letting down the prohibitions against Communist participation; since the Communists were undoubtedly the most active political organizers at the time, this meant that the Labor Farmer Party would probably become increasingly influenced by the Communist leaders.

Rid of Communist infiltration, the seceding social democrats were finally free to form their own party. Their group consciousness on the political plane can be traced back to October 17, 1925, when they resigned en masse from the Society for the Study of Politics because of what they considered the predominance of leftist members from the Student Social Science Federation and the Council of Japanese Labor Unions. As described above, the General Federation did withdraw just before the Farmer Labor Party was formed. As soon as the government had eliminated that party, the former right-wing members of the Society for the Study of Politics took positive action in setting up the Independent Labor Society (Dokuritsu Rōdō Kyō-kai), on February 6, 1926, at which time Isoo Abe was elected Director. Other important members included Kagawa, Yoshino, Shima-naka, and Katayama.

The Independent Labor Society had also been instrumental in setting up the Labor Farmer Party, with Abe and Kagawa as Advisors. They actually spearheaded the drive to exclude the leftists and Communists and sought to broaden the class basis of the party by moderating its policies. The Communists wanted to restrict the party's objectives to those of the "proletarian class," although even their definition of proletarian included the tenant farmers and various types of propertyless agricultural workers. As opposed to this, the right-wingers advocated a "democratic party" (*minshūteki seitō*—the Japanese word used here means "democratic" in the sense of "popular" rather than "self-governing"). They wanted a platform that would appeal to the lower middle class or petty bourgeoisie, made up of the small shopkeepers as well as the salaried white-collar groups, all of whom were somewhat wary of associating themselves too closely with industrial or manual workers or with tenant farmers—to whom they felt socially superior.

The Society set in motion on July 16, 1926—even before quitting the Labor Farmer Party—a campaign to establish a new popular or democratic party at a time when the dispute over the open door policy was just beginning. With the approval of the General Federation leadership and even with the assent of the Central Executive Committee of the Labor Farmer Party that it planned to replace, the Society set up a Preparatory Committee for the Establishment of a Democratic Party. The new Social Democratic Party (Shakai Minshū-tō) was duly inaugurated on December 5, 1926, only one week before the first convention of the senior Labor Farmer Party.[17]

The intellectuals and labor leaders who became the officers of this new party gradually coalesced over the years into a clearly identifiable clique that came to be known as the *Shaminkei,* an abbreviated word which means "that group of leaders who were once associated with the founding of the Social Democratic Party." For the purposes of this study they will be called the Socio-Democratic clique or faction or the Socio-Democrats, to identify them as a group long after the original Social Democratic Party had ceased to exist.[18]

The non-Communists, however, were far from united. A right-wing agrarian leader, Rikizō Hirano, who had taken part in the formation of the Labor Farmer Party, had bolted it two months earlier in order to organize his own more right-wing Japan Farmers' Party (Nihon Nōmintō). Then, shortly before the Social Democratic Party was formed, a number of the young leaders of the General Federation, who had supported the expulsion of the Communists but who had now become dissatisfied with the top leadership of the General Federation, joined with some of the right-wing Japan Farmers' Union leaders and founded their own party on December 9, 1926, which they called the Japan Labor-Farmer Party (Nihon Rōnōtō). They, too, came to form a clique called the *Nichirōkei,* from an abbreviation of the party name. In this study they are called the Japan-Labor clique or faction, or the Japan-Laborites. The cliques are de-

17. See Appendix II, p. 407: "Proletarian Party Convention Dates." The founding convention is usually counted as the first convention, but the new leaders of the Labor Farmer Party considered its founding convention not truly representative of the party as it had developed. Their public reason for not counting the founding as the first convention was that it had not been a sufficiently grand affair. Some 224 delegates attended the much publicized official first convention. Hakuyōsha (White Sun Company), ed., *Nihon Musan Seitō Shi* (A History of the Japanese Proletarian Political Parties) (Tōkyō, Hakuyōsha, 1931), p. 479.

18. Japanese abbreviations do not result in initials of the words or names as in English. They tend to take one character (or syllable) from each compound word or each important compound part. Sha-kai Min-shū-tō can be abbreviated to Sha-min-tō. This process is similar to some Russian usage, as in the case of Communist International which becomes Comintern. In translating the names of the various factions I have tried to approximate this system. This enables me later to discuss the Socio-Democrats as members of the Socialist Masses' Party after the Social Democratic Party has been dissolved.

picted graphically in their various political manifestations in Chart I of the Appendix.

The formation and composition of these cliques and their subsequent activities will be described and analyzed in the following chapters. Here it is sufficient to note that they formed the two main currents in what had become the noncommunist left or the social democratic movement in Japan. To them were added a number of other factions and groupings which will also be treated in detail.[19] These subdivisions within the social democratic movement itself can, after further clarification, serve as threads of continuity through the patchwork of organizational changes, outlining the twists and turns of policy development. And they can be used to sort out and measure comparative support given by social democratic leaders from labor, agrarian, and other groups.

Organizational change was most kaleidoscopic between 1926 and 1932, as may be seen in the Lineage Charts in the Appendix. By 1932, however, the social democratic movement achieved a measure of unity. It then became possible for the various splinters to merge in the formation of the Socialist Masses' Party (Shakai Taishūtō), which remained in existence for eight years until all Japanese parties were disbanded in 1940. Anticommunism, along with anticapitalism and antifascism, formed one of its basic principles. Actually, in the course of time, the communist issue lost its importance. It was in the years from 1926 to 1929 that the Communists were most active and successful. Continuous governmental suppression was largely responsible for the decline of the Communists after the proletarian movement split.

COMMUNIST DECLINE

The Communist Party of Japan did not progress steadily upward after its formal founding in 1922. Due to the arrests of the following year and also to the fact that the party's highest theoretician, Hitoshi

19. As indicated earlier, the purpose of the present chapter has been to describe the process by which the social democrats became differentiated from the Communists. When the term "Communist" is capitalized, it refers to members of the clandestine Japanese Communist Party. When "Social Democrats" is capitalized, the reference is to actual members of the Social Democratic Party during the time it existed, but when "social democrats" is used, it can mean persons associated with any part of the legal noncommunist left except those clearly identified as anarchists or national socialists.

Yamakawa, came to feel that the working class in Japan was too immature to find a Communist Party useful as yet, the party was dissolved in 1924. With the aid of the Comintern and Profintern, however, it had been revived and reorganized by the end of 1926. During the following two years it was active through student, labor, and proletarian party organizations—the Student Social Science Federation, the Council of Japanese Labor Unions, and the Labor Farmer Party.

The Communists ever since 1925 had aimed to create a united labor movement and a single proletarian party but had been frustrated by their own policy of attacking the moderate and right-wing social democratic leaders. Another policy contradiction involved the aims of building both an illegal Communist Party, on the one hand, and a legal, mass party (the Labor Farmer Party), on the other.[20]

When the Labor Farmer Party achieved a measure of success, securing the largest support at the polls of all the proletarian parties, the government cracked down. On the morning of March 15, 1928, a mass roundup of Communists, sympathizers, and other leftists numbering about 12,000 was carried out. Some 500 were held and prosecuted. On April 10, 1928, the Labor Farmer Party, the Council of Japanese Labor Unions, and the All-Japan Proletarian Youth Federation, already crippled and disorganized after most of their leaders had been arrested and their premises searched and sacked, were officially ordered disbanded under terms of the Peace Preservation Law.

Despite this heavy blow all these organizations proceeded to reorganize. A number of the top Communist Party leaders had evaded arrest. Contact was reestablished with the Comintern and its aid received. To take the place of the disbanded Council of Japanese Labor Unions, the National Conference of Japanese Labor Unions was organized on December 25, 1928. By March of the following year, active Communist Party membership surpassed its previous peak. Once more the police conducted nationwide arrests on April 16, 1929, and more than a thousand suspects were rounded up. Gradually thereafter the top Communist leaders were arrested one by one in private homes, or in secluded tea houses, or while passing in or out

20. For a discussion of these contradictory policies, see Robert A. Scalapino, "The Labor Movement in Japan," unpublished manuscript, Chap. 5, "The Era of Division," pp. 15–16 and 24.

of the country. By the summer of 1929, the party had again been reduced to a small group. Moscow now attempted to reorganize the
party with Russian-trained replacements, but they were all gradually
apprehended by the police. By 1932 the trials of the top Communists
arrested in 1928 and 1929 came to an end with convictions for all.
The following year, several of the best-known Communist leaders,
such as Manbu (Gaku) Sano and Sadachika Nabeyama, wrote from
their prison cells recantations which were publicized by the government. This started a wave of recantations among the lower levels of
the party. The Communist movement had become almost totally ineffective in Japan.

The social democrats had, in a sense, come into existence through
their struggle against the Communists when the latter had tried to
take over the leadership of the General Federation. Then their own
attempt to survive within the bounds of legality necessitated cutting
loose from the illegal Communists and contributed to the destruction of the organized Communist movement in Japan. Thereafter,
the social democrats, it is true, moved forward to their greatest victories in terms of numbers of votes at the polls until they confronted a
strident nationalism. Nevertheless, the struggle between the Communists and the social democrats drained the burgeoning proletarian
movement of much of its strength and dynamism. It entailed the sacrifice of solidarity within the labor, agrarian, and other social movements, crippling them at their birth in the 1920s when world and
domestic conditions otherwise were most conducive to their growth.
Furthermore, the disruption of a common front among those seeking
to represent the nonpropertied masses inevitably weakened them
against their common antagonists, the established parties and the
various segments of the state bureaucracy. Because of their weakness,
some of the social democratic leaders became susceptible to appeals
from the increasingly assertive military. This, as we shall see, led
them down the path of ultranationalism. If in this period from 1922
to 1932 the social democrats' contribution to social stabilization in
the eyes of the authorities was to prevent the various social movements from going too far left, their role in the succeeding decade was
to drag these movements into the orbit of support for aggressive
war.

In concrete terms, the one issue that most crucially divided the social democrats from the Communists throughout the presurrender period was their stand on the question of the "emperor system" (*tennōsei*). This at first may appear strange, inasmuch as antimonarchism was a cardinal principle of the early democratic movements in the West. In the Japanese context, however, the Meiji oligarchs had used loyalty to the throne not only as the slogan for the Restoration but also as their Archimedean lever in creating a "modern" state. According to official interpretation, the uniqueness of Japan lay in its being ruled over by emperors "in a line unbroken for ages eternal." The theory of the spiritual omnipotence of the Emperor, if not his divinity, was part and parcel of the "national polity" (*kokutai*)—the "basic essence" or "unwritten constitution" of Japan. If the emperor system were taken for granted in any plan for the construction of a socialist economy, then it followed that the uniqueness of Japan would remain. Although this line of reasoning did not inevitably lead to the ideology of "national socialism" at home and the "imperial mission" abroad, that path was thus made much easier.

4: Toward War and Totalitarianism: 1931-1941

To combat the rising liberal, socialist, and labor union movements, a number of reactionary, ultranationalistic groups sprang up after the end of the First World War. Only a few succeeded in gaining at least a moderate mass following; most consisted of a sprinkling of determined followers.[1] Tracing their spiritual heritage back to the Sea of Genkai Nada Society (Genyōsha) of the early Meiji period and acting in concert with the Amur River Society (Kokuryūkai, often erroneously translated as the "Black Dragon Society"), they exerted pressure for Japanese expansion abroad and at times resorted to violence to stem social change at home. While some had connections in high places, many were organized on the lower levels by such people as building contractors who demanded feudalistic obedience of their followers. Sometimes they threatened moderate statesmen, but far more frequently they engaged in strikebreaking activities or violent attacks against leftist individuals, trade unions, or farmers' organizations, or against minority groups such as the "special community

1. A convenient reference for the names, aims, leaders, lineages, dates, and strengths of these and almost all other nationalistic organizations in Japan (and abroad) is Hanji Kinoshita, *Gendai Nashonarizumu Jiten* (Dictionary of Contemporary Nationalism) (Tōkyō, Kantōsha, 1951).

people" (former Eta social outcasts) and Korean laborers. Such activities suggest that these groups grew out of the almost inevitable reaction against "modernization" or "Westernization" pure and simple.

A more complicated motivation characterized other nationalistic groups which began to appear at this time and which, in addition to harboring leftist antipathies, were interested in positive programs for change toward the radical right. Their leaders were men who had been deeply influenced by various types of socialistic thought which they had combined with elements of ultranationalism or imperialism. Because of similarities to the early forms of Italian Fascism and German National Socialism, their theories have generally been regarded in Japan as Japanese versions of fascism.[2]

Although the majority of the conspirators or agents in the assassinations and bombthrowings of the 1930s were uneducated farm boys or young officers and noncommissioned officers, a few intellectuals were to be found among the fascist or national socialist ranks. They had almost invariably been baptized in leftist socialist thought. Outstanding examples were Ikki Kita, Dr. Shūmei Ōkawa, and Motoyuki Takabatake. Kita was the most important "theoretician" and activist; Ōkawa promoted Kita but soon broke with him in a fashion typical of the factionalism that plagued the ultra-right wing, as it did the left; Takabatake, originally known for his translations of Marx, became an admirer of Mussolini and supported the proletarian right-winger, Rikizō Hirano.

The years from the First World War until 1931 have been called the period of preparation for Japanese fascism; that is, the period when its various ideological elements were being formed and disseminated and personal contacts made. As with European fascism, it

2. For interpretations of prewar fascism, see Ivan Morris, ed., *Japan 1931–1945: Militarism, Fascism, Japanism?* (Boston, D. C. Heath, 1963). The best recent study in English that covers prewar Japanese fascism is Richard Storry, *The Double Patriots: A Study of Japanese Nationalism* (London, Chatto & Windus, 1957). Storry points out that the Japanese versions of fascism differed from European fascism in never getting significant mass support and being averse to open dictatorship. Ibid., p. 6. Among the most important Japanese scholars of this subject are Masao Maruyama and Hanji Kinoshita. See the former's *Gendai Seiji no Shisō to Kōdō* (Thought and Behavior in Modern Politics) (2 vols. Tōkyō, Miraisha, 1956–57). This has been edited in English by Ivan Morris as *Thought and Behaviour in Modern Japanese Politics* (London, Oxford University Press, 1963). See Kinoshita's *Nihon Kokkashugi Undō Shi* (History of the Japanese Nationalist Movement) (2 vols. Tōkyō, Iwasaki Shoten, 1952), and *Nihon no Uyoku* (The Right Wing in Japan) (Tōkyō, Yōshobō, 1953).

was a blend of traditional thought with specific radical propositions. While Kita proposed the nationalization of important industries and the confiscation of private fortunes, his greatest emotional appeal was for "removal of the barriers between the nation and the Emperor," echoing the cry of the Meiji Restoration, "revere the Emperor." [3]

The year 1931 marked the opening of a new era for Japanese fascism. Radical elements of the army then for the first time took an active part in a series of attempted uprisings. The most noted of these in the following year was the so-called "May 15th incident" in which Prime Minister Inukai was murdered and the Bank of Japan was bombed by navy and army officers. This trend reached its climax in the February 26, 1936, abortive uprising in which some 1,400 troops, under the influence of the Army's Imperial Way Faction (Kōdōha), assassinated select high-ranking officials and occupied the new Diet building, the War Ministry, the Metropolitan Police office, and other points in downtown Tōkyō in a vain effort to create a situation in which the army chiefs would be compelled to take over the direction of the government. An appeal by the Emperor helped bring the incident under control by the fourth day. Kita was executed for complicity in this plot.

Thereafter the opposing Control Faction (Tōseiha) gained the upper hand in the army by purging leaders of the Imperial Way Faction and by employing severe measures to prevent any further radical uprisings from below. Instead of losing power because of this incident, the army turned it to its own advantage by demanding concessions from the Diet and the bureaucracy in return for keeping the young army hotheads under control. By this process the army eventually became so powerful that it was able to place the Control Faction leader, General Hideki Tōjō, in the premiership in 1941. Thus a form of "military fascism" or totalitarianism took hold of the country by stages, as Japan prepared for all-out war.

SOCIAL DEMOCRATIC REACTIONS TO THE MANCHURIAN INCIDENT

What was the role played by the social democrats in this process? Did they prove effective in resisting the radical fascist trends in

3. See Sōgorō Tanaka, *Nihon Fashizumu no Genryū: Kita Ikki no Shisō to Shōgai* (The Fountainhead of Japanese Fascism: The Life and Thought of Ikki Kita) (Tōkyō, Hakuyōsha, 1949).

Japan, did they compromise, or did they even to an extent get in step with them?

The occupation of Manchuria by Japan's Kwantung Army after September 18, 1931, shocked and initially bewildered the Japanese social democratic parties. Despite clear-cut antiwar planks in their platforms, they found it difficult to take an unequivocal stand on the issue. Already factions were rising within the parties ready to support national socialism at home and expansion abroad.[4]

In the Social Democratic Party at this time such a faction was led by Katsumaro Akamatsu. He soon proved to be an inveterate opportunist who ran the gamut of the political scale from communism to fascism within a decade. In 1922 he had been one of the supporters of the Japan Communist Party, when it appeared that communism was the wave of the future. By accident he was not arrested along with the other Communist leaders, and, as the possibility of a revolution occurring in Japan appeared increasingly remote, he was soon counted among the conservative right-wingers of the General Federation leadership. He took part in the founding of the Social Democratic Party in 1926, instead of going along with most of the other young intellectuals, who instead formed the Japan Labor-Farmer Party at the price of expulsion from the General Federation. With the ebb of the revolutionary tide in Germany, the solidification of Mussolini's regime in Italy, and the growing power of the Nazis in Germany, Akamatsu's ideas became more rightist and his popularity grew. On March 15, 1930, he was elected Secretary-General of the Social Democratic Party.

With the outbreak of the Manchurian incident, Akamatsu and his followers pressed the party to adopt the following stand: "All peoples have the obligation to demand an equal right to existence. It is unthinkable that only the Japanese be restricted to an island country and that only they be bound to sacrifice themselves for the sake of 'world peace.' "[5] In openly supporting Japanese aggression in Manchuria, Akamatsu's position did not differ from that of the "bourgeois" parties. But beyond that he did disassociate himself from them, for he called for "an end to bourgeois control over Manchuria

4. Probably the most detailed account of the rise of fascist trends within the social democratic movement is to be found in Kinoshita, *Nihon Kokkashugi Undō Shi*, especially Part II, Chap. 4 and Part VII, Chaps. 3 and 4.

5. *Nihon Minshū Shimbun* (The Japan Democratic News) (October 15, 1931). This was an unofficial organ of the Social Democratic Party edited by Akamatsu himself.

and Mongolia and a conversion to national socialist control." This demand aligned him with the ultranationalist or military fascist groups which were crying for "an end to the exploitation of finance capital in Manchuria and the establishment there of the Kingly Way (Ōdō)." [6]

The majority opinion within the Social Democratic Party was less radical and somewhat closer to that of the bourgeois parties. Yet despite some theoretical differences between them, both factions were in fundamental agreement on the justice of Japan's actions in Manchuria. The heightened patriotism resulting from the victories of Japanese arms in Manchuria, combined with the increasingly frequent acts of violence perpetrated against "unpatriotic" individuals or groups in the semi-wartime atmosphere, certainly formed the background in which these decisions of the Social Democratic Party were reached.

But in order to understand why the party reacted to the situation as it did, a more detailed sociological analysis of its support is necessary. This will be undertaken at appropriate points in subsequent chapters. Here it is sufficient to mention that most of the party's organized labor support was drawn from two groups: (1) the comparatively well-off segments of labor (sometimes called the "labor aristocracy," if that term can be applied to Japanese labor at all), composed of the merchant marine unions, and the army, navy, and government workers' unions; and (2) the comparatively backward sections of labor that worked in relatively large factories such as textiles, and formed what were virtually company unions or at least ones which fully supported the principle of labor-capital "harmony."

At the head of these sections of labor, many of the Socio-Democratic leaders were able to strengthen their position as a result of the Manchurian affair. Their advocacy of class harmony had greater relevance and their bureaucratic control over their unions seemed more justified than in the slough of the depression before the outbreak of hostilities. They emphasized labor peace in the following statement at the twenty-first national conference of the General Federation held November 15–17, 1931, shortly after the outbreak of hostilities in Manchuria: "The policy of the General Federation has always

6. See Naimushō Keihokyoku (Home Ministry Police Bureau), ed., *Shuppambutsu o Tsūjite Mitaru Nihon Kakushinron no Genkyō* (The Present Situation Concerning Ideas for Renovating Japan, as Seen Through Publications), marked *"Hi"* (confidential) (Tōkyō, December 1933), p. 553.

been to keep the number of strikes down to the lowest possible limit. The General Federation is dead set against turning strikes into political struggles or provoking them recklessly." [7] Mild as this statement was, taken in the context of the post-Manchurian crisis it could easily be interpreted as betraying a desire on the part of the General Federation's leaders to share in the prosperity about to be created by increased orders for military goods and by the new economic expansion in China.

While the more conservative majority of the Social Democratic Party welcomed the increased chance for labor peace, the radical rightist minority led by Akamatsu was getting impatient for more forthright action. Even before the Manchurian affair, the civilian rightists, including Shūmei Ōkawa and the so-called "young officers," had already planned an uprising to overthrow civilian rule and substitute military dictatorship under General Kazushige Ugaki. Some three hundred bombs and sufficient funds had been collected, but when General Ugaki backed down the plot was abandoned.

Akamatsu then renewed his contacts with Ōkawa, who had been a classmate of his older brother, and set up the Japan Institute for the Study of Socialism (Nihon Shakaishugi Kenkyūjo) together with Hanji Matsunobu, a close follower of Ōkawa, and Tatsuo Tsukui and Junjirō Ishikawa, two disciples of Takabatake, the translator of Marx turned fascist. The purpose of the Institute was to create a theory of national socialism for Japan and also to try to coordinate the various fascist organizations in the country. It had a considerable amount of money at its disposal, and one of its main aims was to convert proletarian organizations to national socialism.[8]

Akamatsu persuaded his Institute to start a magazine called *Japanese Socialism (Nihon Shakaishugi)* after he learned of the failure of the "October (1931) incident," in which Ōkawa and others had planned to assassinate the whole Cabinet and install General Araki as Premier. This plot was actually the revival with expanded objectives of the abortive coup that was to have taken place in March and as such was a more important failure. Akamatsu was convinced that before "renovationist" actions could succeed, a wider understanding of their aims and greater support were needed. Shortly thereafter, on

7. *Rōdō (Labor)* (November 1932), p. 17. This magazine was the official organ of the Social Democratic Party.

8. Kinoshita, *Nihon no Kokkashugi Undō Shi, I,* 211.

November 29, 1931, Akamatsu organized a Socialist Youth League (Shakai Seinen Dōmei) within the Social Democratic Party but mainly under his faction's influence. He intended either to convert the whole party to national socialism or split it wide open.

Despite basic agreement in attitude toward the Manchurian incident, majority opinion in the Social Democratic Party wanted to maintain the principles of social democracy. Isoo Abe expressed this sentiment at the Central Committee meeting on April 15, 1932, when the party finally did split:

> I interpret democracy as a very broad concept. Thus, I hold that it may be altered somewhat in accordance with objective conditions, whether they be problems of internationalism or of the Diet. Like the pendulum of a clock, it may swing to and fro for a certain distance; but it is absolutely opposed to dictatorship. I will devote my life to the cause of democracy as against dictatorship.[9]

During the course of events leading to the split it appeared at times that the Akamatsu faction would be dominant. At the sixth party convention held on January 19 and 20, 1932, both factions submitted proposals. Tetsu Katayama, representing the majority faction, proposed the Three Antis Platform (Sampan Kōryō): (1) anticapitalism, (2) anticommunism, and (3) antifascism. Akamatsu submitted what was called the New Campaign Policy, containing many of the fascistic overtones of the time, such as "reverence for the national polity," the nationalist as opposed to the internationalist position of the Japanese proletariat, and deemphasis of parliamentarianism.[10] Oddly enough, in the tense atmosphere, both proposals passed despite obvious contradictions.

In April, however, the conflict between the two factions came to a head. A Central Executive Committee meeting was held to consider whether to amalgamate with the other proletarian party, the National Labor-Farmer Masses' Party, which united within itself all the hitherto disparate remaining legal proletarian factions. Akamatsu agreed with the majority faction on dissolving the Social Democratic Party, but he was for setting up a new party based entirely on the

9. Quoted in Rōdō (May 1932).
10. The text of the New Campaign Policy may be found in Nihon Rōdō Nenkan, 14 (1933), 452.

spirit of the New Campaign Policy, that is, "national socialism" (kokumin shakaishugi) or "state socialism" (kokka shakaishugi).[11] He was backed up by the Secretariat of the Party Headquarters, the Socialist Youth League, and also the Hirano faction whose organized base was the newly formed Japan Farmers' Union (Nihon Nōmin Kumiai—not to be confused with the earlier, larger organization of the same name). The majority faction, as represented by Katayama and Komakichi Matsuoka supported by the General Federation, persisted in their support of the Three Antis Platform and social democracy. When put to the vote, Akamatsu's proposal won, twelve to eleven. It now appeared that the majority faction was becoming the minority.

Such a close vote, however, was not felt to be binding and the issue was raised in precisely the same form at the meeting of the larger Central Committee on April 15, 1932. Here the earlier decision of the Central Executive Committee was reversed by a clear majority of 61 to 52 in favor of "social democracy." Thereupon, Akamatsu, Shirō Koike, and his other sympathizers stalked out of the room indignantly. It is interesting that the groups that these men led out of the party were mainly white-collar workers (including only a small number from the General Federation) with the exception of a landlord-backed farmers' group led by Hirano.[12]

All the proletarian political groupings to the left of the Social Democratic Party had united into one party just before the Manchurian incident. Officially set up on July 5, 1931, it was called the National Labor-Farmer Masses' Party (Zenkoku Rōnō Taishūtō). The leaders of the former Japan Labor-Farmer Party or the Japan-Labor clique, together with some Labor-Farmer factionists, formed the backbone of the new party. They had been joined by the remnants of the reorganized Labor Farmer Party which had moved to the right with the continued arrests and defections of Communists and Communist sympathizers. The party had also attracted several smaller parties which had been largely influenced by the Labor-Farmer faction, another left-wing group to be described below. (These shifts are depicted graphically in Chart 1, "Lineages of

11. These two terms were used almost interchangeably by Akamatsu and others at this time in Japan.

12. A list of the organizations and their leaders may be found in Kinoshita, Nihon no Kokkashugi Undō Shi, 1, 222.

Japanese Social Democratic Parties," found in the Appendix.)

With the outbreak of Japanese aggression in Manchuria, this party was quick to condemn the "imperialistic" policy being pursued by the government and the military. It demanded the withdrawal of all Japanese troops from China and set up a committee to work out tactics to effectuate this demand and struggle against the spread of the fighting.

At its annual convention held on December 5–6, 1931, the National Labor-Farmer Party attacked its rival in the following terms:

> The Social Democratic Party's social democracy (in practice, class collaboration) . . . is quickly becoming bankrupt in the present conditions of capitalism. It can be said that socialism has already become the generally accepted goal within the proletarian class movement, but in the end it can only degenerate into social fascism (or national socialism) if it tries to avoid a head-on clash with bourgeois imperialism. The sight of the Social Democratc Party excitedly pandering to the recent trend toward fascism unmercifully exposes its corrupt nature to the masses. For the sake of the liberation of the workers and peasants, such supporters of bourgeois reaction must be completely obliterated.[13]

A proposal was made at the convention to "oppose the imperialistic war," and a stirring message supporting it which had been written by Toshihiko Sakai, one of the "grand old men" of the party who was ill and near death, was read. But Chief Takeuchi of the Atago Police Station, present at the convention in accordance with the law, would not allow any other speakers to be heard on behalf of this proposal. When the convention, chaired by Asō, unanimously adopted the proposal, the Police Chief ordered that the word "adopted" be excised from the minutes and closed the convention.[14]

In these circumstances, the party's antiwar campaign appears to

---

13. The convention statements are found in *Nihon Rōdō Nenkan*, *13* (1932).

14. As all the reports by the party officers had not yet been delivered, the police chief allowed them to finish, and thus the odd spectacle took place of party officers gravely intoning their reports after the convention was officially over. Masao Naka, *Senkusha no Keifu: Shakaitō Zenshi* (The Genealogy of the Forerunners: The Prehistory of the Socialist Party) (Tōkyō, Shakai Shichō Henshūkyoku, 1949), pp. 167–68. As the delegates were leaving the hall a number of them were arrested, and that night bamboo sticks and knuckles rained on their heads at the Atago Police Station. Mosaburō Suzuki, *Ai to Tōsō* (Love and Struggle) (Tōkyō, Rōdō Bunkasha, 1949), p. 102.

have been limited to one rally at the Honjo Public Hall in Tōkyō. Although this policy had the full backing of the delegates at the open convention, behind the scenes a clash of opinion among the leaders further stymied the campaign. A few of the Japan-Labor clique leaders had begun to get in touch with civilian fascists and young officers soon after the March 1931 plot, and apparently contact men from the military actually visited the majority of National Labor-Farmer Masses' Party leaders after the outbreak of war in Manchuria and attempted to persuade them to support the army's actions.[15] The right wing of the party was led by Asō who was supported by such men as Shōzō Ōya and Yoshitsuru Yamana; a little more to the center were Mitsu Kōnō, Jusō Miwa, and Teruaki Tadokoro; and on the left were Mosaburō Suzuki and Hisao Kuroda, formerly of the Tōkyō Proletarian Party, and Kanjū Katō who was originally associated with the Japan-Labor clique but who was becoming more leftist.

The frayed bonds of leadership were first severed on the left by the defection of Katō and his supporters. An explanation can be found both on the party level and on the lower level of trade union support. At the party level friction had developed between Katō and Asō because each of them considered the Fifth District in Tōkyō as his own constituency. While it was theoretically possible for both of them to be elected, since four Diet seats were assigned to this district, their rivalry would undoubtedly divide the proletarian vote probably defeating them both.

On the trade union level the explanation is more complicated. A policy difference had developed between Katō and others, including Asō, all of whom were leaders of "National Labor" (Zenrō), the abbreviated name for the National Labor Union Federation (Zenkoku Rōdō Kumiai Dōmei). National Labor was led by the Japan-Labor clique (see Chart 2 in Appendix). In June 1931 the majority of its leaders decided to respond to an overture from more right-oriented unions (affiliated with the General Federation) to join in forming a kind of liaison office, called the Japan Labor Club (Nihon Rōdō Kurabu). Katō, however, branded the club "a social fascist manifestation of the new fascist trend." By November he had formed a group within National Labor with the descriptive title of the National Labor Struggle Combination to Boycott the [Japan Labor] Club (Zenrō Kurabu Haigeki Tōsō Dōmei). The leadership majority thereupon expelled this group known as the "Boycott Combina-

15. Ibid., p. 99.

tion" (Haidō), from National Labor, and since National Labor constituted the main pillar of support for the National Labor-Farmer Masses' Party, it soon became impossible for Katō and his supporters to remain in the party. His group's future attempts at a more leftist type of unity were to eventuate in the "popular front" of 1937. In the immediate situation it simply indicated that the party was veering to the right.

As the Manchurian affair dragged on and as the crisis atmosphere pervaded the country, a number of party leaders began to feel that the party was not moving to the right fast enough, that is, was not going along with the times, and a series of fascist-oriented deviations began to take place.

The first of these was the actual defection of the General Alliance of Japanese Labor Unions (Nihon Rōdō Kumiai Sōrengō), led by Kōsaburō Sakamoto. At the party's convention on December 6, 1931, Sakamoto stated that his organization was not an "auxiliary" of the party, that it "reserved independence of action and freedom of criticism," and that it was, therefore, withdrawing its support from the party.[16] Very shortly afterward, four party functionaries in the Kyōto region also bolted the National Labor-Farmer Masses' Party, after criticizing it for not being sufficiently national-socialist. Both Sakamoto and these four functionaries joined Yasaburō Shimonaka and his following in January 1932 in preparing for the formation of a Japanese "national socialist party" (kokumin shakaitō).

The severest shock to the party's already fainthearted opposition to the war in Manchuria, however, came from a statement issued by

16. The background and subsequent action of this organization is illustrative of the drastic shift that was taking place in the labor movement. With an announced 25,437 members in 1931, the General Alliance had been organized and led from the beginning by Sakamoto singlehandedly. It began as a radical, anarcho-syndicalist organization. Being syndicalist it did not join the Communist-led Council of Japanese Labor Unions; nevertheless, being also radical, it supported the Council as an outside organization during the latter's existence. With the increasing governmental pressure against the left wing, as manifested in the mass arrests of March 15, 1928, and April 16, 1929, the General Alliance modified its policies, affiliated with the Japan Labor-Farmer Party, and remained with it through its reorganization into the National Labor-Farmer Masses' Party in July 1931.

After withdrawing his support from the party in December 1931, Sakamoto was afraid of becoming isolated and seized the opportunity of the appearance of the national socialist movement to form, with Yasaburō Shimonaka, the Preparatory Committee for the Organization of the National Socialist Party (Kokumin Shakaitō Soshiki Jumbikai) on January 17, 1932, which will be discussed below. The history of this organization, therefore, describes an arc from anarchism to Communism and then through left-wing social democracy to national socialism or fascism.

Yojirō Matsutani, one of the party's two representatives in the Diet, when he returned to Japan from an inspection tour in Manchuria with several other Diet members.[17] He unequivocally supported Japan's actions there, saying that it was not "imperialistic" to dispatch troops to protect Japanese interests, but he went on to argue that these interests should be taken from the capitalists and given to the peasants and workers and that the two million unemployed in Japan should be sent as settlers to Manchuria. It was rumored that he was pressured by the army to take this stand.[18] A movement for Matsutani's expulsion from the party immediately got underway, but it was not successful due to intrigues from such national socialists outside the party as Akamatsu and Shimonaka, in collaboration with leaders within the party, such as Tadokoro.

Furthermore, Matsutani's position appeared to be vindicated by the general election of February 20, 1932. He was reelected to the Diet from his constituency in Tōkyō. The party did hold on to one more Diet seat, though it passed from Kenzō Asahara of Fukuoka to Motojirō Sugiyama of Ōsaka. But worst of all, the party's popular vote melted away. It received only some 135,000 votes compared to the aggregate of almost 269,000 garnered by its predecessors in the election of 1930. Matsutani himself commanded no real mass organizational backing. He was a lawyer who had joined the party after becoming known for his achievements in the field of civil liberties as a member of the Liberty Lawyers' and Judges' Guild (Jiyū Hōsōdan). His support for the military in Manchuria appeared to be an important aspect of his appeal to the electorate.

Following the electoral reverses, a considerable section of the party's organized support broke away as a result of the conversion of five top Japan-Labor clique leaders to national socialism: Hitoshi Imamura, Bunroku Fujioka, Sakaru (Sakan) Aki, Genji Mochizuki, and Zensaku Iwauchi. On March 11, 1932, they wrote a joint memorandum to the Central Executive Committee which implied that the party should cooperate with the military and attempt to gain power by the tactic of spreading confusion.[19] This was a telling blow in

---

17. Matsutani had been elected to the Diet on the Japan Masses' Party (Nihon Tai-shūtō) ticket in 1930 and with the formation of the National Labor-Farmer Masses' Party received the honorary post of Advisor to the party.

18. Kinoshita, *Nihon no Kokkashugi Undō Shi, 1*, 225.

19. The whole memorandum is quoted in ibid., pp. 225–28.

favor of national socialism. These men were top leaders in the party's strongest supporting organization, National Labor.

On March 24, 1932, the Central Executive Committee, while issuing special statements opposing both the Second and Third Internationals and the Japanese Communists, nevertheless also confirmed its policy opposing fascism. These leaders then attempted to withdraw National Labor support from the party under the name of "freedom of political affiliation," but at the National Labor's Central Committee meeting on May 5th and 6th, they lost by a one-vote margin, six to seven. The next day, led by Shōzō Ōya (who had earlier switched from the Socio-Democratic to the Japan-Labor clique) they seceded from the party, taking with them sizable labor support, which then transferred to the national socialist movement under Akamatsu's leadership. Even after the defection of this opposition, the stalwarts who remained were not able to maintain the party's original stand against Japan's role in Manchuria.

It is obvious that at this period the social democratic movement was serving to a certain extent as a recruiting ground for the fascist or national socialist movement.[20] An examination of Japanese national socialism can therefore help clarify the nature of social democratic ideology, leadership, and activity.

JAPANESE NATIONAL SOCIALISM

Along with Akamatsu, Yasaburō Shimonaka was the most active social democratic convert to national socialism at this time. Born in Hyōgo prefecture, his first job was teaching in an elementary school in Kōbe. Later he went up to Tōkyō and became leader of a teachers' union. He was apparently an anarchist until the sharp defeat on September 30, 1922, of the anarcho-syndicalist attempt to unify the labor movement. Shimonaka then became an editor of the Hei-

20. It should perhaps be pointed out that "fascism" (rendered either as *fassho* or *fashizumu*) was used as a term of opprobrium and, being a loan word, had a foreign flavor. It was only natural that the nationalistically inclined Shimonaka, Akamatsu, and other "national socialists" and "Nipponists" objected to being "dismissed" as "facists." The term, nevertheless, became popularly accepted in Japan to mean just such people and it stuck. For a discussion by Akamatsu on the points of agreement and disagreement between his form of national socialism for Japan and German Nazism and Italian Fascism, see Katsumaro Akamatsu, *Shin Kokumin Undō no Kichō* (The Keynote of the New Nationalist Movement) (Tōkyō, Banrikaku, 1932), pp. 106–51. Akamatsu praises Nazism for its activism and for recognizing the fundamental unity of national interest but criticizes it for not being sufficiently anticapitalist.

bonsha, a large publishing house in Tōkyō, and by his sponsorship there of popular publications directed to the masses gained considerable influence. After abandoning anarchism, he gradually came to a right-wing social democratic position and joined the Social Democratic Party, but left it considerably earlier than Akamatsu.

Shimonaka began his campaign for the formation of a national socialist party a month after the outbreak of the Manchurian war, together with Kametarō Mitsukawa, a close associate of both Ikki Kita and Shūmei Ōkawa. He felt that a new base for fascism could be found among: (1) proletarian and labor organizations in conjunction with certain right-wing groups, (2) journalists, teachers, government and business office workers, artists, doctors, lawyers, small tradesmen, and manufacturers, and (3) small farmers and landlords with small and medium-sized holdings.[21]

Akamatsu requested Shimonaka to hold up the formation of the new party until Akamatsu himself could gather more forces from the social democratic camp with the aid of Ōya, who had just bolted National Labor. After setting up several preparatory committees and study groups, the formal inauguration of the new party was planned for May 29, 1932; but on that day just before the ceremony was to take place, the two main factions fell out over the party name and over assignment of posts. Negotiations broke down and two separate parties were formed: Akamatsu's faction set up the Japan State Socialist Party (Nihon Kokka Shakaitō), while Shimonaka's followers organized the New Japan Nationalist Federation (Shin Nihon Kokumin Dōmei). The former advocated "state socialism" and the latter "Nipponism"; but their platforms were almost identical.[22]

The growth of national socialism of this variety in Japan was stunted almost from birth. Henceforth, both factions split up even more. The process need only be surveyed here. Early in 1933 Akamatsu was converted to Nipponism. He was then expelled from his own postmen's union and bolted the Japan State Socialist Party which he had helped organize. Together with Tatsuo Tsukui, he formed the Nationalist Movement Association (Kokumin Undōsha) which later became the Nationalist Society (Kokumin Kyōkai) and attempted to spread the spirit of Nipponism. Akamatsu was elected to the Diet in

21. Kinoshita, *Nihon no Kokkashugi Undō Shi, 1,* 233, n. 1.
22. The platform of the latter is quoted in ibid., *1,* 235, and of the former in ibid., *1,* 240–41.

1937 as a candidate from the Society. After helping to form several other organizations, he ended up in the Imperial Rule Assistance Association in 1940.

Others of Akamatsu's associates also split up. The Hirano group, leading the Japan Farmers' Union of 1931, took its own course and entered the Imperial Way Association (Kōdōkai). Koike, who had bolted the Social Democratic Party with Akamatsu on April 15, 1932, split with him a year later when Akamatsu shifted to Nipponism. Still unwavering, Koike at first organized the Standing Conference for the Resurrection of the State Socialist Party (Kokka Shakaitō Kōsei Jōnin Kaigi) but later also went over to Nipponism, changing the name of the group to the Patriotic Political Federation (Aikoku Seiji Dōmei).

The Japan Labor Federation (Nihon Rōdō Dōmei), which under Ōya's leadership had withdrawn from National Labor and which supported Koike's state socialist philosophy, also experienced a split-off by a faction converted to Nipponism, which then proceeded to organize the Japan Industrial Army (Nihon Sangyō Gun) in 1933. Succumbing to appeals by Yojirō Matsutani, the Japan Labor Federation supported the formation of the Japan Party of Devoted Labor (Kinrō Nihontō) in 1934,[23] but later, under pressure from below for a united labor front, the Kantō unions of the Federation rejoined National Labor and the Kansai unions (led by Ōya) joined the Japan General Federation of Labor, both of which were supporting the Socialist Masses' Party at the time.

Thus by 1935 it appeared that the radical fascist movement was on the wane and parts of its former mass support were returning to the social democratic fold. What had happened in these few years? Was there still a future for social democracy? Why did radical fascism not rise out of social democratic groups in any real strength? The answers lie partially in a further analysis of the dynamics of the radical fascist movement in Japan.

23. Matsutani, as we have seen, was elected to the Diet as a member of the Japan Masses' Party in 1930 and was reelected in 1932, this time as a member of the reorganized party, the National Labor–Farmer Masses' Party. But he had been a strong supporter of Japan's interests as "defended" in the Manchurian incident. He did join the new Socialist Masses' Party and became an Advisor when it was formed in 1932, but he soon bolted it over his stronger views on support of Japanese expansion; thus he was in a position to form this new "nationalist socialist" Japan Party of Devoted Labor in 1934, after a flirtation with Adachi's Nationalist Federation (Kokumin Dōmei).

The "military fascism," if it can be called that—there is no scholarly consensus on this point—that became dominant in Japan in the 1930s until 1945 took its form not in a revolutionary manner but through a modification of the existing political structure. It was led by the military, the most aggressive and violent segment of the great bureaucratic Japanese state which revolved organizationally and spiritually about the imperial institution. Thus Japanese fascism differed from the German variety. The latter rallied the masses through a struggle against other political parties and eventually, as a party, gained control of the whole apparatus of government. It developed outside of the state structure and took it over, whereas in Japan military fascism was more of an attitude or political orientation that eventually saturated the state structure. While it was not brought about by mass demonstrations, the successively attempted coups d'état by military groups served as pressures against the political arm of the government.

In Germany, the people had experienced the downfall of the Hohenzollern monarchy, had voted the Social Democrats into a plurality in the Reichstag, and had supported strong labor organization. Similar occurrences had never taken place in Japan. The fascist appeal in Germany had to be to the masses. It had to stir them and direct their energies to its own ends. It had to capture segments of labor as well as the petty bourgeoisie. But in Japan the emperor institution became the cynosure of all fascist thought and action. Anachronistic sociopolitical attitudes made this so. Traditional social relationships continued to exist, especially in rural areas, despite the rapid growth of the great zaibatsu trusts, whose power lay in their modern industrial combines. This above all created the peculiar conditions in which the centralized bureaucratic state apparatus, capped by the Emperor and supported by a prefeudal mythology, could be transformed into a pseudo-totalitarian fascist system wherein elements of modernism were fantastically mixed with antiquated shibboleths and behavioral patterns. Thus Japanese military fascism resulted from the reactions of a traditional, orthodox political structure to the depression, Chinese nationalism, and the worldwide loss of faith in capitalism and democracy.

Elements of Western fascistic thought began to receive serious acceptance among certain segments of the civilian and military bureaucracy with the onset of the great depression in 1929–30. Particularly affected were the young army officers whose background was rural and whose only education was narrowly military. They were able to secure large-scale support from rural areas because the army was popular among the villagers, a popularity based in part on two of its characteristics that were pseudo-democratic. Firstly, the officer class had been open to recruitment of the younger sons of even very small landlords throughout Japan. It had not been a preserve of the aristocracy, such as the Junkers in Germany. And secondly, all civilian social distinctions and family background were completely disregarded *within* the army, being replaced by military grades and ranks that were theoretically open to all on the basis of ability, training, and experience.

As we have already seen, certain intellectuals such as Ikki Kita, armed with fascist ideas from abroad, attempted to utilize the susceptibility, and popularity of the young officers to create a revolutionary movement "from below." [24] When funds and confidential information were received by them from military or bureaucratic–political sources, they flourished. But actually the various right-wing factions within the military and the bureaucracy utilized the sudden bursts of energy of these radical organizations for their own advancement within the existing power structure. When the army leaders found them no longer useful, they repudiated them. The February 26 (1936) incident sealed the doom of the radical fascist movement.[25]

24. See Maruyama, *Gendai Seiji no Shisō to Kōdō*, pp. 28, 32, and passim. By "from above," Maruyama and others meant not only the military and bureaucracy but also the politicians and the zaibatsu and other powerful financial interests. But "from below' also has a wider meaning: the small-scale business class, foremen, and lower white-collar workers, schoolteachers, and others who would wax militantly patriotic and xenophobic. Ibid., p. 59. Here we are referring only to the small numbers—the radical rightists or fascists—who wanted' to take revolutionary action to "rectify" the situation at home and abroad.

25. How the radical fascists felt after the incident is shown in the following quotation: "According to my observations, it seems that after that incident [the February 26 (1936) incident] a feeling of melancholy and emptiness began to eat away at the hearts of not only the members of the February Club (Nigatsukai) but of all the fighters in the whole renovation movement (*kaikaku undō*). . . . The distinctions between right and wrong, good and bad, came to an end and such things as election campaigns and the nationalist movement lost all their strength in an instant like dewdrops exposed to the heat of the sun. . . . It seems that the military braintrusters feel that it was more advantageous to entrust the great work of domestic renovation to the Hirota Cabinet than to the advocates of Nipponism. Thus, fortunately or unfortunately, it appears that the relationship of the Nipponist movement with the military has returned to a blank

Thereafter the government took action against some of these radical fascist groups for obstructing bureaucratic control. In the period of the culmination of the totalitarian structure in Japan (from the time of the second Konoe Cabinet to the end of the war), some of these organizations actually resisted the totalitarian trend by calling for "freedom of expression" for the "demands of the masses." Such organizations were either suppressed or forced off the political stage.[26]

The conversion of segments of the social democratic movement to fascism took the same course. The dramatic shift of Sakamoto's General Alliance from the National Labor-Farmer Masses' Party to Shimonaka's national socialist group helped turn the whole labor movement more toward the right.[27] But the General Alliance soon lost favor with the military, as the latter found less need for civilian radical groups. Unhappy at being jolted by the military, the General Alliance leaders turned to flirtations with the fascist organizations which were advocating Nipponism, but this was like the halt joining the halt and shortly led to their disappearance from the political scene altogether. The course of this organization is typical of those social democratic groups that embraced fascism around the time of the Manchurian incident.[28]

It is apparent that fascism in Japan lacked large-scale support from

once more. . . . At present we are without strength; in some respects even more so than the proletarian parties. . . . Since then I have felt more and more strongly like getting away from actual activity." From Tatsuo Tsukui (a member of the so-called "idealistic right wing" (*kannen uyoku*), "Nihon Kokkashugi Undō Shiron" (On the History of the Japanese Statist [Nationalist] Movement), *Chūō Kōron* (May 1937), pp. 190–92.

26. Perhaps the most outstanding example was Seigō Nakano's Eastern Association (Tōhōkai) which opposed the bill to give Tōjō full power to control speech and assembly; the Association was soon ordered disbanded, and Nakano was arrested. See Taketora Ogata, *Ningen Nakano Seigō* (The Man Seigō Nakano) (Tōkyō, Masu Shobo, 1952), pp. 40–56.

27. For instance, on March 25, 1934, at the third Executive Committee meeting of the Congress of Japanese Labor Unions, the social democratic unions consisting of about 270,000 members were intimidated by the General Alliance of Japanese Labor Unions, which had only about 27,000 members—the publicly announced figure, probably heavily padded—into withdrawing the slogan opposing fascism from the coming May Day demonstration. See *Ōtsuki Shakai Rōdō Mondai Geppō* (The Ōtsuki Monthly Report of Social and Labor Problems) (April 1934).

28. Another case was that of the Postmen's Brotherhood (Teiyū Dōshikai). After having expelled Akamatsu from its leadership because he switched from state socialism to Nipponism, the Brotherhood gave the union presidency to Seigō Nakano, originally a politician in the Seiyūkai who had been converted to fascism and helped Adachi form the party he represented in the Diet, the Nationalist Federation—later to become

independent antigovernmental mass organizations and that the radical fascist groups could not survive without aid and abetment from the ranks of the young officers.

According to an analysis by Professor Maruyama,[29] the social exponents of fascism in Japan were to be found in the unorganized masses of the lower middle classes, among the "pseudo-intelligentsia," rather than among the more highly educated segment of the economically lower middle-class. They consisted of local community leaders and occupational superiors with enough education to place them in a position of authority among the less informed masses but whose level of education, especially of a Westernized content, was not high enough to isolate them from the masses. In this category also were the owners of small factories, the bosses of town workshops, building contractors, owners of small retail shops, master carpenters, small landlords and those ranging down to owner-cultivators, schoolteachers, especially at the primary level, employees of village offices and lower grade civil servants in general, Buddhist and Shintō priests, and all those with a certain "status" within the local community. Wielding a paternalistic authority by which they dominated

---

the Eastern Association. Other social fascist organizations considered Nakano's group too "bourgeois" and shunned the Postmen's Brotherhood. See Matsuta Hosoya, *Nihon Rōdō Undō Shi* (A History of the Japanese Labor Movement) (2 vols. Tōkyō, Dōyūsha, 1948), 2, 145. With the rise of the government-sponsored Patriotic Industrial Movement, the union was suppressed by the authorities on the grounds that, being an independently run organization, it obstructed governmental control. The chairman and two others of its leaders were discharged from their jobs in the postal system "because of resisting orders and disturbing discipline." See Teishinshō (The Ministry of Post and Telegraph), *Teishin Jigyō Shi* (A History of the Work of the Post and Telegraph) (2 vols. Tōkyō, Tsūshin Bunka Shinkōkai, 1949), *1*, 550, and for a detailed history of this union by the same source, see *Teishin Rōdō Undō Shi* (A History of the Postal and Telegraphic Labor Movement) (2 vols. Tōkyō, Tsūshin Bunka Shinkōkai, 1949, 1951), *1*, 3–94.

29. See "Nihon Fashizumu no Shisō to Undō" (The Japanese Fascist Movement and its Ideology), in Shigeki Toyama, Korefusa (Shisō) Hattori, and Masao Maruyama, *Sonjō Shisō to Zettaishugi* (Absolutism and the Ideology of Revering the Emperor and Expelling the Barbarians), Tōyō Bunka Kōza (Monographs on Oriental Culture), 2 (Tōkyō, Hakujitsu Shoin, 1948), 149. This was reprinted as Chap. 2 in Maruyama, *Gendai Seiji no Shisō to Kōdō*, pp. 25–82. It was first translated in English in an abridged version by Maruyama himself as "The Ideology and Movement of Japanese Fascism," *The Japan Annual of Law and Politics*, *1* (1952), 95–128. It has been retranslated by Andrew Fraser as "The Ideology and Dynamics of Japanese Fascism" in Maruyama, *Thought and Behaviour in Modern Japanese Politics*, pp. 25–83. Incidentally, in using the term "totalitarian" in the present book I am referring more to the *attempts* by Premier Konoe and others than the actuality, since Japanese "totalitarianism" (*zentaishugi*) always fell short of the goal.

their followers, employees, tenants, debtors, or "inferiors," they helped manufacture anti-leftist public opinion and fostered the excessive reverence for the Emperor in whose name the political assassinations and attempted coups d'état were carried out by the various fascist or ultranationalist groups.

The social category which, according to Maruyama, abhorred rightist or fascist movements consisted, on the other hand, of the better-paid salaried men in the metropolitan areas, the nonofficial intelligentsia, the independent professionals (such as professors and lawyers), and the more highly educated student class, as well as workers in the larger, modernized industries. It was from among these strata that the leaders of the communist and social democratic movements were recruited, as will subsequently be shown in greater detail, and consequently also those leaders who turned from leftist thought and then attempted to create an organized basis for fascism in Japan. Yet these converts were never really successful, as they coupled their support with anticapitalist demands that were too extreme for the more conservative Control faction which gradually got the upper hand within the army and the nation and which needed the cooperation of important capitalist groups in order to supply the military needs and exploit Japanese acquisitions on the mainland of China.

While the pseudo-intelligentsia of the first category continued the generally unorganized support for Japanese aggression abroad and totalitarianism at home, a large part of those of the second, more highly educated category at first actively opposed these trends and then during the total war period evinced a passive resistance in the form of "culturism." For example, at the time of the most promising phase of fascist development around 1931 when the extreme leftist labor unions (notably the National Conference of Japanese Labor Unions or Zenkyō) had been forced underground, the pro-Communist intellectual magazine *Battle Flag* (*Senki*), organ of the All-Japan Conference of Proletarian Fine Arts Organizations (Zen Nihon Musansha Geijutsu Dantai Kyōgikai) was maintaining a circulation of some 23,000 copies with an estimated readership of 100,000 and could continue to count on raising sufficient funds.[30] Furthermore, the cry for academic freedom continued to be heard in

30. See Seizaburō Yamada, *Puroretaria Bungaku Shi* (A History of Proletarian Literature) (2 vols. Tōkyō, Riron Sha, 1954), 2, 264–65. Also see George T. Shea, *Leftwing Literature in Japan* (Tōkyō, Hōsei University Press, 1964), p. 200.

the universities, even long after the staggering setback of the arbitrary dismissal in 1933 of Professor Takigawa of Kyōto Imperial University for alleged Marxist views.[31]

Even among labor unions which had officially espoused national socialism, Nipponism, or some other variety of fascist dogma, the older trade union philosophy still retained an underlying vitality. The workers in such unions often opposed the "industrial peace during foreign crisis" philosophy of their leaders by demanding wage increases, protesting against job controls, or making various political demands. An example of this was the unprecedented wildcat strike at the Toshima Post Office in May 1933 by members of the Postmen's Brotherhood, which by this time had long since switched its political support from social democracy and now supposedly eschewed such "disruptive activities" as strikes.[32] In other cases, some union leaders who had been converted to Nipponism were still forced to maintain a policy of "trade unionism" with regard to their own unions. Organized labor, like the intelligentsia, appeared unable to provide the mass basis for a fascist movement that was seen in Germany or Italy.

The situation was somewhat different with regard to the organized agrarian movement in Japan. The first farmers' group to be converted from the social democratic camp to a brand of fascism was led by Rikizō Hirano. In January 1931 his farmers' union had merged with that of the Socio-Democrats to form the Japan Farmers' Union (as may be seen in Chart 3 in the Appendix). When he was converted to national socialism—just before he joined the Japan State Socialist Party with Akamatsu—the minority led by the Socio-Democrats bolted the Japan Farmers' Union; [33] but otherwise only two local sections of the union, those of Kanagawa and Saitama, protested the farmers' union's conversion to fascism.

Hirano also succeeded in taking with him a substantial following when he later switched his support to the Imperial Way Association

---

31. It was Home Minister Ichirō Hatoyama (later a postwar Prime Minister) who ordered the dismissal in May 1933. As it disregarded established procedures, the President and a large section of the Kyōto faculty resigned in an attempt to preserve "academic freedom" and the "independence" of the University.

32. Teishinshō, *Teishin Rōdō Undō Shi*, pp. 545–52.

33. After the Socio-Democratic-led farmers bolted the Japan Farmers' Union in April 1932, the Union had 26 local federations and 38,000 reported workers. As against this, the Socio-Democrats, who had reformed their General Federation of Japanese Farmers' Unions, had only 12,000 of whom 8,000 had paid dues to the Social Democratic Party. *Nihon Rōdō Nenkan, 14* (1933), 446.

(Kōdōkai) in 1933. Even in the period of decline of the radical fascist organizations he did not lose his organized mass support among
small landlords and well-to-do farmers, although their political demands had to be phrased in terms that relegated agrarian class lines
to the background. During the agricultural crisis of 1931–32, when
tenant-farmer disputes were breaking out all over Japan and when
tenant farmers were turning against their landlords with demands
for full possession of the lands they tilled, Hirano's demands were as
follows: "Return to the agricultural villages the exploitation taken
by the big cities; lend money to agriculture without collateral; and
overthrow capitalism which is selfishly exploiting the agricultural
villages." [34] The attempt here was to deflect the anger of the tenant
farmers at their distress away from the landlords and direct it toward
the cities.

This same point may be further clarified by recalling that many of
the fascistically inclined young officers of the Japanese army had
originally come from landlord and relatively well-off farming families and that the vast majority of the soldiers in the regular army
were from the villages. The civilian groups that worked with them,
moreover, were composed of farmers' sons; an example was the Blood
Brotherhood (Ketsumeidan) that took part in several plots in early
1932 culminating in the May 15th incident of that year, when Premier Inukai was assassinated. Thus, the most active elements in the
radical fascist movement arising from the agricultural communities
were those who vociferously attacked the "ruling circles of finance
capital," that is, the zaibatsu and their "tools," the political parties,
but who were ultrareactionary in wanting to return to the past and
to reestablish the nation again on the principle of "agriculture-is-the-
base" (nōhonshugi), an ideology tied up with Shintō nationalism,
exalting the values of rural life and opposing the evils of urbanism
and industrialization.[35]

Although Hirano's organization was eventually dissolved to make

34. These demands were put forth at the August 19, 1932, convention of the Kyūshū
Federation of the Japan Farmers' Union (Nihon Nōmin Kumiai Kyūshū Dōmeikai).

35. This ideology had a long history going back to the Meiji period when it expressed
a reaction against the attempted introduction of large-scale capitalistic agriculture. By
this time it had become more virulently anti-urban and ultranationalistic, though various aspects of it were espoused by different factions, some of which were not much
concerned with world problems. See Dore, Land Reform in Japan, pp. 60–64, 77–78, and
92–93.

way for Japan's totalitarian structure, it was able to maintain up to
the end a certain mass organization with a stability never achieved
by the fascistic organizations composed of the urban middle strata
and labor union officials.

UNIFICATION OF THE SOCIAL DEMOCRATS AND SUBSEQUENT REACTIONS TO FASCISM AND WAR

With defections to national socialism from the ranks of both the
National Labor-Farmer Masses' Party and the Social Democratic
Party, pressure for their unification mounted. Both parties had made
a poor showing in the 1932 Diet election, and this was attributable
partly to their attacks on each other. The National Labor-Farmer
Masses' Party was no longer much to the left of the Social Democratic
Party inasmuch as some of its leftists, such as Kenzō Asahara, had
embraced fascism while others, notably Kanjū Katō and his following, had withdrawn from the party and had been expelled from National Labor. Both parties were almost equally targets for the attacks
from the illegal leftist National Conference of Japanese Labor Unions in its last burst of energy in 1932.

Within the labor movement personal rancor was clearly a barrier
to immediate unification among the labor federations. But the two
parties realized that greater cooperation between their respective
supporting trade union organizations was desirable in the event of a
merger. They decided that the Japan Labor Club, with which both
organizations were connected, should be strengthened and reorganized for this purpose. Two months after the party merger the reorganized Japan Labor Club took the name of the Congress of Japanese Labor Unions (Nihon Rōdō Kumiai Kaigi) on September 25,
1932. This opened the way to the eventual unification of the federations in 1936 (see Charts 1 and 2 in the Appendix for elucidation of
this point in visual terms).

The merger ceremony of the two parties took place on July 24,
1932, at the Kyōchō Kaikan (Harmonization Hall) in Shiba Park in
Tōkyō. The new party was called the Socialist Masses' Party (Shakai
Taishūtō) and in its "Terms of the Merger" it took a clearly antifascist stand, "opposing imperialistic wars" and "strengthening the
anti-fascist front." As a socialist party it was also dedicated to "the
overthrow of the declining capitalist system" and still spoke in the

radical phrases of opposition to "class collaborationism" and "parliamentarianism"—by which term they meant "elections as the only form of political activity." The party was obviously not opposed to campaigning for office but wanted to supplement this with street demonstrations that would gradually build up the militancy of the masses. It aspired to be the single proletarian party and to promote cooperation between labor and the farmers.[36] Isoo Abe was elected Chairman of the Central Executive Committee, while Hisashi Asō became Secretary-General.

In the beginning the Socialist Masses' Party clearly opposed fascism, but it gradually came to support a war policy and then the whole structure of military fascism or totalitarianism in Japan. The first step seemed almost innocuous: it reversed its stand in 1933 on the question of "military orders inflation" which was one of the government's methods of getting out of the 1931 depression and consisted of expanding military orders and of large-scale deficit spending for military purposes, a policy that made necessary the "dumping" of goods abroad to secure imports. The party's reversal, contained in "A Policy for Rebuilding Japan in a Period of Change" [37] adopted on July 22, 1933, declared, "The lower classes find mass inflation desirable." This trend became even more apparent at the Second Party Convention held December 8–10, 1933, at which proletarian "dogmatism" was repudiated and a conscious policy of appealing to the broad middle strata was adopted. This was an important step in the reorientation of the Japan-Labor clique and was strongly opposed by Mosaburō Suzuki and other Labor-Farmer faction supporters within the party on the grounds that blurring class lines was conducive to "social fascism."

But the Labor-Farmer faction was fighting a rearguard action. The following quotation indicates the drift away from the tenets of social democracy:

> Our class movement is not a narrow one. It does not overlook the permanence of the nation nor does it stand for those selfish class interests which cause tension between class and people . . . Now and in the future, we must treat the problem

36. The "Terms of the Merger" were published in the *Nihon Minshū Shimbun,* June 15, 1932. Jōtarō Kawakami was Chairman of the Merger Committee.

37. "Tenkanki Nihon no Kensetsu Seisaku," *Shakai Taishutō Pamfuretto* (A Socialist Masses' Party Pamphlet) (Tōkyō, Shadaitō Shuppambu, 1933).

of war much more carefully and concretely. We must stop simply opposing it in our writing and speeches and overcome our mechanical, dogmatic, and anarchistic way of treating the problem.[38]

With regard to labor policy, the Socialist Masses' Party (particularly the Socio-Democratic clique within it) called for industrial peace and greater cooperation between labor and management. The government and the military were very much interested in this campaign, and through it the party's labor leaders increased their contacts with the authorities and began to advocate governmental control over industry and labor. The Congress of Japanese Labor Unions on December 16, 1933, met with representatives from the government, from proletarian and bourgeois political parties, from business, and from the academic world to consider the problem.[39] This trend was eventually to develop, some six years later, into what was called the Industrial Patriotic Movement (Sampō Undō) in which labor was brought under governmental control for the purpose of prosecuting the total war effort.

There are indications that the Socio-Democratic clique had secret financial connections with various capitalist and zaibatsu groups and that the Japan-Labor clique gradually established such connections with the military (Imperial Way faction) and the "new zaibatsu." [40] In any case, it was not long before Asō was advocating closer connections between the proletarian classes and the military.

38. From the *Shakai Taishūtō Undō Hōshin Sho* (Campaign Policy Paper of the Socialist Masses' Party) (Tōkyō, Shadaitō Shuppambu, 1934).

39. The government was represented by interested officials from the Home Ministry, the Metropolitan Police Board, the army, navy, communications, etc., mostly of vice ministerial rank. Also present was Shigeru Yoshida representing the Harmonization Society.

40. See, for instance, Ken Itō, *Shikin Ami Monogatari* (Stories of Fund Raising) (Tōkyō, 1935), which claimed that, of the Socio-Democratic clique, Bunji Suzuki obtained funds from Mitsui and Mitsubishi managements and Komakichi Matsuoka secretly received ¥20,000 in 1927 as election funds from the Noda Soy Sauce Company where he had led a strike only a few months previously. Itō further claimed that Asō, leader of the Japan-Laborites, and Kanichirō Kamei, his close friend, although a Socio-Democrat, received financial aid from General Kazushige Ugaki who was implicated in the March 1932 plot, an unsuccessful coup d'état plotted by the young officers of the Cherry Society and civilians including Shūmei Ōkawa and Kanichirō Kamei himself. Ugaki also had much to do with encouraging military production in Korea and elsewhere and thus had close contacts with the "new zaibatsu." Through Ugaki, Asō was said to have special connections with such zaibatsu, particularly in the Kansai area.

The occasion was the so-called "army pamphlet incident." In October 1934 the Press Section of the Ministry of War issued a propaganda pamphlet entitled "The Essence of National Defense and Proposals to Strengthen it." [41] Opening with the phrase, "War is the father of creation and the mother of culture," the pamphlet went on to say that the army was the prime driving force behind the nation. It advocated Japan's development in the direction of a totalitarian economy based on a nationalistic systematization of the elements of defense, adoption of further governmental controls over business, and reform of the structure of the national economy. The pamphlet was fundamentally a declaration of war against the party system in Japan, and with the prestige of the army behind it its influence was considerable. The stock market fell, and the bourgeois parties dared to criticize the military on the floor of the Diet for bringing out such a pamphlet.

Asō, however, speaking as a leader of the Socialist Masses' Party, openly defended the military's action. "Although we resisted the fascistic reactionary forces at the time of the Manchurian affair and the May 15th incident," he said, "considering the situation in Japan and inferring from the true nature of the Japanese army, we firmly believe that fascism is impossible here. . . . The situation in Japan makes necessary a rational alignment of the proletarian classes with the army, if a social reformation is to be achieved by the overthrow of capitalism." [42] Furthermore, on the floor of the Diet, Asō declared,

> Recently the Ministry of War put out a pamphlet . . . [which] states that military preparations alone are insufficient for our national defense in the future. Our national defense must be based on a real stabilization of the people's livelihood. . . . We indeed agree with the principle of national defense in the broader sense. However, if we examine the budget which has been submitted since then, it seems to us that even the military has, in a certain sense, trampled on the idea of national defense in its wider meaning. . . . Above all, if in the future a war occurs among

41. *Kokubō no Hongi to Sono Kyōka no Teishō.*

42. From the party organ of the Socialist Masses' Party, *Shakai Taishū Shimbun* (The Socialist Masses' News) (October 28, 1934), quoted in Jōtarō Kawakami, representative (of the Committee for the Publication of the Biography of Hisashi Asō), *Asō Hisashi Den* (The Biography of Hisashi Asō) (Tōkyō, Asō Hisashi Den Kankō Iinkai, 1958), p. 457.

the great powers of the world, it cannot be a simple war such as the Sino-Japanese or Russo-Japanese Wars of the past. Although we have experienced one world war, in another such, if it should arise, I feel that probably all countries will be thrown into great confusion. In such a severe war, I consider it impossible for a country to stand the severe strain or to protect its people unless it possesses a solid national structure built on principles making for national unity. . . . Knowing capitalism's lack of a sense of nationality . . . I cannot help but feel that unless Japan today develops a real unity worked out in a system based on the principle of unity between the military and the people, real national defense cannot be carried out.[43]

Asō used this advocacy of the need for reform in the capitalistic economy of Japan as a reason for wooing the military clique. In the same speech, he then turned to address the bourgeois parties: "It is quite possible for you to shout me down. But why did you of the Seiyūkai who had 303 Diet seats become so petrified with fear at the time of the May 15th [1932] incident? If you really had the trust of the masses of the people, you would have had no need to fear the 'pistols' of the military."

Criticism of Asō's support for the army pamphlet bubbled up within the Socialist Masses' Party, adding heat to the growing friction between the Japan-Labor and Socio-Democratic cliques.[44] Thus, though strongly seconded by Tadokoro, approbation of the pamphlet did not become official party policy.

Despite the continuing friction within the Socialist Masses' Party on this and other points, the emphasis on proletarian unity did not abate, and the story of the unification of the social democrats would

43. "Asō's Interpellation of a Minister of State," Stenographic Transcription #5, Proceedings in the Lower House of the Diet, May 9, 1936 (in Japanese).

44. Some members of the so-called Labor-Farmer faction were still found in the party, as indicated in Chart 1 of the Appendix. At the third party convention held on January 20–22, 1935, they were the most vocal critics of Asō for his defense of the army pamphlets, but they did not find much support for their position among the other party delegates. It was subsequently decided to have the party appoint a committee to study the meaning of the army pamphlets and how they might be used to gain adherents for the party among members of the Army Reservists' Association (Zaigō Gunjinkai), the Young Men's Association (Seinendan), and the Industrial Guild (Sangyō Kumiai), all of which were ultrapatriotic groups but appeared to be responsive to the anticapitalistic propaganda of the army, which the party now wanted to utilize for strengthening itself. See Nihon Rōdō Nenkan, 17 (1936), 501.

not be complete without commenting on the merger of the General Federation, led by the Socio-Democrats, with National Labor, led by the Japan-Labor clique. By the middle of 1935 the cry within organized labor for labor unity had become so great that, on July 18, 1935, the "three elder statesmen of labor"—Abe of the Socialist Masses' Party, Bunji Suzuki, Advisor to the General Federation, and Iwasaburō Takano, Advisor to National Labor—published a joint statement urging unification. The usual struggle over the top positions, as well as the question of outside unions joining, held up unification for the rest of the year but on January 15, 1936, the two large federations did succeed in uniting under the name of the All-Japan General Federation of Labor (Zen Nihon Rodō Sōdōmei) with Komakichi Matsuoka as President and Mitsu Kōno and Suehiro Nishio as Vice Presidents. The combined membership was reported as over 85,000.

The question of outside unions joining had political implications. This was a period when the situation in Germany served as a strong warning to organized labor throughout the world that, if it wished to maintain its independence, it must achieve strength by unity and subordinate partisan considerations to the larger issue of antifascism. In the early part of 1935, some of the independent unions, which had hitherto stayed out of the larger federations—such as the Japan General Alliance of Transport Workers (Nihon Kōtsū Rōdō Sōremmei) —called for an overall unification of antifascist unions accompanied by their democratization internally and their reorganization into industrial unions. The problem that faced the leftist unions was how to achieve unity with the bigger rightist-controlled federations without compromising their basic policies to such an extent as to render the unification meaningless.

As for National Labor, despite the profascist learnings of some of its leaders, its appeal had always been in more radical terms than that of the General Federation and, as it was weaker than the latter, it supported the addition of non-General Federation forces in the new merged body. The General Federation, conversely, was wary of accepting additional unions in the fold if they appeared to be disruptive or to pose a threat to the established leadership. A compromise proposal by the "three elder statesmen" to the effect that outside organizations would not come in at the time of the merger but would gradually be accepted subsequently made the merger possible (allowing an easier division of top posts).

In sum, it may be said that this whole trend toward social democratic unity meant a consolidation of power in the right wing with
the formerly somewhat more leftist Japan-Laborites taking at times
an ultrarightist position, advocating closer ties with the military in
order to strengthen the proletarian movement vis-à-vis the main established political parties and the government (specifically the
Home Ministry and the police)—and to strengthen their own position relative to the more entrenched Socio-Democrats. Nevertheless,
in maintaining various principles of social democracy and in drawing
a line between themselves and converts to national socialism, social
democratic unity continued to have strong antifascist connotations
which cannot be overlooked in the electoral successes for the Socialist
Masses' Party in 1936 and 1937. That they remained "connotations"
rather than an open stand will become clearer from an examination
of what was called the "popular front."

Confronted with the success of the Nazis in 1933, the continued
strength of Italian fascism, and the growing fascist movements in
their own countries, European social democrats and Communists
were beginning to suppress their mutual hostility and to take unified
action in concert with as large a number of groups as possible on certain issues. This cooperation took most notable form in the popular
fronts in France and Spain and attracted broad support by protests
against the drift to world war, against the rise of military cliques,
against the suppression and curtailment of speech and assembly,
against the oppression of independent trade union activity, and
against the terrorization of minority groups. The idea of a popular
front with its implication of power derived from the cooperation of a
wide variety of political, social, and economic groups was appealing
to all those who were suffering from increasing restrictions on political expression, on the economic struggle, and on cultural development, and as such, it could not help but find some fertile soil in
Japan.

The intelligentsia were undoubtedly the Japanese most sensitive
to developments abroad. The European popular front movements
were reported in detail and polemically praised in the journal literature they read (and wrote) during this period.[45] Through the chan-

45. Among the journals editorially committed to the popular front at the time were
the following: *Doyōbi* (Saturday), *Gakugei* (The Arts and Sciences), *Gakusei Hyōron*
(The Student Review), *Jikyoku Shimbun* (Current Affairs News), *Jiyū* (Freedom), *Rekishi
Kagaku* (Historical Science), *Rōdō Zasshi* (Labor Magazine), *Sararīman* (The Salaried

nels of journalism the idea of the popular front infiltrated to a certain extent into the socialist and labor movements.

Communist influence in promoting a popular front appears to have been slight. Although the Japanese Communists had been able to revamp their strategy after the clarification of their position in the so-called 1932 Thesis, their membership was gradually dispersed by continuous police oppression. By the end of 1933, it will be recalled, most of the top leaders had been tried and imprisoned, and a number had recanted.[46] With the arrest of Satomi Hakamada, the last of the Central Committee members who remained loyal, the Communist organ Red Flag (Akahata) ceased underground publication and all party organization was crushed. Thereafter, scattered Communist groups tried to rebuild the party, but they were always arrested before they could accomplish anything substantial.

This was the state of affairs in Japan when the tactic of the united front against fascism was adopted at the Seventh Comintern Congress in July and August 1935. In February 1936 Sanzō Nozaka, who had escaped from arrest in Japan in 1931 and had just been elected at the Congress to the Presidium of the Comintern, wrote in collaboration with Kenzō Yamamoto, the Japanese representative to the Profintern, what they called "A Letter to the Communists of Japan," explaining the new tactic, and sent it to Japan via the United States.[47]

Man), *Sekai Bunka* (World Culture), *Shakai Hyōron* (The Social Review), *Shimpo* (Progress), *Taishū Seiji Keizai* (Popular Political Economy), *Yuibutsuron Kenkyū* (Studies on Materialism); in addition, there were two directly affiliated with the Japanese Communist Party: *Ikita Shimbun* (The Living News) and *Zudon* (Bang).

46. For the effects of these confessions in Communist Party ranks, see Yamamoto and Arita, *Nihon Kyōsanshugi Undō Shi*, pp. 382 ff. Somewhat abbreviated texts of the Sano and Nabeyama confessions may be found in ibid., pp. 376–81.

47. The main points in the policy outlined in the "Letter" were as follows: (1) The "overthrow of the emperor system" should be deleted from the present program and the "overthrow of the military fascist dictatorship" should replace it. (2) All party sectism should be done away with to strengthen the movement to create a popular front through the achievement of a broad unity among the farmers (including the rich farmers and small landlords), the petty bourgeoisie, and the intelligentsia. (3) All legal means of struggle must be utilized, and for the purpose of turning the Socialist Masses' Party to the left every effort must be made to join it and all social democratic labor and farmer unions. (4) All the various daily needs and demands of the masses that are being suppressed by military fascism must be brought to the fore and fought for; Communists should not try to make the form of struggle too extreme but should rather attempt to arouse the masses on as broad a basis as possible and lead them into organized and united action. For the text, see "Nihon no Kyōsanshugisha e no Tegami" in Yamamoto and Arita, pp. 411–19.

Since this was almost a directive, it must have been read by many of the remaining Communists as a guide for their activities.

Among other things, it proposed infiltrating the Socialist Masses' Party and other social democratic labor and farmer organizations. But it is not clear what effect this and the report of the Seventh Comintern Congress had in Japan, as they were circulated clandestinely. Furthermore, even among the few remaining Communists there was confusion as to how this tactic should be applied to Japan. For example, Shigeo Kamiyama argued against making the popular front "center around" the Socialist Masses' Party, much less the more sectarian Japan Proletarian Party formed in 1937 by Katō.[48] Communist participation was reduced not only by their own confusion but also by the bar against suspected Communists maintained by both of those parties.

The Japan Proletarian Party claimed to be the driving force behind the antifascist popular front in Japan, and yet it encountered considerable opposition based on the counterclaim that instead of uniting the proletarian front, with its own small and more radical following it was disruptive.

The origins of this party can be traced back to Kanjū Katō's defection from the National Labor-Farmer Masses' Party shortly before it joined the Social Democratic Party in setting up the Socialist Masses' Party in 1932. As time passed Katō, by his more openly antimilitarist, antifascist stand, attracted supporters away from the Socialist Masses' Party. For instance, in the February 1936 election, several important functionaries in the Socialist Masses' Party, instead of supporting their candidate in the Fifth District in Tōkyō, Asō, backed Katō, who was the leader of the National Council of Japanese Labor Unions formed in 1934. In that election Katō received 53,000 votes, more than any other single candidate, demonstrating that the idea of a popular front could have great appeal. The Socialist Masses' Party functionaries who supported Katō were expelled from the party in March.

As a consequence, a number of labor and farmer organizations which had been willing to follow Katō's leadership in rallying an antifascist popular front began to withdraw their support from him when it became apparent that he was planning the creation of a new

48. See Shigeo Kamiyama, *Gekiryū ni Kōshite* (Resisting the Fierce Current) (Tōkyō, Chōryūsha, 1949), pp. 145–47.

political party together with Mosaburō Suzuki, who had long since
bolted the Socialist Masses' Party. The objection to creating a new
proletarian party was simply that this would disrupt the degree of
unity already achieved in the proletarian front. Katō and Suzuki,
nonetheless, went ahead with their plans and in July 1936 reorganized the Labor-Farmer Proletarian Conference (Rōnō Musan Kyōgikai) into a political action group. This Conference had been set up
in May, while Tōkyō was still under martial law because of the February 26 (1936) incident, to act as a liaison organ for a number of
labor unions in the Tōkyō area and for the National Farmers'
Union. (Martial law continued into June 1936.) In September and
until the end of the year, Katō in behalf of the Conference and its
supporting organizations negotiated with the Socialist Masses' Party.
He proposed a merger in order to create a stronger antifascist popular front. The Socialist Masses' Party's reply was always that if the organizations supporting the Conference switched their support directly to the Socialist Masses' Party, the problem would be solved.
The offer to merge was refused.

Unwilling to accept anything other than a formal merger, either
because they felt that only in this way could they be sure the resulting new party would be antifascist or, as their opponents claimed,
because they were trying to sell their strength at too high a price,
Katō and Suzuki formalized their organization on February 20, 1937,
by changing its name to the Japan Proletarian Party (Nihon Musantō). In the April 1937 elections, only party chairman Katō, of the
five candidates it put up, was elected to the Diet.

The Socialist Masses' Party, however, leapt from 24 to 38 members
in Diet representation and thereby became the third largest parliamentary party. Much speculation appeared in the press concerning
this advance. Noting the tenseness of the situation in North China,
some observers argued that this was a protest reflecting dissatisfaction
with the lack of party cabinets since 1932, the increasing number of
scandals associated with the main, established political parties, and
opposition to the possible outbreak of hostilities. In this sense the
vote constituted implicit support for the popular front idea.

While conceding that the people were worried by the war clouds,
others argued that the mass of manual and white-collar workers and
tenant and small farmers who had voted for the Socialist Masses'
Party accepted the necessity for defending Japanese interests on the

continent but voted for the Socialist Masses' Party because they were convinced that it might be able to do something for them within the context of a politics of weak and greedy parties and of an economy in many ways preparing for war. The party appeared to have exhibited unprecedented stability for the last five years, and to have representatives in the Diet who interpellated the government on increasingly specific issues rather than roundly denouncing it in a dogmatic manner.

When headlines of the China incident splashed across the front pages of the daily papers following the exchange of fire on the night of July 7 at the Marco Polo Bridge (Lukuoch'iao) in North China, the proletarian party leaders were faced with the necessity of taking a stand. Behind closed doors a peculiar reversal took place. The Socio-Democratic leaders who had been so quick to support Japan's actions in the Manchurian incident of 1931 were now worried about foreign reactions against Japan that could lead to international isolation, and they were wary of the increasing power of the military. In contrast, the Japan Laborite leaders, who had braved the police and flouted dominant public opinion in criticizing the military moves in Manchuria as "imperialistic," this time demanded that the party pledge all-out support for the cabinet in promoting national unity. While Asō and others had had contacts with elements of the military, as we have seen, what convinced the majority of the party's leadership to support this stand was consideration of the sharp electoral reverses suffered in 1932 by those opposed to the army's actions in Manchuria. At that time the proletarian popular vote fell to less than half that of 1930.

As the self-avowed champion of the popular front against fascism and war, the Japan Proletarian Party could hardly condone the army's advance into China, but in the tense atmosphere, it did not dare to make a public condemnation. Its position was one of eloquent silence. The party did, however, express concern for the welfare of families deprived of their breadwinners and for the morale of troops in the field.

As war fever heightened, however, more positive "patriotic" support was demanded of all Japanese subjects. The Home Ministry decided to move resolutely against opinion-makers suspected of possible "disloyalty," especially all those involved in the "plot" of the popular front. On December 15, the police arrested hundreds of leftist labor leaders and even nonparty intellectuals. Katō and Suzuki were, of course, included. (Later they were to argue that their attempt to form a popular front proved to be the last flash of democratic activity before the Pacific War and the ensuing catastrophe for Japan.)

Obviously the trend of events in Japan made practically impossible an effective antiwar campaign. There were, nevertheless, certain subjective factors within the Japan Proletarian Party itself that abetted the defeat of the antifascist popular front.

First, its numerical weakness was of crucial importance. The party's most direct, organized support came from Katō's National Council of Japanese Labor Unions—known by its abbreviation, National Council (Zempyō)—composed of five area councils and forty unions with a total membership of about 12,000.[49] This was only about one eighth of the almost 95,000 members in the All-Japan General Federation of Labor which supported the Socialist Masses' Party. Furthermore, the National Council's members were scattered throughout the country, organized in small-unit unions varying in membership from a few dozen to several hundreds and representing workers in small and medium enterprises. With such a composition it was incapable of generating a powerful influence.

The only real foothold the Japan Proletarian Party had in the industrial working class was the support of two large unions which possessed the strongest fighting traditions in the "legal left wing." They were the Tōkyō Transport Workers' Union (Tōkyō Kōtsū Rōdō Kumiai) with 1,100 members and the Tōkyō Automobile Workers' Union (Tōkyō Jidōsha Rōdō Kumiai) with some 1,400 members. Within these unions were many secret members of the illegal National Conference (Zenkyō), the underground Communist-led federation whose full name was the National Conference of Japanese Labor Unions (Zenkoku Rōdō Kumiai Kyōgikai), and also a large number who supported the right-wing social democrats. These two groups struggled constantly for hegemony within the unions. The National Conference members had long kept the unions from shifting to the right. This contest between the extreme leftists and the right-wingers enabled the legal left-wingers to climb into leadership positions where they held the balance of power.

49. These and the following trade union strengths are rounded figures from the more precise ones reported in *Nihon Rōdō Nenkan, 19* (1938), passim, but they must be taken as relative approximations inasmuch as there was no effective check on their accuracy.

Besides these two relatively strong unions there was the Tōkyō Municipal Workers' Union (Tōkyō Shi Jūgyōin Kumiai), but with 800 members it had little real strength. Within the National Farmers' Union the followers of Hisao Kuroda still pressed for the formation of a popular front, but that organization was not active enough politically to concentrate the farmers' drive for land into political channels.

Besides being weak, the Japan Proletarian Party and the force it led had no well worked out program. The police had forbidden publication of its campaign policy. In its other statements, it did not even hint at measures that went beyond the pale of the very restricted sphere of "legal" activities at that time. In addition, its partisan political stand alienated a number of organizations that might otherwise have favored a popular front. Furthermore, its electoral competition with the Socialist Masses' Party automatically cut off collaboration with the antifascists within that party, such as Kiyoomi Taman.[50] Finally, the party's quick cessation of all activity as soon as the hostilities started in China deprived of leadership whatever latent antiwar protest existed.

Even before the Japan Proletarian Party was ordered to disband, the Socialist Masses' Party, like Peter before the cock crowed thrice, disowned its founding principles. This came in a Diet speech by Kanichirō Kamei who stated categorically: "Our Party is neither social democratic nor socialist." [51] While the denial did not actually represent the truth, the political social democratic movement had reached a crisis. Its formal termination awaited the decision by party leaders to initiate the campaign to dissolve all political parties.

The first move in this direction would be for the Socialist Masses' Party to demonstrate its willingness to dissolve itself. Such a policy was actually proposed as early as December 1937 by Diet Representative Suejirō Yoshikawa, a Socio-Democratic member of the party's Central Executive Committee. He reasoned that since national unity was needed to carry out Japan's mission in Asia, "politics" should be abandoned, and this could begin with the party's own dissolution.

50. Taman's position was that instead of setting up a party to compete with the Socialist Masses' Party and thereby antagonizing it, those who supported a "people's front" should join the Socialist Masses' Party and help make it more antifascist. See his article, "Taishū Sensen to wa Nani ka" (What Is the People's Front?), *Gakusei Hyōron* (The Student Review), *1* (September-October 1936), 46–50.

51. Quoted in *Nihon Rōdō Nenkan*, *19* (1938), 288.

The membership, however, was not yet ready for such a move. In fact, Yoshikawa was expelled from the party late in December at the same time, ironically enough, as were the party's two strongest supporters of a "popular front": Hisao Kuroda and Toshio Ōnishi, leaders of the National Farmers' Union, who had been arrested in the December 15 roundup.

The idea of a totalitarian "reorganization" of the people was nevertheless gradually gaining adherents. Public opinion turned more and more against the "corrupt politicians." The idea in the beginning was that the Diet should be done away with entirely, but since its existence was sanctioned by the Constitution which had been given to the people by the Meiji Emperor himself, the proposition of a single totalitarian party came to supersede it.[52]

Prince Konoe, who had become Prime Minister a month before the Lukuoch'iao incident on July 7, 1937, early indicated that he was favorably inclined toward this solution. From the latest biography of Asō, it appears that he had some secret liaison with Prince Konoe. In later criticism this was likened to Ferdinand Lassalle's relationship with Chancellor Bismarck.[53] In the Konoe case the relationship was somewhat closer and involved the use of violence in a typically Japanese fashion. On February 17, 1938, some three hundred bullies of the Anti-Communist Protect the Country Corps (Bōkyō Gokokudan), led by Tamakichi Nakamizo who had been a tool of the Seiyū-

52. Strangely enough both those who favored dictatorial government and those who opposed it came to support the single party idea from diametrically opposite principles. See the prophetic article by Tsunego Baba, "Seifu to Seitō" (The Government and the Parties), *Chūō Kōron* (April 1938), as reprinted in the same journal (November 1960), pp. 394–99.

53. See Kawakami, *Asō Hisashi Den*, pp. 474, 476, and 478. For Ferdinand Lassalle's relationship with Chancellor Bismarck in the early 1860s, see, for instance, Gustav Mayer, *Bismarck und Lassalle* (Berlin, 1928), based on letters exchanged between the two. It appears that Kanichirō Kamei was a go-between for Asō and Prince Konoe. Kamei's qualifications were his background: he was related to nobility, the family of a Kyūshū Daimyō, and thus had some social entrée to the Prince. Kyūshū was Asō's "home country" (*kuni*). Teruaki Tadokoro had been Asō's strategist and Asō usually followed his advice. He first made contact with the military for Asō; specifically, Tadokoro hoped to work through Major General Tetsuzan Nagata, head of the army Control faction and friend of Shūmei Ōkawa. Nagata advocated national planning. That sounded like socialism to Tadokoro. But Tadokoro died in 1934 and in the following year Nagata was murdered by a member of the Imperial Way faction. After that Asō could find no one in the Japan-Labor clique to replace Tadokoro. He did, however, become a close friend of Kamei, who became his right-hand man and confidant.

kai, attacked the headquarters of the two big parties, the Seiyūkai and the Minseitō, in an attempt to pressure them to dissolve. Then on June 12, the Socialist Masses' Party leaders quietly decided to draw up "a proposal overcoming the crisis," to be delivered by Asō. It took Asō two months to prepare this proposal and he secretly worked with Nakamizo! It turned out that Konoe had clandestinely arranged that Nakamizo make the attacks against the major parties. From this time on Asō gradually brought the party around to full support of Konoe's policies. He believed that a socialist revolution could not be engineered entirely from below but, like the Meiji Restoration, needed support in high places.

On the first anniversary of the Lukuoch'iao incident, July 7, 1938, the Socialist Masses' Party proposed forming a "national party" (*kokumin no tō*) as the means for achieving "national unification" (*kyokoku itchi*), overcoming class conflict, factional strife, and mutual misunderstandings. To this end the party itself was taking an attitude of "self-effacement" (*onore o munashū shite*), as all other special interests should, to help prosecute the "holy war." [54]

Since the major parties responded lukewarmly to this idea, Asō, Miwa, and other Socialist Masses' Party leaders thought they might speed the process by merging with other minority parties in the Diet. The next move was the joint declaration in February 1939 by Isoo Abe, as head of the Socialist Masses' Party, and Seigō Nakano, leader of the ultranationalistic Eastern Association (Tōhōkai), declaring that their two parties should each dissolve and together organize a "unitary, national, totalitarian party" in the spirit of Yamato (the classical name for Japan).[55] This was clearly a move toward fascism, since Nakano had just returned from a trip to Germany and Italy, convinced of the need for such a party. Nevertheless, Abe and the Socio-Democratic clique within the party reacted coolly and Nakano later admitted that basic ideological differences rather than a quarrel

54. See *Nihon Rōdō Nenkan*, 20 (1939), 248–49. Among the characteristics the Socialist Masses' Party considered necessary for the new "national party" were the following: (1) It should be based on the principle of totalitarianism and express the national will. (2) It must not be just a collection of the various existing forces but should become a renovationist (*kakushinteki*) force striving for the reform of capitalism and the construction of a new East Asia. (3) More specifically, it should bring planning into production, develop defense in the broad sense, secure the people's livelihood, and aim at the complete renovation of Japan.

55. This joint declaration may be found in Ogata, pp. 153–54

over posts brought the move toward merger to an end, after it became clear that no other large group in the Diet would join the venture.[56]

While the future of the party was being debated, opinion within the organized labor movement favoring the dissolution of independent labor organizations was already strong. The idea was that both the workers and management in all enterprises should join the Industrial Patriotic Association (Sangyō Hōkokukai) where together they would submerge their own class interests to those of the nation in its hour of crisis. Within the All-Japan General Federation of Labor this idea was championed by the Japan-Labor clique leaders (who had formerly led National Labor), while the Socio-Democratic (former General Federation) leaders favored retaining independent labor organizations as the better way to cooperate with the government and the war effort. Friction between the two factions grew until the organization split on July 24, 1939. The old National Labor elements joined the Industrial Patriotic Club, while the remaining forces changed the name of the organization back to the Japan General Federation of Labor (see Chart 2 in the Appendix). Although the two factions parted ways on officially amicable terms, their latent antagonism was soon to be reflected in the councils of the Socialist Masses' Party.

Within the party the Japan-Laborites held the Socio-Democrats largely responsible for the failure of the merger with the Eastern Association, and in February 1940 they took advantage of a seemingly unrelated incident to expel leading Socio-Democratic leaders from the party. On February 2, Takao Saitō, a Minseitō leader, made a speech in the Diet criticizing the objectives of the Japanese army in China since the outbreak of the China incident. As he spoke, shouts of indignation drowned out scattered cries of support. As a result, the Speaker of the House had half the speech expunged from the record. Attempting to cash in on the popularity of the military, the Socialist Masses' Party that very afternoon issued a statement attacking both Saitō and the Minseitō. Gradually war supporters from all the parties joined the clamor for punishing Saitō. The Socialist Masses' Party Central Executive Committee decided, 12 to 5, to vote in the Diet for Saitō's expulsion. Five Seiyūkai Diet members who opposed the expulsion were asked to leave that party, but some mediators stepped

56. Ibid., p. 155.

in and they were allowed to remain. The Socialist Masses' Party also expelled eight of the nine party members who absented themselves from the chamber at the time of the vote expelling Saitō, but although they protested there was no mediation to bring them back in.[57]

Party leader Abe, who had also been absent but who was not expelled because he had been too ill to attend the Diet, resigned from the party on March 21, 1940, and simultaneously announced his intention to form a new party. In the following month preparations were made and the name chosen was the Nationalist Labor Party (more literally, the Industriously Toiling People's Party—Kinrō Kokumintō). Just before its inauguration, however, the Home Minister prohibited the formation of the party on the grounds that, being "socialist" and "based on the proletariat," it was potentially disruptive to the peace.

Rid of the Socio-Democratic leaders, the Socialist Masses' Party again sought to take the lead in the direction of a "reorganization of the people" and issued an appeal in June 1940 to all the other political parties to dissolve in order to make way for a new unitary totalitarian structure dedicated to serving the state.

When it became clear that Prince Konoe considered the time ripe for his becoming the leader of a "new structure," the Socialist Masses' Party formally made its decision, on July 6, 1940, at the Kyōchō Kaikan in Tōkyō, to dissolve. Asō, having arisen from his sickbed to address the party, attempted, as Chairman of the Central Committee, to make it appear that the totalitarianization of the nation was what the social democratic movement had striven for all along, saying, "Now our call for the organization of the people has become the call of the nation and our advocacy of dedication has become the advocacy of the race. I rejoice that the day has come when our simple wishes have spread abroad and our sacrifice has opened the road to renovation." [58]

Two days later the General Federation, with 28 years of activity behind it, dissolved voluntarily rather than be ordered to disband, as

57. The eight were Tetsu Katayama, Yoshio Matsunaga, Chōzaburō Mizutani, Suehiro Nishio, Ken Okazaki, Bunji Suzuki, Eiji Tomiyoshi, and Mitsusuke Yonekubo. Also absent was another proletarian representative, Jiichirō Matsumoto, who cooperated with the Socialist Masses' Party within the Diet.

58. Naka, p. 238. The other parties in the Diet all dissolved themselves within the next month and a half.

had been feared ever since the abortive Nationalist Labor Party had been prohibited on May 7, 1940. The General Federation had promised its support to the formation of that party.

On July 16, Premier Yonai submitted the resignation of his cabinet so that the second Konoe cabinet might be formed, and almost simultaneously the Seiyūkai, the Minseitō, and the Kokumin Dōmei, as well as the remaining smaller parties all dissolved themselves. The agrarian movement soon came to an end with the dissolution of the Japan Farmers' Union and the General Federation of Japanese Farmers' Unions.

When Premier Konoe appointed the Preparatory Committee for the New Structure (Shin Taisei Jumbikai), Asō was included in the membership,[59] but on September 6 he died. When the Imperial Rule Assistance Association (Taisei Yokusankai) was formally inaugurated on October 12, 1940, several leaders of the late Socialist Masses' Party were appointed officials of the organization. Among them, Jōtarō Kawakami became a member of the Secretariat, Jusō Miwa, Chief of the Liaison Section of the Organization Board, Inejirō Asanuma, Vice-Chief of the Section on Research on the Lower House Special Election System of the Diet Board, and Mitsu Kōno, Vice-Chief of the Lower House Screening Section of the Diet Board.[60] All were Japan-Laborites.

On the surface, the "new political structure" was a great success and the former proletarian leaders were incorporated into it in strategic positions. The party organizations of their bourgeois political rivals, who had enjoyed superior financial backing from big business, were dissolved. Prince Konoe had always wanted to bring the China war to an end and now he was Premier again.

Fundamentally, however, the "new political structure" was a failure. Plans for it had been formulated during the first Konoe cabinet (June 1937–January 1939) under the terminology of a "reorganization of the people." Konoe's advisors had thought in terms of fashioning a new political instrument, based overtly on fascist and covertly on communist models of one-party systems, which would be able to control the military. It was thought the military would support it in return for the dissolution of the venal, decadent political

59. For a list of the membership see Yasaburō Shimonaka, ed., *Yokusan Kokumin Undō Shi* (A History of the Nationalist Movement of Imperial Rule Assistance) (Tōkyō, Yokusan Undō Shi Kankōkai, 1954), p. 82.

60. Ibid., pp. 141, 148, 150, and 151.

parties they had so often castigated. At the apex the strong charismatic leader, Prince Konoe—whose varied characteristics would make him acceptable to the military, the aristocracy, the civilian bureaucracy, the intelligentsia, and other main segments of Japanese society —would be able to make real concessions to the nationalist aspirations of the Chinese, win them over on the basis of a regional, cultural, and racial mutuality of interests against the Western colonial powers, and establish a genuine East Asian "cooperative body." But as it turned out, Konoe was not a strong or resolute enough leader. He talked about making concessions to Chinese nationalism before he had the power in Japan to deliver on them. The military were not willing to give up their own independence and indeed were able to produce a stronger leader in General Tōjō. Those who saw in the Imperial Rule Assistance Association an attempt to prevent dominance of the country by the military probably realized that it was stillborn when the army refused participation in the central headquarters of the organization, before it was even officially inaugurated.

Since the aim of bringing the military to heel could hardly be overtly proclaimed for the IRAA or its predecessors, the "new structure" and the "reorganization of the people," it is difficult to judge how conscious were Asō's actions in supporting this movement. (After the war, all political leaders, with the social democrats not the least among them, attempted to place the most antimilitarist construction on their own motivations, if not actions—all of which complicates the problem of motivations.) In any case, a totalitarian structure was created which was not really totalitarian, since the military retained its independence of action and in fact attempted to use the structure, with revisions, for its own ends in the prosecution of the Pacific War when it broke out on December 8 (Japanese date), 1941.

During the war the activities of former social democrats in the Diet, as far as they related at all to their former position, aimed at bringing the attention of the authorities to the plight of labor by pointing out that poor working conditions rendered industrial workers inferior soldiers and that some welfare facilities should be arranged for the good of the war effort. For instance, at a meeting of the Committee for a Bill on Special Wartime Administration Regulations in 1943 former Socialist Masses' Party member Jōtarō Kawakami rose and in an interpellation of Premier Tōjō said:

I do not mean to deny the proposition that farming-villages constitute a source of sturdy soldiers. However, if factories are
incapable of supplying them, too, such a defect should be rem-
edied . . . In the past farming-villages and cities have been opposed to each other. I should think it necessary to take measures
to do away with this opposition and to enable both factories and
villages to supply sturdy soldiers.[61]

As even Tōjō's reply showed, the industrial worker was looked down
upon and the farmer idealized in Japanese fascist thinking, and thus
there was some role for the former social democrats to play in trying
to see that free and conscript laborers were not subject to such conditions as would make them highly inefficient.

An election became mandatory during the war four years after the
last election of April 30, 1937, but the Tōjō government extended
the life of the Diet for exactly one extra year for the first time in its
history. In the 1942 election, a number of the former social democrats
ran; eight of those elected had government blessing and eleven did
not.

Even with government support no Diet members were allowed to
form any organization in competition with the Imperial Rule Assistance Association. When Premier Tōjō took over the helm of state, he
tried unsuccessfully to reorganize the association in such a way as to
give him firmer control over the country, such as Hitler had through
the Nazi Party. The IRAA was finally dissolved on June 13, 1945,
after the National Volunteer Army (Kokumin Giyūtai) had been set
up to prepare for "eternal resistance" against the enemy who was expected to land on Japanese soil any day. Throughout its existence
and throughout the life of the Imperial Rule Assistance Political
Society (Taisei Yokusan Seijikai) set up on May 20, 1942, by Tōjō,
former social democrats served, mostly from the Japan-Labor
clique; [62] and this led to their temporary purge from political life by
the Supreme Commander of the Allied Powers early in the American
Occupation.

61. This is quoted from the Diet records in Maruyama, *Gendai Seiji no Shisō to Kōdō*,
pp. 50–51, and translated into English by Maruyama in "The Ideology and Movement
of Japanese Fascism," p. 111. Also found in Tōyama, p. 137, and in Maruyama, *Thought
and Behavior*, p. 49 (though the translation in the text is mine).
62. Shimonaka, pp. 458–60.

Leadership, Cliques, and Factions

1. The three sponsors of the Social Democratic Party of 1926: Sakuzō Yoshino, Isoo Abe, and Kiichi Horie. (Photo © *Asahi Shimbun*.)

2. The Labor Farmer Party Convention of December 1927.
Ikuo Ōyama is at the speaker's desk, presiding. Slogans on the wall call for freedom for all of the people, for immediate dissolution of the Diet, and for opposition to those who oppose a united front. On one side stands a box for congratulatory messages from friendly organizations. Notice the police watching the speaker and the police circulating through the hall. One person standing may be asking Ōyama a question from the floor. Most people are wearing overcoats because the building is poorly heated. (Photo © *Asahi Shimbun*.)

3. Some of the 24 proletarian party members of the House of Representatives in April 1936. Reading from left to right, first row: Shigezō Tsukamoto (Ōsaka), Yasutarō Kawamura (Ōsaka); second row: Jiichirō Matsumoto (Fukuoka), Ken Okazaki (Kanagawa), Kiyooto (Seion) Kawamata (Akita), Haruki Satake (Kōchi); third row: Eiji Tomiyoshi (Kagoshima), Kenji Yamazaki (Shizuoka), Jōtarō Kawakami (Hyōgo), Inejirō Asanuma (Tōkyō); fourth row: Hisao Kuroda (Okayama), Kiyoomi Taman (Ōsaka), Chōzaburō Mizutani (Kyōto), Hisashi Asō (Tōkyō), Kanichirō Kamei (Fukuoka); fifth row: Bunji Suzuki (Tōkyō), Isoo Abe (Tōkyō), and Motojirō Sugiyama (Ōsaka). All those named were members of the Socialist Masses' Party, except Matsumoto and Tomiyoshi. (Courtesy of Mr. Tamio Kawakami, son of Jōtarō Kawakami and now a professor at Tōkai University.)

4. Hisashi Asō as Secretary-General of the Socialist Masses' Party. (Courtesy of Mr. Yoshikata Asō, son of Hisashi Asō and now a Democratic Socialist member of the House of Representatives.)

5: The Socio-Democratic Clique (Shaminkei)

In pursuing the story of Japanese prewar social democracy from its radical beginnings to its ultimate accommodation to ultranationalism, one may wonder by what devious path of logic its advocates reached the end of the line or at what point others refused to go further and either turned off the narrowing legal path or were forced to cease their journey by physical arrest. The study of social democratic ideology and tactics is addressed to this question. But before we can begin to answer it, we must become aware of internal complexities, of the ideological differences, of the factionalism that characterized Japanese social democracy; at all times we must bear in mind that the concept of "social democracy" itself is only a tag used for purposes of analysis and seldom if ever designates a movement of ideological or organizational unity and consistency.

This chapter and the two following attempt to answer the "who's who" question in Japanese social democratic ideological leadership. As this is a pioneer attempt to analyze the competing factions or cliques, it may be useful to say a few words about the methodology and procedure. In the literature on this subject, the author found considerable confusion in the application of the ideological labels "right," "left," and "center" and also marked ambiguity in the use of faction labels derived from the names of political parties. The first step, therefore, appears to be to clarify these terms by recapitulating in simplified accounts how the three main leadership factions came into being and their relation to one another. It will be possible then to examine them one by one, pinning them down as much as possible by lists of names and illustrating their main characteristics by introducing representative individuals. It must be emphasized, however, that we are dealing here with the behavior of groups of human beings and have space to describe only the general patterns; we cannot go into the more erratic minor changes of individual allegiances. Also since there is no way to measure in precise terms the amount of leadership exhibited by any individual, we shall take account of only those men whose names appear in positions of prestige with the greatest frequency. Finally, it may be pointed out that in this and the next two chapters in which leadership composition is emphasized, ideology and strategy are treated in such a way as to bring out the most striking differences among the factions; the common content of the various ideological positions and the concrete reactions to specific issues can then be examined in more detail.

With the advantage of hindsight, we have been able to discern the main lines of cleavage in social democratic leadership stemming from the groups formed by the end of 1926. We shall examine them in the following order: (1) the group of leaders who organized the Social Democratic Party (Shakai Minshūtō) and who well into the post-World War II period were still called the *"Shaminkei,"* a term, it will be remembered, that we are translating as the "Socio-Democratic" clique; because of their ideological position in 1926, they were known as the "right wing" of the proletarian movement; (2) the group who organized the Japan Labor-Farmer Party (Nihon Rōnōtō) and who equally long were referred to as the *"Nichirōkei"* or "Japan-Labor" clique; in 1926, they claimed to be the "center" between the anticommunist Social Democrats and the more procommunist elements; and (3) the groups which successively emerged from the Communist movement and turned against it after each blow of governmental suppression, and yet who continued to maintain an uncompromising, antigovernmental stance; they were known as the "left wing," or the "legal left" to distinguish them from the Communists who were illegal. This last category included more than one group, but, as will be explained, the most important of these was the Labor-Farmer faction (*Rōnōha*).

These three important lines of leadership cleavage persisted, even though their ideological positions changed and their theoretical differences blurred, rendering the distinctions "right," "left," and "center" meaningless. In addition, individual leaders emerged from time to time who were strong enough to organize their own parties but not to maintain them for long or to avoid temporary associations with the important groups.[1]

In order to distinguish these three main elites from each other, they will be described in terms of general labels, the definitions of which will be further refined in subsequent chapters. For purposes of analysis, the distinguishing characteristics of each may be listed under four headings: composition, ideology, role, and style of behavior. The first of these will be emphasized in this and the following two chapters.

Functionally the Socio-Democratic clique was composed of three types: (1) the "prestige element," made up of men who had achieved some position in Japanese society before the organization of the Social Democratic Party, men who were "respectable" despite their interest in socialism, democracy, and the labor movement; (2) the "administrators," composed of union officials who, despite their lack of higher-school education, had risen from the ranks to important union posts through their activities in the labor movement; and (3) the "agitators," composed mostly of university graduates who had decided to devote themselves to socialism as a result of their participation in the post-World War I student movement. Although the agitator or propagandistic element was actively engaged in giving coherence to ideology and hammering it into a concrete political program, the moderate tone of the clique's political position was furnished by the prestige element.

1. The actual personnel in these groups, cliques, and factions have been determined largely by studying the lists of candidates put up by the various proletarian parties in the prefectural and Diet elections between 1927 and 1939. The most convenient source for this material is Naka, *Senkusha no Keifu: Shakaitō Zenshi*. This book is arranged chronologically with each chapter devoted to one or two years from 1925 to 1945. I nevertheless checked names with actual participants or scholars. Most helpful in this connection was Professor Tamio Kawakami (son of Jōtarō Kawakami, belatedly associated with the Japan-Labor clique), who told me that one of the surest ways the participants themselves identified faction members was to observe attendance at funeral ceremonies, for these tended to be factional affairs.

A series of descriptive terms is sufficient to give a preliminary impression of the idelogical tenor of the Socio-Democrats. Such a list would include: Christian reformism, gradual socialism, parliamentary democracy, political participation combined with business unionism, class collaborationism, and an attitude of compromise toward forces above but of dictation to inferiors.

Such an ideology was necessary for the role this group wished to play. It would enable the Socio-Democratic labor leaders to appeal to and organize the more stable strata of Japanese workers—those with a degree of job security, rather than those who were temporary or excessively underpaid. Such a basis would allow broader appeals for middle-class support during elections. With sufficient votes from outside the working class, even labor leaders in the clique might climb to positions of respectability, prestige, and political prominence.

To play this role the elite tended to bend with the prevailing winds. Its attitude was one of caution and only token resistance to the tide toward war and totalitarianism in Japan, except where its core of trade union support, organized mainly in the General Federation, was jeopardized. Its top leaders were more cooperative with the advocates of expansion and militarism at the time of the Manchurian incident but far less so thereafter than the Japan-Laborites, but most of the Socio-Democrats were able to hold their own in the shrunken sphere of wartime political activity. In addition, they were able to maintain a middle ground between local management and labor even after the formal disappearance of the independent labor unions.

The above threefold classification of the Socio-Democratic clique at the time of its birth is to be understood as representative rather than exclusive and absolute. Furthermore, with the passage of time its composition was altered by age, deaths, new blood, and changes of allegiance. The Socio-Democratic label very clearly designated certain leaders at the top but became less distinct as it was applied to persons lower in the hierarchy. Other proletarian political or labor leaders were too briefly or spasmodically associated with this clique to be classified with them in any meaningful way. The listing of prominent leaders in each category will be presented as it existed in 1926, taking note of those who left the groupings during the period 1926–40.

THE PRESTIGE ELEMENT: WELL-KNOWN PERSONS

The prestige element of the Social Democratic Party in 1926 consisted of the following: [2]

NAME AND DATES	EDUCATION	OCCUPATION	NOTES *
Isoo Abe 1865–1949	Dōshisha, Hartford Theological Seminary	Professor at Waseda U., earlier at Dōshisha U.	An "old socialist" moderate, Christian; Diet 1928, 1932, 1936, 1937; but failed 1930.
Tsunego Baba 1875–1960	Dōshisha and Waseda U.	Journalist	Retired from politics in the middle 1930s until after the war.
Kiichi Horie 1876–1927	Keiō U.	Professor at Keiō U.	Had changed from laissez-faire to nationalization.
Toyohiko Kagawa 1888–1960	Meiji Gakuin and Kōbe and Princeton Theological Seminaries	Author	Switched cliques several times; famous for his devotion to Christianity; better known in America than in Japan. Diet candidate 1930.
Tetsu Katayama 1887–	Tōkyō U.[3]	Lawyer	A protégé of Abe; Diet candidate 1928, 1930, 1932, 1942; elected 1936, 1937.
Yūzō Shimanaka 1881–1936	Tōkyō Hōgakuin (predecessor of the present Chūō U.)	Journalist	Diet candidate 1930, but left the clique for national socialism in 1932.
Bunji Suzuki 1885–1948	Tōkyō U.	Union leader	Founder of the Friendly Society; Diet 1928, 1936, 1937; failed 1930, 1932.
Sakuzō Yoshino 1876–1933	Tōkyō U.	Professor at Tōkyō U.	Led in introducing concept of "democracy."

* "Diet" means election to the Diet.

2. Information for this and the subsequent lists dealing with leadership has come principally from the following sources: (1) Shinnosuke Abe, *Gendai Nihon Jimbutsu Ron* (On Personages in Contemporary Japan) (Tōkyō, Kawade Shobō, 1953). (2) Hideo Aragaki, *Sengo Jimbutsu Ron* (On Postwar Personalities) (Tōkyō, Yakumo Shoten, 1949). (3) Evelyn S. Colbert, *The Left Wing in Japanese Politics* (New York, Institute of Pacific

The general tenor of thought that held this group together and dominated the Socio-Democratic clique was the feeling that there existed profound injustices in contemporary Japanese society; that it was not a radical or dangerous thing to be interested in the welfare of the poorer classes; and that the remedy lay in transforming the capitalistic economy of Japan into a socialistically oriented one through parliamentary legislation.

Protestant Christian ethics either motivated or influenced most of these men and helped to link them with social currents in the more economically advanced and democratic nations of the West. Isoo Abe's life was indicative of the Christian current in the whole Japanese socialist movement.[4] The son of a samurai who was suddenly reduced to poverty as a result of the Meiji Restoration, Abe studied the new learning from the West at Dōshisha University and was baptized as a Congregationalist Christian in 1882. Later he came to America and attended the Hartford Theological Seminary in Connecticut. While here, his disappointment at the inadequacy of the social settlement work he saw in New York City put him into a frame of mind so receptive to Edward Bellamy's *Looking Backward* that when he closed the book, after staying up all night to read it, he decided he was a "socialist." He never wavered in this conviction, although the content of his ideas underwent considerable change.[5]

Relations, 1952), Appendix A. (4) Korefusa (Shisō) Hattori, ed., *Gendai Nihon no Jimbutsu Jiten* (A Dictionary of Personages in Contemporary Japan) (Tōkyō, Jiyū Kokuminsha, 1952). (5) Mainichi Shimbunsha, ed., *Nihon Jimbutsu Jiten* (A Biographical Dictionary of Japanese Personages) (Tōkyō, Mainichi Shimbunsha, 1952). (6) Fusakichi Myōga, *Nihon Seitō no Gensei* (The Present Situation of the Japanese Political Parties) (Tōkyō, Nihon Hyōronsha, 1929). (7) Ripōtosha, ed., *Musan Seitō no Enkaku, Gensei* (The History and Present Circumstances of the Proletarian Political Parties) (Tōkyō, Ripōtosha, 1929). (8) Shisō no Kagaku Kenkyūjo (The Institute for the Scientific Study of Thought), ed., *Tenkō: Kyōdō Kenkyū* ([Political] Conversions [or Recantations]: A Collaborative Study) (3 vols. Tōkyō, Heibonsha, 1959–62). (9) Personal interviews by the author.

3. Tōkyō U. refers to the Tōkyō Imperial University. Since the war, "Imperial" has been dropped from the names of all government-established universities.

4. Information on Abe: an interview with his widow, Komao, and daughter, Mrs. Ōinoue, in the spring of 1953; his autobiography, *Shakaishugisha to Naru Made* (Until I became a Socialist) (Tōkyō, 1932; reprinted by Meizensha, 1947); Tetsu Katayama, *Abe Isoo Den* (The Biography of Isoo Abe) (Tōkyō, Mainichi Shimbunsha, 1958); and from standard references.

5. While it is safe to say that Abe did not waver in his basic conviction, it must be understood that this was very vague and utopian. An indication of this is that he lists as the books which formed his ideas the following: William Morris's *News from No-*

Upon returning to Japan, Abe became a Unitarian, as did many of the Japanese who had become interested in social problems, and he joined in the study of Western socialist thought. He was to have by far the longest political career in Japan of all his associates who took part in the formation of the abortive Social Democratic Party of 1901.

During the Russo-Japanese War of 1904–05, Abe became the embodiment of the united front between the socialists and the Christians for the purpose of opposing the war. At that time he went so far as to say he could bear seeing his own country ruined by a foreign army if the reason the Japanese did not fight was their support of the principle of nonresistance.[6] During the First World War, however, Abe, like the antiwar European socialists, retreated from this idealist position. Yet he did not support Japan's aggression on the Chinese mainland in the 1930s nor her attack on the United States in 1941. He at least maintained a position which he could claim was not one of full support. But as a young man completely outside the government in the decade of 1900–10, Abe was a far more trenchant critic than he was as a silver-haired veteran Diet member in the 1930s.

Known as "The Second Abe" because he was a close follower and admirer of the older man, Tetsu Katayama, helped carry on the Christian trend in the Japanese socialist movement.[7] After World War II, he became Japan's first Christian, as well as her first Social Democratic, Premier. A stocky man with a serious mien, he was at his best when making speeches. They were not fiery but had a grand air about them. He was certainly not in his element in round-table discussion or at quick repartee in interpellations. But he has always been known as a common sense politician with a sense of humor. His greatest fault, which proved at times to be an asset, has been his inability to make up his mind or to take a firm stand. He came to be re-

_____
where; Tommasso Campanella's *Civitas Solis;* and Sir Thomas More's *Utopia.* See Kenichi Yarita, *Dai San no Taiyō: Nihon Shakaishugi Undō Shi Kōwa, Dai Ichibu* (The Third Sun: The History of the Japanese Social Movement, Part I) (Tōkyō, Shakai Shichō Henshūkyoku, 1948), pp. 18–19.

6. Katsuzō (Kanson) Arahata, *Sa no Memmen: Jimbutsu Ron* (Faces on the Left: Biographical Essays) (Tōkyō, Hayakawa Shobō, 1951), p. 16. Also see Cyril H. Powles, "Abe Isoo and the Role of the Christians in the Founding of the Japanese Socialist Movement: 1895–1905," *Papers on Japan* (Harvard University), *1* (June 1961), 89–129.

7. The following sketch of Katayama is taken from the chapters on him in Aragaki, pp. 46–54; from standard references; and from personal conversations.

ferred to in the political journalism of early post-World War II Japan as "Guzu Tetsu" (dilly-dallying Tetsu).

Katayama's affiliation with Christianity dates back to his days at the Third Higher School in Kyōto just after the Russo-Japanese War. Later he graduated from the Law Department of Tōkyō Imperial University and began his career as a lawyer. He tried to make the law more accessible to the common people by setting up a side practice at the Tōkyō YMCA where he acted as a civil law consultant for the nominal fee of 50 *sen* a case. His entrance into the labor movement dated from his appointment as legal advisor to the General Federation in 1920. This in turn led to his participation in founding the Social Democratic Party of 1926, through which he made his debut into politics. Subsequently, he became a constant Diet candidate. Elected in 1936 and 1937, he failed in 1942 when he was not "recommended" by Tōjō. Perhaps one reason for this failure was his Christian affiliation. If in the 1920s and early '30s it had proved to be somewhat of an asset because of the ethical aura it bestowed, it became a liability during the war.

Christian influence in the General Federation did not originate with these two political leaders. Rather, it dates back to the founding of that organization in 1912 under the name of the Friendly Society (Yūaikai) and can be illustrated by the life of Bunji Suzuki, a student of the famous professor of political science at Tōkyō Imperial University, Sakuzō Yoshino.[8] Son of a well-to-do family which had gone bankrupt, located in the same village as Yoshino's, Suzuki, while attending Tōkyō Imperial, formed a close attachment to the older man. Although Suzuki's family was Catholic, through Professor Yoshino's influence he affiliated with the Hongo Protestant Church. He soon joined the Tōkyō Unitarian Society, editing its influential journal (*Rikugo Zasshi*), which stressed social problems. A club for workers which he organized in the Unitarian Society's Hall in Tōkyō evolved into the Friendly Society for the promotion of mutual aid among workers, with such Christian advisors as Dr. Clay Macaulay (missionary), Isoo Abe, Taku Naitō (an army instructor), and Sakusaburō Uchigasaki (an Oxford-trained Waseda professor).

Suzuki remained president of the organization from its founding until 1932 when he was succeeded by one of his own protégés,

---

8. Details on the relationship between Yoshino and Suzuki come mainly from Suzuki's autobiography entitled *Rōdō Undō Nijū Nen;* cf. Preface, which was written by Sakuzō Yoshino, pp. 1–13.

Komakichi Matsuoka, also a Christian. Suzuki saw the friendly society evolve from a vehicle for Christian social work in 1912 to the dominant and militant Japan General Federation of Labor in the early 1920s. He also presided over the organization as it split again and again, isolating most of the Christian influence within the Socio-Democratic clique.

The Christian aspect of the clique helped to attract at least temporarily the well-known Toyohiko Kagawa.[9] As a brilliant young man troubled with personal and family problems and an acute sense of pity for the poor, Kagawa found himself spiritually through preaching and practicing Christianity in the slums of Kōbe. From settlement work he gradually moved into trade-union organizing, while continuing to proselytize. The profits from a book about his life in the slums [10] helped him lead and finance the Kawasaki Shipyard strike of 1921.

But Kagawa's interest was not fully taken up by the labor movement. The agrarian movement was just beginning to take shape; here the social gospel served as an inspiration. Of the seven most important organizers of the Japan Farmers' Union, three were Christian ministers (Kagawa, Motojirō Sugiyama, and Keizō Ogawa), and one a "newly awakened" Christian layman and tenant farmer (Takeo Yamagami).[11] Sugiyama became president of the Farmers'

9. Kagawa described his youth and life in the Kōbe slums in his novel, *Shisen o Koete* (Across the Deathline). This was translated into English by I. Fukumoto and T. Satchell, under the title *Before the Dawn* (New York, George Doran, 1924). A somewhat fictionalized biography is Akira Asano, *Aganai: Kagawa no Shōsetsuka* (Redemption: A Biographical Novel of Toyohiko Kagawa) (Tōkyō, Tōkō Shobō, 1952). A more scholarly work is by Shunichi Yokoyama, *Kagawa Toyohiko Den* (A Biography of Tyohiko Kagawa) (Tōkyō, Shinyaku Shobō, 1950); it contains a bibliography on Kagawa and a chronology of his life. In English there is a biography by William Axling, *Kagawa* (17th rev. ed. New York, Harper and Bros., 1946). Shorter sketches of Kagawa in English include: Margaret Baumann, *Kagawa, An Apostle of Japan* (New York, Macmillan, 1936); Kenneth J. Saunders, *Whither Asia? A Story of Three Leaders* (Gandhi, Hu Shih, and Kagawa) (New York, Macmillan, 1933); Helen Topping, *Introducing Kagawa* (Chicago, Willett Clark, 1935); and Victor Marriott, ed., *Kagawa and Cooperatives* (pamphlet, Chicago, 1935).

10. This was *Shisen o Koete*, mentioned in the preceding note.

11. The other three were Denzō Furuse, a reporter specializing in agricultural administration, Chōzō Yukimasa, who had taken part in the Kawasaki Shipyard strike with Kagawa, and Zensaku Iwauchi, a labor leader. Cf. Tatsuo Morito, *Nihon ni okeru Kirisutokyō to Shakaishugi Undō* (Christianity and the Socialist Movement in Japan) (Tōkyō, Ushio Shobō, 1950), pp. 62–63. According to Morito, himself a Christian social democrat, the Christian influence was so great that certain landlords propagandized against the Farmers' Union by telling the peasants that if they joined it they would become Christians and thereby betray their ancestors. Ibid., p. 63.

Union and remained a pillar of the right wing of the agrarian movement. Kagawa, however, although always a fervent Christian, enjoyed embarking on new enterprises and soon veered off from the Socio-Democratic clique. Later he affiliated more closely with the Japan-Labor group. He was often known as "the holy speculator" and from the success of his books and lecture tours abroad, he usually had enough money to enable him to be one.

On discovering that Christianity was a *primum mobile* in the agrarian, labor, and socialist movements in Japan, it is only natural to wonder if Buddhism and Shintoism also served as inspirations for social democratic activity. Throughout the literature on the socialist movement in Japan there is little mention of these two religions except as traditional elements in the environment and as impediments to progress.[12] In a number of cases the sons of Buddhist priests, as a result of an interest in social problems developed at school, went into the socialist movement instead of carrying on the priestly succession. Katsumaro Akamatsu of the agitational element in the Socio-Democratic clique is an example.[13] In contrast to the Christians, the Buddists had little to offer in the way of social policy. For instance, in 1926, the Federation of Christian Churches in Japan set up articles of faith on social questions and, among other things, called for equality of opportunity, an end to racial discrimination, prohibition of alcoholic beverages, and a minimum wage law; the Buddhists on the other hand, seldom made explicit their attitude toward the social movement.[14]

12. Cf., Seidō (Masamichi) Takatsu, *Musan Kaikyū to Shūkyō* (The Proletarian Class and Religion) (Tōkyō, Taihōkaku Shobō, 1929), and Kenryō Toyoda, *Bukkyō to Shakaishugi* (Buddhism and Socialism) (Tōkyō, Shigekawa Shoten, 1924). This point is discussed further in detail in George O. Totten, "Buddhism and Socialism in Japan and Burma," *Comparative Studies in Society and History*, 2 (April 1960), 293–304.

13. Akamatsu's father and uncle were Buddhist priests and his older brother taught Buddhism at Ryūkoku University. But Akamatsu's younger brother, Iomaro, and his younger sister, Tsuneko, both entered the labor and socialist movements.

14. Sangendō Miura, *Sayoku Sensen to Bukkyō* (The Left-Wing Front and Buddhism) (Tōkyō, Taihōkaku Shobō, 1933), p. 22. This book was written by a young Buddist priest to try to get Buddhism to emulate Christianity in taking a positive approach to social problems. Christianity influenced the socialist movement but here the case is reversed: the socialist movement has influenced Buddhism (at least in the case of Miura). It has been pointed out that some of the leaders in the agrarian movement were Christian ministers. Miura shows how different was the attitude of the Buddhist priests toward a tenant farmer–landlord dispute. The priest would stay out entirely, plead neutrality, or preach harmony. He would never become a local leader in solving the dispute. Ibid., Chap. 1. Miura himself, however, helped influence a group of "special

If Christian influence is the most prominent characteristic that distinguishes the Socio-Democratic from the Japan-Labor clique, the Labor-Farmer faction, and other socialists, the emphasis on "democracy" is the second most prominent factor. This is best illustrated in the life of Professor Yoshino himself. As a young instructor, Yoshino spent the years 1910–13 abroad, where he had three experiences that converted him to democracy.[15] First, in Great Britain he observed the political struggle which succeeded in limiting the powers of the House of Lords. Secondly, in Vienna he actually marched in the great labor demonstration against price increases and was impressed by his observations that public order was not destroyed and that labor won the confidence of the nation. And thirdly, in Belgium in 1912 he witnessed the preparation for the general strike. He claimed these experiences convinced him that a people's movement could be both powerful and just.

When he returned to Japan he began formulating his ideas on how democracy might be adapted to Japanese conditions and expounded his position to the Japanese intelligentsia through magazines and newspapers. He resurrected the word *"mimponshugi"* (people-based-ism) which could be traced back to Mencius, as a translation for democracy, rather than using *"minshushugi"* (people-rule-ism), so as to avoid the charge of lèse-majesté.[16] He called for immediate universal suffrage and a restriction of the prerogatives of the House of Peers, the Privy Council, and the military clique. Together with Professor Tokuzō Fukuda and others, he founded the Dawn Society

community people" of the former outcast (*Eta*) minority to take part in the socialist movement.

15. Sakuzō Yoshino, "Mimponshugi Kosui Jidai no Kaiko" (Recollections on the Period of Propagating Democracy), *Shakai Kagaku, 4* (1928), 134. Also see Yoshino's article "Minshūteki Jii Undō o Ronzu" (On Democratic Demonstrations), *Chūō Kōron, 29* (Spring 1914), which was based on these three experiences. For a sketch of Yoshino's life, see Gakusei Shobō Henshūbu (Student Library Editorial Staff), ed., *Tatakau Hyūmanisuto* (Fighting Humanities) (Tōkyō, Gakusei Shobō, 1948), chapter on Sakuzō Yoshino written by Tōmin Suzuki; and Katsumaro Akamatsu, ed., *Ko Yoshino Hakase o Kataru* (Telling About the Late Dr. [Sakuzō] Yoshino) (Tōkyō, Chūō Kōronsha, 1934). A full-length biography is Sōgorō Tanaka, *Yoshino Sakuzō* (Tōkyō, 1958). In English, see Totten, *Democracy in Prewar Japan;* Bernard S. Silberman, "The Political Theory and Program of Yoshino Sakuzō," *Journal of Modern History, 31* (December 1959), 310–24; and Walter Scott Perry, "Yoshino Sakuzō 1873–1933: Exponent of Democratic Ideals in Japan," (Ph.D. dissertation, Stanford University, 1956; University Microfilm 17,734).

16. Yoshino, "Mimponshugi," p. 127. For a discussion of the whole question of translations for "democracy" at this time, see Seizaburō Shinobu, *Taishō Seiji Shi* (A Political History of the Taishō Era) (Tōkyō, Kawada Shobō, 1952), pp. 1372–73.

(Reimeikai) in December 1918 to try to enlighten the Japanese people. Yoshino's most responsive audience was a group of his students who formed the New Men's Society (Shinjinkai) and soon took positions much to the left of his own. Two who became more moderate joined him in forming the Social Democratic Party: Katsumaro Akamatsu, who married his daughter Akiko, and Ryūsuke Miyazaki.

To Yoshino, democracy meant the representation of the people's interests in the Diet. Since the workers and poorer masses of people had no direct Diet representatives, he felt it his duty to fight for their right to vote and to organize a moderate, parliamentary, proletarian party. With the establishment of the Social Democratic Party, he became less active politically. Especially after the Manchurian incident, he saw his ideas come increasingly under attack until his death in 1933, which in effect coincided with the decline of "democracy" as an important element within the ideology of the Socio-Democratic clique.

Along with Christian socialism and an emphasis on democracy, the prestige element of the Socio-Democratic clique was characterized by the stress it placed on the "principle of legality" (gōhōshugi). Bunji Suzuki can also serve as an example of this aspect of the clique's ideology.

In dress and manner Suzuki resembled a dedicated businessman rather than a union leader. Although an intellectual, he was not a "theorist" but a practical man, anxious to keep the organizations he led moderate and their activities within the bounds of law. This was not always easy. When the Friendly Society was born, any organization the purpose of which was to carry out united action to raise wages was illegal under Article 17 of the Peace Police Law of 1900. Yet, as the First World War progressed, the demand for labor outdistanced the readily available supply, especially in the skilled categories. Member units of the Friendly Society actually began to press for higher wages to counteract the effects of inflation. But since the law was not being strictly enforced, and because trade unions and union activity in the allied Western nations were generally regarded as legal, and since Suzuki himself advocated the abolition of Article 17, he countenanced illegal activity. Without such restrained boldness it is doubtful that the Friendly Society could have become the foremost champion of labor in Japan, openly declaring itself the Friendly Society Greater Japan General Federation of Labor in 1919. But beyond this, Suzuki opposed all other illegal activity, whether in the form of "direct action" along syndicalist lines or political action as advocated by the "Bolsheviks." Legality became the one tenet of the Socio-Democratic clique on which it never again wavered.

This principle served to preserve and protect the General Federation, which after all constituted the bulwark of organized strength under the clique's leadership. Suzuki had founded the Friendly Society and it had been his whole life. On the one hand, he resisted official pressure to dissolve the organization when the Harmonization Society was set up in 1919. On the other, he did consent to strong action against the radicals in order to maintain his position within the General Federation.

THE ADMINISTRATOR ELEMENT: WORKER ORIGIN

Rallying around Bunji Suzuki and increasingly influencing him were his beneficiaries, his *kobun,* the workers who had risen to positions of prestige even without a university education. They shared with him the emphasis on both "legality" and "unionism." It was they who supported him in expelling nearly half the membership—including some leaders—of the General Federation in 1925 and 1926. These men were the administrators and supplied the staff for running the General Federation and the political parties led by the Socio-Democratic clique, either alone or in coalition with other groups such as the Japan-Labor clique. The most important of them are listed in the table below.

NAME AND DATES	EDUCATION	OCCUPATION	NOTES *
Naosaku Doi 1900–	Elementary; Japan Labor School, 1922; Mita English School, 1924	Union official	Received his education after he had joined the Friendly Society in 1917; Kanagawa Prefectual Assembly.
Toraichi Hara 1897–	Elementary; Waseda Trade School	Union official	Became member of Tōkyō Municipal Assembly; ILO.
Ryōji Inoue 1898–	Elementary; Ōsaka Labor School, later taught there.	Union official	Left Socio-Democratic clique in 1928; joined Japan-Laborites, but made up after 1932; Ōsaka Assembly 1931; Diet 1937; failed 1942; ILO.
Ushirō Itō 1894–	Elementary	Union official	Elected to Fukuoka Prefectural Assembly. Diet candidate 1937, 1942.

NAME AND DATES	EDUCATION	OCCUPATION	NOTES *
Yonekichi Kanemasa 1892–1963	Elementary	Union official	Diet candidate 1942; ILO.
Komakichi Matsuoka 1888–1958	Elementary	Union official; originally a metal worker.	Succeeded Suzuki as president of the General Federation in 1932; Diet candidate 1930, 1932, 1942; ILO.
Jirō Miki 1885–1963	Elementary	Union official; originally a metal worker.	Elected to Kawasaki Municipal Assembly; ILO.
Suehiro Nishio 1891–	Elementary	Union official; originally a metal worker.	Most important leader of General Federation in Kansai; Diet 1928, 1930, 1937, 1942; failed 1932; ILO.
Shōzō Ōya 1893–1962	Nishinoda Night Trade School in Ōsaka	Union official	Feuded with Nishio in 1929 and bolted General Federation and SDP; Diet candidate 1930 (NDP), 1932 (NLFMP); turned to national socialism in 1932 but returned to social democracy in 1934.
Mitsusuke (Manryō) Yonekubo 1888–1951	Tōkyō Mercantile Marine Higher School, 1914	Captain; official in Seamen's Union.	Wrote popular novels of sailor life; Diet, 1937; failed 1928, 1930, 1942; ILO.

* "Diet" means he was elected to the Diet. "ILO" means he went to a conference at the International Labor Organization in Geneva at least once. "NDP" means National Democratic Party. "NLFMP" means National Labor-Farmer Masses' Party.

Nearly all these leaders were practically the same age, the variation being only a dozen years. This is a manifestation of the fact that the labor movement in Japan mushroomed just after the First World War but soon reached a standstill. In spite of little formal education, these men were able to improve themselves sufficiently to discharge such political duties as making speeches, writing reports, and deciding policy. For them the labor movement became a ladder on which to rise in the world to positions of prestige in Japanese society. Over half of those listed above were able to travel abroad to attend International Labor Conferences.

The Socio-Democratic was thus distinguished from the other social democratic factions by the large number of men who had risen from the ranks of labor. Only among the Communist or pro-Communist groupings was this characteristic as apparent. From the evidence, it appears that workers who had risen to positions of leadership in the labor movement tended to be either very radical or very conservative, often veering from left to right but seldom the reverse—at least until after World War II. The radical ones at this time joined the Council and its successors, and the conservative ones the Socio-Democratic clique.

Komakichi Matsuoka and Suehiro Nishio, two men who contrasted greatly in personality and ability, can serve as excellent examples of the caliber and temperament of the Socio-Democratic leaders whose forte was their administrative and organizational ability and perseverance. At seventeen Matsuoka started work in a steel factory in Muroran, Hōkkaidō.[17] Nishio, likewise, went to work just after graduating from primary school, first in a small factory and then in the Sumitomo steel works.[18] They both first came in contact with the Friendly Society in 1915; Matsuoka joined it immediately, but Nishio, more distrustful of its intellectual leadership in far-off Tōkyō, held off until 1919.

Matsuoka was moderate as a young man and gained the reputation in his later years of being a "real gentleman." He managed to stay out of prison even in his first attempt at leading a labor dispute in Muroran in 1912. By contrast, Nishio was fiery and outspoken, had the reputation of lacking graciousness, and, outside the Socio-Democratic clique, was usually widely disliked and feared. He was more militant in his strike activities and was arrested in 1921 at a time when police interference in labor disputes was relatively less frequent than usual. At that time he was close to being a Communist, but after the "white terror" at the time of the 1923 earthquake he quickly changed and sided with the conservative elements in the General Federation. By 1925 he was organizing a metal workers'

17. Information concerning Matsuoka was obtained from personal interviews by the author, plus standard references, in particular the chapter on Matsuoka in Aragaki, pp. 123–30.
18. Ibid., chapters on Nishio, pp. 70–78. Information is also from Nishio's autobiography entitled *Taishū to Tomo ni: Watakushi no Hansei no Kiroku* (With the Masses: A Record of Half of My Life) (Tōkyō, Sekaisha, 1951).

union in collaboration with management. He did this by convincing
the president of the company that the kind of union Nishio would
organize would be even more to the president's interest than having
no union at all.[19] In the first manhood suffrage election of 1928,
Nishio was elected to the Diet as a candidate from the Social Democratic Party, but he was already reportedly receiving money secretly
from the Ōbayashi Gumi, a construction company, for future returns.[20]

Neither of the two men had a reputation for being particularly religious. Matsuoka became a Christian at seventeen while working at
Maizuru, because he was impressed by the character of the Christian
family with which he studied English.[21] Unlike Abe, however, his
Christian affiliation was not generally known, particularly in the
1930s.[22] Nishio, on the other hand, maintained his family's affiliation with the popular Shingon Sect of Buddhism.

The two men had different personalities. The more fiery character
of Nishio helped him to achieve greater success at the polls during
Diet elections, but at times it got him into trouble, as, for example,
when he was expelled from the Diet in 1938 for a speech demanding
a "strong man like Hitler, Mussolini, or Stalin" as Premier. This incident has been cited to show his lack of a clear political philosophy;
nevertheless, he was considered more of a theorist than Matsuoka.
Their differences were, basically, more of degree than kind. They
both alternately attended International Labor Conferences in Geneva at quite regular intervals, first as advisors and then as actual
labor delegates. Both held the double position of secretary and treasurer of the General Federation, Matsuoka in the Kantō area and
Nishio in the Kansai region. These positions as keepers of the purse
strings gave them both great power and expedited the birth of the
Japan-Labor clique, as will be explained.

Although rivalry was reported between the two, they stuck together to maintain intact their basis of power, the General Federa-

19. Ibid., pp. 304–07.

20. Arahata, Sa no Memmen, pp. 149–50.

21. From the author's interview with Matsuoka.

22. From the author's interview with Sōichi Ōya, commentator on political personalities and a former participant in several social movements. At the time of the interview, Ōya was preparing a book which later appeared as Kamen to Sugao: Nihon o
Ugokasu Hitobito (Masks and Bare Faces: The People Who Influence Japan) (Tōkyō,
Tōzai Bummeisha, 1953).

tion. It was Matsuoka who succeeded in replacing Suzuki as President of the General Federation in 1932, when Suzuki was elevated to the honorary position of advisor. But both Matsuoka and Nishio, together with the whole Socio-Democratic group, displayed their solidarity in 1940 when they tried to resist the dissolution of the General Federation and all political parties into the government-sponsored imitation of the Nazi *Arbeitsfront,* called the Industrial Patriotic Association.[23] For this they were expelled from the Socialist Masses' Party by the then dominant Japan-Laborites who, having closer ties with the military and bureaucracy, had more to gain from the "new structure." Yet both Matsuoka and Nishio, and almost all of the administrator element of the Socio-Democratic clique, were able to find places for themselves in the Imperial Rule Assistance Association (IRAA) of 1940 or the Imperial Rule Assistance Political Society (IRAPS) of 1942. This group of leaders who had risen from the ranks of labor was the backbone of the Socio-Democratic clique. As real power within the elite concentrated in their hands, the prestige elements tended more and more to become mere figureheads. This trend was reinforced by the gradual defection of the university graduates, the next object of inquiry.

THE AGITATOR ELEMENT: UNIVERSITY GRADUATES

The university graduates, whose forte lay in their skill at propaganda or agitation and who decided to devote themselves to the socialist movement as a result of their participation in the student movement, may be listed as follows:

NAME AND DATES	EDUCATION	OCCUPATION	NOTES *
Katsumaro Akamatsu 1894–1955	Tōkyō U.	Journalist	Originally a Communist; abandoned the clique in 1932 with Shimanaka. Diet candidate 1928; elected 1937; failed 1942.
Hyō (Hyōnosuke) Hara 1894–	Tōkyō U.	Professor at Hōsei U.	Studied under Yoshino and Abe; combined teaching and political activities; Diet candidate 1942.

23. Sangyō Hōkokukai, abbreviated to Sampō. For explanation and a sympathetic comparison between it and the Nazi *Arbeitsfront* see Tatsuo Morito, *Doitsu Rōdō Sensen to Sangyō Hōkoku Undō: Sono Honshitsu Oyobi Nimmu ni Kansuru Kōsatsu*

NAME AND DATES	EDUCATION	OCCUPATION	NOTES *
Kanichirō Kamei 1892–	Tōkyō U., Fordham U., and Columbia U. in 1920	University lecturer; diplomat in Foreign Office—first such to enter proletarian movement.	Originally he had worked in the foreign service in consulates in New York and Tientsin. A latecomer, he resigned teaching at Keiō in 1928 to enter politics; later he became a close personal friend of Asō. Diet 1928, 1932, 1937; failed 1930, 1942.
Shirō Koike 1892–1946	Tōkyō U.	Engineer; mine chief 1923; author; founded publishing company; organized salaried men.	Diet candidate 1928, 1930, elected 1932; followed Akamatsu out of clique in 1932 for national socialism. Thereafter, Diet 1936, failed 1937, 1942.
Yoshio Matsunaga 1891–1955	Tōkyō U.	Lawyer, author, agrarian union official	Remained faithful to the Socio-Democratic clique; Tōkyō Municipal Assembly; Diet 1937; failed 1930, 1932, 1942.
Ryūsuke Miyazaki 1892–	Tōkyō U.	Lawyer; China expert	Expelled in 1928; worked for merger of 1932; bolted in 1939 for Eastern Assn. Diet candidate 1928, 1930, 1942.
Masaru (Katsu) Nomizo 1893–	Morioka Agricultural Higher School; Hōsei U.	Politician; veterinarian	Switched to Japan-Labor clique in 1930; member of Japan Farmers' Union. Diet 1937.
Haruki Satake 1896–	Chūō U.	Lawyer	Remained with the Socio-Democratic clique. Diet 1936, 1937; failed 1930, 1942.

* "Diet" means election to the Diet.

(The German Labor Front and the Industrial Patriotic Movement: Observations Concerning Their Fundamental Characteristics and Their Functions) (Tōkyō, Kaizōsha, 1941).

This list shows an age variation of only about five years as contrasted with the ten-year spread in the ages of those in the administrator element. The university-trained agitators and the worker administrators were essentially of the same age as contrasted with the older prestige element. How these university men came into the labor movement will be discussed in Chapter 6.

At this point a few words on the relationship between the worker-leaders and the young university men may be useful. It was partly the antagonism and rivalry between the working-class leaders and the young intellectuals in the Labor Farmer Party and the General Federation that caused their split into the Socio-Democratic and Japan-Labor leadership factions. But when the worker-leaders were accused of being antagonistic to the intellectuals they could point to their support of Suzuki, a genuine Tōkyō Imperial University graduate. They believed Suzuki had proved himself in his dedication to help the less fortunate, but they distrusted the "young intellectuals," who, they felt, were motivated too greatly by romanticism and adventurism.[24]

This attitude seems to have been justified, considering how few of the intellectuals who sided with the Socio-Democratic clique at its founding continued as loyal members in later years. As is shown in the list above, only three out of these eight members remained in the clique throughout the fifteen-year period. By the time Professor Yoshino died, his brilliant young student and son-in-law, Akamatsu, had abandoned social democracy for national socialism and "scientific Japanism," and had taken with him Shimanaka, whose brother was the president of the important magazine *Chūō Kōrōn*. Miyazaki, who was said to have been like a twin brother to Akamatsu in the student movement, moved to the left and was expelled from the Socio-Democratic group, though he moved right again subsequently. A little later, Nomizo switched allegiance to the Japan-Labor clique and Kamei almost did so because of his friendship with Asō. Tsunego Baba drifted away from politics in the 1930s, retaining his reputation as a liberal journalist. These changes of allegiance, together with the deaths that occurred among the older men of prestige—Horie in 1927 and Yoshino in 1933—tended to leave what we have called the administrator element of working-class origin as the most characteristic of the Socio-Democratic clique.

24. From an interview with Matsuoka by the author in the spring of 1953.

In this analysis of the composition of the Socio-Democrats, characteristics of its ideology, role, and style have also been touched upon. It was ideology, as well as long personal association within the General Federation, that held this group together. The various aspects of its thought were represented in the lives of leaders in the prestige element: Christianity by Abe, Yoshino, Katayama, and others; socialism by Abe; democracy by Yoshino; and legality and trade unionism by Suzuki and his protégés from the laboring class, particularly Matsuoka and Nishio.

The function of the clique for its own members was to provide them with respectability (association with professors), prestige (travel abroad as governmentally appointed representatives of labor), and political prominence (election to the Imperial Diet). In terms of the labor movement as a whole, the role of this clique was to supply the very moderate or conservative leadership desired by the more stable sections of the labor force, and also to provide an obstacle within the labor movement to the growth of anarchist, communist, and other radical forces. Above all, it strove for "respectability" in the eyes of both governmental authorities and private industrial leaders. Thus, it could repudiate rightist or fascistic developments within the labor movement, such as national socialism, but it was unable to offer resistance to the trends toward Japanese military adventures abroad or totalitarianism at home when these trends were endorsed by "respectable" Japanese statesmen. With reluctance the clique complied with the government's demand to dissolve its independent political party and its trade union base in the fateful year of 1940.

6: The Japan-Labor Clique (Nichirōkei)

In contrast to the Socio-Democratic, the Japan-Labor clique was composed almost entirely of intellectuals whose experience in the student movement had persuaded them to devote themselves to the newly awakening social movement. ("Intellectuals" are here understood to mean university graduates and those who were either expelled or voluntarily withdrew before graduation.) In a more specific sense, however, this clique originated as the merger of two groups: (1) a section of the General Federation leaders (of the same type as the "agitators" of the Socio-Democratic clique); and (2) a section of the Japan Farmers' Union leaders who wanted to disaffiliate from the Labor Farmer Party, as the General Federation leaders had already done, because of its increasing radicalism.

It was the Labor Farmer Party's adoption of the "open door" policy that finally convinced the General Federation to walk out and consider the establishment of their own party. All apparently proceeded well on November 20, 1926, at the first meeting of the preparatory committee for the Social Democratic Party. Two days later, however, some of the intellectuals in the General Federation at the instigation of Hisashi Asō met secretly with certain right-wing Japan Farmers' Union leaders to discuss whether to form still another new party. On the basis of an affirmative decision, a formal promoters' meeting was hurriedly held the next day, and this led to the founding, on December 9, of the Japan Labor-Farmer Party, four days after the Social Democrats were organized.

The majority of the General Federation's Central Committee was highly indignant at those leaders—including some from the Central Committee itself—who had signed their names as promoters of the Japan Labor-Farmer Party, and demanded that they resign. The dissidents refused and were expelled from the General Federation. The unions under their influence then followed their leaders out of the General Federation. The new organization formed as a basis for the Japan Labor-Farmer Party was named the Federation of Japanese Labor Unions and its announced membership was twelve thousand (though in actuality it may have been as low as five or six thousand).[1]

The reasons for the establishment of this new party help explain the characteristic differences between the Japan-Labor and the Socio-Democratic cliques. For some time, workers who had risen from the rank and file, such as Matsuoka and Nishio, had been elbowing the university graduate leaders out of the positions of real power within the General Federation, causing friction and dissatisfaction between the workers and young intellectual elements.[2]

The best example of this process can be seen in the case of Asō, undoubtedly the leading personality among the university group. After giving up his work as a newspaper journalist, Asō had organized the Miners' Union; its members, backward and impoverished, were always far behind in paying union dues to the General Federation. The activities of this union were scattered and it was forced to depend heavily on the finances of the General Federation. The

1. Nishio, *Taishū to Tomo ni*, p. 253.

2. This friction is interestingly described in a letter written by Asō to Kotora Tanahashi in Hisashi Asō, *Reimei* (Dawn) (Tōkyō, Reimei Shoin, 1949), pp. 180–86. Tanahashi, after graduating from Tōkyō Imperial University, became a kind of apprentice legal prosecutor, but in response to the *"v'narod"* (to the people) student movement, he gave up his career and entered the General Federation. After working there a few years he decided he could no longer stand the antipathy demonstrated by his colleagues from the working class because of his university background. He quit the labor movement and returned to his native village. Asō wrote him this letter to try to convince him to return to the movement. Later Asō inserted it in his own autobiographical history of the labor movement, written in the style of a novel and analyzing in detail the development of feelings of resentment by the working-class leaders toward the university men.

former laborer, Matsuoka, as secretary treasurer, held the purse strings, and the financial position of the Miners' Union gave him ammunition for ridiculing the university-educated Asō and the other intellectuals.

Added to this friction between the conservative former laborer group and the more radically inclined intellectuals was the realization that there was a need for leadership representing unions and public opinion that might otherwise go far to the left because of discontent with the conservatism that at the time dominated the General Federation leadership. Those who felt this most keenly were the more moderate leaders in the Farmers' Union, such as Motojirō Sugiyama, who saw their own organization giving strong support to the Labor Farmer Party which the pro-Communist Council members were joining. At the same time the Farmers' Union leaders could not feel happy about entering the preparatory committee for the establishment of the Social Democratic Party, a committee dominated by General Federation leadership. Tempers were still running high over the mutual recriminations between the General Federation and the Farmers' Union concerning particularly the communist issue in the Labor Farmer Party. This was the situation that led to the secret negotiations between the dissatisfied intellectuals of the General Federation and a section of the Farmers' Union leaders to form the Japan Labor-Farmer Party.

As the "center" between the Social Democratic and Labor Farmer Parties in 1926, the Japan-Labor clique fashioned for itself an ideological position marked by revisionist Marxian concepts as contrasted with the Christian and democratic socialist eclecticism of the Socio-Democrats and the more Leninist Marxism of some of the vocal leaders of the Labor Farmer Party. If the Socio-Democrats could be said to reflect a respect for what the British Labor Party stood for, the ideology of the Japan-Laborites betrayed an admiration for the German Social Democrats. In the 1920s the name of Marx certainly had an appeal that the Japan-Labor leaders wished to exploit. After the turn of the decade, however, the glamor of Marxism began to fade, and particularly after the Manchurian incident in 1931 the Japan-Labor clique perceptibly deemphasized this aspect of their thought. This opened the way for realignment with their old associates, the Socio-Democrats, in the Socialist Masses' Party in 1932 and their eventual repudiation of "socialism."

During this period the role of the Japan-Laborite leadership changed. At first it gave expression to mass discontent with current conditions, a function at which it appeared more adroit than the Socio-Democratic leaders. More precisely, it represented those labor unions dissatisfied with the authoritarian and conservative bossism of the General Federation and yet not discontented enough to follow more radical leadership, which might invite governmental suppression. When the two cliques were realigned in one party after 1932, they together represented the noncommunist, nonfascist discontent with the status quo. Their function became less one of giving voice to that discontent than of redirecting it into nonradical channels. After 1937, however, friction again appeared between the two cliques. As earlier indicated, the Japan-Laborites represented more and more the forces which sought salvation in a totalitarian state, whereas the Socio-Democrats continued to reflect a certain undercurrent of uneasiness about this trend.

If the general style of the Socio-Democratic clique was one of caution, that of the Japan-Laborites, by contrast, was one of militancy. The Socio-Democratic leaders possessed a stable basis in the General Federation but Japan-Laborite support was more diverse, made up partly from labor and partly from the agrarian movement. With basically unstable support, it became increasingly imperative for the Japan-Labor clique to cast about for sources of strength from other quarters than from the labor and agrarian movements.

Finding it impossible to change Japanese society with the very small portion of the working population in their movement, the Japan-Labor clique began to make overtures to sections of the military on the basis that the army, too, was dissatisfied with capitalism and sought to realize an ideal society in Japan. However, the Japan-Laborite leaders discovered that closer ties with the military and pro-military groups, such as the Imperial Way Association, were hindered by Socio-Democratic leaders who supported the status quo and were wary of military adventurism. Consequently, in 1939 the Japan-Labor clique led the unions under its control out of the old General Federation (with which they had amalgamated in 1936), and in 1940 utilized the Takao Saitō Diet incident to expel the important Socio-Democratic leaders from the Socialist Masses' Party and set the pace for the big parties by being the first to dissolve, thus consummating the clique's trend toward totalitarianism.

LEADERSHIP HOMOGENEITY

The most striking characteristic of the composition of the Japan-Labor clique was its homogeneity in terms of educational background. The clique's top leaders, listed below, were, with only two exceptions, all university men:

NAME AND DATES	EDUCATION (STUDENT ORGANIZATIONS)	OCCUPATION	NOTES *
Inejirō Asanuma 1897–1960	Waseda U. (Founders' Federation)	Politician, agrarian leader	Originally a Communist supporter; Secretary of Farmers' Union; in party organization sections; Tōkyō Municipal Assembly; Diet candidate 1928, 1930, 1932, elected 1936, 1937; IRAA.
Hisashi Asō 1891–1940	Tōkyō U. (New Men's Society)	Newspaper reporter, author, union leader	Leader of the clique; led labor disputes; later supported military and war; Diet candidate 1928, 1930, 1932, elected 1936, 1937; IRAA; IRAPS.
Michio Hosono 1897–1955	Tōkyō U. (New Men's Society)	Lawyer, translator, writer	Active in agrarian movement; one of the few of the clique's adherents to translate from Marx. Diet candidate 1930.
Kanjū Katō 1892–	Japan U.	Union leader	Left the clique in 1932 and finally formed the Japan Proletarian Party in 1937 with Labor-Farmer faction leaders. Diet candidate 1928, 1930, 1932, elected 1936, 1937.
Ryōzō Katō 1899–	Middle School	Farmers' union official	Gifu Prefectual Assembly 1931, 1935; Diet, 1937, failed 1942.

NAME AND DATES	EDUCATION (STUDENT ORGANIZATIONS)	OCCUPATION	NOTES *
Jōtarō Kawakami 1889–1965	Tōkyō U.	Professor at Kansei, Meiji, and Rikkyō U.; lawyer	Christian; close friend of Tatsuo Morito; elder brother-in-law to Kazuo Nagae; Diet 1928, 1936, 1937, 1942, failed 1930, 1932; IRAA; IRAPS.
Seion (Kiyooto) Kawamata 1899–	Waseda U. (Founders' Federation)	Agrarian leader, author	Farmers' union leader; Diet candidate 1930, elected 1936, 1937, 1942; IRAA; in a Ministry committee during war.
Tadao Kikukawa 1901–1954	Tōkyō U. (New Men's Society)	Union leader, author	Wrote book on student movement; one of founders of Japan Labor Club, 1931.
Mitsu Kōno 1897–	Tōkyō U. (New Men's Society)	Reporter, professor, Union leader, author	Translated Marxist works; led in move to promote government-supported labor front; ILO; Diet candidate 1930, elected 1936, 1937, 1942; IRAA; IRAPS.
Junzō Matsumoto 1894–1946	Keiō U.	Author	Propagandist; Tōkyō Prefectural Assembly.
Jusō Miwa 1894–1956	Tōkyō U. (New Men's Society)	Lawyer	Translated Marxist works; first Secretary-General of Labor Farmer Party; supported labor front (Sampō); Diet 1937; IRAA.
Shōichi Miyake 1900–	Waseda U. (Founders' Federation)	Agrarian leader, author	Leader in Farmers' Union; Diet candidate 1932, elected 1936, 1937, 1942; IRAA; in a Ministry committee during war.
Genji Mochizuki 1902–	Elementary, later labor school	Union leader, strike leader	Organizer of Federation of Japanese Labor Unions in 1926. In 1932 he went over to national socialism.

NAME AND DATES	EDUCATION (STUDENT ORGANIZATIONS)	OCCUPATION	NOTES *
Kazuo Nagae 1902–	Kansei Gakuin College	Local labor leader, politician	Student of Jōtarō Kawakami and his brother-in-law; Kōbe Municipal Assembly; Diet 1937, failed 1942; IRAA.
Masaru (Katsu) Nomizo 1898–	Aomori Agricultural School; Hōsei U.	Politician, agrarian leader, author	Switched from Socio-Democratic clique in 1930; Diet 1937 (SMP); favored Imperial Way Association.
Motojirō Sugiyama 1885–1964	Ōsaka Agricultural School, Tōhoku Theological Seminary	Agricultural technician, Christian minister, dentist, agrarian leader	A founder of Farmers' Union; Diet candidate 1928, 1930, elected 1936, 1937, 1942 (recommended by Tōjō); IRAPS.
Kō (Yoshimi) Sunaga 1894–1946	Left Oita Middle School before graduating	Agrarian leader	Leader of Japan Farmers' Union and National Farmers' Union. Organized Japan's first proletarian village in 1925. Diet candidate 1928, 1930, 1936, 1942, elected 1937.
Teruaki Tadokoro 1900–1934	Left Waseda U. before graduating (Founders' Federation)	Author, labor leader	Originally a Communist; intellectually close to Labor-Farmer faction; later became Asō's right-hand man, especially in early relations with military.
Haruji Tahara 1900–	Waseda, Missouri, and Denver U.	Newspaper journalist	Came late to Japan-Labor clique; during war studied immigration to Southeast Asia for Navy; Diet 1936, 1937, failed 1942; as a "special community person" he was in National Leveling Society.
Kotora Tanahashi 1889–	Tōkyō U.	Lawyer; union leader of big strikes in 1918–19	Friendly Society leader; led the Federation of Japanese Labor Unions; Diet candidate 1930, 1937.

NAME AND DATES	EDUCATION (STUDENT ORGANIZATIONS)	OCCUPATION	NOTES *
Yoshitsuru Yamana 1891–	Tōkyō U. (New Men's Society)	Author	At first worked for Home Ministry; later Ōhara Institute of Social Reasearch; born a baron, his title was nullified by the government; in 1932 he joined Akamatsu in conversion to national socialism.

* "Diet" means elected to the Diet.

"IRAA" means membership and position in the Imperial Rule Assistance Association (Taisei Yokusankai) and "IRAPS" means position in Imperial Rule Assistance Political Society (Taisei Yokusan Seijikai).

"ILO" means attendance at an International Labor Conference at least once.

In educational background and age, this group resembled the agitator element in the Socio-Democratic clique. Only three out of the 21 listed had not been university students, though only one had studied abroad. They averaged a few years younger than the working-class administrators of the Socio-Democrats. But no figureheads or prestige names presided over this clique. Its acknowledged leader until his death was Asō who was only 35 in 1926, the average age of his clique at the time. The occupational category is also indicative of the intellectual characteristics of this group; several had either taught at universities or had worked on newspapers. Actually most did some writing, for magazines or newspapers, but very few did more serious studies or translations, since they were so busy with their work in connection with labor, agrarian, and socialist movements that they did not have time.

Perhaps concealed in the "Occupation" category of the table are the important sacrifices these men made for the proletarian movement—the long hours of toil and drudgery they devoted to their specialties. About one third of them specialized in the labor movement, one third in the agrarian, and one third in journalism. Only two practiced law. Kawakami gave up his university position in 1927 to go into the movement on a full-time basis. These positive aspects must be borne in mind when perusing the notes, which single out the later right-wing tendencies brought about under the duress of changing times, very much *because* these men had been so active in radical activities.

Only two were well known as Christians—or three, if we add Kagawa who, despite his participation in the organization of the Social Democratic Party in 1926, was subsequently for a while considered closer to the Japan-Labor than to the Socio-Democratic clique. Christianity was respected among the Socio-Democrats even by those who were not converts but was only tolerated by the younger members of the Japan-Labor clique.[3]

In spite of some differences in philosophical orientation, personal ties within the Japan-Labor clique were strong. Asō more than once described himself as someone to whom "feudalistic" interpersonal obligations were very important. This observation reflects his childhood environment in Kyūshū, the most feudalistic area in Japan with regard to the concept of personal loyalty.[4] Within the clique it was generally considered that to compromise one's personal opinions was less reprehensible than to endanger the solidarity of the group.[5] Consequently, as can be seen from the list, of twenty-one members two went over to national socialism, but Katō's was the only defection to the left and even this came about largely through a misunderstanding with Asō.[6]

Partly because of the close-knit character of this elite, the majority of its members were able, after the dissolution of all parties in 1940, to secure positions in the Imperial Rule Assistance Association, posts that conferred considerable status. For instance, Kawakami's position as a member of the General Council of the IRAA placed him along with persons of the highest prestige; in addition he was made a member of both the Committee of Inquiry on Price Policy and the Committee on Central Price Fixing. Kōno became Director of the IRAA's Political Affairs Institute, and Miwa, Chief of the Liaison Section of the Organization Bureau.[7] These men were young radicals in the student movement some twenty years earlier; now they were sitting with their former conservative university classmates on

3. A conversation between Asō and Kagawa, reported in Aso's autobiography, illustrates this point. Asō tells Kagawa he thinks Christianity is a deception and Kagawa replies that, for himself, he believes in it and will continue to do so even if no one else does. *Reimei*, pp. 227–28.

4. Ibid., p. 14.

5. From an interview by the author with Mitsu Kōno.

6. Katō returned to the clique after World War II. There were leftward defections of less important members, however.

7. Their old classmate from Tōkyō Imperial University, Katsumaro Akamatsu, was also working there as Chief of the Organization Section of the Planning Bureau.

the highest wartime committees after they had helped in a drive to dissolve all political parties, including those they themselves had founded.

STUDENT MOVEMENT BACKGROUND

The Japan-Labor clique stemmed in the main from the student movement. Almost two thirds of its members in their younger days joined either the New Men's Society (Shinjinkai) or the Founders' Federation (Kensetsusha Dōmei). These two organizations were important sources for the mainstreams of the social movement in Japan: the New Men's Society, organized at Tōkyō Imperial University in 1918, pouring out young men into the labor movement; and the Founders' Federation, almost simultaneously organized at Waseda, channeling them into the agrarian. Such social awareness resulted from several post-World War I conditions: the Christian emphasis on human dignity and its interest in social work; the popularity of democracy as a result of the "victory of democracy" in the war; the prior existence of the Friendly Society; the Russian Revolution with its emphasis on workers and peasants; the Rice Riots in Japan in 1918; and the revision of the curriculum in the leading universities, providing greater freedom in study, thought, and activity.

One of the founders of the New Men's Society, but not while he was at the University, Asō first became interested in the socialist movement at the time of the Kōtoku Treason Trial in 1911, when he was attending the Third Higher School, located in Kyōto (one of the two finest higher schools in Japan, the other being the First, located in Tōkyō).[8] Upon entering Tōkyō Imperial University in 1914, Asō invited graduates from these two schools to form a weekly discussion club. Gradually the topics of conversation became more and more political and their tenor increasingly serious. The war was going on; business was booming; and workers were organizing and striking in violation of what was to them the infamous Article 17 of the Peace Police Law of 1900.

Just as Asō and his classmates graduated, the world was shaken, first by the March Revolution and then more violently a few months later by the October Revolution in Russia. Asō was so moved by

8. Most of this material on Asō comes from his autobiographical work, *Reimei; Asō Hisashi Den;* and also Shisō no Kagaku Kenkyūkai, ed., *Tenkō 1,* 94–113 and 2, passim.

these events that he wrote a long newspaper series under the title "From Peter to Lenin," [9] attempting to refute the prevalent opinion that the Russian Revolution would be short-lived because it went against human nature. He predicted that the changes it wrought would be permanent ones, because they were as much a response to Russian conditions and as in tune with the Russian soul as were the reforms of Peter the Great. For about a year Asō's discussion club had called itself the Wednesday Society (Suiyōkai). Among those who came to discuss and study social problems were Yamana, Tanahashi, and even Sanzō Nozaka. Asō was not proficient in foreign languages, but so much of the literaturre on socialism and momentous world events was not available in Japanese that he had either to struggle with German, English, and French or to rely on his more scholarly friends. He was the most dynamic of the group, however. When fishing village housewives touched off the great Rice Riots in August 1918 and they spread to Tōkyō, Asō led his group in the demonstration that ended up rioting in Ueno Park. Had there been an organized political party to lead it, Asō and his friends felt, the people's fury against existing conditions could have been turned into a revolution like Lenin's.

Three months later, Asō joined with Professors Yoshino and Fukuda and others to organize the Dawn Society (Reimeikai) to awaken the Japanese people and prepare them for the postwar era. The tumultuous debate between Professor Yoshino and four members of the ultranationalist Rōnin Society (Rōninkai) on whether "democracy" was a dangerous doctrine or not, stirred the student audience into cheering as if at a sports event. Mitsu Kōno, a young student at the time, walked away from the meeting convinced he should dedicate himself to the cause of the masses.[10] Other students who felt this way, notably Akamatsu and Miyazaki, sought the advice of Asō. Combining with the Wednesday Society under the sponsorship of Professor Yoshino, they together organized the New Men's Society in

9. "Pītā yori Rēnin Made" appeared serially in the Tōkyō Nichinichi Shimbun just after the Revolution in 1917, Asō, p. 10.

10. Tadao Kikukawa, Gakusei Shakai Undō Shi (A History of Student Social Movements) (Tōkyō, Kaikō Shoten, 1947), p. 46. The student movement is well described in this and the following books: Kenji Sugiyama, Nihon Gakusei Shisō Undō Shi (A History of the Japanese Student Ideological Movements) (Tōkyō, Nihon Kirisutokyō Seinen Dōmei Gakusei Undō Shuppambu, 1930); and Etsuji Sumiya, Suehide Takakuwa, and Jōji Ogura, Nihon Gakusei Shakai Undō Shi (A History of Japanese Student Social Movements) (Kyōto, Dōshisha Daigaku Shuppambu, 1953).

November 1918 on a two-point program: "(1) We shall attune ourselves to the new movement ascendant in world culture today, the movement for the emancipation of mankind, and endeavor to promote it. (2) We shall take part in the movement for the rational reform of present-day Japan." [11] This vague platform expressed only the naïve, albeit fervent, desire of the students to take part in building the new age which seemed to be dawning in the world.

The organization of the New Men's Society at Tōkyō Imperial was as surprising as "lightning from a clear sky" to use the words of the society's organ, *Democracy*.[12] Ranking highest in the country in terms of prestige, this university had been created by the archconservative bureaucracy to replenish its own ranks. Among its student body were found sons of some of the leading families. Radical activities at the Imperial Universities can be partly explained by the fact that the tuition was low and standards very high. Thus, brilliant sons from poor families could go there, and they often keenly felt the unjust contrast between wealth and poverty.

At any rate, it was through choice, not force of circumstances, that students went into the labor and agrarian movements after the First World War. They sacrificed good careers and in some cases bore social ostracism from their families in order to devote themselves to the same labor movement that was a stairway to fame and prestige for some laborers, such as those in the Socio-Democratic clique.[13]

In the 1930s when Asō traveled in various parts of Japan to make political speeches, he could say that the head of the prefectural police had been only a freshman when he, Asō, was a senior; or that the governor of the prefecture had had poorer marks than he when they were at Tōkyō Imperial. In this way, Asō could drive home the point that he had given up a prestigious career leading to high rank as a bureaucrat to devote himself to the socialist movement. This would impress his audience, because in Japan great respect is paid both to universities and to rank. University ties between senior and junior graduates (*sempai-kōhai*) from the same university were very strong. The fact that governmental officials had been senior or junior class-

---

11. Kikukawa, p. 53.

12. *Demokurashī*. The name of the organ was soon changed to *Senku* (*Pioneer*), as "bourgeois democracy" became passé to the students who were turning more radical.

13. Mitsu Kōno described to the author how he was socially ostracized by his family when he decided to enter the socialist movement.

mates of the Japan-Laborite leaders meant that it was comparatively easy to find places in the wartime structure for the clique.[14]

The significance of the New Men's Society at the time of its birth, however, was that it became more than a students' organization. It became a group where students, workers, radical intellectuals, and old socialists could meet. In practical terms, "the democratic movement" at the time meant agitation for universal suffrage—in particular, extending the vote to the laboring classes. Workers who wanted the vote attended mass meetings of the Society, where they found students telling them it was more important for them first to organize unions. Starting with the Nagamine Celluloid Works in Tōkyō in 1919, students helped workers organize, articulate their demands, and carry through strikes.

The workers' encounter with the students excited both sides and opened new worlds to each in a way that can happen only where there has been a recent, rapid industrialization in an economically backward nation. The navy-blue uniformed students editorially proclaimed they had "found a new lover" in the strong but grimy workingman.[15] In conscious imitation of the Russian students of the 1860s, they were acting upon the slogan "V'narod!" (To the people!).[16] In this atmosphere of meetings, labor disputes, and police searches of the students' publications, the new leadership for the socialist movement was born.

There was a place in the expanding labor movement for these young university men who could provide the leadership in organizing trade unions which the inexperienced and unlettered workers themselves could not. To organize a union meant formulating demands to rally the men and precipitating a dispute with management. But there was also need for men with courage who would not balk at self-sacrifice. A dispute or strike often meant a riot because management would hire gangs of hoodlums or ultranationalists to create violence, for which the police would arrest the workers and their leaders. For instance, in 1919, when Asō organized the miners at the Hitachi Mines in Kyūshū, he and his assistants were arrested and given prison sentences.

14. This point was verified for the author by Sōichi Ōya, mentioned above.
15. Kikukawa, p. 68.
16. The poem by Takuboku Ishikawa, "V'Narod!" is reprinted in ibid., pp. 80–82. The young students made fervent speeches telling the workers labor was being exploited by capitalism and the workers asked them what "exploit" and "capitalism" meant.

Paralleling the New Men's Society which had its center at Tōkyō Imperial and which concentrated on the labor movement, the Founders' Federation was developed at Waseda University and focused on the agrarian movement. Professors Shinjirō Kitazawa and Ikuo Ōyama played roles analogous to those of Professors Yoshino and Fukuda. Although Waseda was not a national university, it had been founded by the Meiji statesman Shigenobu Ōkuma and had become the school for the conservative politicians who peopled the big parties in the Diet. The program of the Founders' Federation was to "build a new, more rational society." It soon succeeded in taking over the university oratorical society and set out to defeat all debating clubs which did not support socialism.[17] In fact, since there was so much competition in public speaking at this university, those who belonged to the Founders' Federation were given the uncomplimentary name of "vocal socialists." [18]

Unlike the New Men's Society, the Founders' Federation recruited members from other universities and one of these was the curious figure of Rikizō Hirano from the Colonization University (Takushoku Daigaku) and later Waseda itself. Hirano never affiliated long with either the Japan-Labor or Socio-Democratic cliques and sometimes headed his own agrarian and nationalistic parties—having enough money and following to be desired by several leadership groups but not the personality to achieve a position of importance within them.

A typical "vocal socialist" who started out in the Founders' Federation was Inejirō Asanuma, who in the early years was often associated with Hirano in the agrarian movement.[19] A year after graduation from Waseda in 1923, Asanuma joined the Japan Farmers' Union. However, his interest was not entirely absorbed by tenant-farmer affairs, and he volunteered to help Asō, who, with Tadokoro,

17. Inejirō Asanuma, "Waseda no Yūbenkai: Shichi Nen no Kokoro no Furusato" (The Oratorical Society at Waseda: My Old Sweet Home for Seven Years), *Bungei Shunjū, 13* (February 1953), 136–39.

18. From an interview with Sōichi Ōya, mentioned above.

19. Information on Asanuma was verified in his biography by Asanuma Tsuitō Shuppan Henshū Iinkai (Asanuma Memorial Publication Editorial Committee), ed., *Bakushin: Ningen Kikansha Numa San no Kiroku* (Dashing Forward: A Record of the Human Locomotive, Mr. Asanuma) (Tōkyō, Nihon Shakaitō Kikanshikyoku, 1961); Tadashi (Choku) Ōmagari, *Asanuma Inejirō: Sono Hito, Sono Shōgai* (Inejirō Asanuma: The Man and His Life) (Tōkyō, Shiseidō, 1961); Aragaki, pp. 168–72; and from a personal interview.

was leading the mineworkers' dispute at the Ashio Copper Mine. For his efforts he was sentenced to five months' imprisonment, despite the strenuous efforts of Tetsu Katayama who acted as his lawyer.

A dynamo of energy in party administration, Asanuma figured among the leading proletarian party officials throughout the kaleidoscopic history of party splits and mergers. His party career began as Secretary-General for the abortive Farmer Labor Party of December 1925, and his public officeholding started with election to the Tōkyō Municipal Assembly in 1933, where he was voted Vice-Speaker. He rose to membership in the Imperial Diet in 1936, to which he was continuously reelected for the rest of his life, except for the so-called Tōjō election of 1942.

Even among the rival, conservative leaders, Asanuma appears to have been especially well liked, despite a husky voice, bulky proportions, gruff mannerisms and plebeian dress. He had a way with people and thus became more of a compromiser than a taker of sides in internal party squabbles. Policy formulation and the refinement of ideological positions he left to others. As a result, he was characterized as "Mr. Well, well" (*Mā, mā San*). (His greatest fame was to be attained in postwar Japan, capped by his dramatic and tragic death on October 12, 1960, while speaking as Chairman of the Social Democratic Party of Japan. He was stabbed by a young ultranationalist, and the gory scene, recorded by television cameras, was quickly rushed around the world. The deciding factor for the assassin supposedly was Asanuma's statement in Peking that "American imperialism" was a common enemy to Japan and Communist China. Yet despite these strong words, a balanced view of the 35 years of his career shows that within the social democratic movement Asanuma was usually drawn to a moderate position.)

The agrarian wing of the Japan-Labor clique did not spring exclusively from the Founders' Federation. The outstanding representative of the other agrarian leaders in the Japan-Labor clique was Motojirō Sugiyama.[20] When the Founders' Federation was becoming interested in the agrarian question, Sugiyama came in contact with the newly founded Ōhara Institute of Social Research (Ōhara Shakai Mondai Kenkyūjo) where for the first time he studied the tenant-farmers' movement. Up to this time Sugiyama had been prac-

20. Besides the standard references special material on Sugiyama comes from Yarita, passim.

ticing dentistry in a poor farming community. He had also been engaged in social work and had successfully converted a poor rice paddy into an orchard, thus winning the confidence and respect of local farmers, which he needed inasmuch as he was also proselytizing for Christianity. Although he had been born of a poor tenant-farmer family in Ōsaka, he had been able to attend the Ōsaka Agricultural School (Ōsaka Nōgakkō), and later the Tōhoku Gakuin.

For ten years he was pastor of a church in Odaka Machi, Fukushima. At the time of the First World War, Sugiyama moved to Ōsaka where, as a result of his contact with the Ōhara Institute, his orientation began to change from social work to social action. He led a large tenant farmers' dispute at the Fujita Farms, and in 1921 was among the founders of the Japan Farmers' Union and became its first president. It was in this capacity that he took the lead in organizing the first "proletarian political party" in Japan, which was to be an alliance of tenant farmers and the urban working masses. Undaunted by the immediate disbandment of the Farmer Labor Party on December 1, 1926, Sugiyama again took the initiative in forming the Labor Farmer Party the following March.

Although their backgrounds were quite different, the role Sugiyama played in the agrarian movement was somewhat analogous to that played by Bunji Suzuki in labor. Yet, in spite of his Christian affiliation, Sugiyama became an initial member of the Japan-Labor clique rather than of the Socio-Democratic, the main reason being the bad feeling that had arisen from mutual recriminations between the Farmers' Union and the General Federation during the process of the radicalization of the Labor Farmer Party.[21] It seemed to Sugiyama that the dictatorial and cliquish General Federation leaders did not welcome "outsiders" in the leadership of the Social Democratic Party which they were about to organize, and yet he felt out of place in the increasingly militant Labor Farmer Party. When Asō and other dissatisfied General Federation leaders called on him secretly in Ōsaka to propose forming a new centrist party, halfway between the Labor Farmer Party on the left and the Social Democratic Party on the right, he welcomed the suggestion.

21. In Sugiyama's opinion the General Federation had done nothing constructive while supporting the Labor Farmer Party but instead had only tried to subvert it. Motojirō Sugiyama, "Rōdō Nōmintō no Bunretsu ni Tsuite" (About the Split in the Labor Farmer Party), *Shakai Keizai Taikei, 1* (December 1926), 391–99.

By the time the Japan Labor-Farmer Party was formed, most of its leaders were already acquainted with each other through the various organizations that had campaigned for the establishment of a proletarian political party.[22] As has been pointed out, many of the leaders were friends from their university days as well. Participation in the student movement had persuaded them to devote themselves to the emancipation of the working classes.[23] It also gave them an idological point of departure: Marxism imported from Weimar Republican Germany.[24]

The constant "spiritual advisor" of the Japan-Labor clique was Iwasaburō Takano, director of the Ōhara Institute of Social Research. He had been a professor at Tōkyō Imperial and had actually had some members of this clique in his seminar as students. His brother, Fusatarō, before his early death after the turn of the century, was a moderate labor organizer and worked with Sen Katayama. Professor Takano was a specialist on labor problems and himself a student of Marxism.

A short examination of the place of Marxian thought in the student movement will help in understanding the ideological characteristics of the Japan-Labor clique, so many of whose adherents had been converted to socialism while still attending university. Student interest in Marxism stemmed partly from the fact that the German Social Democratic Party was heading the state in postwar Germany. The additional facts that Marxism was considered the philosophical basis of the German Social Democratic Party and that, in the Japanese popular conception, the Germans were the most cultured and the most philosophically advanced people in Europe combined to raise interest in Marxism among Japanese students who always craved to know about the latest things in Western civilization. Be-

22. For example, the Society for the Study of Politics (Seiji Kenkyūkai) organized in June 1924.

23. Besides Sugiyama, Jōtarō Kawakami was also an exception to those who became socialists through the student movement. Older than the students, he had been emotionally stirred by the antiwar activities of the socialists at the time of the Russo-Japanese War. At Tōkyō Imperial he had been influenced by Iwasaburō Takano and through him became involved in studies undertaken by the Ōhara Institute of Social Research when Kawakami was teaching in the Ōsaka-Kōbe area. Kawakami gave lectures at the newly created labor schools in the area and actually led a strike at a textile plant. Gradually he became more and more deeply committed to the socialist movement. This information is from Professor Tamio Kawakami.

24. It is also relevant that already in the 1920s study of the German language was especially popular on the higher school (kōtō gakkō) level.

cause of the university market, Motoyuki Takabatake, an early Japanese authority on Marxism (though he changed and became an admirer of Mussolini), was continually besought by magazine publishers for any scraps of his translations of Marx. By 1924 he had published a full translation of the three volumes of Marx's *Capital*.

Members of the New Men's Society and other student groups also found a ready market for their translations. Miwa, for instance, published his college translation of Kautsky's *Commentary on the Erfurt Program*.[25] The demand for writings by Karl Marx himself and by every variety of Marxist theoretician expanded even more in the late 'twenties and only began declining after the Manchurian incident of 1931. Of all the Japan-Labor clique intellectuals, Mitsu Kōno did the most translation and writing on Marxism. He contributed to the ambitious 28-volume project, *The Collected Works of Marx and Engels*.[26] Of the translators for this set only four were definitely from the Japan-Labor clique,[27] none were from the Socio-Democratic, but some 20 were associated with the Labor-Farmer faction, which will be examined in the next chapter. Besides the works of Marx and Engels themselves, much was translated of every variety of Marxist literature, including particularly works by Lenin, Bukharin, Kautsky, Plekhanov, and Liebkneckt. In addition, numerous commentaries were written by Japanese. Kōno translated Heinrich Cunow's *Commentary on Marx's Thory of History, Society, and the State* and wrote *An Essay on Marx's Theory of the State*.[28] The majority of the Japan-Labor clique, however, were too busy with practical politics to spend much time translating and writing on theory. The clique may be described as being composed of "intelligentsia" but not of "rarefied intellectuals."[29]

It is interesting to note that almost all the salient characteristics of the Japan-Labor clique seem to stem from the fact that they were

25. Jusō Miwa, translator, *Kautsukī Erufuruto Kōryō Kaisetsu* (A Commentary on the Erfurt Program by [Karl] Kautsky) (Tōkyō, Kaizōsha, 1930). Original German title: *Das Erfurter Programm in seinem grundsätzlishen Theil, erläutert von Karl Kautsky* (Stuttgart, 1892).

26. Kaizōsha, comp., *Marukusu, Engerusu Zenshū* (28 vols. Tōkyō, Kaizōsha, 1928–33).

27. Michio Hosono, Tadao Kikukawa, Mitsu Kōno, and Jusō Miwa.

28. *Marukusu Rekishi Shakai Kokka Gakusetsu* and *Marukusu Kokka Ron*. The Cunow book has not, so far as I am aware, been translated into English. Its original German title is *Die Marxsche Geschichts-, Gesellschafts-, und Staats-theorie: Grundzuge der Marxschen Soziologie* (2 vols. Berlin, 1920).

29. While translations are not included, most of the indigenous Marxist theoretical

university graduates, in contrast to the main elements of the Socio-Democratic clique. Their dedication to the labor and socialist movements undoubtedly involved a certain amount of sacrifice. Their motivation was of an altruistic, humanitarian nature and, as such, it differed from that of the worker–leaders, risen from the ranks, who were fighting for their class and in so doing rising in the world themselves. Furthermore, the Japan-Laborites' university background and their interest in ideology from abroad—particularly in the organized body of socialist thought imported from Germany—gave them a more radical and less practical approach than that of the Socio-Democratic working-class leaders, who feared the competition of these glib, better-educated intruders. At the same time the working-class leaders felt they could run both the unions and the political parties quite competently themselves.

Antipathy toward the university graduates, however, was not widespread among the rank and file workers. In fact, so many unionists in the General Federation were dissatisfied with the lack of militancy on the part of the working-class leaders that the majority of the university-educated leaders were able to split the General Federation and set up their own trade union federation and proletarian party. But as the temper of the times changed and made it less possible to be militantly leftist, the trade union basis of the Japan-Labor clique became less and less stable in contrast to that of the Socio-Democrats.

Insufficient organized support was a strong factor in inducing the Japan-Laborite leaders in the mid-1930s to make overtures to the militarists on the common ground that they were both against the "selfishness" of the capitalists and that both favored national control of the economy. By that time similar attitudes also characterized the government bureaucracy. If one takes into consideration not only this new-found similarity in outlook, but also the old common university background, it is easier to understand why the bureaucrats were willing to place many of the Japan-Labor clique politicians in high positions in the Japanese wartime structure.

Finally, this clique was especially characterized by what the Japanese called *"kanjō"* (emotion) and "personal relations." They were held together in later years by the romanticism of their early "awak-

---

writings may be found in Cecil H. Uyehara, *Leftwing Social Movements in Japan: An Annotated Bibliography* (Tōkyō and Rutland, Vt., Charles E. Tuttle, 1959), especially Chap. 4, B and C.

ening" to the social problems that lay at the base of society and to the possibilities of fundamental social change. Asō, as a strong personality, could capitalize on this; and it was undoubtedly his initiative, both overt and covert, that led the Japan-Labor clique toward support for the military and then the "new structure." He never fully articulated his reasons before his death, but certainly one was that he felt that the proletarian movement needed help from men in high places. Aware for some time that he had heart disease and a limited time to live, he preferred to exhaust his last years in a burst of energy rather than to live a quiet, longer life. This energy seemed to infuse the whole clique and to express itself in the constant speechmaking they undertook throughout Japan. The Socio-Democrats were far narrower in their governmental and political contacts, in their public appeal, and in their organized support; while they had a firmer trade union foundation, their agrarian support was negligible. Thus, as the Socialist Masses' Party matured, the Japan-Labor clique came to dominate it and to determine its last actions.

7: The Labor-Farmer Faction (Rōnōha) and Other Leftist Groupings

As compared with the social democratic elites previously described, those to be treated in this chapter did not coalesce into closely knit cliques. That is one reason why the less precise terms "faction," "group," and "grouping" are used to designate them. For purposes of analysis, these leaders will be grouped and interpreted in the following order: [1]

I – The Labor-Farmer Faction
II – The Proleterian Masses' Party Leaders
III – The Mizutani Group
IV – The New Labor Farmer Party Leaders
V – The Popular Front Groups

Leaders operating under Communist direction are not classed as "social democrats" in this study, although their supporters are, inasmuch as the latter supported them as proletarian party candidates and usually did not know they were Communists. The Labor Farmer Party leaders, therefore, are not here considered "social democrats" but the "legal left" after the withdrawal of the General Federation

1. These groupings are graphically portrayed in Chart 1, "Lineages of Japanese Democratic Parties," in the Appendix.

leadership cliques. Ikuo Ōyama was head of the party. Although he was never a Communist Party member, we shall only count him as a social democrat when he diverged from the Communist line. This he did when he led the "New" Labor Farmer Party into a merger with definitely anticommunist groups. But he and his close associates are not to be confused with the Labor-Farmer faction, whose name does not derive from either the earlier or reorganized Labor Farmer Party.

Groupings II through V were influenced to various degrees by the Labor-Farmer faction whose Marxist ideology was more orthodox, or at least far less "revised," than that espoused by the Japan-Labor clique. In fact, these leaders did not like to be called social democrats at the time, because they considered that designation too conservative. They thought of themselves as an independent communist faction without international ties. Nevertheless, the nature of their opposition to contemporary Communist strategy and tactics placed them, from 1926–32, in what is generally considered the "left wing" of the social democratic movement, in contrast to the "right-wing" Socio-Democratic and the "centrist" Japan-Labor cliques. Their conceptual framework was often the same as the Communists' but their theoretical differences became explicit through their drawn-out polemical controversies with Communist thinkers over conflicting analyses of Japanese capitalism.

As a consequence of their ideological position, the role of these leaders in the whole proletarian party movement was to channel the most radical sections of labor and the tenant farmers into legally permissible courses of action. In this they were sometimes aided by governmental arrests of rival Communist labor and agrarian leaders.

Since the "members" of the Labor-Farmer faction had only informal, unorganized connections with each other, their style of activity tended to be disconnected, erratic, and individualistic. So many of them aspired to be theoreticians in their own right that they argued among themselves as much as with other groups. Their political alignments were unstable. Existing as they did just within the pale of legality (the Communists as such being outside), and under pressure from the other elites on the right, they sometimes allied themselves for safety with the Japan-Labor or Socio-Democratic cliques in a "united front" party—although occasionally they were expelled. As the country became more and more involved in war they were forced farther and farther to the right. When they stepped out of line to protest the drift to war, they were jailed.

The Labor-Farmer faction did not spring from a reformist, charitable organization as did the Socio-Democratic clique (from the Friendly Society), nor did it develop from radical student organizations as did the main elements in the Japan-Labor clique (from the New Men's Society and the Founders' Federation). Rather, its origin lay in the Communist camp. Whenever the great police hammer of the Japanese state came down upon the growing Communist movement, some pieces were likely to split off into what are here called the Labor-Farmer leadership factions.

The groups associated with the Labor-Farmer faction all appeared later than the Socio-Democratic and Japan-Labor cliques, which formed their own parties in December 1926, after parting ways with the Labor Farmer Party. As this party became a legal haven for the Japanese Communists, those individuals and groups that subsequently splintered off from it tended to be attracted to the Labor-Farmer faction which had earlier split directly from the Communist Party.

THE ORIGINAL LABOR-FARMER FACTION

The Labor-Farmer faction proper was a product of the government's first blow against the illegally formed Communist Party of Japan. As mentioned earlier that blow came on June 5, 1923, eleven months after the party was organized. Several arrests were made and, after short sentences, those jailed promised to, and did, dissolve the party. The Comintern urged its reorganization but was opposed by a faction called the "dissolutionists" led by Hitoshi Yamakawa who was against the ultraleftism of Kazuo Fukumoto. This faction's break with Communism was not complete, however, until it refused to accept the criticism of the Comintern embodied in the so-called "July 1927 thesis" which criticized both Fukumotoism and Yamakawaism. Yamakawa and his followers at first considered that the thesis vindicated their own position and began publishing articles in the "bourgeois" press attacking Communists and sympathizers who continued to hold that a Communist Party organization was necessary. One evening in November 1927, Yamakawa and his followers gathered at the house of Professor Yoshitarō Ōmori in Kamakura and formed what was at first called the "Labor-Farmer Faction Group" (Rōnōha Gurūpu).[2] They undertook the publication of a magazine, *Labor-Farmer (Rōnō)*,[3] and began attacking the Communists who had been recently recognized by the Comintern. Their attack was directed against the Comintern's strategy for revolution in Japan, not against the objectives or desirability of revolution. This was the origin of the Labor-Farmer faction in its strictest sense, and in it were such people as:

Grouping I

NAME AND DATES	EDUCATION (STUDENT ORGANIZATIONS)	OCCUPATION	NOTES *
Katsuzō Arahata (Pen name: Kanson Arahata) 1887–	Elementary and thereafter self-taught	Journalist	In original CP; veteran socialist.
Tsunao Inomata 1889–1942	Waseda, Wisconsin, Columbia, and Chicago Universities	Lecturer at Waseda U., author	In original CP; wrote voluminously on Japanese capitalism; a leading theorist.
Hisao Kuroda 1899–	Tōkyō U. (New Men's Society)	Lawyer	Specialist on tenant-farmer movement and a leader of Farmers' Union.
Yoshitarō Ōmori (Pen name: Mitsuo Naruse) 1898–1940	Tōkyō U.	Professor at Tōkyō U.	Wrote voluminously on dialectical materialism.
Toshihiko Sakai (Pen name: Kosen Sakai) 1870–1933	First Higher School, Tōkyō	Author	In original CP; veteran socialist.
Mosaburō Suzuki 1893–	Waseda U.	Newspaper journalist	Had probably been a member of a group connected with the American CP.

2. Yamamoto and Arita, *Nihon Kyōsanshugi Undō Shi,* p. 117.
3. The first issue is dated December 1927.

NAME AND DATES	EDUCATION (STUDENT ORGANIZATIONS)	OCCUPATION	NOTES *
Hitoshi (Kin) Yamakawa 1880–1958	Dōshisha U. but left for socialist movement before graduating	Author	In original CP; the leading personality and theorist in the Labor-Farmer faction.

* "CP" — Japan Communist Party.

As time passed, this group expanded and the term "Labor–Farmer faction" became far more indefinite than either Socio-Democratic or Japan-Labor. The list below includes people considered as belonging to the faction. Particulars concerning their lives are omitted here, since some of them had only indirect contact with the proletarian political parties and others will be discussed below.

Isamu Abe (Pen name: Kazuo Tachibana)
Hiromi Arisawa
Kenzō Honda
Junzō Inamura
Tomoyuki Ishihama
Kōdō (Yoshimichi) Itō
Etsuzō Kawai (Pen name: Sōnosuke Kimura)
Tamizō Kushida
Sōji Okada
Hyōe Ōuchi
Shintarō Ryū
Itsurō Sakisaka
Hiroo Sassa
Iwasaburō Takano
Takao Tsuchiya
Tadayuki Tsushima (Pen name: Kihachi Yokose)
Kikue Yamakawa (wife of Hitoshi Yamakawa)
Kōzō Uno

The outstanding personality in the Labor-Farmer faction was undoubtedly Yamakawa.[4] Having left Dōshisha University before graduating, he entered the socialist movement in Tōkyō where he worked with Toshihiko Sakai, Arahata, and other "veteran socialists." Because of his espousal of Bolshevism and opposition to "anarchism" after World War I, it was only natural for him to become one of the founders of the Japan Communist Party in July 1922. As we have seen, the article he published in August 1922 entitled, "A Change of Direction for the Proletariat," had tremendous repercussions

4. Material on Yamakawa is from a personal interview as well as from other common sources. Also, Shisō no Kagaku Kenkyūkai, ed., Tenkō, 2, 468–92 and passim. For a chapter on his wife, Kikue, see Aragaki, Sengo Jimbutsu Ron, pp. 198–203

throughout the socialist and labor movements and was interpreted in various ways. In the article, Yamakawa qualified himself as the leading Communist theoretician; however, after the first dissolution of the Communist Party, he proposed that it not be reestablished until the masses were ready for it and that they could be prepared for it only through the creation of a broad proletarian party, embracing the poor farming population as well as the urban masses. This thesis was attacked by Fukumoto who soon usurped his leadership.[5] Nevertheless, as Yamakawa moved out of the Communist fold, many of his followers accompanied him and helped found the Labor-Farmer faction.

Yamakawa wrote prodigiously until his retirement from political activity after the Manchurian incident in 1931, when he settled down on a farm in Kamakura with his wife, Kikue, who, like her husband, was an outspoken polemicist and had the reputation of being "too intelligent." In front of their house the police erected a small shelter for themselves, and three policemen always trailed the Yamakawas,[6] keeping notes on their activities. In spite of failures, retirement, arrests, and attacks from the left as well as from the right, the Yamakawas never changed their ideological position. (In postwar Japan, Mrs. Yamakawa was the first woman to become chief of a bureau in a ministry in the Japanese government, while her husband proved to be as prolific a writer of advice to the labor and socialist movements in postwar Japan as he had been in the 1920s. Until his death he remained the leading representative of the Labor-Farmer faction, which continued to supply theory for the noncommunist left wing in the postwar social democratic movement.)

If a distinction were to be made between the Labor-Farmer faction and the "legal left" up until its disappearance in 1930, it would be between those, on the one hand, who had made up their minds to cut their ties with the Comintern-recognized Communists, and others who had not yet definitely decided whether they should go along with the illegal Communist Party. Those who broke away from

5. Kazuo Fukumoto in his autobiography entitled *Kakumei wa Tanoshikarazu ya?* (Isn't Revolution Fun?) (Tōkyō, Kyōiku Shorin, 1952) mentions his attack against Yamakawa on p. 63.

6. Actually the Yamakawas were on good terms with the police; Yamakawa told me during an interview that the policemen who "trailed" when they traveled helped carry their bags.

the current of the Communist movement had either to work together, if they wished to have any independent strength, or to join with the Japan-Labor or Socio-Democratic cliques, if they wanted to be safe from arrest. Although the Labor-Farmer faction, which was the first to break away, was made up of only a few intellectuals in the beginning, the later groupings all possessed at least some organized support in the labor movement. As the Communist movement grew and as governmental suppression drove more groups out of it, these defecting factions joined and formed local proletarian parties. There were two reasons for this: the amount of support they could muster was limited, and the government's attitude toward local parties was more lenient.

SUBSEQUENTLY INFLUENCED GROUPINGS

Until April 1928 when ordered dissolved by the government following the mass arrests of "Communists" on May 15, the Labor Farmer Party was considered the "legal left" of the socialist movement. Thereupon, a group of "legalists" who had decided definitely to cut their ties with the Communists conferred with certain members of the Labor-Farmer faction and together with them formed the Proletarian Masses' Party (Musan Taishūtō) in July 1928. It was rumored at the time that these Labor-Farmer faction people had secretly conferred with the Japan-Labor clique leaders and had come to an understanding that the Proletarian Masses' Party would at an appropriate time amalgamate with the much larger Japan Labor-Farmer Party.[7] This rumor seemed to be substantiated a half year later, in December 1928, when such an amalgamation actually occurred, forming the Japan Masses' Party (Nihon Taishūtō). This was an example of the influence of the Labor-Farmer faction in gradually detaching organized support from the Communist-influenced "legal left."

The important leaders in the Proletarian Masses' Party, including some from the original Labor-Farmer Faction Group, made up what we have called Grouping II:

7. Nenshi Kankōkai Henshūbu (Editorial Department of the Yearly History Publishing Society), Shōwa San Nen Shi (The History of 1928) (Tōkyō, Nenshi Kankōkai, 1929), p. 142.

NAME AND DATES	EDUCATION	OCCUPATION	NOTES *
Kenji Daidō 1890–1940s(?)	Elementary	Worker, labor leader	Leader of Tōkyō Municipal Workers' Union; was member of Executive Committee of the Labor–Farmer Party.
Yoshiki Hayama 1894–1945	Self-taught after year at Waseda preparatory school	Novelist	Representative to the Party from Labor–Farmer Artists' League; working class background.
Junzō Inamura 1900–1955	Tōkyō U.	Author, translator	See Grouping I (expanded): Labor–Farmer faction.
Jinji Kobori 1901–1959	Self-taught after middle school	Novelist, translator	Translated Lenin's *State and Revolution,* etc.; husband of the authoress Taiko Hirabayashi.
Hisao Kuroda 1899–	Tōkyō U. (New Men's Society)	Lawyer, agrarian leader	See Grouping I: specialist on tenant-farmer movement and a leader of Farmers' Union.
Akio Mochizuki 1887–1962	Elementary	Worker, labor leader	A devout Christian; later became a small shopowner.
Sōji Okada 1902–	Tōkyō U. (New Men's Society)	Author, agrarian leader	See Grouping I (expanded): Labor-Farmer faction; Japan Farmers' Union.
Yoshitarō Ōmori (Pen name: Mitsuo Naruse) 1898–1940	Tōkyō U.	Professor	See Grouping I: wrote voluminously on dialectical materialism.
Mosaburō Suzuki 1893–	Waseda U.	Newspaper journalist	See Grouping I: originally close to CP.

* "CP" — Japan Communist Party.

Of the leaders listed here, Suzuki, Ōmori, Kuroda, Okada, and Inamura were charter members of the Labor-Farmer Faction Group (Grouping I). The newcomers Daidō and Mochizuki, when they withdrew from the Labor Farmer Party, brought with them organized labor union support, and Inamura, Kuroda, and Okada, who were leaders of the Japan Farmers' Union, brought with them agrarian support.

The central figure of Grouping II became the outstanding representative personality of the Labor-Farmer faction in the political sphere. Mosaburō Suzuki combined in himself what were very distinct elements in other elites: he was a university graduate although the son of a rickshaw puller.[8] He tried his hand at all the types of "Arbeit"—the German word used by the students—available to an impecunious student in Japan, making just enough to enable him to graduate from Waseda University, where he studied political economy.

In spite of his leftist orientation, Suzuki maintained connections with such important figures in the Japanese financial world as Toshi Hiraga and Baron Seinosuke Gō. He became acquainted with Baron Gō when, as a reporter, he specialized in financial news. From such men he obtained information for his serious theoretical books on the zaibatsu and Japanese monopoly capitalism which were characterized by the typical Labor-Farmer faction approach.[9] In the spring of 1928, when, because of his open participation in the socialist movement, he was discharged from his position on the Tōkyō Nichinichi newspaper, he visited Baron Gō and informed him of his intention to devote himself completely to the proletarian party movement. The Baron reportedly exclaimed, "I thought only hoodlums were involved in such movements, but when I hear that such a serious minded person as you has decided to do such a thing, it's not hard for me to surmise the future of Japan, and even I will have to get ready for it." [10]

A fellow member of the Labor-Farmer faction, Arahata, later criticized Suzuki for his declining theoretical contributions [11]—a criticism indicative of the importance given to theory by the Labor-Farmer faction.

Grouping III was much less close to the Labor-Farmer faction

8. Material is from Arahata, Sa no Memmen, pp. 5–23 and 93–100; Aragaki, pp. 83–92; and from interviews by the author.

9. See his Nihon Dokusen Shihonshugi no Tembō (The Outlook for Japanese Monopoly Capitalism) (Tōkyō, Hakuyōsha, 1931); Nihon Zaibatsu Ron (On the Japanese Zaibatsu) (Tōkyō, Kaizōsha, 1934); and Nihon Dokusen Shihon no Kaibō (An Analysis of Japanese Monopoly Capitalism) (Tōkyō, Gakugeisha, 1935).

10. Arahata, Sa no Memmen, p. 11.

11. Ibid., p. 14.

than Grouping II. It came into being when the government directed a second blow at the "legal left," or the left that was trying to be legal. The remnants of the Labor Farmer Party, which had been dissolved in April 1928, tried to reestablish themselves as a party on December 24 of the same year, but the party they formed was forcibly dissolved the same day by the government (as explained below in connection with Grouping IV). The groups that gave up the attempt and broke away this time organized a number of local proletarian parties (as had been advocated by the Labor-Farmer faction), the most important of which was the Labor-Farmer Masses' Party (Rōnō Taishūtō), a local party under the leadership of Chōzaburō Mizutani, organized in Kyōto on January 17, 1929. Mizutani was the only leader of importance in Grouping III:

NAME AND DATES	EDUCATION	OCCUPATION	NOTES *
Chōzaburō Mizutani 1897–1960	Kyōto U. (Labor-Student Society)	Lawyer, agrarian leader	Associated with the Communist-influenced "legal left" up to this time. Had been elected to Diet 1928 (LFP); thereafter failed 1930 (LFMP), 1932 (NLFMP), but won 1936 (SMP), 1937 (SMP), 1942. IRAA.

* "LFP"—Labor Farmer Party.
"LFMP"—Labor-Farmer Masses' Party. For other abbreviations, see NOTES, p. 164 below.

At Kyōto Imperial University from which he graduated in 1921, Mizutani joined the Labor-Student Society (Rōgakkai) whose members had helped persuade Akamatsu and Miyazaki to organize the New Men's Society at Tōkyō Imperial.[12] Mizutani entered the labor movement while at university by becoming head of the legal department of the Kyōto Branch of the Friendly Society. In 1921 he started graduate study at Kyōto Imperial under the well-known Professor Hajime Kawakami, who at that time, in middle age, was becoming a proponent of Marxism.

In 1925, Mizutani became an advisor to the Japan Farmers' Union which spearheaded the movement for the first proletarian political party (which became the abortive Farmer Labor Party). When the Labor Farmer Party was successfully formed he was made a member

12. Material is from the usual sources including the chapter on Mizutani in Aragaki, pp. 131–34 and from a personal interview.

of its Central Executive Committee and Chairman of its Kyōto Branch, and on its slate he was elected, amid great rejoicing, to the Imperial Diet in 1928. But after the party had been severely hit by police arrests because of suspected Communists within its ranks, Mizutani withdrew and formed the Labor-Farmer Masses' Party mentioned above. This caused great bitterness between him and his former associates, including Professor Kawakami, who stuck with the remnants of the Labor Farmer Party. It appeared to be a breach of *on* or obligation when Mizutani ran against his former professor in the Diet election of February 20, 1930, in Kyōto. In thus dividing the proletarian vote, both lost.[13]

Mizutani's following, now organized in the Kyōto-based Labor-Farmers Masses' Party (Grouping II), was soon joined by members of Groupings I and II who had bolted or been expelled from the Japan Masses' Party in which they have been in uneasy alliance with the Japan-Labor clique. Among those who had already been expelled from the Japan Masses' Party during the period from May to June 1929 were persons influenced by the Labor-Farmer faction, such as Mosaburō Suzuki, Kuroda, Inomata, Daidō, and the venerable Toshihiko Sakai. After being defeated in an internal leadership struggle against Hisashi Asō, who at the time was supported by Rikizō Hirano, they had organized local parties, such as the Tōkyō Proletarian Party (Tōkyō Musantō) headed by Sakai and Kuroda with one Inosuke Nakanishi. It was on March 17, 1930, that they joined Mizutani and together with his party formed the National Conference for a United Proletarian Party Front (Musan Seitō Sensen Tōitsu Zenkoku Kyōgikai). The poor showing of the proletarians in the February 1930 election combined with the theoretical imperatives of the class struggle and the dwindling competition from the Communists to strengthen the drive for a united front.

This drive was strong enough to overcome the factional antipathy toward the Japan-Labor clique held by the more orthodox Marxist-oriented Labor-Farmer faction and those it influenced (Groupings I and II), and now together with it and Mizutani (Grouping III), they reorganized on a national basis as the National Masses' Party (Zenkoku Taishūtō) on July 20, 1930.

13. Hajime Kawakami mentions his relationship with Mizutani in his autobiography, *Jijoden* (My Autobiography) (5 vols. Tōkyō, Iwanami Shoten, 1952), *1*, 231–32 and *2*, 121 and 126. The extension of this autobiography is entitled *Gokuchū Nikki* (My Diary While in Prison) (2 vols. Tōkyō, Iwanami Shoten, 1952).

With this much momentum, the coalition of factions was able to attract remnants of the "New" Labor Farmer Party, causing another reorganization a year later, on July 5, 1931, creating the new, even more unmanageable party name: National Labor-Farmer Masses' Party (Zenkoku Rōnō Taishūtō).

But before discussing the genesis of the new group—which we call Grouping IV—a few words on the subsequent course of the Mitzutani faction can dispose of this strand which continued into the grand unification of the Socialist Masses' Party in 1932. In that party, curiously enough, Mizutani, while always maintaining a somewhat independent flexibility and a small but faithful following, gradually became friendly with those he had castigated most in his early days in the Labor Farmer Party, namely the Socio-Democratic clique. He sided with them in the last days of the existence of the Socialist Masses' Party, being counted among those expelled in the Takao Saitō affair in 1940. He then joined in the abortive attempt to form the Nationalist Labor Party but despite this was accepted shortly thereafter in the Imperial Rule Assistance Association and its successor the IRAPS.[14]

To return to our story in 1931, before the Socialist Masses' Party came into being, what was the genesis of Grouping IV, remnants from the New Labor Farmer Party? It will be remembered that the original Labor Farmer Party was ordered disbanded by the authorities on April 10, 1928. Meeting on that very day, the angry, indignant, and defiant leaders formed the Preparatory Committee for the Organization of a New Party (Shintō Soshiki Jumbikai). On December 24, they proclaimed the formation of the Worker Farmer Party (Rōdōsha Nōmintō), but the authorities ordered it disbanded immediately. In consternation, the assembly set up the Labor-Farmer Federation for Securing Political Liberties (Seijiteki Jiyū Kakutoku Rōnō Dōmei), calling on the support of all who believed in the preservation of civilized political processes and opposed arbitrary bureaucratic behavior.

This organization was tolerated by the police, but within it a pro-Communist group began to mock the idea that anything really effective could be done if the resultant new party was to confine itself to

14. Mizutani became active in postwar politics in the right wing of the Social Democratic Party. Journalistic opinion of Mitzutani in postwar Japan was that he had an open personality and charm but also a certain toughness and a sharp tongue at round-table discussions and on the air; it was said that he had a medicine for general problems but no specifics. See, for example, Aragaki, p. 133.

limits of "legal" activitiy. This group argued that the most effective protest and resistance to the government's arrogant political interference would be to swell the ranks of the underground Communist Party. This argument won the day in the councils of the Federation, but as it was about to be carried into action the government moved again to crush the Communist Party by mass arrests on April 16, 1929. Although the Federation was pitifully weakened by the losses the arrests had caused, those who remained, the "right wing" of the organization, decided to organize a "legal" party. Founded on November 1, 1929, with the name Labor Farmer Party, it was commonly known as the New Labor Farmer Party (Shin Rōnōtō) to distinguish it from the old.

Grouping IV was thus composed of the leaders of the New Labor Farmer Party, which lasted from November 1, 1929, to July 5, 1931:

NAME AND DATES	EDUCATION	OCCUPATION	NOTES *
Kanemitsu Hososako 1896–	Tōkyō U.	Lawyer	Diet candidate 1930; did not enter NLFMP. Underwent temporary jail "conversion" to patriotism; elected city mayor.
Susumu Kamimura 1883–	Waseda U.	Lawyer	Diet candidate 1928, 1930; did not enter NLFMP; Secretary of the Liberty Lawyers' and Judges' Guild.
Hajime Kawakami 1878–1946	Tōkyō U.	Professor and editor of own magazine	Diet candidate 1930; did not enter NLFMP, entered CP instead; until then ideological leader of New Labor Farmer Party; editor of its organ.
Takaichi Nakamura 1897–	Waseda U.	Lawyer	Entered NLFMP; then SMP; later East Asiatic League; Diet candidate 1930, 1936, 1942; elected 1937.
Ikuo Ōyama 1880–1955	Kōbe Commercial, Waseda U.; postgraduate at U. of	Professor at Waseda and newspaper edi-	Leader of "legal left" (Labor Farmer Party and successive organizations)

NAME AND DATES	EDUCATION	OCCUPATION	NOTES *
	Chicago and U. of Munich	torial writer	until dissolution of New Labor Farmer Party; Diet candidate 1928, elected 1930; entered NLFMP.
Kanji Shindō 1896–1940s(?)	Self-taught while a non-commissioned officer in the Army	Lawyer	Diet candidate 1928, 1930; did not enter NLFMP.
Hideo Yamahana 1904–	Elementary	Labor leader	Friendly Society; Council; entered NLFMP; later Japan Proletarian Party; arrested for popular front activities.
Kenji Yamazaki 1902–1956	Gotemba Agricultural School	Farmer's Union leader	Entered NLFMP and then SMP; Diet 1936, 1937; IRAA, IRAPS.
Tsunekichi Yamazaki 1891–1961	Elementary	Tinsmith, union official, owned business	Entered NLFMP; in 1937 joined splinter Patriotic Proletarian Party; Diet 1937, 1942; IRAA; IRAPS.

* "NLFMP" — National Labor-Farmer Masses' Party.
   "SMP" — Socialist Masses' Party.
   "CP" — Japan Communist Party.
   "Diet" — elected to the Diet at least once.
   "IRAA" — Imperial Rule Assistance Association.
   "IRAPS" — Imperial Rule Assistance Political Society.

The new party was not in existence long before the same polarization that had plagued its predecessors once more took place. Again came the proposal for dissolving the party and supporting the Communist Party instead. For advocating this, a number of leaders, such as Hajime Kawakami, Kamimura, Hososako, Shindō, and Iomaro Akamatsu (Katsumaro Akamatsu's younger brother), were expelled from the party during September and October 1930. Of those who remained, the only well-known figure was Ikuo Ōyama, who had been elected to the Diet in 1930 from the famous Fifth District in Tōkyō. Kenji Yamazaki and Nakamura, who also remained, later became Diet members, but only after they had become identified with the Japan-Labor clique. (Nakamura became well-known in postwar Japan as a right-wing Socialist.) The only leader who entered into a coalition with the other elements of the social democratic movement and yet moved leftward again was Yamahana, who later appeared in the "popular front" with the Labor-Farmer faction in 1937.

After the withdrawal or expulsion of the more militant elements, and with the remaining ones determined to keep the party strictly legal, the New Labor Farmer Party became passive and ineffective. For example, it led the large strike at the General Motors plant in Ōsaka in December 1930, but even from within the thinned ranks of the party came the criticism that the handling and solution of the dispute compromised the workers.[15] The party gradually seemed to be losing its raison d'être, when Ōyama finally took the same path he had castigated others for taking and joined with the Japan-Labor clique in forming the National Labor-Farmer Masses' Party.

Called "Our shining (warera no kagayakeru) party leader," Ōyama was the representative figure of Grouping IV for indeed he had led the "legal left" throughout its existence.[16] A man of high scholastic background, he had graduated from both the Kōbe Commercial School in 1901 and from Waseda University in 1905 before spending four years abroad doing postgraduate work at the University of Chicago and the University of Munich. On his return, he taught at Waseda University 1915–17. During the following year he worked as an editorial writer for the Ōsaka Asahi Newspaper where he developed a popular and fluent style. In 1919 he put out a magazine called We (Warera) in collaboration with Nyozekan Hasegawa, known as a liberal, and Tamizō Kushida, a Marxist who had studied in Germany and, though a student (deshi) of Hajime Kawakami, was associated closely with the Labor-Farmer faction. Ōyama then returned to Waseda until his political activities took him away from teaching again. He gained a high reputation as a public speaker and, though he stammered somewhat, it was said that the flow of his argument "would break stones." Nevertheless, he was criticized by his closest companion in the New Labor Farmer Party, Professor

15. Yamamoto and Artia, p. 178.

16. A 409-page biography of Ōyama has been written collectively by a committee composed of people who know him well: Shinjirō Kitazawa, Hiroshi Suekawa, and Yoshitarō Hirano, comp., Ōyama Ikuo Den (The Biography of Ikuo Ōyama) (Tōkyō, Chūō Kōronsha, 1956).

Kawakami, editor of the party organ, who said, "Mr. Ōyama likes speech-making better than eating or anything else. At street corner speeches, the bigger the crowd the higher his spirits. He doesn't worry about anything else." [17]

In the negotiations in 1931 leading up to the New Labor Farmer Party's merger with the party led by the Japan-Labor clique, the question came up as to who should be party leader (i.e. Secretary-General), Asō as the central figure in the Japan-Labor faction or Ōyama as the more distinguished in age, intellectual background, and popular reputation. Due to his factional backing, Asō won; Ōyama was to be made an Advisor, but he refused, saying he wanted to work as "a common foot-soldier" in the party. However, learning of a plot on his life by certain ultranationalists, Ōyama decided to flee to the United States, where he obtained a position as Research Associate at Northwestern University through the sponsorship of Professor Kenneth Colegrove. He remained there until after the war.[18]

As part of the price for the Social Democratic Party's merger with the all-inclusive National Labor-Farmer Masses' Party to form the Socialist Masses' Party, the chairmanship of the Central Executive Committee—and thus of the party—was given to Isoo Abe, but greater power fell into the hands of Hisashi Asō as Secretary-General. The Socio-Democratic clique was represented by such men as Abe, Bunji Suzuki, Yoshino, Tsunego Baba, Hyō Hara, Tetsu Katayama, Matsuoka, and Nishio; the Japan-Labor clique by Asō, Sugiyama, Jōtarō Kawakami, Sunaga, Asanuma, Tadokoro, Miwa, and Mitsu

17. Kawakami, *Jijōden*, 2, 26.

18. That Ōyama's life was in danger there was no doubt; but many other proletarian leaders had been threatened—in fact even conservative government and business leaders —so that perhaps Ōyama's more fundamental reason was that he was tired of the struggle and at the time saw only the bleakest future ahead.

The story of how Ōyama came to Northwestern is an interesting one. Before he left Japan he had received a letter containing a check in dollars from Professor Kenneth Colegrove, who was teaching constitutional law at Northwestern, requesting information on certain conditions in Japan. When Ōyama got to Evanston he called on Colegrove and returned the money with his apologies for not sending the report. Professor Colegrove entreated him to stay and made a place for him at Northwestern. Ōyama reportedly wanted several times to return to Japan before it was too late, but Colegrove pointed out that he might be killed or imprisoned, and convinced him to remain. The work given Ōyama at Northwestern was to collect material on the Japanese Constitution and to translate Tatsukichi Minobe's *Kempō Seigi* (A Commentary on the Constitution). This work he did not complete. Kitazawa et al., *Ōyama Ikuo Den*, pp. 252–62.

Kōno; the Labor-Farmer faction (Groupings I and II) by Mosaburō Suzuki and Hisao Kuroda (the former expelled in 1936 and the latter in 1937 for "popular front" activities); Grouping III by Mizutani (expelled in 1940); and Grouping IV by Yamazaki and Nakamura of the New Labor Farmer Party. (Now that Ōyama had fled, the latter two tended to side with the Japan-Labor clique on policy issues.)

However, harmony did not continue to reign in the "one big party," despite its impressive electoral gains in 1936 and 1937. The defections and expulsions that occurred were indicative of the new problem facing the socialist movement: the anti-fascist popular front.

The popular front that actually emerged was essentially a coalition of the followers of Katō (the former Japan-Labor clique leader) and various elements of the amorphous Labor-Farmer faction (Groupings I and II plus new people). The first public call for a popular front made by a mass organization in Japan was that of the Labor-Farmer Proletarian Conference in July 1936, five months after the country had been rocked by the February 26th attempted coup. It was Jiichirō Matsumoto, an independent Diet member representing the National Leveling Society, and Kuroda, on the fringes of the Socialist Masses' Party and leader of the All-Japan Farmer's Union, who acted as mediators in the vain attempt to effect a merger between the Conference and the party on the basis of a popular front. Soon after the Conference reorganized as the Japan Proletarian Party, it signed up over 7,000 members and set up a number of local branches. On its platform, Mosaburō Suzuki was elected to the Tōkyō Municipal Assembly in March and attracted considerable, but insufficient, votes in the April Diet election, though Katō held on to his Diet seat. All too swiftly the tidal wave of the China incident washed away the antifascist people's front before it could become firmly rooted.

While the first arrests in the popular front incident occurred on December 15, a wider net was cast to bring in what was called the "Academicians Group" six weeks later, on February 1, 1938. Approximately 400 persons were jailed in these roundups. Coming from what can be classified as four different groups, they were all influenced by Labor-Farmer faction thinking. The leading figures, whom we have designated as constituting our Grouping V, can be listed as follows:

A. From the Japan Proletarian Party:

NAME AND DATES	EDUCATION	OCCUPATION	NOTES *
Kanjū Katō 1892–	Japan U.	Union leader	Switched from the Japan-Labor clique in 1932; Diet candidate 1928 (JLFP), 1930 (JMP), 1932 (local); elected 1936 (local), 1937 (JPP); S-3 yrs.
Jinji Kobori 1901–1959	Self-taught after year at Waseda preparatory school	Novelist, translator	See Grouping II: started in Proletarian Masses' Party and later joined the Socialist Masses' Party from which expelled in 1936 for aiding Katō instead of Asō in election; S-2 yrs. 6 mos.
Zengorō Shimagami 1903–	Elementary	Union leader	On Central Committee of Labor Farmer Party in 1926; S-2 yrs.
Mosaburō Suzuki 1893–	Waseda U.	Journalist	See Groupings I and II: originally close to CP; Labor-Farmer Faction Group; also in the Proletarian Masses' Party of 1928. Diet candidate 1937 (JPP); S-5 yrs.
Minoru Takano 1901–	Waseda U. but left for socialist movement before graduating	Union leader	Originally CP; came into political arena through the Labor-Farmer Proletarian Conference; S-3 yrs.
Seidō (Masamichi) Takatsu 1893–	Expelled from Waseda U. for radical activities (Founders' Federation)	Author	Originally CP; Labor-Farmer faction; Diet candidate 1930 (local); in Association of Friends of Peace in the Far East in 1932; S-2 yrs.
Hideo Yamahana 1904–	Elementary	Labor leader	See Grouping IV: from New Labor Farmer Party; a leader of National Council of Japanese Labor Unions; S-2 yrs. 6 mos.

NAME AND DATES	EDUCATION	OCCUPATION	NOTES *
Shikaichi Yasuhira 1902–	Elementary	Labor leader	A leader of the National Council of Japanese Labor Unions, 1934; elected to Tōkyō Prefectural Assembly, 1936; S-2 yrs.

B. *From the National Farmers' Union (Zenkoku Nōmin Kumiai):*

Junzō Inamura 1900–1955	Tōkyō U.	Author, translator, agrarian leader	See Groupings I (expanded) and II: Labor-Farmer faction; Proletarian Masses' Party; S-2 yrs. ss.
Hisao Kuroda 1889–	Tōkyō U.	Lawyer, agrarian leader	See Groupings I and II: Labor-Farmer faction; member of Socialist Masses' Party at time of arrest; elected to Diet 1936 (local), 1937 (SMP); S-2 yrs.
Sōji Okada 1902–	Tōkyō U.	Author, agrarian leader	See Groupings I (expanded) and II: Labor-Farmer faction; Proletarian Masses' Party; S-2 yrs. ss.

C. *From the Labor-Farmer Faction Group itself:*

Katsuzō (Pen name: Kanson) Arahata 1887–	Self-taught	Journalist	See Grouping I: veteran socialist; in original CP; S-3 yrs.
Tsunao Inomata 1889–1942	Waseda, Wisconsin, Columbia, and Chicago Universities	Instructor, author	See Grouping I: in original CP; wrote voluminously on Japanese capitalism; a leading theoretician; his wife was a Polish revolutionary.
Yoshitarō Ōmori (Pen name: Mitsuo Naruse) 1898–1940	Tōkyō U.	Professor	See Groupings I and II: wrote voluminously on dialectical materialism.

NAME AND DATES	EDUCATION	OCCUPATION	NOTES *
Itsurō Sakisaka 1897–	Tōkyō U.	Professor, author	See Grouping I (expanded): after expulsion from Kyūshū U. in 1928, devoted himself to *Labor-Farmer* and battled Communist theoreticians over Marxian interpretations; S-2 yrs.
Hitoshi (Kin) Yamakawa 1880–1958	Dōshisha U. but left for socialist movement before graduating	Writer	See Grouping I; in original CP; the leading personality and theorist in the Labor-Farmer faction; S-5 yrs.

D. From the Academicians Group (Gakusha Gurūpu):

NAME	PROFESSOR AT	SENTENCE (AT TŌKYO)
Isamu Abe (Pen name: Kazuo Tachibana) **	Hōsei U.	S-2 yrs. ss.
Hiromi Arisawa **	Tōkyō U.	S-2 yrs. ss.
Toshio Hayase	Yokohama Higher Commercial School	
Kinji Minami	Hōsei U.	Ng.
Ryōkichi Minobe	Hōsei U.	Ng.
Hyōe Ōuchi **	Tōkyō U.	Ng.
Hyōe Serizawa	Sugamo Higher Commercial School	Ng.
Masao Takahashi	Kyūshū U.	S-2 yrs. ss.
Kōzō Uno **	Sendai U.	
Yoshitarō Wakimura	Tōkyō U.	Ng.

* "CP" — Japan Communist Party.
"JLFP" — Japan Labor-Farmer Party.
"JMP" — Japan Masses' Party.
"Local" — local party or union.
"S-no. yrs." means "sentenced to a certain number of years of imprisonment at hard labor for popular front activities." Appended "ss" means "sentence suspended." "Ng" means "found not guilty." (These sentences were meted out at the Tōkyō Court August–September 1942 but subsequently appealed. Those indicted at other courts are not indicated here.)
** See Grouping I (expanded).

The official reason given by the government for the arrests was that the popular front was carrying into effect the new program of the Comintern, spreading antiwar propaganda, and not cooperating with imperial policy.[19] It was difficult for the government to prove its case in the courts.[20] Gradually most of the arrested were released on bail, although the court proceedings had not been completed by the time Japan surrendered, and then, of course, they were dropped.

The most outstanding political figure of this Labor-Farmer faction-influenced grouping was Kanjū Katō, who had originally been one of the Japan-Labor clique.[21] Like most of the adherents of that clique, he was an "intellectual," but he had graduated from Japan University and thus did not have close university ties with the majority who had attended either Tōkyō Imperial or Waseda universities. Like Mosaburō Suzuki, Katō suffered from poverty. He worked as an errand boy for a clothier when he was eleven. At seventeen, he entered the Japan Middle School but had to quit for two years because of lack of funds. At twenty-one he was drafted and after military service, he studied law, at night, at Japan University. Once more, before graduating, he was recalled to the service and sent to

19. For an abridged quotation of the official reason, see Hosoya, *Nihon Rōdō Undō Shi*, 2, 195, and for Home Minister Suetsugu's interview with the press on the reason for the arrests, see Shōzō Mori, *Fūsetsu no Hi: Shōwa Junnansha Retsuden* (A Storm Memorial: Biographies of Martyrs in the Shōwa Period) (Tōkyō, Masu Shobō, 1946), p. 102. For a complete list of those sentenced in the Tōkyō court for popular front activities, see Naka, pp. 243-44.

20. With regard to the Labor-Farmer faction, the government prosecutor changed his accusations twice. At first he charged that the faction was following orders from the Comintern transmitted by the Chinese Communist, Kuo Mo-jo, who had visited Japan in 1936. After a short investigation this charge was dropped. Then the prosecutor alleged that it was a secret organization set up to alter the national polity and reject the system of private property, thus violating the Peace Preservation Law of 1925. His position was that the program of this secret group was the blurb Yamakawa had written in the first issue of *Labor-Farmer (Rōnō)* in 1927 giving the reasons for establishing the magazine, and that subsequent policy was expressed in disguised form (or Aesopian language) in the pages of that journal. However, this charge, too, was dropped and a new one leveled: that although the Labor-Farmer faction was not a secret organization, still its adherents were Marxists, and as such had the long-range aim of altering the national polity and denying the system of private property. The cases were tried in the summer of 1942 and sentences of one or more years of hard labor were handed down, but they were then appealed to the Supreme Court, which, however, was obliterated by bombs in 1945 before the cases were finally settled. This material is from an interview by the author with Hitoshi Yamakawa.

21. For material on Katō, see Aragaki, pp. 139-43; Ichirō Akasaka, *Musantō o Ugokasu Hitobito: "Jimmin Sensen" to wa Nani ka?* (The Men Who Lead the Proletarian Parties: What is the "Popular Front"?) (Tōkyō, Okabe Shobō, 1936), pp. 61-63; and Shisō no Kagaku Kenkyūjo, *Tenkō*, passim.

Siberia in the medical corps; his experience there, he later claimed, gave him a personal basis for attacking Japan's preparations for more war. After that, he led the great strike on the *Teito* newspaper in August 1919. In 1920 he took part in the first Yawata Iron Mill strike of some 25,000 workers, an event that marked the beginning of his wide experience in mine disputes, parallel to that of Asō. He gained great acclaim for his exploits, as, for example, leading the Besshi Copper Mine strike of 1925, 5,000 feet above sea level in snow and wind for 112 days.

When a leader of the General Federation, Katō was considered a "centrist" and as such displaced the right-wing Matsuoka temporarily as Secretary of the General Federation at the time of the split which led to the formation of the Council in 1925. In his opposition to Matsuoka, he joined Asō in organizing the Japan Labor-Farmer Party, becoming an original adherent of the Japan-Labor clique. In time he came to oppose Asō as well, as we have seen. It began with a misunderstanding that resulted in the two battling each other in Tōkyō's Fifth District in the election of February 1932, thus splitting the proletarian vote so that neither won. Nonetheless, Katō had a firm footing in the labor movement and remained until 1932 in the National Federation of Labor Unions, the trade union basis of the Japan-Labor clique.

After November 1931, Katō had led a protest movement in the National Federation against what he claimed to be its fascistic tendencies. By 1934, when Asō praised the army's pamphlet, the break between Katō and the Japan-Labor clique was complete, and he then organized the National Council of Japanese Labor Unions. Katō received encouragement in his decision to resist fascism from some members of the American Federation of Labor during a three-month trip he took to the United States in 1935 at their invitation.

Katō's attempt to organize a popular front is hard to reconcile with his apparently, at the same time, taking a somewhat cooperative attitude toward Japan's adventure in China. For example, he was arrested for popular front activities in 1937 just as he landed in Nagasaki on his return from China, where he had been visiting the troops as an Imperial Army Comfort Officer! Katō was imprisoned for about two years. During his trial he met Baroness Shizue Ishimoto, who had been arrested for her activities on behalf of birth control. His wife had recently died, and when Baroness Ishimoto secured a divorce from her husband in 1944, she married Katō. In time she was to become a strong influence in turning him more to the right.[22]

A few more observations may help clarify the characteristics of the Labor-Farmer faction. Although all those listed may be considered "adherents of" or "influenced by" the Labor-Farmer faction—that is, they held certain opinions or rather a *Weltanschauung* in common—they were at no time all members of a single organization. The Labor-Farmer Faction Group itself had no organization: no officers, discipline, program, or headquarters. In the political sphere it supported the Japan Proletarian Party in 1937 but all of its "members" did not belong to that party. It had adherents in labor and farmer unions, among the intelligentsia, and even among some members of the Socialist Masses' Party. In contrast, the Japan-Labor and Socio-Democratic cliques were both completely organized in political parties, sometimes in opposition to each other, sometimes together.

Also in contrast to the other elites, the Labor-Farmer faction-influenced groups were intellectually top-heavy in that so many of them were engaged in spinning out theory and writing books, articles, and tracts on many of the problems of the day. As a group, they held a leading position in Japanese academic life and in the most important intellectual monthly journals, such as *Chūō Kōron* and *Kaizō*, which were suppressed in 1943. And finally it can be said that the Labor-Farmer faction represented a way of looking at things but had no very specifically worked out program of action. They were invariably outdone by their rivals, especially the Communists, in organizing demonstrations, collecting signatures for petitions, putting on spectacular publicity stunts, or engaging in violence.

In spite of the fact that those arrested in connection with the popular front came from labor, farmer, proletarian, and academic circles, they were all influenced by the writings of the Labor-Farmer faction. They were not part of a "popular front" in the sense of a front containing widely divergent points of view united on a single issue; in fact they were just a faction of the social democratic movement as a whole.

22. After the war Katō was criticized by his old friends for making money from a war goods factory which enabled him to build an elegant house while the war was still on. Mori, p. 112. During 1945–6, he and Suzuki resumed their close collaboration, but thereafter Katō drifted back into the Japan-Labor clique and the Right Socialists, while Suzuki became leader of the Left Socialists and later of the united Socialist Party.

In comparing the three main factions or cliques, we have argued that, if the Socio-Democratic clique was composed mainly of leaders who had risen from the working class, and the Japan-Labor clique of university graduates, the Labor-Farmer faction was composed of a mixture, but was noteworthy for having by far the largest proportion of "braintrusters."

The Socio-Democrats had the firmest trade-union basis. The Japan-Laborite leaders' union support was less stable but their agrarian strength was greater. The Labor-Farmer faction as a whole had no organized following but would gladly furnish the theory for any mass group it could find. It advised Katō, for instance, and urged him to action when he led a section of labor out of the Japan-Labor clique's trade union federation. The Labor-Farmer faction as a whole had many armchair generals but few sergeants in the field.

While the basic ideology of the Socio-Democrats derived from trade unionism—at first having the additional elements of socialism and democracy; and while the Japan-Laborites were inspired by revised Marxism in the beginning—gradually changing to military fascism; the Labor-Farmerites can be said to have been far more uncompromising in adopting orthodox (non-Stalinist) Marxism and holding fast to it.

If the function discharged by both the Japan-Labor and Socio-Democratic cliques was eventually to help give the wartime government of Japan some semblance of a national front by cooperating in the "new structure" as the former representatives of the labor and tenant-farming classes, the role played by the Labor-Farmer faction was to resist this trend within the limits of the law, until those limits became so narrow all opposition was snuffed out.

Finally, in somewhat more personal terms the difference between the Japan-Labor clique and the Labor-Farmer faction can be epitomized by Asō and Yamakawa. Asō was the romantic, the adventurist; he wanted to make history and change society but had no clear set of principles; thus he could approach the military at one point and Konoe at another, feeling that a popular movement needed support from high places. Yamakawa, on the other hand, was the cool theorist; consistency in thinking was of utmost importance to him, and unwillingness to compromise, a virtue. When the tides began to run swiftly against the socialist movement, he turned to quail raising, but Asō sought somehow to ride with the current and eventually master it. He ended up by associating his faction most closely with the war effort. As a result, at the end of the war the Socio-Democrats, together with Labor-Farmer faction people, were best able to take the lead in reorganizing the movement, while many of the Japan-Laborites were caught in the Occupation's purge of ultranationalists.

Ideology, Tactics, and Policies

8: Class Concepts and Strategy and Tactics

All socialist factions shared a common aversion to capitalism and the common goal of its overthrow. While even the thoroughgoing Marxists had to admit that it had played a progressive role in transforming Japanese feudalism into the bustling industrial economy of post-World War I Japan, they argued that the peculiar way it had developed in Japan added to its virulence, for they saw the benefits of this "modernizing" process as accruing almost entirely to a small minority of "capitalists" and their political, bureaucratic, and small business lackeys who together with the partially commercialized landlords of the countryside made up the "bourgeoisie" or "propertied class" (*yūsan kaikyū*).

Economic changes had in fact come about so quickly in Japan, bringing with them such great physical and psychological stresses, that the majority of the people probably had some sense of the temporal nature of this phenomenon, unlike in the West where it had developed so much more gradually and spread its largesse among so much larger a middle class that it had been accepted naturally and was by many thought of as well-nigh immutable. In Japan aversion to capitalism was widely shared by many who could hardly be termed socialists, including members of the aristocracy, landed interests, and the military. Indeed this common aversion drew the young officers and elements of the social democratic movement to one another at least temporarily. When it came to the question of what should be done to eradicate this evil, however, not only did those who held in common the distant goal of socialism become differentiated from the majority of society but also cleavages among them appeared. Differences in concepts and practice overshadowed common goals.

Perhaps the most basic difference concerned the proper class orientation of the proletarian parties. Although some attention has already been given to this subject, it must be touched upon here again, because it is the starting point from which various strategies and tactics arise. The actions of an army, for instance, will depend in large measure of the type of soldiers it is composed of—whether infantry, cavalry, armored divisions, or various combinations of these. The passage of manhood suffrage and the possibility of appealing to the poor for votes brought the socialists face to face with this fundamental question. They never ceased wrangling over it. (If anything, it was intensified after the Second World War.)

CONCEPTS OF CLASS APPEAL

In their interest in and support for the extension of the suffrage such advocates of "democracy" as Sakuzō Yoshino and Kiichi Horie desired to see the interests of the whole nation represented, for they felt that the loyalty of the people could not be counted on unless they believed they had some stake in government. And the feeling of having a stake in government could only be obtained through political participation, i.e. voting for one's own representatives in the Diet. Their main consideration was that state policies should be determined from the viewpoint of the whole people, even if this redounded to the disadvantage of substantial owners of private property.[1] They aimed not at abolishing private property as an evil, but at seeing that even the interests of those who did not have property should be taken into consideration in the formulation of public policy; without representation, they argued, the interests of the masses would be neglected.

1. Kiichi Horie, "Senkyo Jichi to Seiji Kyōiku" (The Institution of Suffrage and Political Education), *Kaizō* (February 1925), p. 109; cited in Edward C. Griffin, "Ideological Conflict in the Japanese Proletarian Parties: 1926–1932" (M.A. thesis, Columbia University, June 1951), p. 17.

Although Horie died shortly after the founding of the Social Democratic Party and Yoshino in 1933, this idea of political rights for all, whatever class a person belonged to, did not disappear from the thinking of the Socio-Democratic clique. There is no indication of any proposal to deprive capitalists of the right to vote, for instance.

The support of organized labor was the predominant factor in all the proletarian parties except those which claimed only to represent the farmers, such as Hirano's Japan Farmers' Party. But because of their obvious potential in Japanese politics, the farmers found their way into the names of the Labor Farmer Party, the Japan Labor-Farmer Party, and others. At the time of the formation of the Social Democratic Party in December 1926, two names were proposed. One was "Japan Labor Party" (Nihon Rōdōtō). It was suggested by Bunji Suzuki, representing the wishes of the General Federation and other labor unions. The other, proposed by Katsumaro Akamatsu, was, of course, the "Shakai Minshūtō" which has here been translated as the "Social Democratic Party," but, as noted earlier, *"minshū"* means democratic in the sense of "Demos" or "the people" rather than democratic in the sense of "government by the sovereign people" or "popular rule" (which would be *"minshu"* without the diacritical mark). The latter name was chosen because it seemed to accord better with the Japanese social structure, in which labor was not as important an element as in Britain, where, of course, the social democratic party is called the Labor Party.

In its founding statement, the party claimed to represent the interests of "the workers, the farmers, the salaried employees, the small storekeepers, and the professional people, who together represent the majority of the nation" as against "the peerage, the clans, the landlords, the capitalists, and the established parties which are the puppets of these privileged classes." "Small entrepreneurs" (*shō kigyōsha* were also to be included.[2]

From the very beginning the Socio-Democrats took up and attempted to popularize the concept of the *"kinrō kaikyū,"* literally, the "devotedly laboring class," which connotes salaried workers as differentiated from *"rōdōsha kaikyū,"* literally "workers class," which tends to be limited to wage earners. Isoo Abe utilized this concept to modify the term *"musan kaikyū"* or "propertyless class" by saying

2. Hakuyōsha, ed., *Nihon Musan Seitō Shi*, pp. 252, 267.

the *"kinrō"* class includes all who are dependent on their own labor for their income. This concept is then wider than propertyless in the strictest sense, since many people in it would own a certain amount of property but not enough to live on without working. What the whole class has in common, then, is not necessarily lack of property, but lack of security; even though one owns a nice house, if he depends on his income to maintain it, and he dies, his family is deprived of its breadwinner and consequently suffers.[3] Such people need social welfare policies that can be instituted by the state. On this basis, the Social Democratic Party opened its gates to the white-collar class. Abe considered the intelligentsia of special importance to the party, yet so many of them did not think of themselves as proletarians that it was necessary to develop the idea of a common united front of all those who lacked basic "security of livelihood" (*seikatsu no antei*). Such a united front Abe estimated would make up 95 per cent of the electorate.

On the left, the leaders of the Labor Farmer Party looked with contempt on the term *"kinrō."* It was not part of the Marxist vocabulary, and they felt its very vagueness blurred the clarity of class lines. As Marxists, Labor Farmer Party leaders sought the impetus for social change first and foremost in the class that capitalism itself was forming for its own destruction, namely, the industrial working class. Capitalism was depriving them of the tools of production, alienating the expression of their personalities in their work, and yet gathering them together in factories where they could learn to act collectively and gain a sense of class consciousness and solidarity. Although capitalism was fashioning the proletariat into a lever for advancing history into its next stage of development, i.e. socialism, as Marx claimed, the proletariat still sought leadership and political expression, as Lenin had demonstrated, and that was why it needed a mass party wherever this was feasible. In its political and economic struggle it had to have allies. The most important potential ally in Japan, as had been the case in Russia, was the peasantry or farmers—more specifically the tenant farmers, the partly tenant and partly independent, and the small, independent farmers. Thus, the Labor Farmer Party was to be the political representation of an

3. See Isoo Abe, "Masa ni Umaren to Suru Shin Musan Seitō ni Tsuite" (Concerning the New Proletarian Party About to be Born), *Chūō Kōron* (December 1926), pp. 121–28; cited in Griffin, p. 13.

alliance between labor and the farmers, with labor taking the lead. The Labor Farmer Party leaders made a distinction between *"musan kaikyū"* and *"puroretaria"* or *"puroretariāto,"* all of which are loosely translated into English as "proletariat." The first term, literally "the propertyless class," included tenant farmers and the poor in general, whereas the latter two designated for the Labor Farmer Party people, "the vanguard of the working class" (*rōdōsha kaikyū no zen'ei*).[4]

Nevertheless, the party was not interested in excluding any categories of people who agreed to work for its aims. This was, of course, the "open door" policy by which members of the Council and three other leftist organizations (except certain known Communist leaders), had been allowed into the party. But aside from the political question of the Communists, the party was not exclusive in its appeals and attempted to involve as many classes and strata from the petit bourgeoisie as possible.[5] Even the lower strata of the bourgeoisie itself were sought out.[6] However, the party's clearly stating its priority of interest in the proletariat gave the other proletarian parties some basis for claiming that one weakness of the Labor Farmer Party was that it did not appeal to the white-collar workers and the intelligentsia.

These two polar positions of the social democratic movement in the late 1920s were opposed by the Japan Labor-Farmer Party leaders during the period they sought to play a "centrist" role. Their slogan was "class solidarity of the masses," and they asked, in the policy statement of November 1927, "Why do we have to be a class party?"[7] Their own answer was that in contemporary conditions where the capitalist class was desperately attempting to stabilize itself, only a party representing the alliance of workers and farmers

4. Editorial: "Subete no Rōnō Seitō no Gōdō Kyōgikai o Teishō Su" (We Advocate a Joint Conference of All Labor-Farmer Political Parties), *Musansha Shimbun* (The Proletarians' News) (November 15, 1927), quoted in full in Hakuyōsha, p. 531. The Communists considered their party the "vanguard of the proletariat" (thus the vanguard of a vanguard)!

5. This was made clear in the detailed accounts of the activities of the Council on behalf of the Labor-Farmer Party, written by one of the top Council leaders, Zentarō Taniguchi, in *Nihon Rōdō Kumiai Hyōgikai Shi*, passim.

6. Ikuo Ōyama, "Gikai oyobi Sōsenkyo ni Taisuru Rōdō Nōmintō no Taido" (The Labor Farmer Party's Attitude Toward the Diet and the General Election), *Chūō Kōron* (February 1928), p. 87; cited in Griffin, p. 16.

7. "Nihon Rōnōtō Hōshin Sho" (The Policy Statement of the Japan Labor-Farmer Party), Part 2, quoted in Hakuyōsha, pp. 55–58.

was strong enough to resist international capitalist reaction. "Class" (*kaikyū*) in Japanese also has the connotation of "militant" (*tōsō-teki*) as against "conciliationist" (*kyōchōteki*), the pejorative label the Japan-Laborites pinned on the Socio-Democrats. They claimed their class emphasis was what divided them from the latter.

The next question was: "Why do we have to be a 'mass' party?" They professed to see two meanings in this term. One would include, along with workers and farmers, and under their combined leadership, the middle class or semi-proletariat composed of the majority of the people in Japan (given the peculiar social structure developed by Japanese capitalism). It further included such strata as the small shopkeepers, the lower government officials (*kakyū kanri*), the salaried employees, independent farmers, and the partly independent and partly tenant farmers, all of whom should go along in the common political struggle against the plutocracy. The other meaning of "mass" was the opposite of the "vanguard" which is created by the dialectic of refinement through division; rather, they thought, a large, inclusive, democratic force was needed to resist the plutocracy. This differentiated them from the Labor Farmer Party which they alleged to be a "vanguard party," despite protestations to the contrary.

When the Socio-Democrats and the Japan-Laborites (and a few elements from the New Labor Farmer Party) united to form the Socialist Masses' Party in 1932, they explained the meaning of a party entirely in class terms.[8] The first of the two principles of the party was, "Our party fights for the sake of protecting the livelihood of the workers, the farmers, and the masses of working people (*kinrō tai-shū*) in general." Here the party had adopted the term the Socio-Democrats were fond of, and yet their platform declared that social reform was possible only under the leadership of the allied workers and farmers; it did not designate the *"puroretariāto"* as the vanguard of the working class.

The Socialist Masses' Party explained the existence of other parties solely in terms of their representing class interests, asserting that the established parties, the Minseitō and the Seiyūkai differed only in

8. Shakai Taishūtō Jigyōbu (Operations Section, Socialist Masses' Party), *Musan Kaikyū no Shin Nihon Kensetsu Taikō* (The Proletarian Class's Constructive Program for a New Japan) (Tōkyō, Shadaitō Shuppambu, 1933).

degree and both represented an alliance of capitalists and landlords. By this time other rightist parties had come into existence: the Kokumin Dōmei (Nationalist Federation) and the national socialist parties. They were characterized as "facist" and as representing "the middle and small industrial capitalist and consumer middle classes."

Even before the "army pamphlets" came out in 1935, Asō began to see in the military establishments a force that could be harnessed to bring about the goals of the proletarian movement more quickly than had hitherto been thought. He pointed out that the military was clearly critical of capitalism, and he reasoned that this in itself was an indication of the weakness of the capitalist structure. He furthermore believed that the military had matured politically since the May 15 (1932) incident when they had thought in dictatorial terms. Now they had become more "democratic" and preferred to proceed in a legal manner. Already the pamphlets had had an effect and would further severely shake the decadent status quo; this, he argued, should be taken advantage of.[9] The sharp questioning of Asō at the 1936 Party Convention revealed that this position was far from fully supported, but it was generally agreed by the press to be a sign of the party's rightward trend and a change in its evaluation of the Japanese sociopolitical structure. Thereafter the Asō faction was often referred to as "facist" because of its belief that dissatisfied military forces could help bring about socialism. Nevertheless, Asō continued to emphasize legal methods rather than arbitrary dictatorship. Recognizing the military as an ally was part of the process of blurring the concept of classes in the totalitarian idea of the whole people (including the capitalists) serving the nation in unity.

The emphasis on classes all but disappeared, however, at the end of 1937 in the Socialist Masses' Party revised platform: "workers" and "farmers" were completely left out, only the term *"kinrō taishū"* ([devotedly] working masses) remained as descriptive of those whom the party purportedly represented. The new goal became "the progress and development of the Japanese people (*kokumin*) on the basis of the cardinal principles of the national polity." An "explanation" of the new platform stated, "though our movement has up to now emphasized class interest and striven hard for it, class interest was not its be-all and end-all, but only one policy in the process by

9. See Asō's statement as quoted at length in *Nihon Rōdō Nenkan, 16* (1935), 440–41.

which we hoped to advance the development and growth of all the toiling masses of the entire nation." [10] The explanation did its best to make it appear that the party had not in fact made a turn-about or change of direction. However, in subsequent statements, it became clearer that a class position had been abandoned, and that the party was not to be considered "social democratic" any longer. Nevertheless, during its active life, the Socialist Masses' Party was considered a class movement.

BASIC STRATEGY: THE QUESTION OF LEGALITY

Given the desire of the social democrats prior to 1937–38 to represent the interests of certain classes, and given the differences in interpretation as to the relative importance of these classes, how did they think these interests could be furthered and fought for?

In its most fundamental sense, the problem of means comes down to a decision as to revolution or reform, quick revolution or gradual evolution, violent or peaceful means, illegal or legal methods, or the use of any means versus a limitation to parliamentarianism. In Japan the Communists in the 1920s and 1930s were dedicated to the former alternative in each case, while the right-wing socialists clearly adhered to the latter; the left-wing socialists (including the Communists who were acting as legal left-wingers) were more ambiguous. Like the Communists, they did not see these as issues of principle but rather as choices of methods under given circumstances. They differed from the Communists in their interpretation of the circumstances existing in Japan at certain periods. The Communists all along saw no circumstances warranting entirely legal means, whereas the left and center socialists did.

The platform principles adopted at the founding of the Social Democratic Party in 1926 clearly state that the party "abjures . . . the radical parties which ignore the process of social evolution . . . and proposes . . . reform . . . by legal means." In expounding the meaning of the platform, Abe wrote,

10. See the Supplementary Statement in *Shakai Taishū Shimbun* (The Socialist Masses' Newspaper) (December 15, 1937), quoted in ibid., *19* (1938), 289. An English translation of this statement appears in Wm. Theodore de Bary, Donald Keene, and Ryusaku Tsunoda, comps., *Sources of the Japanese Tradition* (New York, Columbia University Press, 1958), pp. 828–32; the section on social movements was contributed by Hyman Kublin and George O. Totten.

A revolution can be carried out by a minority of people, but without the support of the majority, it would have no prospects of permanence. The important thing is whether or not the majority is obtained. If that support is obtained, the goal of social reconstruction can be fully reached even through parliamentary policies. Where is there any need for revolution at all? . . . The old saying goes, "If you're in a hurry, don't take a shortcut!" Perhaps parliamentary policy is a bit round-about, but it might, however, reach the goal sooner.[11]

Thus, a "revolution" could be brought about by parliamentary means.

"Revolution" for Abe's various Marxist rivals, however, did not necessarily imply violence. Certainly it meant a complete or fundamental change in society. But even the Japanese Communists did not choose to use violence, except perhaps for the so-called "armed interlude" from February to June 1930 when Seigen Tanaka was the leader.[12] They decided to exercise what they considered was a greater freedom of action than the oppressive, bourgeois-made law actually allowed. Since the Japanese government had modern law enforcement agencies to meet illegal activity, illegal methods could not be peaceful, if met by force. The Communists attempted to use secrecy to keep their activities, whether legal or illegal, from being suppressed by violence, which usually meant arrest (sometimes accompanied by torture). The only type of illegal means that would be peaceful was "passive resistance," like that developed by Mohandas Gandhi in Africa and India. There is no evidence of theoretical support for this kind of pacifism on the part of any of the Japanese proletarian parties from left to right—an interesting sidelight on Japanese social thought.

All except the "vanguard" Communist Party were, of course, legal. That party sought to lead the Labor Farmer Party, which did not officially or in theory accept or acknowledge that leadership. It did, however, provide a milieu conducive to Communist influence, and the Communists made it clear to some voters that certain of the Labor Farmer Party candidates in the 1928 elections were also Communists.

11. Isoo Abe, *Kōryō Kaisetsu* (Commentary on the Program), (Tōkyō, Shakai Minshūtō Shuppambu, 1927), pp. 24 and 26.
12. See Swearingen and Langer, *Red Flag in Japan*, pp. 39–42.

Because Ikuo Ōyama, though leader of the Labor Farmer Party and its successors, was never arrested as a Communist, while many of his cohorts were, it is probably most instructive to examine his line of thought. In commenting on the stillbirth of the Farmer Labor Party before the founding of the Labor Farmer Party, Ōyama asserted his belief that what was needed was a "reform party" rather than a "revolutionary party." He did not base this conviction on principle but rather on his evaluation of the existing social situation in Japan. He struck out against the old anarcho-syndicalist idea of direct action which derived from the rejection of parliamentary means. He did not imply that direct action was reprehensible as such, only that it was illogical in a situation in which manhood suffrage obtained. If terrorism were not used against the proletarian movement, he believed, it would become an irrepressible influence.[13]

Terrorism, however, was used against the Labor Farmer Party, though the prime target was undoubtedly the illegal Communists. It was Ōyama's evaluation of the new situation that led him to part ways with the Communists. The mass roundup on April 16, 1929, removed the most active Communists within the Labor Farmer Party's successor—the Labor-Farmer Federation for Securing Political Liberties—as well as destroying the central Communist Party leadership itself. Many of the young people felt it would be wrong to allow all the energy of the Federation to dissipate just because the Communist leadership had disappeared. They proposed creating another legal party until such time as the Communist Party reorganized, a proposal Ōyama at first opposed but soon came to agree with.[14] The remaining Communist Party members, however, maintained that nothing should be done until Communist strategy had been officially worked out. Under their influence, the Labor-Farmer Federation for Securing Political Liberties continued its illegal existence but changed its name to simply the Labor-Farmer Federation (Rōnō Dōmei). It then expelled Ōyama, Kanemitsu Hososako, Dr. Hajime Kawakami, and others.

The expellees finally launched the New Labor-Farmer Party on November 1, 1929, but in the summer of the following year, frustrated by the lack of effective activity and influenced by the reviving

13. Ikuo Ōyama, "Nōmin Rōdōtō no Kaisan to Shihai Kaikyū Shinri" (The Dissolution of the Farmer Labor Party and the Ruling-Class Mentality), *Chūō Kōron* (January 1926), pp. 134–36; cited in Griffin, pp. 26 and 33.

14. Hakuyōsha, pp. 639–40.

Communists, many in the party began to call for immediate dissolution. Specifically, at an enlarged committee meeting of the Ōsaka Joint Association of Branches (Ōsaka Shibu Rengōkai) on August 29 1930, a proposal for dissolving the party passed; the reasoning was that as a legal entity the party could not adequately support strikes or engage in other activity in the interests of the masses and would tend to "sell out" the workers like the other proletarian parties. Actually from the beginning the party had been formed with the understanding that it would eventually dissolve to make way for an organization of a "higher level," a "militant alliance of workers and farmers" (rōnō tōsō dōmei), by implication a real Communist Party, if possible. This was called "developmental dissolution" (hattenteki kaishō).

But Hososako, Koiwai, and others in August, and Kawakami in October, became convinced that the party should dissolve at once. Quoting from Lenin to support his thesis, Kawakami held that "reformist daily struggle" was an obstacle to revolution.[15] It was his evaluation that the New Labor Farmer Party was only capable of leading reformist struggles, and so was playing a reactionary role and ought to be dissolved as soon as possible. He now went along with Hososako who had advocated that the party members should go into labor unions and lead revolutionary struggles there.[16]

The party's reply (and this meant Ōyama's) was that Kawakami was misreading Lenin and making a false dichotomy between "revolutionary" and "reformist" daily struggle, since a particular struggle —such as the Great Strike in Britain in 1926 led by the Labor and Communist Parties jointly—was both revolutionary and reformist. What Lenin was really trying to say, the party leadership maintained, was that without direction spontaneous labor action tended to be no more than "economic" or "reformist," but with proper leadership could become "revolutionary." The role of the New Labor Farmer Party was to nurture this spontaneous labor and farmer action flaring up throughout Japan and prevent it from being stifled by the "social democrats" (the other proletarian parties).[17] Ōyama did not differ from his opponents in this controversy on the

15. Ibid., pp. 725–26.

16. See Kanemitsu Hososako, "Rōnōtō Kaishō Mondai ni Kansuru Ikensho" (A Statement Concerning the Question of the Dissolution of the [New] Labor Farmer Party), quoted in full in ibid., pp. 712–13.

17. Both the party and Kawakami were quoting from V. I. Lenin's *What Is to Be Done?* which was written in 1902; ibid., pp. 726–29.

ends to be achieved. Both sides wanted to create a "militant alliance of workers and farmers" but disagreed only on the way of attaining this goal. His opponents had no constructive alternative, but the New Labor Farmer Party at least could continue to keep the energy of the masses from being dissipated.[18]

This lack of principle on the matter of legality or illegality certainly led to instability in a situation where the leaders were changing their minds as to the possibilities the narrow limits of freedom permitted. For example, in January 1929 Ōyama denounced Mitzutani when he bolted the Labor-Farmer Federation for Securing Political Liberties and organized a legal party (the Labor-Farmer Masses' Party). In the following month after the Japan Masses' Party had been formed with the participation of Labor-Farmer faction people, Ōyama attacked it for endorsing legal methods. How ironical it was then that Ōyama and his colleagues were denounced and expelled from the Labor-Farmer Federation for Securing Political Liberties in their turn.

In contrasting the basic positions on legality so far, it might be said that the Socio-Democrats had a dogma—legality to the end—whereas the leaders of the "legal left" believed they should periodically reevaluate the desirability of legality. For the "Party-Communists" the problem was simpler since the Comintern would make the decision (though the Japanese Communits would take part in the decision-making process) and the Japanese party, as a local branch of the Comintern, would carry it out. (The Comintern had attacked the formation of the New Labor Farmer Party.) In other words, the non-Marxist Socio-Democrats supported legality unequivocally. The Comintern-recognized Marxists (Communists), although they supported the original Labor Farmer Party, followed the "higher voice" on the question, but the pro-Communist Marxists, such as Ōyama— Kawakami later became a Communist—had to rely on their own interpretation.[19] In all this, what was the position of the self-styled

18. See Ikuo Ōyama, "Iwayuru Tōsōteki Kaitai Ron no Shōtai Bakuro" (An Exposé of the So-called Militant Disbandment Theory), Chūō Kōron (December 1930), p. 81; cited in Griffin, p. 28.

19. Since the New Labor Farmer Party was obviously friendly to communism, the question arises of how to label it. At the conclusion of a study of this period Edward Griffin concludes, referring to the party, "rather than describe it as Communist-controlled or a Communist front, it would seem more accurate to call it pro-Communist.

"orthodox" Marxists who opposed the Japanese Communist Party: namely, the Labor-Farmer faction?

It must be remembered that some of what became the Labor-Farmer faction leaders had originally been founding members of the Japanese Communist Party. However, after Yamakawa had called for dissolution of the party in 1923 and after Kazuo Fukumoto had developed his ideas in opposition to "Yamakawaism," the cleavage grew. The debate centered directly on strategy. While still a Communist, Yamakawa wrote his famous article calling for a "change of direction": he alleged that the advanced elements who had led the socialist movement had become isolated; they should return to the masses and raise the latter's political consciousness. This they must do by taking an active interest in the daily demands and sporadic struggles of the masses and in this way lead them into longer-range revolutionary channels. This implied taking "reformist" political action, including the formation of legal political parties when that became possible.[20]

The other element of Yamakawaism can be found in his advocacy of a "single proletarian class party" (*tanichi musan kaikyūtō*) or "united front party" (*kyōdō sensentō*). Yamakawa asserted that such a party should rally into an independent political force all anti-capitalist groups—the masses of workers and farmers whether they were organized or not, as well as the lowest stratum of the middle class. This would be a legal party, and unlike the vanguard party (i.e. Communist Party) it would not need a maximum program, but

---

In this connection the significance of the position of Oyama . . . cannot be overlooked. To call the [New] Labor-Farmer party a Communist-front would seem, in conventional terminology, to imply that the party's leader was either a non-communist dupe of the official organization, or an agent of that organization. This dissolution controversy of 1930 would indicate that Oyama was not a dupe, since even after the controversy, he avowed adherence to the communist ideal. His rejection of the Comintern interpretation of the way to achieve that ideal, excludes him as an agent of the official organization *after* that time. There is no evidence on which to postulate a change of heart on the part of Oyama in 1930. It seems more justifiable to say that he (a recognized spokesman for the Labor-Farmer Party) had refused out of independent conviction to reject explicitly the official leadership of Communism prior to 1930. However, he was prepared to reject it (and did) at any time when true communism, or Leninism, as he interpreted it, so demanded." Ibid., pp. 59–60.

20. Discussed in greater detail but in a different context previously, this article has been mentioned again to remind the reader of the kernel of the argument. See Chap. 3, note 4, above p. 42.

rather just a minimum action platform for the immediate concrete demands of the masses.[21] Such a party could do things that under the special conditions prevailing in Japan a vanguard party could not do. This is, of course, what the supporters of the Labor Farmer Party and the New Labor Farmer Party also believed. However, Yamakawa considered that the time was not ripe for a vanguard party and in fact that it would be a detriment. Therefore, he called for dissolution (or "liquidation") of the Communist Party.[22] By about 1926, the majority of Communists rallied to Fukumoto who emphasized the theoretical need for an illegal vanguard party on the basis of the dialectic of "division before unity."

Perhaps the most important single incident which separated what became the Labor-Farmer faction from the Communists with regard to the question of strategy and tactics was the publication of the so-called Bukharin or July 1927 Thesis in which the Comintern criticized both Yamakawaism and Fukumotoism. While Fukumoto confessed his "errors," Yamakawa attempted to utilize the document to vindicate his own position, though criticizing certain aspects of it and repudiating the validity of leadership from a source distant from Japan. The thesis criticized the "sectarianism" of Fukumotoism for its tendency to create a party that was nothing more than a rarefied ideological group, isolated from the masses, and attacked the "opportunism" of Yamakawa who went so far in proposing a single broadly based, though leftist, "labor-farmer" party that he simultaneously called for the dissolution of the illegal vanguard party. But the thesis was vague in several points and left room for differences of interpretation. Both sides used it to rationalize their positions.

During the first period of controversy between the Communists and the Labor-Farmer faction, roughly 1927 to 1932—the second period being from 1932 to 1936, which had to do more with the interpretation of capitalism than political strategy and tactics—one of the ablest adversaries on the Labor-Farmer side was Tsunao Inomata who had studied in the United States at Columbia and taught at

21. See Hitoshi Yamakawa, "Musan Kaikyū Seitō no Sho Mondai" (Various Problems of a Proletarian Class Party), *Marukusushugi* (May 1924) cited in Hirotake Koyama, *Nihon Marukusushugi Shi* (A History of Japanese Marxism) (Tōkyō, Aoki Shoten. 1956), p. 28.

22. Yamakawa never again called for the formation of a Communist Party. It appears that even in the changed conditions of postwar Japan, he considered that the Social Democratic Party of Japan could better carry out the tasks he envisioned than the legal "mass" Communist Party.

Waseda. By implication he supported legal proletarian parties although on the surface his position seemed to be more radical than the Communists'. That is, the latter laid greater emphasis on the necessity for a "bourgeois democratic revolution" before the socialist revolution, whereas Inomata saw the two as coming simultaneously.[23]

The Communists belittled the strength of capitalism in Japan, maintaining that it had not yet matured, much less reached its highest stage of development. Nevertheless, since the bourgeoisie was obviously not progressive, the proletariat had to take upon itself the task of doing away with such feudalistic, undemocratic remnants as exploitation in the mode of production on the land, expressed in the relations between the landlords and the tenant farmers. On this exploitation the whole governmental superstructure had been built, its most reactionary elements being the Privy Council, the House of Peers, the General Staff, and above all the imperial bureaucracy itself.

Inomata, on the other hand, in criticizing the 1927 Thesis, maintained that the real political power was in the hands of the monopolist bourgeoisie, not the feudalistic, absolutist remnants (including the emperor system). He saw the First World War as having not only catapulted Japanese capitalism into the giant, monopoly stage but also as having brought about the bourgeois democratic elements of universal suffrage and the party cabinet system. In 1927 he predicted that in a few years civilian supremacy would be openly recognized, the independence of the General Staff would have been done away with, and the big landlords' power would become relatively diminished, transforming them into a true bourgeoisie. He was convinced that the remants of feudalism had lost their raison d'être in contemporary Japan.

This was the reasoning that led Inomata and the Labor-Farmer faction to place so much more emphasis on mass legal proletarian parties than did the Communists. They thought it was foolhardy to organize an illegal party that could be broken up by the police—and they felt themselves vindicated in this attitude when the March 15, 1928, and April 16, 1929, mass roundups of Communists occurred. They considered it was safer to start by organizing local proletarian

23. Tsunao Inomata, "Gendai Nihon Burujoajī no Seijiteki Chii" (The Political Position of the Contemporary Japanese Bourgeoisie), Taiyō (The Sun) (November 1927).

parties which would gradually merge into a mass party, strong enough effectively to pressure for reforms. In time this party might eventually take on a maximum program like a Western Communist party.

This was the rationale on which some of the Labor-Farmer faction followers bolted the Labor Farmer Party in 1928 and organized local parties, including the Proletarian Masses' Party of July 1928 which was located in Tōkyō, and in which Inomata as well as Suzuki and Kuroda were leaders. The proletarian unity they worked toward was not an unconditional one. When they or other Labor-Farmer faction leaders were expelled from the larger parties, they again organized local parties but did not give up their desire to reunite with the Japan-Labor and even the Socio-Democratic cliques.

It is interesting to note, however, that for about a year and a half —from 1931 to the first part of 1932—Inomata and other Labor-Farmer faction leaders agreed in large measure with the Communists. This came about because of their own attitude toward what became known as the 1931 Draft Thesis.[24] This document reached a 180-degree different conclusion from the 1927 Thesis in that it relegated the bourgeois democratic revolution to the background and called for an immediate socialist revolution. The completion of the democratic revolution would not be a necessary prerequisite but actually part and parcel of the socialist revolution. Inomata considered that this thesis vindicated the Labor-Farmer faction position and assumed that the Communists would now have to agree with it.

Nevertheless, bickering continued between the Communists and the Labor-Farmer faction over what tactics were implied. For instance, the Labor-Farmer faction believed that, since the landlords in the countryside had largely lost their feudalistic characteristics, an agrarian revolution (land reform) was not so important; the tenant farmers should direct their struggle against the real enemy—monopoly capital—rather than wasting their efforts in struggles against the landlords. Also, as the emperor was only an ornament of bourgeois rule, he would be swept aside in a socialist revolution and need not be singled out beforehand as a special object of attack, as the Communists had done, an act which more than anything else, in the con-

24. Called "The Japanese Communist Party's Political Thesis—A Draft" (Nihon Kyō-santō Seiji Tēze—Sōan), this document is now thought to have been reproduced by Jōkichi Kazama from memory after returning from a Comintern meeting in Moscow toward the end of 1930. Swearingen and Langer, p. 44.

text of Japanese society, made the Communist Party ipso facto an illegal organization. On these grounds, the Labor-Farmer faction saw no need for illegal activity and were determined to make clear the distinction between themselves and the illegal Communists.

A revision of the 1931 Draft Thesis, known as the 1932 Thesis, (and accepted by the Communists as authoritative, since it had been written at Comintern headquarters by Sanzō Nozaka) again caused the controversy between the Labor-Farmer faction and the Communists to flare up hotly. This document returned to the position that the immediate objective of proletarian struggle was the achievement of the bourgeois democratic revolution and placed great weight on the necessity for destroying the emperor system and carrying out land reform in a thoroughgoing manner.

The spate of polemics on this question, varying in intensity, came to be referred to by both sides as the "capitalism controversy." After about 1930 it became both more academic (and thus more respectable) and more theoretical (and thus more abstract); tracts from both sides began to find their way into the general journals, such as *Chūō Kōron* and *Kaizō*. In addition the Communist side gained a podium with the publication of a symposium or long series of monographs which came out serially between 1932 and 1935, edited initially by Eitarō Noro, a brilliant young economist and former student of Nozaka's at Keiō University.[25] Though Noro was a Communist, many of the authors in the series were not; some favored the Labor-Farmer faction's position. In any case, the debate was also called the "Labor-Farmer faction versus the Monographs faction controversy" *(Rōnōha-Kōzaha ronsō)*.

In upholding their position, the Labor-Farmer theorists stoutly maintained that the bourgeois revolution, while admittedly not very democratic, had been consummated and that monopoly capital now held the Japanese people firmly in its grip, necessitating an immediate socialist revolution without trying to establish "democracy" through an intermediate phase.

On the surface, the Labor-Farmer position appears more radical than the Communist, but that was not really true. In belittling the

25. The symposium was entitled *Monographs on the History of the Development of Japanese Capitalism (Nihon Shinhonshugi Hattsu Shi Kōza)*, published by Iwanami Shoten. For a detailed annotation of this, see Uyehara, *Leftwing Social Movements in Japan*, pp. 148–52. In fact, an excellent summary and bibliography of the whole controversy may be found in ibid., pp. 134–62.

importance of the emperor, the Labor-Farmerites avoided conflict
with the stringent lèse-majesté laws that the Communists had to con-
tend with. Also by arguing that the tenant farmers' main enemy was
"monopoly capitalism," and that the struggle against the landlords
was subsidiary and diversionary, they did not encourage what was the
sharpest, most emotion-laden confrontation in the rural areas: the
farm tenant–landlord disputes. To a certain degree, this played into
the hands of various ultraright-wing groups which were attempting
to pit the farmers as a whole against the "blight" of urban life with
its "spineless materialism" and lack of traditional values.

The controversy was shortly smothered by police and ultrarightist
pressure against the Communists. Noro died while undergoing rough
treatment by the police in 1934 and many other Communists were
apprehended. The Labor-Farmer people by and large were not set
upon by the authorities until three years later in the popular front
arrests.[26]

In summing up the positions of the various proletarian factions on
legality, a few words on the Japan-Labor clique may be added. A
basic difference in the rationale for supporting legal methods existed
between the non-Marxists (Socio-Democrats) and the Marxists (almost all the other factions). The former considered legality a principle and the latter a mere tactic. The Japan-Laborites who counted
themselves the "centrist" group appeared to base their advocacy of
legality on expediency rather than principle but without the emphasis on "stages of development" that the more orthodox Marxists
stressed. The first of the three points of the Japan Labor-Farmer
Party program called for the political, economic, and social emanci-

<hr>

26. An interesting sidelight on this period concerns Labor-Farmer faction influence
on the Communists. It was at this time that the public trials of the Communist leaders
as a group were taking place. Consciously making use of the trials for propaganda purposes, the defense submitted to the court in July 1931 its version of the history of the
Japanese Communist Party; later revised by Shōichi Ichikawa, it became the official
history of the party and required reading for Japanese Communists. It was published
secretly in 1932 by the Propaganda and Agitation Section of the Central Committee of
the Japanese Communist Party; a postwar edition came out in 1946 with Ichikawa as
author, under the title, *Nihon Kyōsantō Tōsō Shōshi* (A Short History of the Struggles
of the Japanese Communist Party) (Tōkyō, Shōkō Shoin, 1946). However, since this
version accorded with the draft thesis of 1931, it interpreted Japanese capitalism to be
in the finance capital stage and called for an immediate socialist revolution, setting up
the capitalists rather than the emperor system as the immediate target. This was in
effect the Labor-Farmer faction position and, in postwar Japan especially, the Communists had to warn their followers of this bias in the history. See Koyama, pp. 60–61.

pation of the proletariat "in accord with the national conditions *(kokujō)* of our country," a phrase that sounded suspiciously like "national polity" *(kokutai)*. The second point demanded reform "by legal means" of the irrational systems concerning production, distribution, and land ownership. The implication was that, given the particular conditions in Japan, it was best to use legal means to effectuate change. The same phrases were repeated in the platform of the Japan Masses' Party of December 1928. By the time the Socialist Masses' Party united all factions, legal means were so taken for granted by all the factions involved that legality was not mentioned in the platform, nor was it put into the 1937 revised platform when reference to the "emancipation of the proletarian classes" was deleted and unequivocal reference made to "the cardinal principles of the national polity."

PROLETARIAN INTERPARTY COMPETITION
AND COOPERATION IN THE DIET

Having examined various aspects of the class nature of a proletarian party and its functions in terms of the legal status quo, we would expect to find these ideas expressed in the degree of inter-proletarian-party competition and cooperation that developed in their tactics.

Communism, or anticommunism, depending upon the angle from which one is viewing the issue, was the most divisive factor in the proletarian movement at least from 1925 to 1930. While this has been emphasized elsewhere, here it can be briefly touched on from the point of view of strategy and tactics. The issue first became central when it was revealed that the Japanese Communist Party had been formed in 1922.

The appearance of the organized Communists forced a theoretical position on what were already called the "right-wing" proletarian leaders. Kenichi Yarita, a Socio-Democratic writer, reconstructs the atmosphere of the time when the right-wing leaders in the General Federation in 1922 realized that the Communists were making a conscious, concerted bid for leadership of the organization. Yarita has a fictional character ask them about their efforts to create a bulwark against "red" influence, saying,

"By doing that, won't you be lining up on the same side as the present ruling class?" If they were asked such a question, they would probably answer in a clear voice after a moment's reflection, "It might appear that way on the surface, but the reason the ruling class puts up a policy of anticommunism and oppresses the left wing is that they are trying to save capitalism at its highest stage, imperialism. On the other hand, we are trying to realize social democracy as our ultimate goal." [27]

Social democracy as an ideology was forced to come into existence in Japan, or at least to take on a clearer form, by the appearance of communism—rather than communism being a reaction to prevailing social democratic ideology—but in action its first manifestation was the rally of right-wing leaders to maintain positions of control in the General Federation. To do this they were willing to sacrifice almost half the organization when the Council was formed and later another large section when what became the Japan-Labor clique bolted. Thus, besides clarifying social democratic theory, anticommunism served as a rationale for the practical struggle against the emergent Communists and pro-communists for control over the trade union federations.

Anticommunism, however, also served as a weapon or tactic that could be used by the social democrats to defend themselves against the displeasure of the conservative governmental authorities. Criticizing the Labor Farmer Party in the context of 1926–27, Akamatsu had this to say:

> Since the Communists adopt special, narrow, arbitrary, and unrealistic campaign policies, [the Labor Farmer Party which they control can only] exist as a minority party . . . and cannot really acquire a mass character. Furthermore, their struggle tactics, recklessly ignoring objective conditions, on the contrary give the ruling class an excuse for suppressing them, and it is probable that they will bring on the destruction of the [Labor Farmer] Party which has not yet acquired real strength.[28]

It seems reasonable to assume that the anticommunism of the right-wing and centrist proletarian parties was intensified by the stern atti-

27. Yarita, *Dai San no Taiyō*, pp. 80–81.
28. Hakuyōsha, p. 266.

tude of the government toward the growth of the Communist movement.

The issue of communism was instrumental not only in splitting up the Labor Farmer Party and establishing the Social Democratic and Japan Labor-Farmer Parties, but in keeping the latter two divided from each other. Yet the very weakness of the proletarian movement as a whole made it abundantly clear that continued division dissipated whatever strength the movement could muster, and each party tried to make political capital among the potential voters by calling for proletarian unity.

The Social Democrats developed the concept of a "grand rally of the right wing" (*uyoku no dai danketsu*), as it was phrased at the 1928 party convention. At that time the party would not consider uniting with the Japan Labor-Farmer Party despite the latter's offer to prove that all the "Fukumotoists" had been purged. The Social Democrats insinuated that, since the Japan Labor-Farmer Party lacked "self-confidence," the offer was only a last resort for self-preservation. They termed the principle of a single party "a plot by the Communists" to increase their strength.

It was true that the pro-communist Labor Farmer Party was the most vocal in favor of "a unified party for the proletariat" in the face of "the united front of the capitalists," but Fukumotoism had advocated ideological purity before coalition. This "division before unity" was an attempt to make strategy and tactics dialectical. At no time subsequently was it thought that solidarity was a cure-all. The main and reiterated condition for unity was the retention of the right to criticize the other elements in the coalition.

Each party, thus, had its conditions for unity and desired to demonstrate its superiority and distinctiveness in comparison with the other proletarian parties. The Labor Farmer Party attempted to monopolize militancy and daring; the Japan Labor-Farmer Party tried to prove itself militant yet tempered with realistic caution; and the Social Democrats emphasized the effectiveness of moderation. Only after the great disappointment in the results of the 1930 and 1932 Diet elections and the defections of the national socialists did the parties swallow their pride enough to unite into the Socialist Masses' Party. After that, the problem came up again when Katō and Suzuki proposed and then campaigned and negotiated for a "popular front" in 1936–37. In rejecting this, the Socialist Masses' Party characterized it as "Communist inspired," despite the fact that the Labor-Farmer faction defined the "popular front" as excluding illegal Communists.

Both the Labor Farmer and Japan Labor-Farmer Parties tried to win *supporters* away from the other parties and their labor and farmer auxiliary organizations by appealing to their rank-and-file members and by denouncing their *leaders*. The left wing employed this tactic against the more intrenched right-wing leaders of the various organizations. All the parties, even the Social Democrats, charged that the other parties and organizations lacked popular or mass support, and especially that they spoke only for a small minority which was in control.

Despite their rivalry and refusals to unify, the proletarian parties did achieve a measure of cooperation within the Diet from the time their first representatives won seats in 1928.

From the outset the parties held to the attitude that the Diet members elected on a proletarian party ticket were subject to the will of the party rather than that the parliamentary representatives should lead the party. This was of course general socialist philosophy. Each of the parties formed its own Diet Policy Committee (Gikai Taisaku Iinkai), and after the first election, convened Emergency National Conventions for Diet Policy (Gikai Taisaku Rinji Zenkoku Taikai) so that the party members as a whole would have some hand in democratically determining the party's policies in the Diet.

Just after the first manhood suffrage election, the four Social Democrats, one Japan Labor-Farmerite, two Labor Farmerites, and one local proletarian party representative jointly set up an informal proletarian Diet members group (musantō Giin dan).[29] Then they went further and, at least on paper, worked out an agreement for a Joint Committee for Proletarian Party Diet Policies (Musantō Gikai Taisaku Kyōdō Iinkai), which would have the right to control the voting of the whole group. These doughty, but still inexperienced, proletarian Dietmen then faced their first tactical test.

The question was what role they should play in the voting for the President (or Speaker) and Vice President of the chamber. Since the two main (government and opposition) parties, the Seiyūkai and the

29. They were: Abe (Tōkyō), Bunji Suzuki (Ōsaka), Nishio (Ōsaka), and Kamei (Fukuoka); Mizutani (Kyōto) and Senji Yamamoto (Kyōto); Jōtarō Kawakami (Hyōgo); and Kenzō Asahara (Fukuoka) from the Kyūshū People's Constitutional Party (Kyūshū Minkentō), respectively.

Minseitō, were of almost equal strength, the proletarian vote could be decisive. The group of eight could not agree. The four Social Democrats decided to vote for the opposition candidate, but the others abstained on the grounds that both candidates were equally reprehensible representatives of capitalism. The result was that the government party candidate won by two votes. Thereupon, seeing how decisive their vote could have been, the four who had not voted before decided to join the others in supporting for Vice President a candidate who was more acceptable since he was not a Minseitō man but an anti-Seiyūkai unity candidate who had been a strong advocate of universal suffrage. He won. Thus, the temptation to play the parliamentary game like a regular "bourgeois" party arose with the very first Diet balloting.[30]

Proletarian cooperation was again put to the test almost immediately following the March 15th (1928) arrests, in the wake of which the government banned the Labor Farmer Party. Although its two representatives, Yamamoto and Mizutani, remained Diet members, the Social Democrats, at an April 12 meeting of the joint committee for proletarian party Diet policies, proposed that the partyless two not attend any more and the committee broke up.

Nevertheless, at the beginning of the next session of the Diet the committee was reconstituted—only to face still another test. One of its members, Yamamoto, was bloodily assassinated in his lodgings on the night of March 5, 1929, by three ultranationalists.[31] That very day he had been the most active of the eight on the Diet floor in protesting the Diet's approval of the Emergency Imperial Ordinance of June 29, 1928, which had put more teeth into the Peace Preservation Law, making subversion subject to capital punishment. Yamamoto was now representing the Labor-Farmer Federation for Securing Political Liberties, the successor to the disbanded Labor Farmer Party. His erstwhile comrade, Mizutani had bolted that group and set up his own Kyōto-based party. There was argument as to who would be the most fitting member of the proletarian group to address the Diet on Yamamoto's death, excoriate the dastardly deed, and warn the

30. Mitsu Kōno, *Nihon Shakaiseitō Shi* (A History of Japanese Socialist Parties) (Tōkyō, Chūō Kōronsha, 1960), pp. 119–22.

31. For a graphic account of Yamamoto's assassination, as well as his interpellations in the Diet, see Yoshio Ichikawa, *Yamamoto Senji wa Gikai de Ikani Tatakatta ka* (How Did Senji Yamamoto Fight in the Diet?) (Kyōto, Sanichi Shobō, 1949), pp. 67–146 and 177–88.

country against the ultranationalist menace. At the last minute Jōtarō Kawakami consented and mounted the rostrum to make an eloquent maiden speech, widely reported in the newspapers.

After that, cooperation among the proletarian minority increased and became a habit. Their legislative proposals, though invariably buried in committee by the major parties, did serve as good campaign material. And no matter how they differed on other points, they always unanimously condemned local police and Home Ministry interference in election campaigns; they also censured those Diet regulations that put minority groups at a disadvantage.

Proletarian unity again dissolved during the 70th session of the Diet, after the 1937 election, when Katō refused to associate himself with the Socialist Masses' Party Diet members. For some time before this Jiichirō Matsumoto of the Leveling Society, while not a member of the Socialist Masses' Party, did cooperate with it fully within the Diet until the Saitō affair of 1940 when the Socio-Democratic clique was expelled.

It is difficult to assess how effective the Diet strategy and tactics of the proletarian parties were. Their main tactic was what they called "exposure" (*bakuro*). By this they meant using the Diet as a forum to denounce and expose various "bourgeois" policies, scandals, and incidents. Through Diet "struggles" they sought publicity for their protests against official measures and for their own counterproposals. It was only after the 1937 Diet election that the Socialist Masses' Party gained enough representatives in the Diet to become a recognized parliamentary negotiating body. This entitled them to send a member to the House of Representatives steering committee and thus gave them a voice in running the House, including the selection of committees, determining the order of interpellations, and so forth.

EXTRAPARLIAMENTARY TACTICS

From the beginning, and to a far greater extent than the other proletarian parties, the Labor Farmer Party relied on extraparliamentary campaigns for various objectives, usually trying to integrate them in the interest of yet bigger objectives, thus creating a concentrated, more effective demand. For instance, when Premier Tanaka declared a bank holiday, the party organized protest meetings for small depositors such as sales people, producers, and salaried men. It attempted to unite with all other movements for freedom of speech and organization involving workers, farmers, and professional people (in schools, the arts, etc.) under the all-inclusive slogan of "fight for political freedom." Ōyama expressed the Party's ideas thus: "Demands for freedom are in themselves demands for a living; and demands for a living are in themselves demands for freedom." [32]

The proletarian representatives usually supported the no-confidence resolutions proposed by opposition parties in the Diet as well as drawing up such resolutions of their own, for it gave them an opportunity to articulate their criticisms of the government. More than simply to garner votes, the proletarian parties pressed their campaigns to petition for the dissolution of the Diet, for the purpose of raising the "political consciousness" of the masses and to facilitate the formation of local party branches. The campaign techniques involved gathering signatures on petitions from people on the streets and distributing handbills. Despite police warnings, a "petition day" was held from time to time in a number of places and signatures collected, houses visited, speeches made, handbills distributed, and forums (*zadankai*) held. These techniques were met by "police sabres and boots." Although the Labor Farmer Party initially was the most energetic in promoting such signature campaigns, it subsequently came to consider this too "naïve" a tactic, easily foiled by the police. But the other proletarian parties—less harassed by the police—continued collecting signatures on a large scale, through 1937, especially in periods of great discontent with the incumbent cabinet.

Each party attempted to coordinate its campaigns with those of its supporting labor organizations. The Labor Farmer Party, of course, utilized the Council of Japanese Labor Unions to the utmost and with its personnel gained hearings in factory representative meetings and works councils. The party also lent its forces to the Japan Farmers' Union campaigns "against preventing tenant farmers from working in their plots" and "opposing the landlords' collecting standing grain," hoping to obtain in return the tenant farmers' support at the polls. Nor did the party neglect the city people. Following the not too successful "depositors meetings," which sought governmental guarantees for small deposits made by retail sales people, small workshop employees, and salaried men, the party led campaigns to organize house tenants to demand 30 per cent reductions in rents.

32. Hakuyōsa, p. 512.

Besides giving aid to strikes waged by their supporting labor organizations, the parties sometimes organized their own "strikes" or boycotts in urban and rural areas. For instance, in campaigns to protest the high utility rates they organized boycotts against the use of electricity or gas and at the same time called for municipal ownership of local utility monopolies. The parties claimed that municipalization would not only lower rates but also aid local finances (though any strong move in either direction would appear to cut into the other objective!). The Social Democratic Party was particularly interested in these public utility campaigns—as a safe kind of municipal socialism—and led most of them.[33]

Each party had its own song and flag, and also held "party days" for increasing membership. Although their financial resources were minuscule in comparison with those of the major parties, they expended a great deal more effort in propaganda work through public speaking, demonstrations, rallies, marches, distributing handbills, putting up posters, showing films, using various cultural media (such as woodcuts, paintings, songs, poetry), and holding entertainment and tea parties as well as formalized panel discussions, because they had in a sense to mold their own constituencies.

As the country became more nationalistic under wartime conditions in the late 1930s, all activity not in conformity with national unity and the war effort was increasingly discouraged. The Japanese language itself became saturated with mystical and irrational terms. Even labor meetings were opened with invocations to the Shintō gods. When the Socialist Masses' Party finally advocated the dissolution of all political parties and independent labor and agrarian organizations, it did so on the rationale that through the central government the efforts of all classes should be "guided" for efficiency in the war effort.

This trend can be illustrated by one extraparliamentary tactic of which the parties took indirect advantage: namely, the May Day demonstration. It had already become a six-year tradition by the time the parties were established and was generally run by the unions rather than the parties. Nevertheless, it was an opportunity to voice economic and political demands championed by the parties on behalf of labor and the farmers. After the parties were formed in 1926, the Japan Farmers' Union ended its separate Farmers' Day on April 9

33. Ibid., p. 370.

and joined in the May Day demonstrations on May 1. Thereafter farmers' slogans and even those of small business were mingled with labor's, just as in the platforms of the proletarian parties.

The vicissitudes of May Day reflected those of the proletarian movement as a whole. The first Japanese May Day was held in 1920, celebrated only in Tōkyō with Bunji Suzuki of the Friendly Society as master of ceremonies. A number of labor unions participated and claimed 10,000 people demonstrated, but the Home Ministry reported only 1,000. Suzuki himself estimated 5,000.[34] Repeal of Article 17 of the Peace Police Law, which prohibited unions, was a prime target. The workers sang labor songs, waved red flags, and marched from Ueno Hirokōji to Manseibashi. Although this is only a half-hour's walk, several fights with the police occurred along the way. This set the pattern.

Thereafter, the number of May Day demonstrations rose to 48 in 1927 and, after a slump, to 70 in 1932. According to Home Ministry figures, the number of total participants rose to 42,330 in 1926, dropped again, and stood at 41,000 in 1932.[35] By 1935 the number had begun to stabilize around 21,600 but the May Day of that year— the sixteenth—was the last one permitted by the authorities before the war. (Consequently, the first one held after the war in 1946 was designated the seventeenth.) [36]

The usual method of demonstrating on May Day was by a rally with speakers on a platform behind which hung long scrolls proclaiming the slogans chosen by the sponsoring committee. These and other resolutions were recited at a microphone and "passed" by the cheers of the audience. Greetings from various unions and proletarian parties were read aloud. A march followed, each union marshaling its own members carrying the union banner or a plain red flag as the emblem of labor—by no means was it confined to symbolizing communism. (In early days the black flag of anarchism was also often carried.) Placards, streamers, and other ingenious attention-catchers would bob above the marchers' heads.

The defiant mood of both the demonstrators and the mobilized

34. See Bunji Suzuki, *Rōdō Undō Nijūnen*, pp. 226–34, and *Nihon Rōdō Nenkan*, 2 (1921), 30–31.

35. Ibid., *17* (1936), 289–90.

36. For a special study of May Day, see Ōhara Shakai Mondai Kenkyūjo Shiryōshitsu (Materials Section, Ōhara Institute of Social Research), "Shiryō: Nihon ni Okeru Mēdē" (Materials: May Day in Japan), *Ōhara Shakai Mondai Kenkyūjo Zasshi* (Journal of the Ōhara Institute of Social Research), *3* (May 1936).

police, who had little regard for civil rights and often looked upon the marchers as "rebels," led to skirmishes. Invariably arrests were made. And very often the demonstrators were divided among themselves, a reflection of the deep rifts between the Communists and the social democrats and among the various brands of the latter. Starting in 1934 as a result of the Manchurian incident and the rise of national socialism within the labor movement, some unions held demonstrations on what they called Japan Labor Day (*Nihon Rōdō Sai*) coinciding with the anniversary of Emperor Jimmu, which fell on April 3rd. One of their slogans ran: "Down with traitorous May Day!"

In places where unions were weak or where the traditional march could not be made, other forms of May Day celebrations were held: union meetings, speeches, forums, mountain-climbing picnics, *sumō* wrestling, entertainment (*iankai*), or simply social gatherings (*shimbokukai*). In a number of agricultural villages tenant farmers gathered together and tilled cooperatively on May Day to demonstrate their solidarity vis-à-vis the landlords.

An examination of the various May Day slogans throughout the period reveals that, although labor and agrarian economic themes dominated, immediate political demands inspired by the proletarian parties, including the clandestine Communists, were often prevalent, especially in 1927 and 1928, and also were more obvious among the left- than the right-wing sponsored rallies. For instance, in 1927, prominent slogans demanded the dissolution of the Diet and an election, freedom for government workers to join a political party, and an absentee ballot for seamen. From 1932 through 1935 antifascist slogans assumed an important place, as well as demands for guaranteeing the livelihood of the families of soldiers on active duty. Thereafter, since no further permission was given for May Day rallies until after the war, the proletarian movement lost one of its most attention-getting and supposedly "muscle-flexing" tactics.

9: Domestic Policies: From Democratic to Totalitarian

The formulation of policy is in a sense the most important function of minority parties. Even though they have no immediate hope of obtaining the reins of administrative power, they can by successfully electing even a few candidates make their voices heard in the halls of the highest public forum in the land. Even cabinet members had to listen to and reply to proletarian representatives' interpellations in the prewar Japanese Diet. These were supposed to embody the policies that had been adopted at the party conventions.

Each of the prewar parties at their founding decided upon a minimum basic program of not more than two or three sentences, which was intended to express their aims and raison d'être. The program of the Labor Farmer Party, adopted on March 5, 1926, before the left-wing influence became strong and before the right-wingers bolted, is typical. It ran as follows:

1. We propose to bring about the political, economic, and social emancipation of the proletarian class in conformity with the national character of our country.
2. We propose to renovate by legal means the unfair land, production, and distribution systems.

3. We propose to displace the established political parties, which
represent the interests of the privileged classes only, and
thoroughly to reform the Diet.[1]

Since this kind of basic program (*kōryō*) was so short, each party
usually accompanied it with a declaration (*sengen*) which might run
to four or five long paragraphs discussing the present political and
economic situation in terms of what the party planned to do or
wanted to be done. While the program usually remained unchanged
throughout the life of the party, declarations might be drawn up at
important junctures. For less important and more specific matters
"statements" (*seimei* or *seimeisho*) were issued by such organs of the
party as the central executive committee.

Specific policies (*seisaku*)—the subject of this chapter—were hammered out or revised at least to some degree at every annual convention. They furnished the basis for many of the election slogans
(*senkyo surōgan*) when put in simplified or catchy language. From
them the party fashioned specific bills to be introduced into the Diet,
proposals for revisions of existing legislation, or riders to be attached
to bills under consideration. They were supposed to reflect the interests and demands of the organized and unorganized masses whom the
parties represented. Perhaps it would be more accurate to say that
the policies articulated the interests of the masses as the party leaders
saw them in terms of their own ideology and also embodied the demands of various organized groups. Thus, the parties' labor policies
usually were taken almost verbatim from their respective supporting
labor federations or else constituted a compromise of the demands of
several labor organizations if more than one supported the party.
The same was true of agrarian and other policies.

For a policy to have any immediate prospects of success, it should
be framed in the context of the specific, concrete situation. This consideration worked upon the proletarian parties in such a way as to
mold their policies into a generally similar pattern no matter how
great the difference in fundamental outlook between the Marxists
and non-Marxists. When we discussed leadership and ideological
orientation, it was helpful for us to treat each of the cliques, factions,
or groupings separately. In analyzing policies, however, we find that

1. Quoted, for instance, in Kyōchōkai, ed., *Saikin no Shakai Undō*, p. 571.

the differences among the Socio-Democrats, the Japan-Laborites, and the various other proletarian groups were not great enough to hinder us from surveying all of them at once. Thus we can concentrate our observations rather on the changes over time, remembering that the more leftist groups suffered under mass arrests at a comparatively early period so that their views were less represented as time went by.

Practical policies, furthermore, are almost invariably compromises in two senses: (1) they represent a consensus among the various factions within a political party and (2) they mediate between long-term goals and the real, immediate situation. Thus, if the implications of various policy demands were to be traced to their ultimate conclusions they might be found to be in fundamental contradiction to one another. These contradictions seldom show up when the policies are phrased succinctly or worked into slogans. All the parties were aware that their policies were compromises with the immediate situation, and they thought of them as therefore "reformist." In their thinking, the role of a proletarian party under capitalism was to work for the alleviation of the suffering of the masses in such a way as to prepare them to fight for a better system: socialism. There was agreement on this point all the way from the Socio-Democrats to the pro-communists. The policies we shall examine in this chapter, therefore, are always the minimum ones, dictated by the situation of the moment, and were acquiesced in by activists of radically differing political shades as long as they did not perceive them to be destroying the possibility of realizing their ultimate objectives. Even the policies of the Japan Proletarian Party in 1937, outside of its call for an antifascist people's front, did not differ from those of the Socialist Masses' Party at the time in any significant way.

At first the policies were jumbled together without much to relate them to each other, as the example of the Labor Farmer Party policies given below will show. But as time went by and the parties accumulated more and more policies, the need for greater systematization was felt. When the Socialist Masses' Party was formed in 1932, a so-called "Constructive Program" [2] was prefixed to the policies, as a first attempt to integrate them into a proposal for a

2. In Japanese, "Kensetsu Taikō." It is quoted in full with an explanation in Shakai Taishūtō Jigyōbu, *Musan Kaikyū no Shin Nihon Kensetu Taikō*, which came out in June 1933 and was 81 pages long; cited above, p. 184 n. 8.

planned or controlled economy. This trend reached its climax in the Socialist Masses' Party's "Wartime Renovationist Policy Outline" [3] adopted at the November 1937 convention, which remained the basic policy with little change until the party's demise in 1940.

We have already seen how the proletarian parties began as "class parties" of varying degrees of radicalism and how, in time, with the suppression of the leftists and the change in the national and international situation, they achieved a united front in the Socialist Masses' Party only to eventually lose their earlier social democratic characteristics. This chapter attempts to document the trend in terms of actual policies.

Before concentrating on separate policy categories, it might be interesting to peruse a typical set of proletarian party policies. They were usually divided into "political," "economic" (and/or "financial"), and "social" sections. Yet the divisions among these sections at times appear surprising. One can also glean something of the tenor of the movement from noting the terminology used. Our example will be the Labor Farmer Party's set of policies which followed the program quoted above.

Political

1. Take full advantage of universal suffrage elections.
2. Abolish the various laws and regulations that oppress the proletarian movement.
3. Eliminate discrimination in the colonies.
4. Reduce armaments and ameliorate the treatment of soldiers.
5. Demand the government assist families and individuals impoverished by conscription, disability, or death in war.
6. Basically reform the tax system, especially eliminate tariffs and consumer taxes on goods for daily use and make property taxes steeply progressive.
7. Establish people's diplomacy (*kokumin gaikō*).

Though almost any demand of a political party could in a sense be called political, items (5) and (6) above might have been more ap-

3. In Japanese, "Senji Kakushin Seisaku Yōkō." For the full text, see Naimushō, Keihokyoku (Home Ministry, Police Bureau), *Shisō Geppō*, (Monthly Report on [Dangerous] Thought) [marked "Confidential"], *43* (January 1938), 88–114. This was the party's most detailed proposal for a planned economy.

propriately placed in the "Economic" section and (3) perhaps in the "Social" section. In any case, the following is what the authors of the policies included in those two sections:

Economic

8. Secure the rights to organize, to strike, and to make collective agreements.
9. Secure the right to till.
10. Enact a minimum wage law.
11. Prevent youths and women from engaging in night work, in work inside mines, and in dangerous tasks.
12. Secure the eight-hour day.
13. Revise the Factory Act, the Mining Act, and the Seamen's Act.

Social

14. Eliminate discrimination toward women in both public and private law.
15. Outlaw traffic in women.
16. Eliminate all restrictions concerning education or occupations for women.
17. Enact an insurance system for unemployment, sickness, old age, and accidents.
18. Compensation by the state to those found innocent and those improperly detained.
19. Compensation from the Treasury for all expenses during the period of compulsory education and occupational training.
20. Secure the right to living quarters.[4]

There is less to quarrel with in these classifications. Nevertheless, in light of the main sources of support for the proletarian parties, a different grouping of policies suggests itself as more appropriate for our study. We shall first consider all those policies concerned with the labor problem, a number of which are included above. Then we shall proceed to the agrarian question, which the above policies are

4. Kyōchōkai, *Saikin no Shakai Undō*, pp. 571–72. For the meaning of the "right to living quarters," see below p. 236.

noteworthy in almost omitting. Finally we can consider the rest of the sociopolitical and economic policies worked out by the prewar proletarian parties.

LABOR POLICIES

With regard to labor, we shall first consider the rights of organization, strike, and collective bargaining, since these form the essence of the democratic aspect of social democracy in a capitalist society. Then we can go on to consider the more technical aspects of arbitration, hours and wages, unemployment insurance, labor exchanges, social insurance, and the type of labor legislation enacted after the China incident. As has been noted, Article 17 of the Peace Police Law of 1900 in effect forbade all labor organization and strikes, and yet this had become more or less a dead letter by about 1918 in the conditions of the war boom.[5]

In 1924 trade unionism was implicitly recognized by the official act of granting to unions of a certain size the right of nominating the workers' delegate and advisers to attend the International Labor Conference. Then in the very year the above policies were fashioned by the Labor Farmer Party, the sections of the Peace Police Act which constituted the greatest obstacles to union activity were repealed.[6] While the Imperial Constitution guaranteed on paper the right of Japanese subjects to form associations, the proletarian parties, as the political champions of labor, called for explicit legal

5. American influence was a factor in this development, because it was just at this time that the principle of the right of workers to organize and bargain collectively was officially recognized in the United States with the creation of the National War Labor Board in 1918 as the major governmental body dealing with industrial relations. Of course, American unions had already had an organizational history of over a century with the emergence of a number of national trade unions in the 1850s. Recognition of labor's rights was late in the United States as compared to Britain, but American prestige in Japan rose at this time because of the entrance of the United States in the war as an ally of Japan and as a leading world power.

6. At the time of the enactmen of universal suffrage, the Peace Preservation Law was passed, as has been mentioned earlier. Although it was aimed at suppressing revolutionary propaganda and not trade unionism, still it affected unions indirectly because of the looseness of administrative interpretations. This was true of another act in 1926 which made it punishable to use mob force or carry arms. Also, as has been mentioned in connection with the assassination of Senji Yamamoto, the Peace Preservation Law was rendered more stringent by an Emergency Imperial Ordinance, approved by the Diet in 1929, making it a capital crime to organize a revolutionary movement.

recognition of labor unions in law together with their right to strike and bargain collectively.

Although industrial disputes had occurred in Japan since about 1897, it was not until the First World War that the number of strikes suddenly doubled in about a year and continued to increase subsequently. After the war they became increasingly organized and disciplined and ceased to be mere sporadic and violent uprisings leading to illegal acts. Strike demands included not only wage increases, shorter hours, and better conditions, but also the recognition of the union and collective bargaining. The latter demand aroused widespread public attention during the Ashio Copper Mines strike of April 1921, after which it became frequent. It was included in the Labor Farmer Party policies, quoted above, but the Social Democratic and Japan Labor-Farmer Parties at the same time, while echoing the Labor Farmer Party's call for the rights to organize and strike, left the demand for collective agreements to their supporting organizations—the General Federation and the Federation of Japanese Labor Unions respectively—which had already made some headway in collective bargaining. Nevertheless, most collective bargaining in Japan was either verbal or based on a natural development of custom. The procedure of signing agreements did not play an important role in prewar Japan.

In the liberal atmosphere of 1925, the year the suffrage was extended, the Social Bureau of the Home Ministry drafted a Labor Union Bill that, among other things, would have forbidden employers from interfering to prevent their employees from joining or remaining in unions. The moderate unions at first welcomed this but when the government revised the bill to conform to pressure from the military and business, even the more right-wing unions opposed it. But in the absence of proletarian representation in the Diet, the bill was defeated by the argument that a labor law, even in the new amended form, was not needed. This was the situation when the proletarian parties were formed and remained so until after the 1928 election.

As representatives of the interests of labor regardless of their long-range differences, the proletarian parties almost invariably demanded legal recognition for trade unions as independent, self-governing organizations.

The Tanaka government that was in power when the proletarians first entered the Diet was totally unresponsive, but the succeeding Hamaguchi cabinet did take notice of these new party demands and sponsored an Inquiry Council on Social Policy which recommended that unions be given legal recognition and some protection. Acting on this recommendation, the Social Affairs Bureau again came up with a new bill not unlike the former one. The Social Democratic and even the other proletarian party representatives were willing to accept it with some reservations and at the same time proposed some improving amendments. Amendments accepted by the government, however, were designed to appease management. The bill finally passed the House of Representatives in 1931, only to fail of adoption in the House of Peers. It would have given "open recognition" to labor unions and put an end to the discharge of workers who were active unionists, but it did not mention strikes or collective bargaining.[7] This was the high-water mark in the movement for a labor union law.

The Socialist Masses' Party labor policy in 1932 called in part for enactment of "an independent labor union law, recognizing the right to organize and to strike." [8] Although collective bargaining was not mentioned here, the party, in addition to a proposal for a labor union law, submitted a collective bargaining bill to the 63rd session of the Diet in 1932, and it continued to resubmit one year after year even though the bill was invariably pigeonholed or died in committee.[9]

After the February 26, 1936, military uprising the government began to revise the Labor Union Bill that had almost been passed in 1931 and had been pigeonholed since. It was reported that the earlier bill was considered too liberal and a new labor control bill, based on the "Japanese spirit," would be formulated.[10] To counter this, labor pressed actively for the enactment of legislation to protect the independence and self-government of labor unions. The Japan Proletarian Party and its forerunner bore the bulk of the petition-signing campaign for such a bill, while the Socialist Masses' Party presented the bill in the 70th Diet session on February 24, 1937. The bill was needed at this time, the party held, in order to bring about industrial

7. For an English summarization of the main points of this bill, see International Labour Office, *Industrial Labour in Japan*, p. 147.

8. Shakai Taishūtō Jigyōbu, p. 47.

9. Both of these bills may be found in ibid., pp. 49–52.

10. *Nihon Rōdō Nenkan, 19* (1938), 484.

conciliation, which was a pressing matter because of the recent boom in military orders and the frequent occurrences of labor speedups and industrial accidents which in turn were causing a deterioration of capital–labor relations. In addition the rise in prices made the situation even more acute.[11] The last time the party presented this bill in the Diet was at the 71st session in July 1937; the revised government bill was never presented.

When the party's national convention opened on November 15, 1937, the whole situation and atmosphere in the country had changed. The advocacy of a labor union law was one of the casualties. There was no mention of this in the Wartime Renovationist Policies Outline which was passed at the convention and which remained with only slight alteration the policy platform until the party was dissolved in 1940. But the Outline did call for collective bargaining legislation, as this was now definitely considered part of the pattern of conciliation. However, no such law was passed until after the war. As a means of fostering cooperation between management and labor, the party proposed industrial conciliation committees (sangyō kyōchō iinkai) nationally and locally. In the following years this idea fused with the Industrial Patriotic Movement which the party supported.

As will be recalled, the Industrial Patriotic Association was formed in 1938 on the basis of conciliation committees in individual enterprises, often fostered by the local police authorities for the purposes of solving or preventing labor disputes. By 1939 there were reportedly 19,601 of these, comprising some 3,000,000 members,[12] and in 1940 the government reorganized them as the Greater Japan Industrial Patriotic Association, officially recognizing it as a national "labor front" on the Nazi model. The original idea of collective bargaining was thus completely perverted. Instead of the two sides bargaining together independently of outside pressure, the local police authorities, through the conciliation committees, could force an

---

11. At the same time Yasutarō Kawamura, a Socialist Masses' Party Diet Member and Secretary of the General Federation of Labor in Government Enterprises, pled for continued recognition of the right of employees in government enterprises to organize, which the army had recently denied. He advocated that unions should be the organizations assigned with the new mission of labor control. The government's reply, however, was that this was contrary to the army's wish but that the government was studying the changing situation. Ibid., *19* (1938), 293–94, 373, 484.

12. Suehiro, *Nihon Rōdō Kumiai Undō Shi*, p. 75.

agreement. Nevertheless, while actively supporting the Industrial Patriotic Movement, the Socialist Masses' Party was not uncritical of it. In 1939, for instance, it called for "correction" of bureaucratic control and capitalist influence in the organization. To the very end, the party, especially the leaders connected with the General Federation, wanted to see the labor federations play a part in the movement rather than be replaced by it. They were less reluctant to see the party lose its identity than to have the General Federation absorbed into a government-controlled organization.

In addition to a Labor Union Law, the Socialist Masses' party (and most of its predecessors) had called for the enactment of a Salaried Men's Law, a Store Employees Law, and a Fishermen's Law.[13] The social democrats considered these classes very different from the manual workers, and they therefore thought in terms of separate laws for them. They wanted all bills to include the rights to organize and act collectively, as well as to provide special protection in the context of their working conditions. (This contrasts with the postwar situation: the Labor Union Law, passed at the beginning of the Occupation, applied to all types of people who earned their livelihood whether they received wages or salaries.) [14] In the prewar situation, probably only piecemeal legislation could be hoped for. For instance, a Shop Law (*Shōten Hō*), providing some protection for store employees, proposed by the government but supported by the Socialist Masses' Party with certain reservations, passed in early 1938.[15] It limited working hours to ten and gave at least one rest day per month and in addition provided for the rationalization of management.

In this regard it is interesting to note the changing attitude on the part of the proletarian parties toward conciliation. In 1926, when so much attention was being paid to labor, a Labor Disputes Conciliation Law was passed. At the time, it was looked upon with suspicion by labor. The proletarian parties tended to ignore it, because it provided compulsory arbitration only in public utility cases and because it specified very restricted conditions under which it could be invoked. It did have a provision for fair representation: it provided for

13. Shakai Taishūtō Jigyōbu, p. 49.

14. This point is discussed in Kyoshi Gotō, *Rōdō Kumiai Hō no Rekishi to Riron* (The History and Theory of the Labor Union Law) (Tōkyō, Zōshindō, 1948), p. 13.

15. For the Socialist Masses' Party's reservations, see *Nihon Rōdō Nenkan, 20* (1939), 257.

conciliation committees to be established, composed of representatives from labor, management, and the public; but this provision was used only once before 1930 and only four or five times thereafter.[16] The law also made available "conciliation officers" (chōteikan) including police officials who acted frequently under this provision, even though conciliation committees were not established. This, in a sense, was interference by the state in disputes between labor and management. The experience of these officials with labor–management relations undoubtedly opened the way for the subsequent development of imposed adjustments in the name of the war effort under the aegis of the Industrial Patriotic Movement.

The New Labor Farmer Party specifically called for the abolition of the Labor Disputes Conciliation Law in 1929, but the Socialist Masses' Party in 1932 did not make this one of its demands. After the China incident, the party came out openly in its Wartime Renovationist Policies Outline for enlarging the system of compulsory arbitration (which by law still only applied to public interest enterprises). The development of the Industrial Patriotic Association brought to an end the need for any other institutionalized conciliation, since the new principle introduced with that movement and openly supported by the party was that both management and labor should bow to the needs of the state in its efforts to prosecute the "holy war."

The original proletarian parties had all called for an eight-hour day, in accordance with the International Labor Convention which had been drawn up at the International Labor Conference held in Washington in 1919. Japan had ratified the Hours Convention but had insisted on the insertion of a special article, applying only to Japan, which in effect vitiated much of the force of the international agreement.[17] In 1932 the Socialist Masses' Party went a step further and demanded a seven-hour working day, together with a living wage. The purpose of this demand, they claimed, was twofold: first,

16. Suehiro, pp. 69 and 100. What labor disliked about this law in particular was a special provision it contained prohibiting so-called third parties (i.e. someone who did not belong to the labor union in question) from interfering or participating in a dispute. Violators would receive up to three months' confinement or be fined up to 200 yen. This was a government counterpolicy to labor's practice of carrying out joint struggles or inviting proletarian party or other leaders from the outside to aid a union in its struggle with management. Ibid., p. 99.

17. This was Article 9. See International Labour Office, pp. 141–42.

to resist the work speedup arising from the Manchurian incident-inspired rationalization of industry, and to help decrease unemployment; they reasoned that if the prevailing nine-and-a-half-hour working day of the 4,700,000 employees in factories employing 40 to 50 or more were reduced to seven, this would provide work for 1,700,000 more.[18] Thereafter, the party gradually dropped the demand for a reduction of hours from among those it was pushing most and let the labor federations take it up.[19] It was not until May 1, 1939, that an ordinance went into effect, based on the National General Mobilization Law, that limited men's hours of work to twelve; and it applied only to very limited categories, such as workers over sixteen years of age in the tool, metal, and shipbuilding industries. The purpose of this ordinance was to prevent the exhaustion of workers from the continuously lengthening workday, especially marked since the outbreak of the China incident.[20]

The social democrats were well aware that hours of work could not be considered apart from wages, and as illustrated in the Labor Farmer Party's policies above, the proletarian parties did call for a "minimum wage." Such a demand, however, would almost have to presuppose a complete revamping of the system of wages in Japan, which was so complicated that it was almost impossible to compute with any degree of accuracy the averages of take-home pay. Basic wages constituted only a fraction of total pay which otherwise derived from midyear and year-end bonuses, family and other allowances, overtime, and various fringe benefits. Both the basic wage and the supplements were influenced by such nonfunctional factors as sex, age, family obligations, and profitability of the enterprise, as well as the more functional criteria of years of experience, efficiency,

18. Shakai Taishūtō Jigyōbu, p. 48. The figures the socialists used were from the Bank of Japan reports. At this time in Japan, only the hours of work of women and young persons in certain categories were regulated by law. They were limited to eleven with a one-hour break when work lasted more than ten hours, according to the amended Factory Act in 1926. A special provision for night work also applied to women and young persons. See International Labour Office, p. 142.

19. For instance, in October 1937 the Congress of Japanese Labor Unions called for an eight-hour day with rest and a maximum of three hours overtime with the sanction of the administrative authorities. The Congress conceded that in the emergency of the China incident workers should not hesitate to sacrifice themselves; but from the point of view of efficiency and health, it held that the government should work out a policy on hours of work. Nihon Rōdō Nenkan, 19 (1938), 183–84.

20. Ibid., 21 (1940), 36–37.

and attendance. Status was more important than actual services rendered in determining pay. In such a context, the demand for a minimum wage was far more abstract than, say, in the United States at the same period.

The intent of the socialists, of course, was to set a floor under wages, raising as many of the lowest ones as possible. After the China incident, wages were frozen and subsequently a complicated series of minimum and maximum wages were set for various occupations, with the intent of curbing inflation. These regulations were promulgated in 1939 in accordance with the National General Mobilization Law. At that time the Socialist Masses' Party advocated adopting a sliding scale of wages based on a cost-of-living index. This was not adopted. Thereafter, although nominal wages rose sharply, when deflated by an index of retail prices, which included elements of black-market costs, it was seen that real wages fell throughout the war.[21]

A strong demand of all the proletarian parties from the beginning was for unemployment insurance, and yet no national system providing for this was ever set up in prewar Japan. The closest thing was the Law for Retirement Reserve Funds and Allowances (*Taishoku Tsumitatekin oyobi Taishoku Teate Hō*) enacted in 1936, but the Socialist Masses' Party continued to the end to call for concrete planning for systematic coverage of unemployment insurance.[22]

A subsidiary labor demand was for an increase in the number of public employment exchanges. In 1932 the Socialist Masses' Party demanded that the exchanges be put under the control of labor unions. The system of public employment exchanges had been set up by law in 1921 and 1922 to not only inform workers of opportunities but to actually pay certain daily wages in advance to save the workers from the clutches of labor bosses (*oyabun* or *oyakata*) who would lend money and then take a cut when the workers were paid, usually once or twice a month. The problem of exchanges became more acute during the depression years, but in the late 1930s the government took a more active interest in the problem. Perhaps that is the reason why the Socialist Masses' Party after 1936 did not include de-

21. Jerome B. Cohen, *Japan's Economy in War and Reconstruction* (Minneapolis, I.P.R. and University of Minnesota Press, 1949), p. 273.

22. After the party's demise, however, some unemployment insurance was incorporated into the Laborers' Annuity Insurance Law (*Rōdōsha Nenkin Hoken Hō*) of 1940 when the latter was revised as the Welfare Annuity Insurance Law (*Kōsei Nenkin Hoken Hō*) of 1942. Suehiro, p. 78.

mands for the extension of the exchanges. The trend toward greater reliance on state direction also tended to preclude any subsequent demands for the exchanges to be run by labor unions.

In the field of social welfare, it is ironic that the government under wartime conditions did adopt some of the policies the proletarian parties had long called for. One of these was the National Health Insurance Law which was passed in 1938. The original Health Insurance Law passed the Diet in 1922 before the proletarian parties came into being, but because of the earthquake it was not enforced until 1926. It was a subject, therefore, for immediate notice by the proletarian parties, and in 1927 they called for some improvements in the law. They all recognized that the principle of compulsory insurance was sound but differed as to how it should be financed, the leftists demanding that the employer should bear the entire cost.

The original Health Insurance Law made insurance compulsory only for persons working in the larger mines and factories, but provided for its extension to other undertakings, such as building, transportation, and engineering, on condition that the employer had obtained the previous consent of more than half the persons to be insured. It provided that health insurance societies (*kenkō hoken kumiai*) could be set up compulsorily by the Home Minister or voluntarily with his permission. The insurance would then be financed by the societies with a 10 per cent subsidy from the state to cover administrative costs. Those workers not organized in health insurance societies were theoretically covered by state health insurance offices, located throughout the country after 1929 in local prefectural governments.

The proletarian parties desired that the system of medical treatment be improved and the scope of insurance be extended. The Social Democratic Party gave the most detailed attention to the problem from the beginning and demanded that health insurance societies be administered solely by the workers and also that the business of drug dispensing be separated from that of prescription writing. The custom in Japan was that the doctor himself sold drugs and pharmaceutical appliances to patients directly, and it was widely felt that the doctors were prescribing unnecessarily in order to make a bigger profit for themselves.[23]

The government considered the original Health Insurance Law as

23. The final legislative separation did not take place until 1957.

one facet of its labor policy, but the Socialist Masses' Party called for extending its coverage to salaried men, fishermen, and the families of those insured. Some extensions were made in 1935, but by then the party had already started demanding a "national health insurance system," which in addition would include the farming population and the small retailers and producers whom labor insurance did not cover. The socialists' aim was to lighten the medical expenses of people of small incomes and in this manner stabilize the national livelihood and aid in the spread of medical facilities. When the government came up with its National Health Insurance Bill in the 70th session of the Diet early in 1937, the party supported it energetically, and, after some concessions had been made to organized doctors and pharmacists, saw its enactment in early 1938, as noted.

The first year or so after the outbreak of the China war witnessed the passage of several governmental social-policy bills related to labor. The Socialist Masses' Party, in company with the national socialist parties, had fought for them under the banner of national "reform" (or "renovationist") policies (kakushin kokusaku), opposing revisions proposed by the major conservative parties. Besides the National Health Insurance Law and the Shop Law already mentioned, they included the revised Seamen's Law, which the party had long called for, and the revised Labor Exchanges Law, as well as the National General Mobilization Law and the Electric Power State Management Law, both of which will be discussed later.[24] Finally, the Seamen's Insurance Law, which the proletarian parties had championed since the first government draft was submitted to the Diet in 1930, passed in 1939. This gave certain laborers for the first time pensions for disability and old age, but on a very limited basis.

In addition, the party strongly supported the creation of the Ministry of Welfare (Kōseishō) in 1938 which took charge of administration in the fields of national insurance, health, social work, and labor, all formerly handled by the Social Bureau of the Ministry of Home Affairs. In the following two years the party demanded that the various labor policy functions still dispersed in other ministries be concentrated here. The real force behind the establishment of the

24. Until this time, the only major labor victories from the standpoint of protective legislation were the revisions of the Factory Act in 1929 with its attendant regulations, and the 1931 Labor Accidents Assistance Law which extended the application of accident compensation to workers in construction, transportation, and some other fields. This latter had hitherto been limited to workers in factories and mines.

Ministry of Welfare was the military, which was interested in using it as an instrument of control, specifically to protect or increase the already low physical stamina and weight of the people and to train and redistribute manpower for the purpose of insuring the supply of conscripts and laborers.

The success of such measures after the China incident, because of the need to stabilize the economy and minimize labor unrest in the face of the rising demands of an extended war situation, gave the Socialist Masses' Party ammunition for contending that its cooperation in the war effort was at the same time fulfilling its proper functions as a proletarian party, even if some of its members were denying it was still either "socialist" or "social democratic."

AGRARIAN POLICIES

Although labor policies had a higher priority in the proletarian party platforms in Japan, agrarian policies were given almost as much weight. Unlike social democrats in some of the industrially advanced countries, Japanese leaders could not disregard the farming population, since it constituted more than half the total population at the time. And although no purely labor party sprang up in Japan, it will be remembered that the Japan Farmers' Party, led by Rikizō Hirano, concerned itself almost entirely with the agricultural villages.

The demand for a Tenant-Farmer Union Law (*Kosaku Kumiai Hō*) ranked highest when the proletarian parties strove to represent the interests of the organized tenant farmers. Its fate paralleled that of the labor union law: it was dropped after the China incident. Despite the activity of the organized farmers, their unions gained no more specific legal recognition in prewar Japan than the labor unions. As with labor, the farmers wanted the rights to organize, to carry on disputes, and to bargain collectively.[25]

Closely connected was a demand for a Farm Tenantry Law (*Kosaku Hō*). Only a few aspects of such legislation can be discussed here, the most important of which was the question of the right of

25. Although tenant-farmer unions had never been as specifically legislated against as labor unions, they experienced great difficulty surviving. They reached their greatest strength in 1927 with 365,332 farmers organized in 4,582 unions, according to Ministry of Forestry and Agriculture figures, quoted, for instance, in *Nihon Rōdō Nenkan, 19* (1938), 236–37.

tillage (*kōsaku ken*). A right of permanent tenantry (*ei kosaku ken*) traditionally existed in Japanese common law and was originally intended to reward someone who opened up undeveloped land owned by another while the owner retained the right to receive a certain rent from that land. The farmers' unions and the proletarian parties, however, went further and demanded that the right of ownership be modified by the right of tillage or cultivation so that the tenant farmer could not be so easily forced off the land he had tilled and so that he would be compensated for improvements he had made. They also sought a legal right to a reduction of rent for various reasons, such as a poor harvest or crop failure. Since agitation for rent reduction was the most common cause of tenant–landlord disputes, legal limits on rent were frequently proposed. Farm tenantry legislation was advocated to protect the tenant farmers from such common occurrences as the landlord's foreclosing the land (*tochi toriage*) in order to get another tenant at a higher rent, or restraining entrance to the land by the tenant (*tachiiri kinshi*), or attaching the crops (*ritsumō sashiosae*).[26]

All the proletarian parties called for a Farm Tenantry Law from the beginning, and as late as February 25, 1937, the Socialist Masses' Party brought up in the Diet such a bill, which, as usual, was pigeonholed. Even after the China incident, while the demand for a Farm Tenantry Law as such was omitted from the new Constructive Program of 1938, still, in supporting the government-sponsored Agricultural Land Adjustment Law (*Nōchi Chōsei Hō*), the party continued to emphasize the need for a comprehensive Farm Tenantry Bill which would include both the right to till and the right to a fair rent.[27]

At this time, too, the party was changing its attitude on the question of the creation and support of independent farmers. This had been the policy of the government since the promulgation of Regulations to Aid in the Creation and Support of Independent Farmers

---

26. Alternative terms for "attaching crops" are: *ine ritsumō kari sashiosae* and *shūkakubutsu no sashiosae*. All these were complicated problems and were in part regulated administratively. For instance, the Socialist Masses' Party in 1936 sought a regulation to put a limit on the landlord's attachment of tenant farmer's crops so as to leave the tenant sufficient rice for his family's consumption for one year. The party could claim to be successful to a degree, because a regulation was revised and such a limitation inserted but only for a three-month period instead of one year. For the regulation, see ibid., *17* (1936), Appendix, p. 17.

27. Ibid., *20* (1939), 252, 257.

(*Jisakunō Sōsetsu Iji Hojo Kisoku*) of May 1926, but all the proletarian parties had opposed this on grounds of its being ineffective in solving the farm tenantry problem. In simple terms, it established financial agencies to lend money under certain conditions to tenants to enable them to become independent farmers in about 25 years. Although the desire to own land was almost universal among the Japanese peasants, the socialists considered that various questions of tenant-farmer rent constituted their immediate problems and gave rise to their most pressing demands. They also feared that individual ownership might create a conservative, rural petit bourgeoisie.

After the China incident, when the national interest was taking precedence over class interests, the party came around to supporting the above-mentioned Agricultural Land Adjustment Law, which passed the Diet in early 1938. Its aim was to secure greater agricultural production through insuring peaceful tenant–landlord relations.[28] To an extent it protected tenant farmers in their tillage rights, as in the case of a tenant being drafted into military service. It also systematized government loans and other means to help tenants to become independent farmers. However, it did not provide for lowering rent nor did it touch on many aspects of tenant–landlord relations that earlier socialist proposals covered. While the party did not abandon its cry for a separate Farm Tenantry Law, it evidently considered that more headway might be made in the direction of transforming tenant farmers into independent cultivators through government ownership (*kokuyū*) of farm tenant land, preceded by increased governmental controls over the land and agricultural production. This would more likely promote collective rather than individualistic tendencies and thus obviate the creation of a conservative petit bourgeoisie.[29] In line with this new policy, the agrarian organizations supporting the Socialist Masses' Party and others merged to form the Federation for Reform of the Land System (Nōchi Seido Kaikaku Dōmei) in November 1939, but the policy was unable to prevent the rapid deterioration of the agrarian movement.

A somewhat similar change of attitude occurred with regard to the Farm Tenancy Conciliation Law (*Kosaku Chōtei Hō*) which went into force in December 1924. This was taken more notice of than the Labor Disputes Conciliation Law, because it was more frequently

28. Ibid., *20* (1939), 425–27.
29. Ibid., *21* (1940), 178.

invoked, especially by landlords. The proletarian parties opposed it mainly on the ground that it was based on individual conciliation and did not recognize tenant farmers' unions or collective agreements.

After the China incident, however, when emphasis was placed above all on national unity and class harmony, the Socialist Masses' Party called for setting up agricultural village conciliation committees which would have important disputes submitted to them first. An old complaint against the Farm Tenancy Conciliation Law was the allegedly unfair treatment the farmers were getting compared to the landlords in the courts where the law referred disputes. Thus, it proposed that special courts for farm tenancy disputes (*kosaku shimpanjo*) be created, but although the Agricultural Adjustments Law of 1938 made some favorable modifications in legal procedure applicable under the Farm Tenancy Conciliation Law, it did not go as far as that.

From the beginning the proletarian parties had been unanimous in calling for government distribution of fertilizers, seed, and farm implements.[30] By 1932 the Socialist Masses' Party advocated state crop, price, and market control of agricultural production. Under the early stimulus of Japanese aggression in China, the production of fertilizer and agricultural implements did increase greatly; for instance, ammonium sulfate fertilizer production reached its peak in 1941. But already the government had begun the system of compulsory delivery of crops provided for by the Rice Control Regulations of October 1940,[31] and in 1942 the Food Administration Law further augmented state monopoly control of all foodstuffs and the checking of prices below the free level. The government had moved in the direction advocated by the social democrats, but because of the demands for munitions it was unable to maintain a sufficient flow of fertilizers and agricultural implements.

Of the many other items going to make up the agrarian policies of the prewar proletarian parties, perhaps the most important remaining ones had to do first of all with credit. An increase in the number

30. Except that the Social Democrats usually limited their demands to government distribution of fertilizers and farm implements, without mentioning seed.

31. This law, incidentally, continued in effect after the end of the war to force farmers to sell their grain to the state at set prices instead of on the sky-high open market.

and functions of agricultural banks was demanded [32] and, as an immediate measure, a government moratorium on all agricultural debts. The Socialist Masses' Party proposed agricultural capital loans on easy terms and that the full crop be used as collateral, or in lieu of monetary collateral the tenant farmer stake his continued right to tenancy. The parties also demanded freer access for poor farmers and tenant farmers to local public lands. Generally they called for the "equalization of city and country," meaning that almost every aspect of the life of the rural population should be raised to urban standards. This meant mechanization of agriculture, rural electrification, improvement of schools, and so forth. The proletarian parties attempted to stimulate and take advantage of what is now called the "revolution of rising expectations" that had hit the rural areas in Japan.

The main trends of the shiftover to wartime policies in 1937 and 1938 involved priority being placed on increasing agricultural production at all costs for the predicted approaching "war of exhaustion," which could last for many years. The resulting Agrarian Patriotic Movement (Nōgyō Hōkoku Undō) paralleled the Industrial Patriotic Movement, both of which the Socialist Masses' Party supported, though at first it tried to prevent the dissolution of the existing tenant-farmer unions. The party also called for cutting consumption and raising more livestock. A new development was the increased emphasis placed on collective emigration of farmers to Manchuria and to areas that were later included in the Greater East Asia Co-Prosperity Sphere. In sum, agrarian policies shifted from an original emphasis on the rights of the tenant farmers to fight for better terms in their relations with their landlords to emphasis on class harmony and boosted production by way of greater government controls.

32. Agricultural credit agencies sponsored by the Japanese government were centered in the Hypothec Bank which in turn was strictly controlled by the Ministry of Finance. They included: the prefectural Agricultural and Industrial Banks; the Hokkaidō Colonial Bank and the Central Bank for Cooperative Associations. "Together these agencies furnished as much as a quarter of the funds borrowed by farmers. . . . Most of the remainder came from local pawnshops, landlords, and merchants at much higher interest rates." William W. Lockwood, *The Economic Development of Japan* (Princeton, Princeton University Press, 1954). The social democrats were trying to save the farmers from the clutches of these latter categories by raising the proportion of government-backed loans at moderate rates, without collateral.

SOCIOPOLITICAL POLICIES

In contrast to labor and agrarian policies, what are here called sociopolitical policies make up a less homogeneous whole. They do not necessarily conform to the classifications the proletarian parties called either "social" or "political." For convenience of presentation the following categories of policies are treated in this section: demands for freedom of speech and action; electoral reform; institutional change; policies on women; educational reform; and arms reduction.

The surprising thing about the reforms in this section is that, whereas none of them were realized in the prewar period, they were all finally initiated under the postwar Allied Occupation, some in more radical form than envisioned by the proletarian parties. This contrasts sharply with the policies in the economic category (examined in the next section), some of which, as with the labor policies, were instituted during or immediately prior to the war, while others remained bones of contention well into the postwar period.

Even the right-wing Social Democratic Party called specifically for the abolition of the Peace Preservation Law, the Peace Police Law, and the Administrative Execution Law as well as revision of the Newspaper and the Publication Laws. Since so many of the socialist leaders, from before the formation of the mass parties, had suffered arrest and imprisonment, it was probably only natural that demands were raised in the party platforms for revision of the trial system and state indemnification for false accusation and improper detention. Stiff penalties were asked for law enforcement authorities who abused their office. The Labor Farmer Party went so far as openly to demand the abolition of secret service funds and the political police.

The Socialist Masses' Party at its founding supported earlier proletarian demands for the repeal of oppressive laws and for penalties for the abuse of office. They called generally for an end to "police rule" (*keisatsu seiji*), and in the following year more specifically for reforms in the procedures of arrest and trial, and also abolition of what was euphemistically termed "education" (*kyōikushugi*) but which was actually official "brainwashing." Gradually, however, the party reached a point after the China incident where all its demands for freedom had been reduced to one: "respect for constructive speech" (*kensetsuteki genron no sonchō*).

It is not surprising to find that demands for electoral reform often headed the list of campaign policies. A liberalization in suffrage had allowed the proletarian parties to come into existence, and their continued survival depended on a more or less impartial enforcement of existing regulations. They all demanded that the suffrage be extended to women. The leftists in Japan did not appear to fear that women would vote more conservatively than men, as did leftists in such Catholic countries as France or Mexico. Still, this demand was not calculated to draw great support under prewar conditions and was thus neglected in the mid-1930s. The Socialist Masses' Party's new Constructive Program of 1937 was silent on the subject. A lowering of the voting age, previously demanded, was also absent. The Labor Farmer Party had called for lowering the voting age from twenty-five to eighteen, but the Social Democratic and later the Socialist Masses' Party had asked only that it be set at twenty.[33] In addition, the Socio-Democrats had been strongly in favor of proportional representation both on theoretical grounds and from the practical consideration that it aided minority parties. This was carried over into the Socialist Masses' Party platform which favored the Hagenbach-Bischoff system and large prefecture-wide election districts.

The so-called "clean election movement" (*senkyo shukusei undō*) of 1936 and 1937, inspired by responsible bureaucrats, helped account for proletarian party gains in those years. Party policies were hammered out to support and encourage that movement in every way. Beyond this, perhaps the most common of the many specific electoral reforms called for by the proletarian parties included state payment of electoral expenses, abolition of the system of candidates posting bonds, and official declaration of voting days as public holidays.

Turning to larger institutional reforms, it is interesting to note that the original draft of policies of the Farmer Labor Party, agreed to by both the left and right wings, included "the abolition of the Genrō, the House of Peers, the General Staff, and the Naval Head-

33. For prefectural and local elections, however, the Socialist Masses' Party called for a voting age of 18. In postwar Japan, the voting age was lowered to 20 for both national and local elections.

quarters." [34] But it was understood that these items were disapproved by the police and they were therefore dropped from the final program of the party, although this did not save it from immediate disbandment. (All these institutions, incidentally, were abolished by the Allied Occupation less than twenty years later.)

The Genrō or Elder Statesmen were already disappearing with only Saionji left, and since he actually played a positive role in stabilizing politics, the demand for abolition of this institution carried less force. Conversely, the star of the military was rising and demands for the abolition of the General Staff and Naval Headquarters became all the more "dangerous." The Privy Council, though not in the above list, was singled out for attack by the Japan-Labor clique parties until the formation of the Socialist Masses' Party. With its formation, however, due to the confluence of various pressures, only the demand for the abolition of the peerage (*kizoku seido*) found common support.

This policy had three aspects. As it was, the House of Peers obviously represented the privileged classes and formed a natural target. Furthermore, according to the thinking of the former *Eta* social outcastes—now called "special community people"—who were giving support to the Socialist Masses' Party, their social emancipation could not be achieved without abolishing the top of the social hierarchy. Consequently, the party called for the abolition of the peerage as part of its demand for the end of all feudalistic status discimination. Finally, the party was beginning to think of reform of the Upper House in terms of functional representation, for even if the Upper House was firmly embedded in the sacrosanct Constitution, its makeup might be changed. Functional representation was called for both in the 1936 election policies well before the China incident and also in the Constructive Program after the party's change of direction.[35] The germ of this idea can be traced back to an earlier proposal by the Japan-Labor clique for an "economic congress," which will be discussed in the next section on economic policies.[36]

34. Kyōchōkai, p. 551.

35. The Japan Proletarian Party, however, openly called for the abolition of the House of Peers during the 1937 election.

36. Functional representation was not included in the postwar reform of the House of Peers into the House of Councillors, but in the way the elections have worked out for this body in the postwar period, a trend toward an informal type of functional representation has been noted by some observers.

On the local level, even the Socialist Masses' Party in the mid-1930s called for the election of prefectural governors and the abolition of prefectural councils, which were made up of appointed local functionaries. As for the prefectural assemblies, which were elective and thus more representative, the party demanded they be given increased powers, such as self-convocation and the right of assemblymen to inspect revenues and expenditures. "Economic congresses" on the prefectural level were also proposed as well as an end to independent prefectural taxes and the establishment of a system of grants-in-aid for social welfare purposes.[37]

Turning now to the feminist question, it should be noted that, owing to the legal disabilities on women in prewar Japan, this was as much political as social. The demand for repealing the law against political participation by women was embodied in the election reform demands already mentioned. But in addition, during the first few years, the parties sought the abolition of all legal and social discrimination against women. Specifically they championed the end of "traffic in women." In their labor policies, they included special protective legislation for women and minors. Legal equality would involve changes in kinship and inheritance legislation and the enactment of a law requiring equal pay for equal work by both men and women. Economically, allowances for working mothers were demanded and pensions for widows and orphans.

It was during the life of the Socialist Masses' Party that the "blackout" on the woman question came. In 1932 the party supported proletarian demands for women. It criticized the 1929 Factory Law revision which forbade night work for women between 11 p.m. and 5 a.m., because in effect its coverage was limited only to large factories. While a number of social democratic leaders, notably Tetsu Katayama and Isoo Abe, continued championing women's rights and in the Diet publicized causes of special interest to women, the Socialist Masses' Party, as a party, became silent on feminist demands and made no mention of them in the new Constructive Program after the China incident. Actually, as will be explained in Chapter 14, the feminist movement flagged rapidly following the Manchurian incident. Thereafter its campaign for acquiring the suffrage gradually changed to a less militant but broader range of activities along na-

37. Except for the "economic congresses," these reforms were carried out in varying degrees in the postwar Occupation period.

tionalistic lines, such as helping the economic home front by exhorting people to eat less polished rice and to rehabilitate worn-out apparel or household articles. By the mid-1930s, the women's sections in most labor unions, which had originally pressured for women's planks in the proletarian party platforms, had become inactive or defunct.

Public education in prewar Japan had a definite authoritarian political orientation, especially pronounced in such courses as "ethics" (shūshin) and history. The proletarian parties hoped to counter this by calling for citizenship training aimed at encouraging greater popular political participation.

The social aspect of proletarian proposals for education reform derived from their underlying desire for equal opportunity in the pursuit of higher education for the poor as well as for the rich. All the parties plumped for raising the educational level of the populace by lengthening the period of free compulsory education and making it less of an economic hardship, through government aid to parents of school children.[38] They demanded that the national treasury cover expenses for pupils' food and materials used in schools and also some of the costs for boarding when necessary to attend school. In rural areas schools were often located beyond commuting distance for many students who would therefore have to board with relatives, friends, or teachers. This was the case even for some elementary school children but was progressively more frequent for students in middle school and above.

In the beginning the Social Democratic Party spelled out its educational proposals in more detail than the others, calling for increases in teachers' salaries in lower schools, civic group participation in compiling government-approved standard textbooks, and public support for vocational and agricultural schools. The Labor Farmer Party emphasized the demand for academic freedom to a greater extent than the others. This contrast was typical of the policy differences between the left and right wings of the proletarian movement.

When the Socialist Masses' Party was formed, the idea of a system of part-time study and part-time work (rōgakusei) was added to the demands for public support of expenses incurred in going to school.

---

38. The period usually demanded for compulsory education was ten years, instead of the then existing six. Under the postwar education reform, the schools were reorganized to conform to the American "6-3-3" system with the first nine years compulsory.

The idea of combining work with study appears to have been inspired by the Marxist conception of the unity of theory and practice as well as the example of Soviet developments in education. But it was not until 1936 that the party for the first time published a proposal for reform of the educational system.[39]

Despite the background of this demand, it was not dropped in the new Constructive Program of November 1938. Here, also, the fundamental principle of equality in educational opportunity remained but was given a nationalistic twist with a demand that the educational system, especially the university curricula, be geared not only to production but to the needs of the state. Otherwise the educational policies remained largely what had become traditional for the proletarian parties: extension of compulsory education to ten years; free provision of elementary school supplies and abolition of fees; education for modern citizenship; and the giving of some kind of special qualification to those who complete their compulsory schooling. Training in the scientific spirit and "social education" were advocated as well as a reorganization of the content and structure of the educational system as compulsory education was extended. A demand for reemphasizing ethics, however, represented a reversal and alignment with the "spiritual mobilization campaign" for the war effort. (Postwar Occupation reforms conformed with the earlier social democratic demands both in revising the content of teaching away from nationalism and in lengthening the period of compulsory education.)

A more sensitive issue than all those so far discussed (and one that has taken on paramount importance in the postwar period) is armaments reduction.[40] In the early days before the Manchurian incident, all the proletarian parties demanded "reduction in military preparations," which in practical terms meant cutbacks in military expenditures in the government's annual budgets. The rationale behind this was that the cause of wars lay in imperialist competition for markets. If the capitalist class, which controlled the state, had at its disposal large military forces, it would be likely to use them in im-

39. *Nihon Rōdō Nenkan, 19* (1938), 290.

40. Here again is a reform the Occupation carried out: it went further and disbanded the military forces. When American policy changed and encouraged rearmament, the question of whether this was constitutional, in light of Article 9 of the New Constitution of 1947, became a burning issue.

perialist adventures that would lead to war. The proletarian class would be called on to do the fighting but would gain nothing from the war. In fact, it could only lose.

Still, none of the parties went so far as to call for the abolition of all armaments. In line with what was considered the inevitably reformist character of political policies possible under capitalist parliamentary government, the proletarian parties sought indirectly to embarrass the military while championing the interests of the proletariat by demanding shorter periods of compulsory service and better treatment for soldiers. Such demands varied slightly from party to party: the Social Democrats called only for pay increases for recruits; while the Labor Farmer Party demanded "recognition of the human rights" of soldiers, one year only of active service in all branches, and elimination of special privileges for a select few while in military service. All demanded compensation to families which encountered financial hardship as a result of the conscription of a family member.

In 1932 the Socialist Masses' Party, made up of groups who had just weathered the storm of defections to national socialism, still retained the planks advocating military reductions in the roster of their policies, although the police forced it to eliminate items concerning the military in the Constructive Program proper. Party policies, however, attacked both the government's "aggressive, militaristic" foreign policy and its tariff barriers as causes of war. In defending their stand on arms reduction, the representatives of the Socialist Masses' Party were the only ones in the Diet in 1933 to oppose the large Manchurian incident-inspired emergency budget.[41]

It is almost superfluous to add that after the China incident the party's change of attitude precluded all talk of military reduction and ending arms races. Actually a gradual change had started earlier. In the 1936 election the party wanted the government to "standardize" military expenditures and in the February 1937 election this was toned down to "rationalize" military expenditures. At the 71st and 72nd sessions immediately following the outbreak of hostilities, the party vied for leadership in supporting the supplementary military budgets. In the Constructive Program of 1938 the party openly stated that it "stood on the principle of national defense in the broad

41. Ibid., *15* (1934), 436.

sense" and called for "the establishment of a system of total defense."
The only proletarian concession asked for was that national defense
should be planned so as to harmonize with the "people's livelihood." [42]

ECONOMIC POLICIES

The questions of taxation, social security, credit, and government
controls over the economy touched the lives of the people perhaps
more deeply than many of the sociopolitical issues; yet, because of
their technical and complex nature, they were less able to arouse
popular interest or stir people to action. Nevertheless, after the dust
of an election campaign settles, a cold look at a party's economic
policies often reveals more about the competence and reasonableness
of the policymakers than such broad demands as freedom of speech
and assembly, however undeniably important they are.

Socialism has traditionally been more an economic than a political
body of thought. Accordingly, one expects to detect more of the socialistic nature of a socialist party by examining its economic policies.
The social democrats in Japan, however, tended to plan for two
levels: their program after the attainment of socialism; and attain-
able goals under the existing capitalist system. Outside of the proletarian parties' demands for the creation of a socialist economy, almost
all policies were conceived of as realizable within a capitalist framework. This was even true of the demands for land reform which
would include government ownership of the land. As with certain
labor reforms, however, the irony of the situation was that some of
the economic demands were partly realized during the war when the
Japanese socialists no longer openly espoused socialism. At the same
time, it is plausible to assume that many social democrats thought
they discerned the approach of socialism in the increase of government controls.

In their labor and agrarian policies, the proletarian parties both
championed rights and worked out measures toward the solutions of
problems as they saw them. In the group of sociopolitical policies just
examined, however, the securing of rights loomed largest. In the economic policies to be dealt with below, it will be seen that measures
were more prominent than rights in the proletarian demands for

42. Ibid., 20 (1939), 251.

transforming the economic system. Big business and the wealthy, however, were the objects of attack and the proposed sources of new revenue. Policies designed to appeal to support from small business gradually developed.

During the period under consideration, a change in attitude toward the state took place. At first the government was thought of as controlled by monopoly capital and therefore basically inimical to the interests of labor, farmers, and small business. Later, along with the change in attitude toward the military, proletarian party leaders began to think of the state as neutral and made up of bureaucrats who were in large part friendlier to proletarian interests than was big business. The Socialist Masses' Party began to conceive of itself as fighting to push through a number of government proposals (even though they were not entirely satisfied with them) against opposition from big capitalist interests represented by the major parties. The party went so far in this that it had to issue statements denying that it was specifically supporting the Konoe Cabinet but was only backing progressive (renovationist) legislation that the bureaucracy had drawn up on the basis of its technical knowledge and in the light of the national interest.

The verbalized main goal of all of the proletarian party policies was "stabilization of the people's livelihood" (*kokumin seikatsu no antei*). Around 1937 another main goal took its place beside the first: "increased productive power" (*seisanryoku zōdai*). (Interestingly enough these together became the chief socialist economic policy slogans in postwar Japan.)

To begin with, all the proletarian parties called for "increased expenditures for the working class"—to use the very words of the Social Democratic Party in 1927. One demand was for a tenfold increase in expenditures for social welfare facilities. As we have seen, all of the parties advocated allowances for needy families with a member in the service and this remained a plank in the late 1930s even after better treatment of soldiers in the service had been effected.

In prewar Japan the term "social security" (*shakai hoshō*) was not in use. It gained acceptance in Japan only after British socialism had refined the concept in the war years to include "full employment in a free society with security from the cradle to the grave."

What can be called the social security goals of the proletarian parties in prewar Japan, short of socialism, were far more limited. They called for social insurance legislation for sickness, old age, accidents, and unemployment. The National Health Insurance, which was eventually enacted, did cover the first three of these items, at least to a certain extent. The Socialist Masses' Party, however, as noted, continued to the very end to advocate unemployment insurance. Also to the end it called for a government-managed life insurance system. High on the Japan Proletarian Party's policy list before its dissolution in 1937 was the demand for a reorganization of the pension and annuity system, which would have involved greatly increased budgetary expenditures.

With regard to health, an important item was the public operation of medical clinics. The New Labor Farmer Party in 1929 outdid its rivals in calling for free hospitalization and diagnosis. Another demand concerning health was for a compensation system for damages caused by industry (such as smoke pollution), or by mines (such as sinking land), and so forth. After the China incident when the army became painfully aware of the poor condition of the people's health as reflected in the high rate of rejects for military service, the Socialist Masses' Party developed proposals for increasing weight through group exercises and improved sanitation.

Public housing projects for workers were sporadically demanded by the proletarian parties, to help free workers from dependence on company block housing and barracks. But in the absence of central or municipal initiatives, the parties insisted on the "right to living quarters" (kyojūken). This had a peculiar meaning. In Japan people often built their own houses on rented land, for houses of wood and paper were cheap but land was dear. If the house burned down, the landowner might rent the space at a higher price to someone else who would build his home there. The proletarian parties wanted to safeguard the tenant's right to rebuild and continue to rent at his former rate.

In contrast to these demands for social security, health, and housing projects—most of which would have involved sizable government outlays—the proletarian parties cited certain items where expenditures could be curtailed. The most important were arms reduction and military cutbacks. Even as late as 1935 the Socialist Masses' Party voiced these demands and proposed that the burden of military support be shifted to the zaibatsu. In addition, it asked that the military forces plan their expenditures so as to bring the greatest benefits to the masses of people by placing construction contracts in areas of severe unemployment. From the beginning the proletarian parties advocated reducing government subsidies and bounties to the zaibatsu and other big capitalists. This continued to be a popular theme, because every cabinet invariably appropriated funds, with the connivance of the major parties, to support the capital structures of the giant banks and industrial concerns.[43]

At the time of the financial crisis of 1935–36, the Socialist Masses' Party detailed another proposal for decreasing government outlays to save money for social purposes: a moratorium (at first for two years) on the payments of capital and interest on government bonds, which the party held was the type of emergency financial policy being carried out in most other countries.[44] This demand was not dropped but rather refined as the 1930s wore on. The party also argued for compulsory conversion of public bonds into lower interest debentures and later on for compulsory retention of bonds for certain periods.

Though the social democrats were ineffective in forcing the government to decrease military and other expenditures or to channel more funds into social welfare, they nevertheless did give thought to the tax structure and made a number of proposals for increasing state revenue. They consistently advocated the creation of a highly progressive general property tax that would go beyond the real estate taxes already in existence and include both movable and immovable property, and even such things as public bonds and antiques. In addition they called for more steeply progressive income, inheritance, and business profits taxes, as well as a tax on interest, which in the prewar period was immune from even the mildly progressive levies of

43. Lockwood, p. 524.

44. The socialists claimed that in the depression the zaibatsu had put their money for safekeeping into government bonds and, by indirectly forcing the government to raise revenue by bonds rather than taxes, lightened the tax burden on themselves. Already the point had been reached where most of the money coming in through taxes was going to pay the interest on these bonds. The people, who bore the brunt of the various taxes on consumption, postal rates, government railroad fares, tobacco, and salt, were indirectly subsidizing the zaibatsu, who paid disproportionately light taxes. Thus, the class interest of the majority of the people was clearly pitted against the zaibatsu monopoly capitalists in the eyes of the socialists. See "Zenkoku Rishi Nikanenkan Shiharai Teishi ni Kansuru Ken" (Item Concerning the Nonpayment of Interest on All National Bonds for Two Years), in *Nihon Rōdō Nenkan, 17* (1936), 504.

the personal income tax.[45] In some policy formulations, this tax on interest was to be part of a proposed general levy on "increases of value": such as exorbitant profits of monopoly capital, capital derived from the increase in value of stocks, the increase of land values derived from surrounding urbanization or industrialization, and windfall profits from speculation on the stock market.[46] With regard to land, the social democrats wanted to "soak the rich" with such special taxes as those on land owned by absentee landlords, on vacant lots, on gardens, and so forth. Directed against the big competitors of the small proprietors was the proposed tax on department stores.

Severe punishment for tax evasion by the wealthy was universally demanded by the proletarian party leaders, because it was well known that many loopholes were taken advantage of, fictitious bookkeeping practiced, and that the laws were loosely enforced.[47] By 1935 the Socialist Masses' Party was calling for taxing "super-profits" from military production inspired by the post-Manchurian incident boom. After the more serious China war started, this demand seemingly took on more moral force, and it became part of the government's 1940 general tax reform which finally made of the income tax an effective means of revenue.

Being opposition parties, however, the proletarian parties were less concerned with the problem of raising government revenue than with decreasing the burden on the wage and salaried classes and people of small means generally. Thus, while insisting on more steeply progressive taxes on income, real estate, inheritance, and business profits, they demanded an upward revision of the exemption levels on these taxes. The Socialist Masses' Party in 1932, for instance, named the figure of 2,000 *yen* per year and demanded an exemption from all taxes for people with an income of less than that. With justice, the social democrats complained about the unfair taxes borne by the proletarian class. They demanded the abolition or at least drastic

45. As much as 40 per cent of corporate dividends and bonuses were not taxed progressively. Interest was taxed at only 4 to 5 per cent (except for the yields on national and savings bonds, which were exempt). Lockwood, p. 524.

46. Lockwood states that the basic rate on corporate profits was only 5 per cent and surtaxes on excess profits raised it no higher than 10 even if a firm made 30 per cent on its invested capital. Ibid., p. 525.

47. "Whatever the legal rates, the taxes paid by Japanese corporations and well-to-do individuals always depended in no small degree on a process of individual negotiation, in which political influence and financial bargaining power carried a good deal of weight." Ibid., p. 525.

reduction of heavily regressive consumption taxes on daily necessities and the lifting of customs duties on consumer goods.[48]

On the local level, they stressed the abolition of prefectural taxes (such as those on public baths and barber shops) and the miscellaneous taxes (on such things as bicycles and carts) that affected the business activity of millions of small industrialists, tradesmen, and professional people. Furthermore, they wanted local house and household taxes abolished or at least shared mainly by the well-off, instead of being borne by the mass of small property owners as was the case.[49] Finally, they agitated for lowering the monopolistic prices charged by government enterprises, such as the railroads, postal and telegraph systems, and tobacco and salt monopolies. In short, the social democrats wanted the government to utilize the power to tax and spend as an instrument for a more equitable redistribution of wealth, for in this respect Japan was backward even compared to the most "capitalistic" nations of the West. Now and again the social democrats did make attempts to calculate in general monetary terms how much their social program would cost and from where the revenue should come,[50] but their main aim in doing so was to try to convince the voters that their program was sound and realistic.

The particular segment of the population the social democrats increasingly strove to impress with their financial soundness and hard-headed realism was the world of small business or what they called "medium and small trade and industry" (chūshō shōkōgyō).[51] However, from the very beginning the proletarian parties concerned

48. During this period, indirect taxes continued to supply 40 per cent or more of the total national revenue, if monopoly profits on tobacco and salt are included. "They weighed more heavily on the wage and salaried classes of the cities," states Lockwood, ibid., p. 524. For instance, the liquor tax alone yielded almost as much as all the national taxes on personal income, business profits and interest in 1933. As for the extensive duties on consumer goods, they cut most directly into real wage rates in the cities. Ibid., p. 543.

49. For a listing and explanation in English of local taxes, see George O. Totten, "Japanese Municipal Government Under Meiji and Taishō (1868–1925)," (M.A. thesis, Department of Public Law and Government, Columbia University, 1949), pp. 95–101. This was published in shortened form in Japanese: "Nihon no Shichōson Seido no Tokushitsu to Sono Seiritsu," Toshi Mondai (Municipal Problems), 44 (June 1953), 669–76 and (July 1953), 833–44.

50. For instance, see Nihon Rōdō Nenkan, 15 (1934), 439.

51. In the postwar period this term has been largely replaced by "medium and small enterprises" (chūshō kigyō), which in Japanese is somewhat easier to say.

themselves with what was a central problem of this class (as it was of the farmers), namely, capital availability or credit. The government was called on to take greater initiative in developing a system of finance or credit facilities (*kinyū seido*) for the proletarian class in its widest sense and to make loans without collateral security.

In Japan the quasi-public Industrial and Hypothec banks pioneered (especially after 1923) in extending low-interest loans to small traders and industrialists with the support of government guarantees and funds from the Deposits Bureau of the Ministry of Finance. The proletarian party policymakers had as a target the huge fund managed by the Deposits Bureau, made up of postal savings, with yearly deposits greatly in excess of those received by the private savings banks. These were the hard-earned savings of the great masses of people and amounted to about one fifth of the entire assets of all other banks and insurance and trust companies combined.[52] From the beginning the Social Democratic and soon the other proletarian parties called for the "democratization" of the use of this fund, suggesting that it might, for instance, be devoted to developing social welfare facilities. Originally in 1927 the Social Democratic Party proposed setting up publicly operated banks for the common people (*kōei shomin ginkō*). The Socialist Masses' Party continued the evolution of this idea, pressing for the establishment of "people's commercial and industrial banks" (*minshū shōkō kinko*), later called "national people's banks" (*kokuritsu minshū ginkō*). In 1936 and 1937 the socialists placed their bill for the establishment of such banks on a par of top priority with their proposed labor union and tenant-farmer union laws, designating them the "three bills."

By this time the party was clearly attempting to appeal to small business or the middle elements of society equally as much as to labor and the tenant farmers. For this purpose it had established an Urban Section (Shiminbu) to hammer out policies directed toward winning over these strata. The reasoning behind this trend, which became evident just before the Manchurian incident, was that the medium and small merchants and industrialists formed a section of society particularly susceptible to fascistic appeals. As one means of fighting this, the party decided on the strategy of winning over these strata to support social democracy and thus preventing them from

52. Lockwood, p. 515.

succumbing to native Japanese fascism "from below." [53] Even after the China incident, in the "renovationist policies" (when anti-fascism was no longer an issue), the party advocated arranging credit for manufacturing and commerce (as well as agriculture) along with the nationalization of the central banks and insurance companies.

With rising inflation and the gearing of the economy ever more to war production, financing became less of a problem. Then the issue of change of employment for small businessmen or conversion of their plants to war work came to the fore in party policies toward small business. The Japan-Laborite leaders in the Socialist Masses' Party advanced an idea for "easy money," which they termed "people's inflation" (taishū infurēshon). It contrasted with the inflationary policies of the early 1930s, which the government had returned to after a brief trial of retrenchment and deflation. The socialists criticized the government-inspired inflation as benefiting only the zaibatsu and capitalist class by draining large resources into armament and shoring up the top-heavy financial structure with "emergency funds" to banks and large companies which had gotten themselves into difficulties through speculation.

By "people's inflation" in 1934 the socialists meant: (1) channeling the flow of investment funds into many welfare projects, such as public works to relieve unemployment in cities and to mitigate distress in hard-hit agricultural areas; (2) raising the level of wages and salaries, while cutting down hours of work; (3) making credit readily available to small businesses; and (4) generally increasing the buying power of the masses and stabilizing their livelihood. They considered that only the state as the largest spender could stimulate this "people's inflation," which would benefit the broad base of the financial system instead of just the apex.

As inflationary policies at the top were continued, and especially after 1937 when the government practiced much less restraint in its power to create credit, the party turned from the people's inflation policy to advocating price controls and rationing. Already at earlier periods the Party had insisted on strong government control over the purchase and selling of rice. Then around 1935 when those farmers who were mainly engaged in silkworm raising were badly hit financially, the party called for government price-setting of cocoons and the rationing of rice to these farmers. Price controls on daily necessi-

53. See Chap. 4, p. 83, n. 24, for a discussion of fascism "from below."

ties, along with a strengthening of the emerging rationing system, finally become top priority items in the Wartime Renovationist Policies of late 1937 and thereafter. These policies, however, grew out of wartime exigencies rather than socialist principles.

More in line with socialist principles is the whole question of nationalization, and yet here, where one would expect to find the clearest demands, we run into a great deal of vague terminology. On the right wing of the proletarian movement in 1927, the Social Democratic Party called for the "socialization" (shakaika) of basic industries and finance, while, contrary to what one might expect, the leftist Labor Farmer Party raised no comparable demands.[54] The Socio-Democrats spelled out "socialization" as the state operation (kokuei) of transportation, electricity, gas, and water, central wholesale markets, and central banks. The term "state ownership" (kokuyū) was used only with respect to the demand for the nationalization of land; it was clear that public ownership, as by the state, prefecture, or municipality, was meant. In the early years all the proletarian parties were active in local struggles against utility rates. They sought first to bring the private utilities into public hands and secondly to lower rates. This was to be achieved through increased popular representation in local assemblies as well as by extraparliamentary pressures.

Still, the terms were not precise in their meaning. When the Socialist Masses' Party was founded, it called for "state management" (kokka kanri) of important industries such as steel, coal, electric power, transportation, communication, and others which were important from the standpoints of social progress, national defense, and the people's livelihood. Later on it was to be "state operation" of important industries; "state management" of credits, insurance, and foreign trade; and "state control" (kokka tōsei) of important agricultural produce. At other times these terms were switched around.

The social democrats explained their policies by claiming that pri-

---

54. It must be remembered that by this time stiff penalties were on the statutes against people who attempted to revise the system of private property. Yet, while the Meiji Constitution specifically protected private ownership, it also stipulated that property rights could be modified by law in the public interest. Perhaps one reason why the Labor Farmer Party was less willing to express itself on this issue than the more "moderate" Social Democrats was that it did not consider it worthwhile to run afoul of the law on this particular long-term issue, when so many immediate issues were more burning.

vate ownership meant exploitation of the workers; competition among capitalists (anarchism in production) resulted in surplus production relative to buying power, and this brought on depressions. When first formed, the Socialist Masses' Party criticized the conservative Seiyūkai and Minseitō proposals for economic "controls" as conducive to further cartelization and trust-building which in the end would limit production. The Kokumin Dōmei (Nationalist Federation), a party which had been formed the same year as the Socialist Masses' Party by the expansionist Kenzō Adachi, was attacked as "fascistic" for its proposal for a government-controlled national economy. The socialists at that time claimed that this proposal was only a refined example of policies advocated by conservative parties and furthermore promoted war mobilization.[55]

Its own program, however, eventually evolved into a plan for industrial mobilization for war. In the Wartime Renovationist Policies (of November 1937), "national economic planning" was clearly advocated as well as the integration of the Japanese economy with that of Manchoukuo and North China. With the new objective of "increasing production" added to that of "stabilizing the people's livelihood," the demands for state control became even more extensive: government operation of basic industries (electricity, coal, oil, and iron and steel); state management of imports, especially rice; state encouragement of exports; state control of foreign exchange; state management of war industries; state management of the central banks and insurance agencies; state supervision of financial (credit) facilities for manufacturing, commerce, and agriculture; and finally government monopoly of rice, fertilizer, sugar, sake, beer, and paper. To direct and coordinate this program, the Socialist Masses' Party called for the establishment of a "national economic planning commission," made up of the braintrusters of each government-managed industry and of each of the government banks, with additional members appointed by the government. The main function of this agency would be the planned development of the nation's power. It would be supervised by the Cabinet and the Diet.

But even the idea of this planning agency was not new. From its founding, the Socialist Masses' Party had inserted in its policies a

55. Shakai Taishūtō Jigyōbu, p. 56. Six years later, the Socialist Masses' Party was to change to such an extent that it planned a merger with the Kokumin Dōmei and the Eastern Association, but this did not take place because of a disagreement ostensibly over the presidency for the new party.

demand for a "National Economic Congress" (Kokumin Keizai Kaigi). This was spelled out in a 1933 proposal.[56] It was to be an organ for legislative investigation and drawing up of bills to be presented by the Cabinet to the Diet, concerning any economic or social questions, including labor and agrarian policies, and any aspect of nationalization. It was to be composed of about 300 representatives from the government, the military, labor, agrarian, and business organizations, the academic world, and others. Any bill it directed to be presented to the Diet a third time, after having been defeated twice before, must be passed. Thus, it would be a kind of supra-Diet planning board.

This proposal was coupled with one for an Oriental Economic Congress (Tōyō Keizai Kaigi), made up of representatives from Japan, the Soviet Union, Manchoukuo, China, Siam, the Philippines, and India. Under Japanese leadership, the Congress would jointly plan the elimination of all obstacles to the political and economic development of underdeveloped countries and would help raise them (including its own members) to a position of equality in the comity of nations. The overriding aim would be the preservation of world peace. These proposals, pushed primarily by the Japan-Labor clique, were resisted by the Labor-Farmer faction and to a lesser degree by the Socio-Democrats, on the basis that they were apt to develop along fascistic lines and depart from the principles of social democracy. They, nevertheless, found their way into the Socialist Masses' Party's policies every year with occasional changes in terminology, and they outlasted the party's avowed rejection of the social democratic label.

Since the socialists had so early proposed a kind of national planning board, it almost seemed as if the government were belatedly taking over an idea of the opposition party when it established the Cabinet Investigation Bureau (Naikaku Chōsakyoku) in 1935. In 1936, in parentheses following the demand for a National Economic Congress, the party called for a basic revision of the Cabinet Investigation Bureau and an end to the Cabinet Deliberative Council (Naikaku Shingikai). As it happened, the government soon expanded the Bureau into the Planning Office (Kikakuchō). When Prime Minister Konoe in October 1937 merged this with the Resources Bureau (Shigenkyoku) and expanded it into the Planning

56. The proposal is quoted in full in *Nihon Rōdō Nenkan, 15* (1934), 436–38.

Board (Kikakuin), as a headquarters for national mobilization, the socialists could only welcome this as a vindication of their own policies. In fact they urged that more powers be given the Planning Board.[57] The proposal for an Oriental Economic Congress was thus a kind of forerunner to what became the Asia Development Board (Kōain) of 1938 which later helped coordinate the Greater East Asia Coprosperity Sphere.

The notion that ever-increasing economic controls and greater economic planning would lead automatically to nationalization and a socialist economy was obviously mistaken at least in the conditions of prewar Japan. Yet in the party's support of the two most important bills to put Japan on a war footing, this kind of reasoning shines through. The social democrats could claim their own precedents for the first of these: the Electric Power State Management Bill (*Denryoku Kokka Kanri Hōan*) of 1938. The Social Democratic Party, for instance, as early as 1931 had drawn up a bill for the nationalization of electric power.[58] Its successor, the Socialist Masses' Party, saw the 1938 bill as the first step in a reform of the whole economy and observed that while water power was not covered in the

---

57. A number of liberal, social democratic, and Marxist scholars were brought into the Planning Board for research purposes. When the Sorge spy ring was discovered in 1941, the police became extremely suspicious and arrested a number of members of the Planning Board (this is known as the Planning Board incident). After World War II, some of these men became important leaders in the Social Democratic Party of Japan, notably Hiroo Wada, Seiichi Katsumada, and Tadataka Sata. The police claimed that the group was attempting to use the Communist idea of the "popular front" to infiltrate legitimate government for the purposes of bringing about socialism through national economic planning and preparing for a war which would result in the spread of Communism. Some of the people arrested had been brought in from the Shōwa Research Association (Shōwa Kenkyūkai) which had been set up in November 1936 to explore and popularize Prince Konoe's ideas. Richard Sorge's Japanese accomplice, Hotsumi Ozaki, was a member of that association; and so was Jusō Miwa of the Japan-Labor clique. Thus, in the late 1930s various strains of social democratic and Marxist thought were not without influence even within high government circles and the leaders of the Socialist Masses' Party was aware of this. Sorge's spy ring, of course, kept itself secret. Whether there was any conscious plot by the others is a moot question. For arguments in favor of the plot thesis, see Takeo Mitamura, *Sensō to Kyōsanshugi: Shōwa Seiji Hiroku* (War and Communism: A Secret Record of Shōwa Politics) (Tōkyō, Minshu Seido Fukyūkai, 1950), pp. 48–53 and 307–24. For a contrary view—that it was concocted by the police—see Shisō no Kagaku Kenkyūkai, ed., *Tenkō*, 2, 74–75. And for materials on the Shōwa Research Association, see Chalmers Johnson, *An Instance of Treason: Ozaki Hotsumi and the Sorge Spy Ring* (Stanford, Stanford University Press, 1964), pp. 114–17 and passim.

58. *Nihon Rōdō Nenkan, 18* (1932), 473.

bill, all sources of power should in the future pass under national control. Party leaders decided to give the bill unreserved support; they agitated for its passage both within and outside the Diet. Their efforts were dramatized by the physical assault on party leader Abe which took place at his home on March 3, 1938, by four thugs of the Anti-Communist Protect the Country Corps, allegedly hired by the wealthy power utilities and members of the major parties who opposed the bill.

Perhaps the single act most regretted by certain social democrats in the postwar period was their voting for the other bill to put Japan on a wartime footing: the National General Mobilization Law (*Kokka Sōdōin Hō*) on March 31, 1938. This was an enabling act which allowed the government to utilize all the nation's resources and business and professional personnel for the purposes of national mobilization during wartime simply by the issuance of imperial ordinances. By its power to regulate production, distribution, prices, wages, exports and imports, and to pay subsidies, build stockpiles, control capital issues, and so forth, it put in the hands of the government a carte blanche which was desired by the military as an instrumentality for bending the nation's economy to its own will.

On the surface, this law appeared fair in that it gave the government control over capital and labor equally, but the effect of the law would depend entirely on how it was administered. The Socialist Masses' Party leaders in supporting the bill added their desiderata that the government would completely overhaul its administrative structure, from the cabinet system down to local government. At the same time they asked for reforms in election procedures and in the powers of the House of Representatives and for functional representation in the House of Peers.[59] They cautioned the government not to endanger the people's livelihood in carrying out the provisions of the bill, and argued for an improved labor policy that would assure the cooperation of labor in the war effort.

It is undoubtedly true that this bill was the framework on which wartime control and planning of the economy were based, and it is also true that planning and government controls are usually associated with theories of socialism. Nevertheless, while the party representatives added their votes, along with those of the conservative and the "national socialist" parties, to the transfer of economic controls

59. *Shisō Geppō* (May 1938), pp. 99 ff.

to the government, their concern with how the people were to control or check the government planners remained hardly more than pious wishes.

In retrospect, it can be seen that many of the policies the Socialist Masses' Party pursued after the start of the China war had precedents in past proletarian platforms. A continuity in policy can be traced, but the emphasis had shifted from independent antigovernment campaigns by organized sections of the people to dependence on government-sponsored measures at the expense of popular controls and safeguards.

10: Foreign Policies: Anti-War to Pro-War

Conscious of their own weakness within the context of Japanese politics, proletarian party leaders undoubtedly derived self-confidence from feeling they were part of a world movement which was riding the wave of the future. This was especially clear in the case of the handful of men who secretly gathered together in 1922 to launch the Communist Party, dedicated, as it was, to the overthrow of the "emperor system" in Japan. How else could they have had such ambition, starting with so little in the way of organized labor strength in Japan?

The world situation also played a decisive role in the thinking of even those right-wing proletarian party leaders who looked to the British Labor Party and other more moderate social democratic movements for inspiration. But in general it appeared that the more leftist the leader or organization, the more important foreign policy statements were considered. The illegal Communists, of course, put top priority on "defense of the socialist fatherland," i.e. the Soviet Union. On the labor federation level, an examination of annual policies reveals that in 1925–28 the Communist-led Council of Japanese Labor Unions, and up to 1937 Kanjū Katō's National Council of Japanese Labor Unions devoted considerable space to foreign policy issues, in contrast to the Socio-Democratic Japan General Federation of Labor until its demise in 1940. The leftist proletarian parties castigated Japan's policies in the Manchurian incident, and in 1937 the Japan Proletarian Party led by Katō and Suzuki saw the popular front largely as a struggle to help prevent the outbreak of a world war.

The more right-wing proletarian parties—and this was true of the Socialist Masses' Party—stressed the idea that internal reform must come before a "people's" foreign policy could be expected. Nevertheless, popular discontent with the government's handling of foreign issues provided good ammunition, and thus even the center and right-wing proletarian leaders did formulate critical attitudes on international questions of the day.

It can be argued that for a political party "horizontal" links necessarily exist among its various foreign and domestic policies at any particular time. When a Japanese proletarian party, for instance, decided that Japan's interests in China should be "protected," it would have to harden its attitudes toward Britain and the United States and also be more respectful of military budgets. It can further be argued, however, that most policies simultaneously reveal "vertical" links with the past. They tend to develop a life and a tradition of their own. When the Socialist Masses' Party, for example, changed its China policy, it had to explain this change in terms of its former positions, using the same terminology to mean something different, and even denying that the policy had been more than slightly altered. The attempt will be made in this chapter, as in the last, to isolate and categorize various policies and detect how they changed over time.

The touchstone of foreign policy attitudes among the proletarian parties, as with those of the Japanese government for that matter, was the China question. Attitudes toward Britain, for instance, were shaped largely in terms of how British policy was affecting Japanese goods in the China market. The emphasis of this chapter, therefore, lies on the China question with its two milestones of change: the Manchurian and China incidents, which, as we have already seen, affected the parties' internal policies, the nature of their support, and in fact their very survival. Thereafter attention will be focused on the proletarian parties' attitudes toward international bodies, their views on the West with regard to migration and colonialism, and their policies toward the Soviet Union. Before examining the particular policies on China, however, the general orientation of proletarian thinking on foreign policy will be discussed, showing how much all four national proletarian parties had in common in 1926.

PEOPLE'S DIPLOMACY

With one voice the proletarian parties demanded "people's (or democratic) diplomacy" *(kokumin,* or *minshū, gaikō).* By this they meant the carrying out of a global policy fashioned by the Japanese people. It would be a policy dedicated to raising living standards throughout the world, because only such a policy would be in the real interests of the masses, whether Japanese or not. It would thus be identified with the underdog as against the powerful; the colored races of the world as against the white; the "oppressed peoples" as against the "imperialists"; and the "have-not" nations as against the "haves." But it also meant a class (or anticapitalist) orientation, and was opposed to official policies which were condemned as "bourgeois." That is, it opposed Japanese capitalist imperialism replacing British and American domination of Asia. But, to insure that Japan would not pursue "aggressive" or "bourgeois" policies, it was emphasized that reform had first to take place in Japan.

An element of people's diplomacy was opposition to secret diplomacy, a concept inherent in diplomacy by and for the people. Here were echoes of Woodrow Wilson's words about "open agreements openly arrived at." This plank was supported by all the left-wing and center proletarian parties up to the time of the Manchurian incident, though it was not a central theme.

Soon after its founding, the Socialist Masses' Party defined what it called "renovationist (or progressive) people's diplomacy" *(kakushin kokumin gaikō),* as a "holy war" based on the "will of humanity" designed to bring light to the dark places of the earth—that is, to bring equality to the weaker peoples who were suffering under exploitation. "Renovationist people's diplomacy" should be the basic moral policy of Japan, as "League diplomacy" was for Britain and France, the "renunciation of war" for the United States, and "nonaggression pacts" for the Soviet Union. In attacking capitalism and imperialism in other countries, this policy contained an implied criticism of Japan. Yet, it was explicitly stated that this policy would not countenance the "decline" of the Japanese people. Through promoting the class interests of the great majority, it would take full responsibility for the people's "continued existence" (ei'ensei). In the long run, it was averred, Japan would be destroyed by capitalism, but by the same token, Japan could be brought to life only by socialism.[1]

After the outbreak of the China incident in 1937, when the Socialist Masses' Party attempted to justify its support of the war as "not a change in direction," it quoted the earlier statement about the party taking full responsibility for the continued existence of the Japanese. From a reading of that tortured rationale against the actual change of policy, it is clear that "renovationist people's diplomacy" had come to mean something different. It was now defined as "planning for the realization of the national ideals (minzoku risō) of Japan, at the dawn of a new structure for peace in the Far East made possible by the occurrence of the China incident." [2] Before the incident the phrase had an antigovernment connotation but afterward it came to mean reforms for the better prosecution of the war.

In 1926 the proletarian parties went on record as opposing "imperialistic" or "capitalistic" war.[3] This meant that with each advance of Japanese arms on the continent, the problem arose as to whether Japan's move was "imperialistic" or "defensive." How such problems were dealt with will be discussed below. At this point it is sufficient to note that the Socialist Masses' Party's main foreign policy goal was world peace. There was little need to change this after 1937, because Japanese forces subsequently overran most of Asia in the name of establishing "peace" in the Far East.

When proletarian party policies were first formulated in 1926 the principle of racial equality was not stated as such, but was implied in such items as the Labor Farmer Party's demand for elimination of

1. Shakai Taishūtō (Socialist Masses' Party), *Kiki ni Tatsu Kokusai Seikyoku* (The International Situation in Crisis) (Tōkyō, Shadaitō Shuppambu, 1936), pp. 2–10: Naimushō Keihokyoku, *Shuppambutsu o Tsūjite Mitaru Nihon Kakushin Ron no Genkyō*, pp. 309–10; and *Nihon Rōdō Nenkan, 15* (1934), 444–45.

2. See *Shakai Taishū Shimbun* (November 30, 1937), p. 2, under "Foreign Policy."

3. There seems to have been no fear by the proletarian parties that the Soviet Union would start a war, but the right-wing social democrats followed the line of the Second International in accusing the Communists of trying to take advantage of wars to spread communism instead of really opposing war. See, for example, Kanichiro Kamei and Suejirō Yoshikawa, *Shakaishugiteki Gaikō Ron* (On Socialist Foreign Policy) (Tōkyō, Kurarasha, 1930), Chaps. 1 and 2.

discrimination in colonial areas and the Social Democratic Party's plank for "liberation of the oppressed races" and freedom for immigration into any country. After the Manchurian incident, the Socialist Masses' Party called upon the world for recognition of racial equality for the Japanese and in addition for equal access to, redistribution of, and freedom to exploit the natural resources of the world. To the plank for "liberation of the oppressed peoples," which its predecessors had urged, the Socialist Masses' Party significantly added one for "aid" to the peoples of Asia. Here again were principles that fitted in with what eventually became the concept of the Greater East Asia Coprosperity Sphere and thus did not have to be dropped, though some modifications were made. When demanding access to raw materials and free trade, for instance, the party originally had protested against the various economic barriers which other countries erected in attempts at autarky, keeping Japanese goods out. But when Japan began to set up her own economic bloc with Manchuria and China, the party supported bloc tariffs on the rationale that Japan was helping her neighbors throw off their backward status— that is, Japan was now actively helping to "liberate the oppressed races."

Up until 1937, the proletarian parties attacked the "dual diplomacy" of Japan, finding the "weak" policies of the Foreign Office at Kasumigaseki equally as objectionable as the "tough" line of the General Staff Office of the military at Miyakezaka. As late as 1936, the Socialist Masses' Party attacked the military's "continental policy" as a "simple-minded survival-of-the-fittest philosophy." [4] But at the same time the party rebuked the traditional Foreign Office policies for simply trailing after the European and American lead, which was not fit behavior for an independent, civilized nation. Thus, they did not advocate replacing the Kasumigaseki with the Miyakezaka approach, or even blending the two, but building foreign policy on the will of the people which should find joint expression in unity between the General Staff and the Foreign Office. They advocated "peaceful means" to achieve the objectives of foreign policy, but by directing their fire equally, at the already declining Foreign Office and the ascendant military, it is an open question as to whether the social democrats did not thereby play into the hands of the latter.

In this fashion, the Japanese proletarian parties attempted to make

4. *Kiki ni Tatsu Kokusai Seikyoku*, p. 5.

it appear that they had maintained a continuity of principles, despite the very real changes in content and significance. This was the background against which more specific policies were rationalized.

ATTITUDES TOWARD THE CHANGING CHINA QUESTION

While the China question was always at the forefront of Japanese proletarian party foreign policy thinking, it developed in three different stages, increasingly vital, during the prewar period. When the parties were called upon to formulate their China policies for their first electoral combats in 1927 and 1928 on the local and national levels, they were faced with a rising Chinese revolutionary movement on the continent which was just beginning to split into the Nationalist and Communist camps. It was easy to attack the Japanese government's response to this as both bellicose and clumsy. During the second period the Japanese government's initiative in the Manchurian incident caused a social democratic agonizing reappraisal. Finally, full acceptance of the China war in 1937 marked the beginning of the last period.

During these three periods social democratic attitudes toward the Chinese Nationalists altered radically. The unanimity of support for the Kuomintang became differentiated among the proletarian parties during the first period by events in China. During the second and third periods, the Socialist Masses' Party became critical of the Chinese Nationalists' lack of understanding of Japan's "legitimate interests" in China. The criticism increased when it appeared that the Kuomintang had again turned to collaboration with the Chinese Communists after the Sian incident in December 1936. This prepared the ground for condemnation of the Kuomintang and acceptance of the Wang Ching-wei regime in Nanking in 1939. As time passed, the party's attitude gradually approximated the government's. It was in the first period that proletarian criticism of official policies was sharpest and most concerned with the Chinese revolution.

Because events in China were stealing the headlines and because criticism of government policies provided such good campaign material, the China issue dominated the foreign policy statements of the proletarian parties during their first electoral tests in 1927 and 1928.

Riding a wave of antiforeign feeling unprecedented in China since the Boxer Uprising of 1900, the Chinese revolutionary coalition of Nationalist and Communist forces swept northward. Starting in July 1926, the first "northern expedition" successfully occupied Hunan, Hupeh, Kiangsi, and Anhwei in three months. In November it was decided at a Kuomintang Central Committee meeting to move the Nationalist government from Canton to Hankow. But many of the rightists and their rising young leader, Chiang Kai-shek, were busy at the battle front and could not attend. Angered, they opposed the decision. Nevertheless, a compromise was soon reached whereby it was decided that the political part of the government, dominated by a coalition of moderates and leftists, would move to Hankow and that the military headquarters would be set up at Nanchang. The "northern expedition" resumed and in March 1927 Nanking was captured, setting off antiforeign riots that caused foreign intervention. The riots may have been touched off by leftists wanting to embarrass Chiang.

Then on March 23, Chiang and his troops approached the suburbs of Shanghai. This action was coordinated with an uprising within the city led by Communists and other leftists, who occupied the police stations and municipal government headquarters, before Chiang's troops marched into the city the following day. At this point the internal alliance between the Nationalists and Communists reached the breaking point. Chiang turned upon the workers and their Communist leaders with merciless fury, succeeding on April 12, by coup d'état in bringing the Shanghai area under his control, except for the foreign settlements. Chiang may have made secret agreements with the foreign powers, including Japan, but they nevertheless reinforced their troops there.

Six days later, on April 18, Chiang set up a new government in Nanking, challenging the left and center Kuomintang government in Hankow—which soon capitulated—and asked for de jure as well as de facto recognition from the foreign powers. By the end of the year the region south of the Yangtse fell under the control of the Nanking government. Subjugation of the various warlords who held North China in their grip remained the main objective of the first phase of the program formulated by Dr. Sun Yat-sen, which was "military consolidation." This was to be followed by a phase of "political tutelage" in order to prepare the people for the exercise of "democracy."

Just at this time, on April 20, 1927, the Seiyūkai Cabinet of General Giichi Tanaka took over from the Kenseikai and announced a new "more positive" policy toward China than that which the preceding Foreign Minister, Shidehara, had enunciated. The first concrete decision announced on May 27 was the sending of Japanese troops to Shantung. This, along with internal troubles, convinced Chiang to call off an immediate expedition further northward. Actually Japanese military actions during the Shidehara period were not as conciliatory as his speeches and under Tanaka not as decisive as the boldness of his approach. In any case, Tanaka's bluntness provoked opposition from the Kenseikai and even more, from the newly arisen proletarian parties.

The leaders of the Social Democratic Party had followed the Chinese revolution closely. One of them, Ryūsuke Miyazaki, knew Dr. Sun Yat-sen personally and was considered an expert on the question. They sympathized with the anti-imperialist position of the Kuomintang, approved of Sun's Three People's Principles due to their own experiences in Japan, and sympathized with Chiang's struggle against the leftists. Even before the Tanaka government came in, the Social Democrats on March 3, 1927, protested the strengthening of Japanese troops in Shanghai in the face of the Kuomintang advance. They demanded nonintervention in the internal development of China, and on April 2 circularized the Foreign Office, the War and Navy Ministries, and the conservative parties to this effect. They heartily approved of Chiang's coup in Shanghai and decided to dispatch Miyazaki and Komakichi Matsuoka to Shanghai early in May. Following a warm welcome by labor unions and the local Kuomintang, they proceeded on to Nanking where they met with Chiang Kai-shek and the venerated revolutionary Hu Han-min and reached an agreement for international solidarity between the Kuomintang and the Social Democratic Party. Upon their return in June, the party issued a long statement attacking Tanaka's decision to dispatch troops to Shantung, maintaining that such a move, by hindering Chiang's northern expedition, only aroused anti-Japanese feeling and brought on boycotts which directly threatened the livelihood of workers in Japan.[5] Although the Japanese troops were not withdrawn until September, no violence occurred.

5. The statement is quoted in Hakuyōsha, ed., *Nihon Musan Seitō Shi*, pp. 288–89. At the same time the party set up a Conference on the China Question (Taishi Mondai

During the summer of 1927, meanwhile, Tanaka held an important conference on continental policy from which the so-called "Tanaka Memorial" was supposed to have emerged. Although that document was not "exposed" by the Chinese until 1929, it was already clear (as stated in the "Memorial") that the Japanese government considered it had "special privileges" in Manchuria and Mongolia. This the Social Democratic Party criticized and advocated that Japan take the lead in returning "imperialistic privileges" in China. Meanwhile, having suffered some military reverses, Chiang Kai-shek resigned his position in the Nanking government and retired to Japan in August 1927 where he remained until called back in January 1928 as Commander-in-Chief. While there he did not publicize any contacts he may have had with Social Democratic leaders. On his return to China he immediately began the northern expedition again, only to be confronted with a transfer of Japanese troops to Tsinan (Shantung) and a dispatch of fresh forces from Japan. Violence broke out on May 9, 1928, when Japanese troops began to expel the newly arrived Chinese from Tsinan by force.

The Social Democrats deplored the "Tsinan affair" but blamed it on the "reactionary" China policy of the Tanaka government. It was, however, the embarrassments caused the Tanaka Cabinet by the assassination on June 3 of Marshal Chang Tso-lin, who was fleeing Peking before the advance of Kuomintang troops, that on July 2 brought about the downfall of the Tanaka government which had dealt so harshly with the Japanese Communists and the Labor Farmer Party in the March 15 arrests. This was cause for great elation among the remaining proletarian parties, as well as in the opposition Minseitō.

The Labor Farmer Party's concern for the Chinese revolution had grown as it became more leftist-oriented in 1926. It maintained that the Japanese proletariat, which stood in the forefront of the struggle for the liberation of the oppressed peoples of the Orient, had great respect and sympathy for the Chinese nationalist movement which was striving against the colonial powers and the warlord "running

---

Kyōgikai) which gained the participation of some important scholars and publicists from outside the party. Among them was Tanzan Ishibashi, who became a conservative Prime Minister after the war (December to February 1957) as well as Professor Sakuzō Yoshino. Other members included Kamekichi Takahashi, Kōtoku Mizuno, Rō Nagano, Hyō Hara, Jikichirō Kawahara, Eiichirō Hirano, and Hidesaburō Suzuki.

dogs" of imperialism. It called for immediate recognition of the
Hankow government and for noninterference of the Japanese government in the internal affairs of China. Then as the Kuomintang
was moving north toward Shanghai in March 1927, the Labor
Farmer Party responded to a call for support from the Kuomintang
branch in Tōkyō to all the proletarian parties by organizing a Federation Against Interference in China (Taishi Hikanshō Dōmei) together with the Japan Labor-Farmer Party on April 28, 1927, which
then attacked Tanaka's China policy.[6]

This was shortly after Chiang had turned on the Communists in
Shanghai. The situation remained confused, however, because the
center and left-wing Kuomintang government at Hankow held on
into the autumn. Although anti-Communist purges were also going
on in Hankow, several Communist uprisings occurred through the
end of the year, before it was finally clear that the Chinese Reds
could not recapture control of at least part of the Kuomintang.
While its ardor for supporting the Kuomintang as such quickly
cooled after April, the Labor Farmer Party stepped up its agitation
against Japanese intervention in China. For instance, in July, the
party, in cooperation with the Federation Against Interference in
China, decided to send observers to China on the basis of support it
had aroused, its targets being workers, farmers, students, women,
Koreans, and members of the Leveling Society. Ritsuta Noda and two
other party and labor leaders took the train from Tōkyō and stopped
along the way to hold rallies. All were arrested before they could actually leave the country; they had agitated under such slogans as
"Hands off China!" and "Pull our troops out!"

The successors to the Labor Farmer Party repeated strongly the
demand for nonintervention in China. Just after the Tsinan affair,
the Preparatory Committee for the Organization of a New Party sent
requests to the other proletarian parties to join it in a nationwide
"opposition week" (May 19–25, 1928) to oppose not only the dispatch of troops to China but also the insertion of the death penalty
in the Peace Preservation Law. But the Social Democratic and Japan
Labor-Farmer Parties would not be prevailed upon to associate
themselves with the Committee so soon after the mass arrests. Alone,
the Committee was unsuccessful in arousing much popular support.[7]

6. Ibid., pp. 496–98.
7. This is on their own admission, ibid., p. 572.

"Noninterference in China" was, however, carried over into the basic program of the New Labor Farmer Party.

The Japan Labor-Farmer Party, shortly after its founding at the end of 1926, gave blanket endorsement to the revolutionary Kuomintang government. It also strongly opposed interference in China and the sending of troops. But true to its role as the "center" of the proletarian front, it decided to lean neither toward left-wing Hankow nor to the rightist Nanking factions when the Kuomintang split in April 1927.

After the fall of the Hankow government, Chiang's ascendancy at Nanking, and the bloody suppression of the leftist Canton uprising, the Japan Labor-Farmer Party leaders gradually reacted against the Kuomintang as a whole. They began criticizing the Social Democratic Party for calling for recognition of the Chinese Nationalist government. They claimed that the Kuomintang represented the "bourgeoisie" of China which was brutally trying to suppress the Chinese proletarian movement. They did not mention the Chinese Communists by name but they implied that the various leftist anti-Kuomintang groups should be supported. They were more concerned, however, with criticizing Japan's actions than with trying to aid any specific Chinese groups.[8] This remained substantially the party's position throughout its various subsequent metamorphoses.

Whatever the factional evaluations among the various proletarian parties concerning the Kuomintang and the course of the Chinese revolution, their public appeal for a military withdrawal from China rested on the reasoning that the presence of Japanese troops in an awakening China could only arouse resentment against Japan. The resultant Chinese resistence in any form, whether boycotts of Japanese goods or physical fighting, would adversely affect the livelihood of the Japanese masses.

In the years following the Tsinan affair, these proletarian warnings proved justified. Some of the radical Japanese military, however, reasoned quite differently from the same set of facts. For them, Chinese resistance only demonstrated the necessity for further penetration of China before it would be too late. Since they decided to take

8. Members of the Labor-Farmer faction, however, remained sharply critical of the Kuomintang even after they joined the party in 1928 when it became the Japan Masses' Party. See Naimushō Keihokyoku, *Shuppan Keisatsu Hō* (Police Reports on Publications) (March 1929), pp. 21–23.

the initiative, it was not long before Japanese troops overran all of Manchuria.

How great a trauma the outbreak of the Manchurian incident caused in proletarian ranks has already been described (in Chapter 4). It was also pointed out that the Social Democratic Party rationalized its acceptance of the situation with less difficulty than its rival, the National Labor-Farmer Masses' Party, and yet the new surge of nationalism caused national socialist breakoffs from both of these parties. A fuller examination of the foreign policy attitudes of these two parties will provide a basis for understanding the degree of change in the policies of their successor, the Socialist Masses' Party.

It will be recalled that the right-wing position within the Social Democratic Party at the time was articulated by Akamatsu, who was soon to bolt to national socialism. While still in the party he argued, "We should be allowed to develop freely on the Chinese mainland or on the American continent. Is it not strange that those who would prevent us from doing so chastize us in the name of 'justice'? We must justify the actions of Japan in the name of the absolute right to exist." At the same time, he advocated in vague but nevertheless forceful terms "an end to bourgeois control over Manchuria and Mongolia and a conversion to national socialist policies." [9]

Yet even the majority within the Social Democratic Party supported Japan's right to obtain colonies. Nishio, for instance, expressed this view at the Sixteenth International Labor Conference in Geneva in April 1932:

> The majority of delegates attending this Conference are of the white race, representing the various countries of Europe. The white race, which once had only one fourteenth of the land of the world, has now taken over more than three fifths of the entire globe and has subjected more than one third of the world's population to its domination. It has concluded anti-war pacts which have guaranteed territorial possessions and permanent peace under conditions extremely unfavorable to the colored races. Are the International Labor Organization and the League of Nations going to set up policies of appeasement, recognizing this illogical state of affairs, this unfair present situation? [10]

9. *Nihon Minshū Shimbun* (October 15, 1931).
10. *Rōdō* (July 1932), p. 6.

He was, of course, referring critically to the Lytton Commission, which the League of Nations had sent to investigate Japan's actions in Manchuria. Furthermore, he was implying a demand for equal opportunity for the Japanese, along with the European "superior races" in the pursuit of colonies.

The Akamatsu and majority factions were able to reach agreement on the justice of Japan's actions in Manchuria on the basis of a report by a delegation sent there by the party, consisting of Tetsu Katayama, Yūzō Shimanaka, and Shirō Koike. This agreement took form in "The Decision Concerning the Problem of Manchuria and Mongolia" drawn up at the Party's Central Committee meeting of November 22, 1931. After rejecting (1) the "bourgeois" policy of taking Manchuria to save capitalism, (2) the "Communist" position of pulling out of Manchuria, and (3) the "liberal" stand advocating "appeasement" of the League of Nations, the decision stated the party's own view that (1) the Chinese were as responsible as the Japanese for the situation, (2) in order to protect the Japanese people's right to survival, Japanese treaty rights should be protected, and (3) bourgeois control over Manchuria and Mongolia must be brought to an end and a socialist state erected to provide a joint economy for both the Chinese and Japanese. The only way they saw for the realization of this foreign policy objective, however, was first to effect the overthrow of capitalism in Japan.[11]

The newly reorganized National Labor-Farmer Masses' Party, on the other hand, took a very different position. While this was indicated earlier, at this point we can note to what extent the party kept to its founding principles, which included opposition to war and imperialism. On September 29, 1931, at a special meeting of the Standing Central Committee, the following statement was approved: "We firmly oppose the imperialistic policy being pursued by the government and the military toward our neighbor, China, since this is pregnant with the danger of bringing on a world war. We demand that the government withdraw the troops and cease interference in the internal politics of China, and we will fight to the end against the ascendancy of the militiary."[12] How prophetic the first part of this statement turned out to be, and how ironic the latter part! Within

11. The whole statement was published in *Nihon Minshū Shimbun* (December 15, 1931). It was also reprinted in *Nihon Rōdō Nenkan, 13* (1932), 475–76.

12. A partial quotation may be found in Naka, *Senkusha no Keifu,* p. 167.

the party, a Committee to Fight for the Withdrawal of Troops from China, headed by Ōyama, was set up ten days after the outbreak of the war. After a reorganization, in which the name was changed to the Anti-War Struggle Committee and the chairmanship shifted to the ill Sakai, the Committee worked out a lengthy policy statement (which was printed but banned by the police).[13]

The statement characterized the Manchurian incident as an attempt by "imperialist Japan" to make Manchuria and Mongolia into colonies. It called Japan's "special interests" there nothing better than "plunder" from the Sino-Japanese and Russo-Japanese wars. Although the statement avoided any discussion of either the Chinese Nationalists or the Communists, it scoffed at the "naïve" slogan of the Social Democrats to the effect that Manchuria should be socialized and transferred to the control of the proletarian masses. Such slogans, it maintained, aided the Japanese militarists by confusing the workers. And even though it appeared that the military had engineered the incident, the only ones to benefit ultimately were the narrow circles of "finance capital."

This policy, it will be recalled, was challenged by Yojirō Matsutani, the party's representative in the Diet who held the post of Party Advisor. On October 16, 1931, about a month after the outbreak of the incident, Matsutani with a group of other Diet members left Tōkyō for a three-week tour of inspection of Manchuria and Shanghai. The report he issued on his return called for support of Japan's interests in Manchuria and Mongolia and advocated that these interests be taken from the capitalists and handed over to the workers and peasants. Since this ran counter to the position of the party leaders, the report caused a sensation within party ranks. The leadership had reasoned that if pressure could be brought against the Japanese government to abandon its special privileges in Manchuria, Japanese capitalism would thereby be weakened and the dawn of socialism brought that much nearer. Matsutani (and his sympathizers in the Social Democratic Party, such as Akamatsu) countered by labeling this position communistic and arguing that giving up Japa-

13. Zenkoku Rōnō Hansen Tōsō Iinkai (Antiwar Struggle Committee of the National Labor-Farmer Masses' Party), ed., *Mammō Mondai to Musan Kaikyū* (The Manchurian and Mongolian Question and the Proletarian Class) (Tōkyō, Zenkoku Rōnōtō Shuppambu, 1932). According to a handwritten marking on the Library of Congress copy of this book, which was confiscated from the Ministry of Home Affairs, it was banned by the police.

nese interests in Manchuria would only strengthen Chinese capitalism and condemn Japan to the status of a third-rate power and the Japanese masses to no hope of raising their standard of living.[14] Matsutani reasoned further that since friction existed between the military on the one hand and the zaibatsu finance capitalists (represented again by Foreign Minister Shidehara) on the other, the military could be persuaded to keep finance capital out of Manchuria so that it could become a socialist state under the leadership of anticapitalist military men. The majority would not go along with this position, however, and Matsutani was read out of the party.

By the time of the party's convention in December 1931, the atmosphere in the country had become so tense that the police in attendance ordered the convention to disband before it was finished in order to prevent the party from officially expressing its "opposition to imperalistic war." Already, however, Asō had begun to make those contacts with civilian fascists and young officers that in 1934 eventuated in his support of the "military pamphlets."

Although the Socialist Masses' Party, when it was formed, did not oppose Japan's actions in Manchuria, neither was its attitude one of positive support. After the establishment of Manchoukuo and its official recognition by Japan in September 1932, the party demanded that the new nation become self-governing and independent and that Japan transfer to it all local Japanese extraterritorial rights. Thus, the party carried over the Socio-Democratic clique's idea that it would not be possible for Japan and Manchoukuo fully to harmonize their economies unless they became socialist. It also opposed the view that Japan and Manchoukuo alone could form a closed autarkic bloc and advocated rather a "joint economy" including China and other nations on a voluntary basis.[15]

In further defining its position, the party opposed the so-called "liberal" view on Manchuria which held that Manchuria should be returned to China, for this erroneously implied that Manchoukuo was merely a puppet state. The party also opposed the so-called "zaibatsu" view that Manchoukuo should be a colonial dependency (zokuryō shokuminchi). The party's position was that Manchoukuo

14. Katsumaro Akamatsu, Shin Kokumin Undō no Kichō, pp. 86–93.

15. See "Tōmen no Kokusai Seisaku Yōkō" (An Outline of Present International Policies), approved October 1, 1932. This is quoted in Nihon Rōdō Nenkan, 14 (1933), 478–79.

should be made into a completely independent nation for the "Manchurian people," based on the principle of self-determination. Government officials in Manchoukuo should not be Japanese nationals but natives preferably of Manchurian descent, free from control by Japan. Japanese rights should be returned to Manchuria and a new friendly relationship should be fostered between Japan and Manchoukuo.[16]

What gave plausibility to the party's position were the statements and activities of the Kwantung Army in Manchuria. Particularly since the start of the depression about 1929, army propaganda had utilized anticapitalist sentiments to attack so-called "zaibatsu-dominated party governments." As soon as the dust began to settle after the Manchurian affair, the army announced that the new Manchoukuo was to have a planned economy, in which entrepreneurs would not be allowed a free hand and the zaibatsu were to be excluded from positions of control. In March 1933 the Manchoukuo government made public an Economic Construction Program that emphasized state planning. The army also set about to foster a "Manchurian" national feeling particularly among the Mongols, Manchus, and settled Chinese (Hans), although in order to keep anti-Japanese antagonism from being expressed, the new state was to observe equality not only among those three "races" but with Japanese, Koreans, and other minority groups. Most important official government posts were duly staffed with Manchus or Mandarin Chinese, although Japanese "advisors" were placed at the elbow of each. Thus, with regard to economic planning and "Manchurian" nationalism, the Socialist Masses' Party was in apparent harmony with the military.

In a fundamental respect, however, the party's attitude differed from that of the military, but this aspect seldom came to the surface in public documents. The difference was with regard to the necessity for war. For the army leaders, the taking over of Manchuria constituted only one step in the expansion of the Japanese Empire. They accepted the prospect that this might in time involve Japan in war with the U.S.S.R. and perhaps also eventually with Great Britain and the United States. We have just seen how, before the creation of the Socialist Masses' Party, the National Labor-Farmer Masses' Party

16. Ibid., *15* (1934), 445–46. Since so few actual descendants of Manchus existed, if taken literally this would mean that Manchoukuo would be governed by a tiny minority. If "Manchurian people" meant simply persons born in Manchuria, this would be a guarded way of saying the Chinese majority.

convention was dissolved by the police to prevent it from officially expressing its "opposition to imperialistic war." The Social Democratic leaders, who had been abroad much more, were equally opposed to the spread of war at this time. When Asō later advocated cooperation with the military, it was at least initially for internal reconstruction rather than in acquiescence in the necessity for war.

Nevertheless, even in other respects, the Socialist Masses' Party tried to promote a "socialist" Manchuria free from zaibatsu control. Public means for financing Manchurian economic development were favored. In criticizing the government's budget in the 65th Diet in 1934, the party's Diet members opposed any increase in military expenditures at the expense of relief measures in Japan, although they did approve of special aid for reconstruction in Manchuria and Mongolia and proposed that this should be financed by low interest public bonds. They also advocated purchasing the Chinese Eastern Railway from the Soviet Union and incorporating it into the South Manchurian Railway system in order that the Manchoukuo economy might better be able to stand on its own feet. The Soviet Union had approached Japanese authorities in May 1933 about the sale of the line, but because of haggling over the terms, the transaction was not consummated until 1935.

The party's basic policies on Manchuria were thus twofold: (1) opposition to the return to capitalistic policies in Manchoukuo and (2) real independence for Manchoukuo.[17] By 1936 the party was becoming alarmed at clear evidences that the army was modifying its policy of keeping the zaibatsu out, at least the "new zaibatsu," for in that year a representative of the latter, Yoshisuke Aikawa, was invited to inspect the progress of economic development there with a view to inducing greater capital investment from private sources.[18] As for the independence of Manchoukuo, the party continued to advocate the transfer of all Japanese rights to the government of Manchoukuo, while at the same time promoting stronger economic ties with Japan for the purpose of "economic construction" in both countries.

These two policies, the party held, constituted a new approach and one which was based on the realistic analysis that Japan was both a

17. Excerpts of all major Socialist Masses' Party foreign policies to early 1936 may be found in Shisō Geppō, 23 (May 1936).

18. F. C. Jones, Manchuria Since 1931 (New York, Oxford University Press, 1949), pp. 147–48.

sea and a land power.[19] As a sea power, Japan's actions were basically "capitalistic." Her taking over Tsingtao and her penetration of Shanghai differed only in cultural respects from what the British did in Hong Kong and Shanghai, or for that matter, what the Chinese capitalist cliques were doing in Chekiang. Continuing along this line, the party argued, would only lead to failure, because Japan's economy was actually weaker than that of Britain and other imperialist powers.

As a land power, Japan was extending its military might to China. Here the nature of the conflict was different. Japan was actually fighting Communists instead of competing with other capitalist powers. Russia was opposing Japan by use of Chinese "Communist bandits" (Kyōsan hi) and they must be rooted out. The difficulty, they recognized, was that the Chinese Reds were actually giving the peasants better local government than the warlords had provided. It was thus necessary for the Japanese army to offer them a still better alternative in terms of local government, economic opportunity, and cultural life. To be successful on mainland China, Japanese policies would have to be progressive and socialist.

This was not yet the case. The military usually did no more than cooperate with the warlords in combating Communist partisans, which was "reactionary." On the other hand, the Foreign Office was cooperating with the Chiang Kai-shek government, which, while being in part used by Russia, was also supported by British capital which was fundamentally antagonistic to Japan. The party held both of these approaches to be wrong. Japan should have a "unified, progressive" policy toward China which must be accompanied by, or preceded by, "socialist, renovationist" policies at home.

Incidentally, it should be mentioned that the Socio-Democratic clique's earlier sanguine view of the Kuomintang had been soured by the mid-1930s. The majority of the party now held that, although the Kuomintang had largely succeeded in doing away with the erratic exploitation of the populace by the scattered warlords, this had been

19. This and the following material is from the interesting report of a five-man delegation, headed by Kanichirō Kamei, which the party sent to China in 1935: *Kiki ni Tatsu Kokusai Seikyoku*, pp. 34 ff. (cited above p. 251, n. 1). The other members of the delegation were Shigeo Abe, Manabu Hirano, Sen Watanabe, and Yoshio Matsunaga. Instead of issuing a report only on their immediate experiences, they worked out a critical evaluation of the whole world situation based in part on their observations in China. This was to serve as the party's explanation of its foreign policies for the next general election which took place in the spring of 1936.

replaced by the more systematic "legal exploitation" of the people by the Kuomintang, which was even worse.

It can be seen that the Socialist Masses' Party had already laid the basis for the subsequent development of its foreign policies, because it accepted the necessity of fighting the indirect influence of both Communist Russia and capitalist Britain in the arena of China and also because it held that it was possible for the Japanese military to carry out a "progressive" policy in China, even though certain military actions were to be criticized.

After the outbreak of the China incident in July 1937, the Socialist Masses' Party gave immediate support to the government in its "holy war" (seisen) in China. The party revised its program, called for "national unity" (kyokoku itchi), and sent a delegation to encourage the soldiers at the front.[20] The party affirmed the immediate cause of the war to be the recent anti-Japanese policies of the Nationalist Government of China, but beyond that saw them as machinations of the Soviet Union and the Comintern to communize China, on the one hand, and of British and American capital to colonize China, on the other. By putting an end to these processes, the party claimed, China could be made self-governing, independent, and true to its indigenous history and national character.[21]

The party advocated the creation of a new structure of peace in the Far East on the basis of an axis of the three countries, Japan, Manchoukuo, and China. Such should be the positive purpose of the "holy war" to which the Japanese people were dedicated in the hope that their sacrifices would be for the benefit of human culture. But in order to make her fit for this high task, Japan must reform internally. On the basis of this rationalization, the party was able to devote most of its attention to specific proposals in its program for domestic renovation.

Because of its international connections, the party felt it could play a role in the war effort by rallying foreign opinion to the side of Japan. Bunji Suzuki, now an Advisor to the party, immediately volunteered to become a "people's ambassador" (kokumin shisetsu) and go to the United States to explain the Japanese point of view to American labor and the American people. He was to represent not only the Socialist Masses' Party, but more importantly for his

20. See *Shakai Taishū Shimbun* (November 30, 1937), p. 2.
21. *Nihon Rōdō Nenkan, 19* (1938), 292.

mission, the Congress of Japanese Labor Unions. The government, too, was anxious to have a nongovernmental labor representative go to the United Sates.

Before his departure on October 27, 1937, Suzuki made a statement of what his message there would be.

> We who have close friendly relations with American labor organizations are sincerely sorry that they have decided to boycott Japanese goods. I believe this was caused by too much faith in the one-sided propaganda from China and the lack of an opportunity for making a fair judgment. It goes without saying that this is truly a war for the defense of Japan, as we could no longer countenance the Bolshevization of China and the deepening of the anti-Japanese movement. We have cast the die in this holy war in the belief that, if we did not, we could not tear out the roots of instability in the Orient.[22]

At about the same time the party also sent Shigeo Abe to the United States as an "observer" (*shisatsu*) to help in the task of explaining the "real meaning" of the China incident to Americans both in and out of government.

Party Chairman Isoo Abe cooperated with the government by making a short-wave broadcast to the United States to explain the China incident, again largely from the official Japanese point of view. His action in this case was a far cry from his association (albeit loose) with the antiwar movement at the time of the Russo-Japanese War of 1904–05. Furthermore, the party was not only concerning itself with influencing opinion in the United States and to a lesser extent in Europe, but also sought to overcome within Japan what it called the "evil propaganda" of the Chiang Kai-shek government which it declared was distorting the meaning of the war.[23]

In contrast to the Socialist Masses' Party, the Japan Proletarian Party and the labor unions supporting it, such as the National Council, adopted a critical attitude toward the China incident, but they did not go so far as to make any mass antiwar or antimilitary demonstrations. Rather, they concentrated their efforts on relief for the families of those called to the colors.[24] In his capacity as a Diet Rep-

22. Ibid., *19* (1938), 190.
23. Ibid., *20* (1939), 246.
24. Ibid., *19* (1938), 218.

resentative, Katō went to Shanghai to visit and encourage the troops of the Imperial Army. It was on his return from this trip that he was arrested in December 1937, after which the party was disbanded.

As the China war dragged on, the Socialist Masses' Party gradually worked out a new "continental policy." The aim was to reconstruct Asia under Asian leadership. As a first step, the party advocated building a "New China" and establishing a "mutually beneficial economic organization" (gokei keizai soshiki) among Japan, Manchoukuo, and China. For China, the party specifically called for (1) a strong, unified government, (2) a five-year plan for the development of North China, (3) a five-year plan for the development of Central and South China, (4) concrete ideological and cultural rapprochements, (5) a planned revival of the agricultural villages, and (6) the formation of a new national political party. Furthermore, political, ideological, and economic bonds should be forged with China in order to bring her into the cooperative unit with Manchoukuo and Japan. That is, the development of raw materials and natural resources and the opening up of the Manchuria–China border regions should be undertaken on the basis of a unified plan.[25] This would involve the establishment of an East Asian Economic Congress (Tōa Keizai Kaigi), as mentioned in Chapter 9. The Socialist Masses' Party was developing an idea here that it had from the time of its founding. It contributed to a trend that culminated in November 1943 in the first meeting of the members of the Greater East Asia Coprosperity Sphere.

In urging the unification of China, the party had in mind the various Chinese puppet provisional governments set up with Japanese help in Peiping, Nanking, and East Hopeh. After failing to persuade Chaing Kai-shek to make use of a statement by Konoe as the basis for opening peace negotiations, Chiang's long-time rival Wang Ching-wei had defected from Free China in December 1938. He wanted to take the initiative, either in bringing about a rapprochement between Tōkyō and Chungking or in winning over to himself the main sectors of the Kuomintang in Nanking with a policy of peace with Japan. Although he was expelled from the Kuomintang in Chungking on the last day of 1938, the Japanese government was reluctant to commit itelf to Wang. Throughout 1939 and into 1940 the Socialist Masses' Party advocated supporting Wang in his various endeav-

25. Ibid., 20 (1939), 249.

ors until he finally officially set up his regime in Nanking on March 30, 1940. The party then called for Japan's immediate recognition of that government as fully sovereign and independent.[26] As the Japanese government, however, was apparently hoping against hope that the threat of recognizing Wang's regime might induce some fissure in Chungking, recognition did not come until November 30, 1940. Ironically this was four months after the demise of the Socialist Masses' and all other regular Japanese parties.

In its final days, the party had turned its attention more to the military aspects of the coprosperity sphere. On June 24, 1940, it had urged "mutual collective security" for Japan, Manchoukuo, and China, but again had held that the achievement of this could only be realized by internal consolidation in each country. For Japan, this meant a single political party to "put political backbone into the state as a structure for total war." [27]

In the fourteen years since 1926, both the Socio-Democratic and Japan-Labor clique leaders of the Socialist Masses' Party had traveled in a wide arc from resistance to government actions in China to an attempt to form vanguard opinion on Japan's mission on the continent, albeit with a "renovationist" twist. In the course of the journey, the Chinese revolution, which at first was seen as the irrepressible drive of the Chinese people for independence and liberation from foreign domination, gradually came to be viewed entirely in terms of big-power politics in which Japan was the most "sincere" player.

FOREIGN CONTACTS AND ATTITUDES TOWARD THE WESTERN POWERS

While the foreign policy attitudes of the proletarian parties were all colored by the degree of their acceptance or rejection of the official Japanese government line on China, each category of issues demanded separate policy formulation. Attitudes toward the United States, Western Europe, and colonial Asia were formulated in terms

26. The Japanese government, through Ken Iunkai, actually completed a secret draft treaty with Wang in December of 1939, which provided that the government he would set up to represent China would be a puppet. "Had Japan really compromised," in the opinion of one expert," and established an independent government under Wang, Chiang Kai-shek might have capitulated, leaving the entire Japanese army free for an attack on Russia." Johnson, *An Instance of Treason*, p. 153.

27. *Rōdō Nenkan* (The Labor Yearbook) (1940), pp. 261, 263. Not to be confused with the Ōhara Shakai Mondai Kenkyūjo's *Nihon Rōdō Nenkan*, this yearbook was compiled by the Kyōchōkai (Harmonization Society), Tōkyō.

of the important questions of international migration, trade, and colonialism, but party orientations toward the Soviet Union raised somewhat separate issues both because of ideology and geographical propinquity. The one question on which it was possible for the parties actually to engage in diplomacy on their own was that concerning which foreign bodies to have contacts with and how close these should be.

Japanese social democratic foreign contacts were not very extensive, compared to their European counterparts, and were confined almost entirely to liaison with foreign labor organizations. Most noncommunist socialist parties were affiliated with the Second International and therefore the Japanese early faced the question of how they should view this organization.

What was called the Second International after 1922 was officially the Labor and Socialist International (L.S.I.) with headquarters in London till 1926, then in Zurich till 1935, and finally in Brussels until its demise in 1940. The Socio-Democratic clique felt quite sympathetic to its program and was probably influenced by its foreign policy outlook, but considering the Japanese government's suspicious attitude toward nongovernmental foreign connections and the misunderstanding in Japan of what the organization was, no formal ties were made.[28] Two of the clique leaders, however, decided to translate into Japanese and publish a long report on all the foreign policy issues discussed at the third meeting of the L.S.I. which was held in Brussels August 5–11, 1928, under the chairmanship of Arthur Henderson of the British Labor Party.[29] Devoted mainly to the colonial problem, the meeting decided to stress antiimperialism to prevent it from being monopolized by the Communists.

The Labor Farmer Party and its successors denounced the Second

28. In 1929, however, there was a rumor that the Socio-Democratic clique's General Federation would join the "Amsterdam International" (a trade union organization). This caused quite a stir in the Japanese labor movement but nothing came of it immediately. In the same year, however, the Japan Seamen's Union joined the International Federation of Transportation Workers and thus became the first Japanese labor union to make such an international connection. Michitarō Watanabe, *Nihon no Rōdō Kumiai* (Japanese Labor Unions) (Tōkyō, 1932). In 1931, however, the General Federation was one of six right-wing organizations that formed a Committee for Promoting a Labor Law (Rōdō Rippō Sokushin Iinkai) and that affiliated with the Amsterdam International. See Katsumaro Akamatsu, *Nihon Shakai Undō Shi*, p. 310.

29. This was the pamphlet by Kamei and Yoshikawa, mentioned above, p. 251, n. 3.

International on the same general basis as did the Third (or Communist) International and apparently succeeded in giving it a black name among many of the intellectuals and rank and file in the Japanese labor movement. It was castigated as being bankrupt of new ideas and as representing Western imperialism in disguise.

The Japan-Labor clique at first also criticized the Second International in only slightly milder terms, holding that it placed too great a reliance on the effectiveness of elections and parliamentarianism, which especially in the Japanese context they judged a great mistake. Later, however, they took a somewhat more sympathetic attitude. In 1931 the National Masses' Party set up a semi-autonomous Research Group on International Problems (Kokusai Mondai Kenkyūkai) for the purpose of gathering news and exchanging materials, especially with the L.S.I.[30] With the outbreak of the Manchurian incident, the Japanese proletarian leaders became more isolated from the world socialist movement.[31] The Socialist Masses' Party's rejection of the international popular front movement, in which many of the European socialists took part, further intensified this isolation.

Attitudes toward the Third International (or Comintern) originally provided the rule of thumb for classifying the parties into left, right, and center. The Social Democratic Party made its attitude of complete opposition abundantly clear from the very beginning, whereas the Japan-Labor clique avoided denouncing it until after the Manchurian incident.

Members of the Labor Farmer Party covertly, and at times overtly (at street-corner speeches, for instance), supported the Comintern. Clandestine Communists within its ranks considered themselves members of the Comintern's Japanese branch. Such contacts have been documented.[32] But the party as such had no foreign affiliations. Its main supporting labor federation, the Council,

30. At that time the International Section (Kokusaibu) of that party was divided into the Chinese, American, and Russian subsections (han), which gives some idea of the areas of the world most important to the party. Starting shortly before the Manchurian incident, from April to September 1931, three party representatives (Asahara, Kimura, and Tahara) traveled to the United States to establish liaison. *Nihon Rōdō Nenkan, 13* (1932), 500.

31. The National Labor-Farmer Masses' Party specifically rejected the Second International, again because of its too great reliance on parliamentarianism. Ibid., *14* (1933), 464.

32. See, for instance, Swearingen and Langer, *Red Flag in Japan*, especially Chaps. 6 and 7.

did officially affiliate with the Communist-supported Pan-Pacific Trade Union Secretariat which was located in Shanghai. In May 1927 two of its members attended a meeting in Hankow and they stayed on for some time in China to try to aid the Chinese labor movement on the basis of their experience in Japan.[33] The Council also had contacts with some other Communist-influenced peace and anticolonialist international organizations before its demise in 1928.

What foreign contacts the other proletarian parties and their supporting organizations developed were less political than these. Rather, they were closely related to trade union affairs and go back to before the proletarian parties were formed. The first big government-approved opportunity for international participation was the naming of delegates to meetings of the International Labor Organization (ILO). Bunji Suzuki, as "advisor" to the Japanese delegation, had attended the meeting that set up the ILO in 1919, but he resented the way the Japanese government had slighted him, and he became increasingly incensed over its arbitrary methods of selecting the Japanese "labor" representatives to the subsequent ILO meetings. The General Federation, therefore, boycotted the arrangements until the government made concessions prior to the Sixth ILO meeting in 1924. As a result, the first real labor union delegate from Japan was Bunji Suzuki himself and he was accompanied by Nishio. By this action, partly prompted by international pressure, the Japanese government, as we have noted, for the first time tacitly gave legal recognition to labor unions in Japan.

The Socio-Democratic clique staunchly supported the ILO, not only because it considered this tacit recognition important, but also because it was aware that official international pressure on the Japanese government would have some effect toward making the Japanese government comply with subsequent decisions taken at ILO conferences to the benefit of Japanese labor.

The ILO also exercised a certain influence on the Japanese labor movement and indirectly on the proletarian parties. For instance, a visit to Japan by the Secretary General of the ILO, Albert Thomas, in December 1928, was made the occasion for a big rally of right-wing unions. Although, as an ILO official, Thomas attempted to be politically neutral, it was widely known that he had been a right-

---

33. See *Saikin no Shakai Undō*, p. 315. Later meetings of this organization were held in Canton in 1928 and in Vladivostok in 1929.

wing leader of the French Socialists. His coming gave prestige to the Socio-Democratic clique leaders because they were the ones most intimate with him. They held several large celebrations in his honor.[34]

The Japan-Labor clique evinced an ambivalent attitude toward the ILO. Despite strong criticism from party platforms, the clique's labor federations were not entirely hostile to it, as demonstated by their participation in the election of the workers' delegate to the Tenth (1927) and Thirteenth (1929) Sessions, although they abstained on other occasions. They originally objected to the method of selecting delegates because they averred that it enabled the right-wing unions to monopolize the posts. After the formation of the Japan Labor Club in 1932, however, these Japan-Labor clique federations put "solidarity" first and joined in the selection of candidates.

The various left-wing unions such as the Council of Japanese Labor Unions, which supported the Labor Farmer Party, were uncompromising in their opposition to the ILO. This attitude was held not only by the two main successors to the council but also by Kato's National Council of Japanese Labor Unions. Although its tone had by then become somewhat milder, the National Council in the 1937 national Diet election campaign portrayed the ILO as an organ of labor–capital "compromise" which served only to pull the wool over the eyes of the workers by making bogus concessions.

The Socio-Democrats, however, remained consistent in their support for the ILO, despite growing international criticism of Japan by other members in that body. At an ILO meeting in Prague in 1938, Japan's aggression in China was denounced by the labor delegates from most of the participating nations. In indignation the Japanese government immediately made known that it was considering withdrawing from that body, as it had already done from the League of Nations in 1933. But the General Federation and other unions in the Congress of Japanese Labor Unions demanded that Japan remain in the ILO; only by so doing, they argued, could Japan's position be positively presented.[35] In pleading against withdrawal they pointed out how deeply Japan had become involved in the work of the ILO. Japan had been one of the founding members of the Organization

34. Ibid., pp. 259 and 262.
35. *Nihon Rōdō Nenkan*, 20 (1939), 171.

and since 1919 had sent representatives 23 times in succession, ratified 14 conventions, and adopted 17 recommendations. Nevertheless,
their plea was not sufficient to deter the government from a move
that had perhaps become inevitable in the international atmosphere
of the times.

Earlier, the Socialist Masses' Party had opposed Japan's withdrawal
from the League of Nations, a stand that constituted indirect criticism of the Japanese military.[36] The Kwantung Army officers had
become incensed over the Lytton Report which was an unequivocal
indictment of Japanese aggression in Manchuria. Foreign Minister
Uchida had sent Yōsuke Masuoka to represent Japan at the League
Council debates on the report. He had been instructed to present
Japan's case but not to go so far as to cause Japan's withdrawal from
the League, inasmuch as that might result in international isolation.
Nevertheless, military pressure mounted until by the middle of
February 1933 the government's decision to withdraw became
known. The central executive committee of the Socialist Masses'
Party hurriedly met and issued a strong statement opposing this.[37]
Such a move they maintained would violate the principle of "peo-
ple's diplomacy" which the proletarian parties had championed from
the beginning.

While the proletarian parties were unable to influence Japanese
foreign policy on the world stage, they did attempt to do something
concrete with regard to regional labor and economic problems in the
Far East. As we have seen, the Council of Japanese Labor Unions
affiliated with and supported the Pan-Pacific Trade Union Secretariat. To oppose this Communist group, the General Federation leader
Bunki Suzuki discussed the establishment of an Asiatic Labor Congress (Ajiya Rōdō Kumiai Kaigi) with S. M. Joshi, the Indian labor
delegate to the ILO in 1925. The purpose of the organization would
be the discussion of subjects of common interest among moderate
labor organizations from various Asian nations. Nothing further
happened until 1928 when Mitsusuke Yonekubo, who was then the
Japanese labor delegate to Geneva, discussed with the Indian delegate, R. R. Bakhale, the possibility of having a meeting the following
year, but it was postponed because the participation of a Chinese
representative could not be obtained.[38]

36. Ibid., *17* (1936), 502.
37. Ibid., *15* (1934), 456.
38. *Saikin no Shakai Undō,* p. 316.

The first meeting of the Asiatic Labor Congress did not take place until May 10, 1934. Representatives from India, Ceylon, and Japan met in Colombo, Ceylon, to promote the "common interests" of Asian labor. Specifically, they wanted the ILO to accord representation to colonies and dependencies and to apply international labor standards to them. They also promised to cooperate with the International Federation of Trade Unions (IFTU). After some disappointing delays, a second meeting was held on May 17, 1937, in Tōkyō, but it was attended only by delegates from India and Japan; no representatives came from Ceylon, the Philippines, or China. A third meeting was scheduled for 1939, but it did not materialize. The Asiatic Labor Congress was finally dissolved on July 19, 1940, along with its mainstay, the Congress of Japanese Labor Unions.[39] All along the Socialist Masses' Party had given its full endorsement to the Congress, but despite a great deal of effort and detailed plans little was accomplished, largely because of the fear of Japan on the part of other Asian trade union movements.

In the broader field of politico-economic international relations the Socialist Masses' Party, at its third central executive committee meeting in 1933, called for an Oriental Economic Congress as mentioned.[40] This followed on the heels of the failure of the World Economic Conference that had met in London from June 12 to July 20, 1933. That Conference had tried to overcome the world economic crisis by stemming the tide toward economic nationalism and substituting international cooperation through new monetary and fiscal policies, reduction of trade barriers and tariffs, a freer flow of international capital, reflation, and international control of shipments of raw materials. Although British defense of imperial preference and American raising of tariffs seriously jeopardized the success of the Conference, Japan also posed difficulties in insisting on recognition of her special interests in East Asia.[41]

In October 1933, the Japanese military through War Minister Araki made a proposal for a Far Eastern Economic Conference to be held among all the powers with special interests in Asia, with a view toward working out a rationale for coexistence in which peace could be maintained. Preliminary negotiations for the recognition of Manchoukuo and the revision of the Washington and London naval

39. *Rōdō Nenkan* (1940), p. 242.
40. See Chap. 9, above, pp. 244–45. The proposal for the Tōyō Keizai Kaigi is quoted in full in *Nihon Rōdō Nenkan, 15* (1934), 438–39.
41. See Yanaga, *Japan Since Perry*, pp. 565–67.

agreements were called for, as well as a Soviet-Japanese nonaggression pact, the implementation of the Pact of Paris and the Nine-Power Treaty, new economic policies for India, and the solution of differences on China. This proposal, however, was overruled by Premier Hirota because of opposition from the Foreign Office.

In general approach, the party's proposal was not very different from that of the military, but it was narrower in scope. The United States and the Western colonial powers were not suggested as participants—which limited the possibilities for revisions of international treaties and agreements. It proposed that the Soviet Union, Manchoukuo, China, Siam, the Philippines, and India be invited, and a permanent Oriental Economic Union be established for continuously attacking such problems as tariffs, trade, investment, and raw materials. The Congress was seen as providing an opportunity for the backward countries of Asia to advance toward equality through cooperation with Japan in order to help insure world peace. Among other problems proposed for consideration were international migration and the independence of the Philippines and India.

It appears that within the Socialist Masses' Party this proposal had been pushed by the Japan-Labor clique along with its idea for a National Economic Congress as mentioned in Chapter 9. These proposals met with some resistance from the Labor-Farmer faction and to a degree from the Socio-Democrats. Those in opposition claimed it was a revival of the Japan-Labor clique's old proposal for a "Far Eastern International" which was called "racialist and nationalistc." They considered that this new proposal was potentially antagonistic to social democratic principles and might encourage fascistic tendencies. The majority of the party leadership, however, was interested in developing a regional economic congress and went along with the proposal.

As nothing concrete was done along this line in the meantime by the Japanese government, the party carried over the idea of a congress into its new Constructive Program of 1937; this time, in line with the latest terminology, it called for an East Asian Economic Congress (Tōa Keizai Kaigi).[42] Not only were the colonial powers not to be invited, but one of the objectives of the Congress and of the New Structure for Peace in the Far East was the expulsion of European and American "capitalism" from the area, specifically the "liberation" of the Philippines and India.

42. *Nihon Rōdō Nenkan*, 20 (1939), 250.

The leading principle behind the proletarian leaders' ideas on migration and colonialism was "racial equality." International recognition of this principle had long been sought by the Japanese government. The Japanese delegation at the Versailles Peace Conference, for example, had attempted to place a racial equality clause in the Covenant of the League of Nations but had not succeeded, due to opposition from the Dominions, particularly Australia, and to a degree from the United States. The issue of racial equality was an emotional one for large segments of the population in Japan and the nonacceptance of it by leading Western nations caused widespread resentment.

Both the demand for an end to racial discrimination and the closely related advocacy of "liberation of oppressed peoples" were shared by all the proletarian parties in Japan in the 1920s. They deliberately left vague what was meant by "liberation." The Communist elements among the leftists undoubtedly interpreted liberation of colonies to include the independence of Korea and Taiwan. Social Democratic Party slogans at its founding included: "Liberate the oppressed races!" and "Establish freedom for world immigration!" The Japan Labor-Farmer Party in 1927 proposed specifically that universal suffrage be extended to the Japanese "colonies" of Karafuto, Taiwan, and Korea.[43]

After the Manchurian incident, the Socialist Masses' Party advocated in somewhat milder terms "friendly cooperation" with the peoples in the colonies of Korea and Taiwan. An end to political, social, legal, and economic inequality was demanded for the indigenous peoples, to put them on the same level as the Japanese.[44] In addition "the liberation of the Asian peoples" was called for.[45] As we have seen, this developed into the idea of a grand economic bloc

43. Hakuyōsha, p. 32.

44. *Nihon Rōdō Nenkan, 15* (1934), 447.

45. With regard to the interpretation of the Socialist Masses' Party's attitude toward the colonies, the author found an interesting handwritten comment in the flyleaf of a copy of *Kiki ni Tatsu Kokusai Seikyoku*, mentioned above as published by the Socialist Masses' Party, which he had borrowed from the Library of Congress and which had come originally from the Japanese Home Ministry. It was as follows: "Underlined by Metropolitan Police Headquarters (Iwanaga); telegraphed [to police] throughout the country. Pages 1, 2, 8 ['revise in next printing' is crossed out] eliminate. Reason: Japan's colonies might be [interpreted to be] included in 'oppressed peoples' and 'oppressed masses.'" Underlined words included *"minzoku"* in the demand for Manchoukuo to be a "national (*minzoku*), independent state" and the phrase, "liberate and cooperate with the oppressed masses of the Orient."

in Asia with Japan as the leader, it being Japan's mission to "liberate" and give "independence" to the other nations of Asia.

The demand for international freedom for migration was prominent among the platforms of all the proletarian parties in the beginning. Only two years before, the whole nation had waxed indignant over the passage of the General Immigration Bill of 1924 in the United States which excluded, with minor exceptions, from American shores aliens ineligible for citizenship. All Japanese and others of the Mongolian race were thus barred from immigrating. This was interpreted by the Japanese as an official insult to Japan, because they felt it implied that Japanese were too "uncivilized" to associate with Americans. They would not have minded being on even the lowest quota but resented the discrimination in kind applied to them and to certain other Asians. While immigration was a problem in Japanese relations with several nations, the Japanese proletarian parties singled out the United States and Brazil as the countries with which the Japanese government should especially take measures to support the rights of Japanese laborer and farmer immigrants.[46]

The United States immigration quota was revised in 1929 and at that time it was discovered that had the Japanese also been put on a quota of the type contaned in the bill, not more than 185 of them would have been admitted to the country. Such a quota would by no means have inundated the United States, while at the same time it would have wiped out the insult to Japan and other countries left out of the quota system.[47] Consequently a renewed drive began to gather momentum in the United States for revising the immigration legislation. This was nearing success when the Manchurian incident destroyed hopes of any immediate moves in this direction.

The fact in the story of Japanese exclusion from the United States that chagrined the Japanese labor and proletarian party leaders most was the involvement, if not leadership, of American organized labor in anti-Japanese agitation. Until the First World War, this agitation had been concentrated most heavily in California and was directed against industrious Japanese farmers more than toward labor. But it had stirred up anti-American sentiment in Japan and worsened official relations between the two countries. When Bunji Suzuki made his first trip to the United States in 1915 as head of the Friendly Soci-

46. Hakuyōsha, p. 480.
47. Yanaga, p. 446.

ety, he conferred with Japanese residents and visitors in America, including Sen Katayama, who had arrived the year before, about organizing Japanese workers in California and elsewhere and about the types of discrimination they faced. Both men wanted to play down the friction between the two nations, though their orientations differed. Katayama was now a militant socialist and assumed an identity of interests between the exploited laboring classes of the United States and Japan in opposing war and discrimination, whereas Suzuki pictured himself as the leader of a moderate, but not a "yellow" or "company," trade union movement, who was interested in arousing the sympathy of organized American labor for the problems of the Japanese workingman and learning from the experience of the more advanced American movement.[48]

Suzuki was extremely successful in making a good impression on his American hosts. On this trip he made friends with Paul Scharrenberg, head of the California branch of the American Federation of Labor (AFL) and Samuel Gompers, the AFL's national leader, and these friendships turned out to be lifelong. During his next trip in 1916 and subsequently Suzuki spoke in English before a number of labor groups, attempting to overcome anti-Japanese discrimination in its various forms and to promote Japanese-American amity. In Japan he and the other leaders of the Friendly Society, and later the General Federation, attempted to use the facts of American discrimination against Japanese labor as an argument to persuade the Japanese government and management to ameliorate working conditions in Japan.

In the long run, however, despite the personal friendships between Japanese and American labor leaders, various positions taken by the mainstream of the American movement vitiated its influence on the Japanese proletarian movement as a whole. Not only was the AFL so long opposed to Oriental immigration, but it roundly denounced socialism. Also there was no comparable tenant-farmer movement. In 1929, for instance, Suzuki invited Paul Scharrenberg to Japan to address a convention of the General Federation, but his argument that anti-Japanese discrimination in America was purely economic and not racial fell flat. The Japanese were too well acquainted with

48. Katayama and Suzuki did not get along. Katayama denounced Suzuki at this time as a "tool of the capitalists" and the Friendly Society as a "paper-union" and a "mere aggregation of names." See Kublin, *Asian Revolutionary*, pp. 224–25.

statements by various other American labor leaders warning of the "Japanese threat" and the "yellow peril."

Only in the mid-1930s, especially with the creation of the Congress of Industrial Organizations (CIO), did the mainstream of American labor become more "progressive" in Japanese eyes. With renewed attention toward organizing the unorganized, many of whom were foreign-born, and with the rise of Hitlerism in Europe, American labor leaders became increasingly convinced of the importance of countering racial discrimination. Among other concrete measures, they took steps to expose some of the baseless propaganda against Japanese laborers in the United States. They invited Kanjū Katō, as leader of the National Council, to come to the United States in 1935 to address both American and Japanese-American audiences on the qualities of Japanese workers and on how to solve the question of racial discrimination among workers. The antileadership group in the AFL paid Katō's expenses, and his itinerary included Seattle, Chicago, New York, Washington, Los Angeles, San Francisco, and Vancouver, Canada, taking 81 days in all [49]

Such efforts were again shattered by Japanese aggression in China in 1937, and the worst was yet to come. After Pearl Harbor most Americans on the West Coast from California to Washington, prepared by long years of anti-Japanese propaganda which insidiously mingled racial strains with the often justified political arguments, countenanced the shameful disregard of human rights entailed in the "relocation" of Japanese and Americans of Japanese ancestry away from the West Coast.

As the decade of the 1930s wore on, in addition to racial discrimination, the Japanese proletarian leaders found themselves faced with questions of tariff discrimination imposed by other countries against Japanese goods, and here again they attempted to interpret the situation in such a way as to produce a solution favorable to Japanese labor. In the new Constructive Program of November 1937, the Socialist Masses' Party placed demands for free trade and equal access to national resources on a par with those for human equality and freedom of migration. Increasingly, restrictions had been placed on imports from Japan. Actually Britain was considered the worst offender. In defense of their actions, Britain and other Western countries accused Japan of "social dumping," of selling below cost by

49. *Nihon Rōdō Nenkan, 17* (1936).

the use of sweated labor in order unfairly to gain footholds in foreign markets. Particularly between 1932 and 1934 markets for British cotton textiles and staple fiber fabrics had been narrowed at an alarming rate due to Japanese competition. The problem of social dumping had assumed such proportions that it became a major subject for discussion at the International Labor Conference of 1934. The question of what attitude the Japanese delegates should take was considered by the Congress of Japanese Labor Unions, which in large measure determined the position of the Socialist Masses' Party on such questions. The arguments used reveal something of Japanese social democratic thinking concerning the relationship of foreign affairs to internal reform.

The Congress attacked those Japanese capitalists who held that to improve labor conditions would place Japanese exports in such a disadvantageous position with respect to international competition that it would prevent Japan's overseas trade expansion—a suicidal act. The labor leaders maintained that Japanese trade was expanding so rapidly that it was becoming a threat to other countries. In these conditions, improving Japanese labor conditions would undermine the abuses of labor in industry, raise efficiency, and improve labor–management relations. Thus, labor peace would be achieved. Japan could then really prove in the forum of world opinion that Japanese exports were not the result of exploited labor, and foreign labor and cultural organizations would have to admit that Japanese trade expansion was not unfair. Consequently, the assembled labor leaders proposed that the question of dumping be solved by raising labor standards in Japan by the following steps: (1) control of exports, with a floor of minimum wages for export industries; (2) establishment of a labor union law recognizing the right to collective bargaining; (3) immediate ratification of the Washington international labor convention on hours, on the prohibition of night work for women and youths, and on days of rest.[50]

Nevertheless, in the face of mounting British trade restrictions, such as the quota system of 1934, the attitude of the Socialist Masses' Party toward England began to deteriorate. This made it easier to adopt the slogan, "Overthrow British and American capitalism in India and the Philippines."[51] After the clash between British and

50. Ibid., 16 (1935).
51. Kiki ni Tatsu Kokusai Seikyoku, p. 2 and Nihon Rōdō Nenkan, 19 (1938), 292.

Japanese soldiers in Tientsin early in the summer of 1939, the party lent its support to the rising tide of anti-British sentiment and supported the military measures taken by the Japanese government.[52]

In looking back over the proletarian policies on migration, colonialism, and international trade, it can be seen that here again "principles" consistently held took on radically different meanings in accordance with changes in international relations.

POLICIES TOWARD SOVIET RUSSIA

Japanese recognition of the Soviet Union took place in January 1925. As the proletarian parties were officially launched only in the following year, they were not troubled by this issue, although it had been a strongly pressed demand of most of the politically active labor and socialist, not to mention Communist-influenced, groups in the preceding period. Thereafter, the maintenance of friendly relations and avoidance of war became the most enduring demands of the proletarian parties with regard to the Soviet Union.

The defense of Soviet Russia as the "country of labor and the farmers" (rōnōkoku) was advocated by the Labor Farmer Party and its successor, the New Labor Farmer Party, but the other proletarian parties felt no special obligation for a pro-Soviet stand. On the other hand, no matter how much the right-wing Social Democratic Party denounced the Japanese Communists, its attitude toward the Soviet Union was not extremely hostile.

An incident occurred in 1924 which revealed that certain General Federation leaders could cooperate with Soviet representatives even before Japan recognized the U.S.S.R. After the great earthquake of September 1923, Leo Karakhan, the Soviet representative in Peking, made it known that the Soviet Union would like to help provide relief for the workers who had suffered in the upheaval by giving to Japanese labor organizations certain rights to the exploitation of lumbering and fishing along the coast near Vladivostok. Under the leadership of the General Federation, an organization was set up to aid worker victims of the earthquake and make plans for taking advantage of the conceded Russian rights and for the distribution of the earned funds through social work. On behalf of this organization, Komakichi Matsuoka went to Peking to discuss the issue in detail

52. Ibid., 21 (1940), 187.

with Karakhan. It was only shortly thereafter, however, that diplomatic relations were reestablished between Japan and the Soviet Union. Fearing that this project would be considered Soviet interference in Japanese internal affairs, the Russians and the Japanese labor leaders agreed to drop it.[53]

Japanese-Soviet relations thereafter ran into no great difficulties until the Kwantung Army overran Manchuria in 1931. As part of their reaction to the situation, the Soviets proposed in December 1931 the conclusion of a nonaggression pact between Japan and the U.S.S.R. While not making an outright refusal, the Japanese government remained cool to the idea, because opinion both within the government and among the military was divided on the question. In September 1932, just as Japan was preparing for the recognition of Manchoukuo, Karakhan, who was now Vice Foreign Commissar, once more raised the question of a nonaggression pact along with the offer to sell the Chinese Eastern Railway. The Socialist Masses' Party immediately demanded that the Japanese government be receptive to both of these offers.

The party held that a nonaggression pact with the Soviet Union would help dispel the tensions that had been raised among the Japanese masses by all the war talk that had been taking place, for such a pact could only promote peace in the Far East. In subjective terms, the party reasoned that since it was a "socialist" party, it had a duty to oppose any possible war with the Soviet Union, which was a "socialist" country. During the next few months, the party mounted a campaign to press for a nonaggression pact. Among other things, a delegation headed by Isoo Abe called on Prime Minister Saitō, War Minister Araki, and Foreign Minister Uchida, handing them a petition which held that the new state of Manchoukuo should be a signatory to the pact as well as Japan and the Soviet Union and that the pact should provide for a demilitarized zone between Manchoukuo and Russia to prevent hostilities from breaking out.[54]

The party envisioned such a pact however, as only part of a much wider system of security in the Pacific area. In the first place, by removing tensions along the Manchurian border, this pact would allow the major efforts in Manchoukuo to go into reconstruction and development rather than defense and thus reduce the burden of mili-

53. *Saikin no Shakai Undō*, pp. 312–13.
54. *Nihon Rōdō Nenkan, 14* (1933), 455, 479, and 481.

tary expenditures both in Japan and Manchoukuo. For broader efforts along this line, the party expressed support for the General Disarmament Conference that had started discussions in Geneva in February 1932. For the most part these discussions dragged on gloomily for several years with only occasional flare-ups of hope. The party's proposal for helping achieve the aims of the Conference was the conclusion of a Pacific collective security pact.[55] But this would not involve complete disarmament. In January 1935, at its third national convention, the party went along with popular nationalistic feeling to the extent of denouncing the naval ratios which had originally been fixed in the Washington Naval Treaty of 1922, then reviewed in 1930, and were to be discussed again in December 1935, but the party did call for the reduction of armaments consistent with a feeling of national security and warned against a naval race.

One of the strongest factors to militate against the conclusion of a Soviet-Japanese nonaggression pact was the signing of the German-Japanese Anti-Comintern Pact on November 25, 1936, by which both contracting parties agreed to exchange information on the activities of the Communist International and to consult and collaborate on necessary countermeasures. The party immediately denounced that pact as ineffective and dangerous in the prevailing international situation, listing a number of detailed reasons: to take the side of fascism to oppose communism would lead willy-nilly to deteriorating relations with the other big powers; the only real way to stop communism is by domestic reform; the reason the masses turn toward communism is that they know their future development cannot be by way of capitalism—therefore, Japan's foreign policy must be anticapitalist as well as anticommunist. The pact, went the party's position, would hinder Japan in her necessary efforts to conclude more trade agreements, and it was far too narrow. Furthermore, collective security required that Japan sign bilateral peace agreements not only with Germany, but also with the Soviet Union, the United States, and China. Although the party was in full sympathy with the aim of opposing communism, it felt that this pact "tarnished the national polity" and exposed the impotency of the Hirota Cabinet.[56]

55. *Taiheiyō anzen hoshō jōyaku*. See ibid., *16* (1935), 444–45, and *17* (1936), 502.

56. See Tōkyō *Asahi Shimbun* (November 28, 1936). For the detailed position of the party formulated by Kanichirō Kamei, see his article "Nichi-Doku Bōkyō Kyōtei to Warera no Taido" (The German-Japanese Anti-Comintern Pact and Our Position on It), *Myōnichi* (Tomorrow) (January 1937), quoted in Naimushō Keihokyoku, *Shuppan Keisatsu Shiryō* (Police Materials on Publications) (February 1937), pp. 44–47.

The party continued to advocate a nonaggression pact with the Soviet Union through the April 1937 Diet elections; after that its policy gradually changed. By 1939 it had not only come around to supporting the Anti-Comintern Pact but actually called for its strengthening. By August 5 of that year, the party advocated its transformation into a military alliance among Japan, Germany, and Italy.[57] This was only weeks before the world was astounded by the announcement on August 23 of the Soviet-Nazi Nonaggression Pact of friendship, neutrality, and commerce, which represented a basic and complete reversal of policy for both contracting parties. Almost before its implications could be grasped, Nazi tanks crossed into Poland on September 1, and two days later, Great Britain and France, honoring their obligation to defend their ally, declared war on Nazi Germany. It was a whole year later and after the party's demise before what the Socialist Masses' Party had called for was brought into being by the second Konoe Cabinet, when on September 26, 1940, the Tripartite Pact with Germany and Italy was signed and Japan became a full-fledged partner in the Axis.

As it turned out, Japan's war was not with Russia—at least until the last few days. This was partly made possible by the signing of the Soviet-Japanese Neutrality Pact on April 13, 1941. Foreign Minister Matsuoka had actually asked for a nonaggression pact but Russia's price was too high. The Nazis who had earlier supported a four-power entente among Germany, Italy, Japan, and the Soviet Union —as the social democrats had advocated and as Matsuoka would have preferred—at this point tried to discourage Matsuoka, who instead surprised the world by emphasizing Soviet-Japanese cordiality. He apparently hoped to strengthen Japan's bargaining position vis-à-vis the United States and at the same time to secure the north in order to push southward.

The reason Hitler now was so cool to the idea was that he was secretly planning the attack on the Soviet Union. He launched it on June 22, 1941, with utter disregard for the Nonaggression Pact of 1939. This posed the alternative to Japan of following suit immediately or putting off an attack on Siberia until the Kwantung Army was further strengthened. The latter course was chosen but could never be consummated because of the cost of the decision to push south first which resulted in the attack on Pearl Harbor. Russia became involved because Roosevelt and Churchill at Yalta urged Stalin to

57. *Nihon Rōdō Nenkan, 21* (1940), 157 and 187.

break the Soviet-Japanese Neutrality Pact and attack Japan three months after V-E Day. This the Soviet Union did on August 8, 1945, according to Japanese reckoning, just two days after the atomic bomb obliterated Hiroshima and six days before Japan accepted the Potsdam Declaration and unconditional surrender.

The irony of social democratic foreign policy was that it eventually came to support a war which was to end in a defeat that in turn provided a greater boost to the social democratic movement and to anti-militarism than would probably have occurred if Japan's rulers had remained cautious enough not to overextend themselves as they did, believing they had the whole nation—including the proletarian representatives—behind them.

Electoral and Organized Support

11: Electoral Support

The most obvious measure of a political movement's strength is the number of votes its political parties obtain. Before the suffrage was extended in 1925 to include all males over 25 years of age, however, it was almost impossible for the Japanese socialist parties to make any showing. For instance, Naoe Kinoshita, well known as the author of the "best selling" socialist novel, *Pillar of Fire (Hi no Hashira)*, and an organizer of the abortive Social Democratic Party of 1901, entered the general election of May 1905 as a socialist candidate but received only 32 of the some 16,000 ballots cast. Although the smallness of his vote was partly due to police interference, Kinoshita's case is illustrative of the fact that an electorate restricted to substantial property holders offers little possibility, in Japan as elsewhere, for the development of a socialist movement.

The quality and quantity of the electoral support that each of the social democratic cliques and factions was able to attract at the polls, after the extension of the suffrage, will be discussed here. Organized labor, agrarian, and other support will be examined in greater detail in the following chapters.

PROSPECTS OPENED BY MANHOOD SUFFRAGE

Universal manhood suffrage was demanded even before the first Diet convened in 1890; it was called for in the Social Democratic Party platform of 1901; and in 1902 it was raised in the Diet for the first time. Subsequently, it was proposed almost annually until it finally passed the Lower House in 1911, only to be quashed by the House of Peers. The Kōtoku High Treason Trial of 1911 and the hysteria it generated not only stifled the socialist movement but also contributed to halting the agitation for widening the suffrage as well.

Both movements, however, were revived toward the end of the First World War, especially after the great Rice Riots of 1918. The conservatives took the initiative and slightly revised the suffrage laws in 1919, reducing the tax qualification to three yen, but at the same time setting up a system of small election districts. This only enlarged the electorate from a million to almost three million and the small election districts increased the government's ability to interfere in elections to the benefit of the party in power. Dissatisfaction with this revision spurred the movement for widening the suffrage, and it appeared as though a bill would pass the Diet in 1920, when suddenly Premier Hara, in opposition to the bill, dissolved the House, crushing hopes for its immediate enactment.

A suffrage bill was introduced in each of the next five years. Gradually the campaign to "protect constitutional government" gained momentum with the promise of universal suffrage until a three-party coalition forced its way into power as no political party or combination had previously done. The promise was fulfilled with the passage of the Universal Manhood Suffrage Law of 1925 under the leadership of Premier Takaaki (Kōmei) Katō, President of the Kenseikai.

This quintupled the electorate to almost fourteen million. Although the election districts were enlarged to "middle size" (three to five representatives), many obstacles still blocked the way of free democratic development—such as the voting age of twenty-five, the total disenfranchisement of women, and one-year domicile requirements which would disqualify many factory workers and city dwellers whose family registration (*koseki*) remained in their native villages.[1] The political threat of the Peace Preservation Bill which

1. The Katō Cabinet estimated that the single restriction of a one-year domicile requirement, which was insisted upon by the House of Peers, would reduce the number

passed the same year must also not be forgotten. Nevertheless, a basis was obviously laid for the development of the social democratic movement in national politics.

Under the liberalized suffrage, six general elections were held before the surrender in 1945: (1) February 20, 1928, (2) February 20, 1930, (3) February 20, 1932, (4) February 20, 1936, (5) April 30, 1937, and (6) April 30, 1942.

The suffrage law broadened the electorate to include much of what the social democrats regarded as the "proletariat." From our discussion of their class concepts we are aware that by this they did not have in mind a homogeneous group, such as "factory workers who do not own the means of production and who have nothing to sell but their labor power." They considered as their potential constituency the whole "propertyless class." In 1929 Sekiguchi, an editorial writer of the *Asahi Shimbun,* expressed the social democratic vision of the class they represented in concrete terms:

> If we ask what part of the population is made up of people who should in general be called proletarians (*musansha*) and if we consider them as those who do not earn enough to pay an income tax, the answer is 97 per cent of the population at present or 87 per cent of the households. Of those who do pay an income tax, 83 per cent have an annual income of less than 3,000 yen [$750 at ¥4 to $1] and cannot be said to be a wealthy class. In any case, at least about 90 per cent of the whole population cannot eat without working and cannot get along very well even when working.[2]

It was unthinkable for a party which attempted to represent the propertyless classes to gain the support of such a high percentage of the population with class appeals. There were many strata within this wide definition that did not think of themselves as proletarian. Professional people, white-collar workers, independent farmers, and small businessmen, for instance, generally considered themselves vaguely middle-class. It must furthermore be understood that Japanese society was filled with patriarchal microcosms where individ-

---

of otherwise eligible voters by some 200,000. See John Jung-shun Lin, "Popular Movements in Japan During the Taishō Era" (Ph.D. dissertation, University of Pennsylvania, 1960), p. 234; for details of the compromises leading to these restrictions, see pp. 218–35.

2. Yasushi (Tai) Sekiguchi, *Rōdō Mondai Kōwa* (A Discussion of the Labor Problem), Asahi Jōshiki Kōwa (Asahi Practical Monographs), 5 (Tōkyō, Asahi Shimbunsha, 1929), 296.

uals, whatever their economic and class status, were often, if not usually, governed by personal obligations in matters such as suffrage. This fact should also be borne in mind to temper generalizations about class behavior in Japan.

As proletarian parties, the newly formed social democratic and Communist-influenced legal leftist parties were organized to appeal first and foremost to the workers and tenant farmers. Of these, however, only males over twenty-five could vote and this was a small number, an estimated three-and-a-half-million plus in 1928 (the year of the first Diet election under manhood suffrage). Although this number rose half a million by 1937, it remained just below 30 per cent of the total eligible voters.[3] Actually the proletarian parties could not by any means count on *all* the workers and tenant farmers to support them. Rather their hopes would have to be placed mainly on those who were *organized,* and these amounted to a combined total that actually dwindled from an estimated 661,803 or 5.3 per cent in 1928 to 625,113 or 4.3 per cent of the total eligible voters in 1937. The number of organized workers rose by over a hundred thousand, but the number of tenant-farmer union members fell by more than that.[4]

Obviously, if the social democratic parties were to get a majority in the Diet they would need to do more than capture the unionized labor and tenant farmers. They would have to promote more labor and farmer organization; compete with the major parties which were now beginning to appeal to the farmer–labor vote; and they would have to win over the fishermen and other economic strata— the intelligentsia, white collar workers, and even small businessmen. An evaluation of election results will indicate to what extent they were successful.

OVERALL RESULTS OF THE SIX ELECTIONS, 1928–42

The actual achievements of the proletarian parties approximated the estimate based on organized labor and tenant-farmer support, as may be seen in Table 1. The differences in support among the social

3. These estimates were made by the author and may be found in Table 1, Chap. 6, of George O. Totten, "Japanese Social Democracy: An Analysis of the Background, Leadership, and Organized Suppport of the Social Democratic Movement in Prewar Japan" (Ph.D. dissertation, Yale University, 1954, Publication No. 11,212, University Microfilms, Ann Arbor, Michigan), p. 173. Hereafter referred to as *JSD.*

4. Ibid., Table 2, p. 174.

TABLE 1. PROLETARIAN PARTY VOTES IN DIET ELECTIONS *

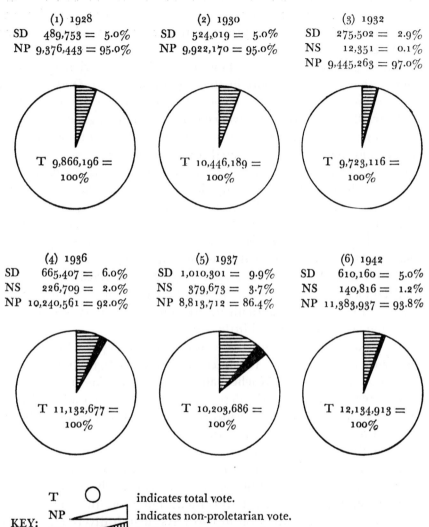

	(1) 1928			(2) 1930			(3) 1932	
SD	489,753 =	5.0%	SD	524,019 =	5.0%	SD	275,502 =	2.9%
NP	9,376,443 =	95.0%	NP	9,922,170 =	95.0%	NS	12,351 =	0.1%
						NP	9,445,263 =	97.0%

T 9,866,196 = 100%

T 10,446,189 = 100%

T 9,723,116 = 100%

	(4) 1936			(5) 1937			(6) 1942	
SD	665,407 =	6.0%	SD	1,010,301 =	9.9%	SD	610,160 =	5.0%
NS	226,709 =	2.0%	NS	379,673 =	3.7%	NS	140,816 =	1.2%
NP	10,240,561 =	92.0%	NP	8,813,712 =	86.4%	NP	11,383,937 =	93.8%

T 11,132,677 = 100%

T 10,203,686 = 100%

T 12,134,913 = 100%

KEY:
T ⬭ indicates total vote.
NP ◸ indicates non-proletarian vote.
SD ◿ indicates social democratic party vote.
NS ◢ indicates national socialist (fascist) vote.

* The statistics for Table 1 were taken from the following sources: both the proletarian votes and Diet seats were from the *Nihon Rōdō Nenkan*, appropriate years. The total vote cast for all parties was from Naikaku Tōkeikyoku (Cabinet Statistical Bureau), *Nihon Teikoku Tōkei Nenkan* (Statistical Yearbook of the Japanese Empire) (Tōkyō), appropriate years, except for 1942 which was from Jiji Tsūshinsha (The Jiji News Agency), *Jiji Nenkan* (The "Jiji" Almanac) (Tōkyō, Jiji Tsūshinsha Shuppankyoku, 1943), p. 95. The areas in black stand for national socialists, regularly listed with the proletarian vote. Percentages were calculated by the author. No proletarian parties as such

democratic parties and also the political affiliations of labor and agrarian organizations will be discussed in detail later; but first the support obtained by the proletarian parties as a whole will be analyzed.

The 1928 election results showed that the proletarian parties received their largest support in the big cities: Tōkyō, Ōsaka, Kyōto, and environs. Over half their votes, 51.7 per cent, came from these industrially and culturally advanced areas. The next greatest number of votes, 12 per cent, came from Fukuoka Prefecture where coal mines and steel mills were located. In the agricultural areas, only two prefectures, Niigata and Kagawa, together accounting for 9 per cent of the proletarian vote, gave any sizable support to the social democratic parties. In Hokkaidō, an area with both mining and agriculture, some 11,000 votes were divided among four candidates with the result that no one was elected. Of the total vote of 489,753, over 300,000 votes were obtained from only nine of the 47 prefectures: Tōkyō, Ōsaka, Kyōto, Kanagawa, Hyōgo, Niigata Kagawa, Fukuoka, and Hokkaidō. In general, support came from workers and intellectuals in the big cities; agricultural regions, with the two exceptions mentioned above, provided little strength.

In 1930, the total number of votes increased slightly, but the percentage of the total vote remained the same. In 1932, however, the proletarian party vote reached an all time low. At first glance it would seem that the world depression of 1929, which affected both Japanese industry and agriculture, should have considerably increased proletarian party strength.

Actually, however, the widespread conditions of poverty dried up party contributions so that the proletarian parties could not afford to run as many candidates nor campaign as effectively as before. The depression did create great discontent but soon the Manchurian incident altered the situation in two ways: first, it diverted attention from the domestic scene to external affairs, and secondly, an inflation caused by the flood of military orders reduced unemployment and raised wages slightly. Although a higher cost of living somewhat counterbalanced the increase in wages, there was an apparent trend

---

existed in the election of 1942, but the figures for that year represent the votes received by former social democrats and former national socialists. They were calculated on the basis of recognizing names from lists and using the figures appearing in the Tōkyō *Asahi Shimbun* (May 3, 1942).

toward prosperity. In the hope that military spending might aid this trend, many former supporters turned away from the proletarian parties whose leaders were equivocating about whether to endorse or condemn Japan's involvement in Manchuria. Attacked by nationalists for not coming out clearly in favor of the war and by leftists, including the Communists, for not resisting it, the social democrats lost support at this time.

By 1936, however, the proletarian parties were regaining support lost in 1932, and in 1937 they polled over one million votes. War-induced prosperity had failed to sustain employment and wages. Many people were losing faith in the major parties due to continual exposés of scandal. Civil liberties were being yet further circumscribed, while militarism and racism grew. The increase in social democratic votes probably represented a reaction against these trends.

Table 2 indicates the degree to which the electoral system worked to the disadvantage of the proletarian parties in proportionally underrepresenting them in terms of the number of seats they received in the Imperial Diet. Tables 1 and 2 also show the appearance of the national socialist elements. In Japanese statistics these were included with the proletarian parties, because, as we have seen, they had originally emerged in large part from the various social democratic groups.

In both the 1937 and 1942 elections the national socialists elected relatively few Diet members in comparison with the social democrats, although by then the national socialist platforms did not differ significantly from those of the social democrats, due to the rightward shift of the latter. The social democrats were beginning to be elected on the basis of "face," that is, familiarity to the voters, rather than policy. In the 1942 elections both groups lost considerable support. Still the former social democrats did not drop below their first election figure of 1928.

A comparison of the results of the prefectural elections with those of the Diet elections reveals that the percentage of social democratic votes at the prefectural level remained both more constant and lower than at the national.[5] They began at 3.9 per cent of the total vote in 1927 and ended at 3.2 per cent in 1939 at the time of the last regular

5. For tables on the proletarian party showings in the prefectural elections, see Totten, *JSD*, pp. 181–82.

TABLE 2. PROLETARIAN PARTY SEATS IN THE DIET [a]

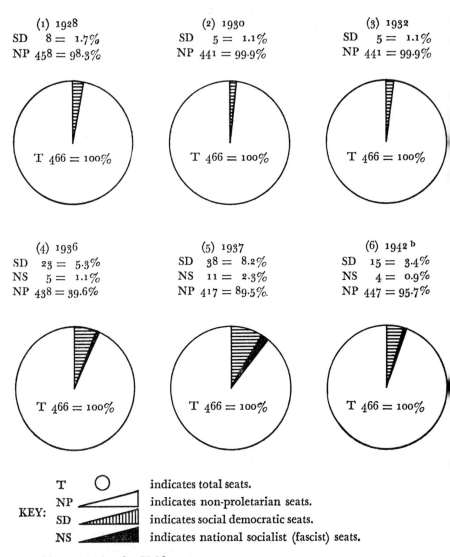

(1) 1928
SD   8 = 1.7%
NP 458 = 98.3%
T 466 = 100%

(2) 1930
SD   5 = 1.1%
NP 441 = 99.9%
T 466 = 100%

(3) 1932
SD   5 = 1.1%
NP 441 = 99.9%
T 466 = 100%

(4) 1936
SD   23 = 5.3%
NS   5 = 1.1%
NP 438 = 39.6%
T 466 = 100%

(5) 1937
SD   38 = 8.2%
NS   11 = 2.3%
NP 417 = 89.5%.
T 466 = 100%

(6) 1942 [b]
SD   15 = 3.4%
NS   4 = 0.9%
NP 447 = 95.7%
T 466 = 100%

KEY:
T   ○   indicates total seats.
NP   indicates non-proletarian seats.
SD   indicates social democratic seats.
NS   indicates national socialist (fascist) seats.

a. Sources same as for Table 1.
b. In the 1942 election no political parties existed, but seats won by former social democrats and national socialists are indicated as proletarian seats.

prewar prefectural election without much variation in between; whereas, from Table 1 it will be noticed that in the national Diet elections the social democratic vote began at 5 per cent in 1928 and thereafter ranged from a low of almost 3 per cent in 1932 to as high as almost 10 per cent in 1937. The percentage of the prefectual vote would be somewhat higher if the results of the elections in the eight prefectures which had been held off-schedule since the great earthquake of 1923 were included in the general prefectural election figures, because among these eight were four strongholds of the proletarian vote: Tōkyō, and the contiguous Kanagawa, Chiba, and Saitama. Nevertheless, the lower percentage in local elections partly resulted from social democrats being more interested in national than in local issues. As to why national election percentages fluctuated so much more than local, the explanation is probably to be found in the fact that Diet elections required far more expensive and highly organized campaigns and, following Diet dissolutions, they could occur more suddenly and more frequently.

An analysis of the type of support in both local and national elections shows a shift in the proletarian vote from the rural to the urban areas. Since this point will be treated subsequently in greater detail, it is sufficient here to note that the biggest such shift took place between the 1927 and 1931 prefectural elections. According to the Ōhara Institute of Social Research, the total proletarian party vote from the cities in 1931 was 39,046 more than in 1927 and from the markedly agricultural regions 34,834 less—the two extremes almost cancelling each other out.[6] Though the total proletarian party vote increased by 20,072, the total vote for all parties shot up by 706,040; in effect, the proletarian party vote percentage remained about the same. What is noteworthy in these two elections is not so much the rise in city votes as the sharp decrease in the countryside vote, due most directly to the forced disbandment in 1928 of the Labor Farmer Party which had the largest rural following. Though at a slower rate, this shift continued in the national Diet elections—with the exception of the 1937 election when the proportion of votes from nonmetropolitan areas again rose to about 40 per cent. Yet even then no votes were garnered in six predominantly agricultural prefectures where the Labor Farmer Party had received a sizable vote in 1928.

6. *Nihon Rōdō Nenkan, 13* (1932), 465.

Despite the 1937 election, when the farmers' unions made a special effort on behalf of the Socialist Masses' Party, increasing support for the social democratic movement as a whole came from the workers, intellectuals, and other middle elements in the cities, whereas support from the tenant-farmer population lagged behind.

DISTRIBUTION OF STRENGTH AMONG THE PROLETARIAN PARTIES

The distribution of votes and support among the various social democratic parties must also be examined in order to show the trends within the movement. The division of votes for all the party elections is graphically shown in Table 3. Subsequent tables for each Diet election provide further breakdowns into numbers and percentages. The factional leadership of each party is indicated, as well as its aspirations in terms of the number of candidates entered. Also illustrated are the results as gauged by the number elected, numerical support, and relative strength by percentages. National socialist strength is shown for purposes of comparison.

An attempt has also been made to estimate what elements of the population supported the social democratic parties in the elections and in what sections of the country social democratic strength was greatest. The available statistics are, unfortunately, neither as complete nor as reliable as one would wish. For example, the number of members per prefecture claimed by each party in 1928 are to be accepted only with reservations. The votes received in the six Diet elections are far more accurate. Combined with information about the places from which the votes came, however, these statistics can give some indication of the kind of support the social democrats obtained.

The Labor Farmer Party won 39.4 per cent of the vote garnered by the proletarian parties in the 1928 Diet election. This was almost as much as its closest two social democratic rivals combined. The year before in the prefectural elections the gap had been even greater, for the Labor Farmer Party cornered 45.6 per cent of the proletarian vote and won thirteen seats in prefectural assemblies compared with 15.1 per cent and three seats each for the Social Democratic and Japan Labor-Farmer, and 15 per cent and four seats for the Japan

	0	1	2	3	4	5	6	7	8	9	10

1928
Labor Farmer Party
(Legal left)

Japan Labor-Farmer Party
(Japan-Labor clique)

Social Democratic Party
(Socio-Democratic clique)

Japan Farmers' Party
(Hirano)

Local proletarian parties

1930
New Labor Farmer Party
(Ex-legal left)

Japan Masses' Party
(Japan-Labor clique,
Labor-Farmer faction)

Social Democratic Party
(Socio-Democratic clique)

Local proletarian parties

1932
National Labor-Farmer
Masses' Party
(Japan-Labor clique,
Labor-Farmer faction,
Ex-legal left)

Social Democratic Party
(Socio-Democratic clique)

Local proletarian parties

Japan National Socialist Party

1936
Socialist Masses' Party
(Japan-Labor clique,
Socio-Democratic clique)

Local proletarian parties

National socialist parties

1937
Socialist Masses' Party
(Japan-Labor clique,
Socio-Democratic clique)

Japan Proletarian Party
(Katō, Labor-Farmer
faction)

Local proletarian parties

National socialist parties

Votes received

in hundred thousands

299

Farmers' Party.[7] From these first two elections it would appear that, had the Japanese government not undertaken the mass arrests on March 15, 1928, and outlawed the Labor Farmer Party, its prospects of future success would have been greater than those of its rivals.

TABLE 4. COMPARATIVE PROLETARIAN PARTY ACHIEVEMENTS IN THE NATIONAL DIET ELECTION OF FEBRUARY 1928 *

PARTY OR GROUP (FACTION OR CLIQUE)	CANDIDATES ENTERED	CANDIDATES ELECTED	VOTES OBTAINED	COMPARATIVE PERCENTAGES
Social Democratic Party (Socio-Democratic clique)	17	4	120,039	24.5
Japan Labor-Farmer Party (Japan-Labor clique)	13	1	85,698	17.5
Labor Farmer Party (Legal left)	40	2	193,047	39.4
Japan Farmers' Party (Hirano)	12	0	44,203	9.0
Local proletarian parties	6	1	46,766	9.5
Totals	88	8	489,753	100

* Statistics from *Nihon Rōdō Nenkan. 19* (1938), 280–81. Slightly different figures—perhaps less carefully checked, immediately after the election—are found in ibid., *10* (1929), 320; still others in *Rōdō* (March 1928), pp. 4–5.

Considering that extreme police interference hindered even these two campaigns of 1927 and 1928, the vote of the Labor Farmer Party is all the more striking. Police officers, who always attended campaign speeches, interrupted and admonished speakers they considered too radical and arrested those who, after being warned, continued their speeches in the same vein. Campaign workers were often jailed on suspicion of election violations such as door-to-door canvassing, and it was not unusual for a candidate to come to local campaign headquarters only to find it empty because all the people there had been taken away by the police.[8] When speakers from another prefecture came to support a candidate, the police deported them as though the prefecture were still a feudal domain. The well-known journalist

7. For these 1928 prefectural election figures, see Totten, *JSD*, p. 189.
8. See Hakuyōsha, ed., *Nihon Musan Seitō Shi*, pp. 552–53.

Nyozekan Hasegawa recounts an incident that occurred on the last evening of the 1928 campaign when he was campaigning for the Social Democrats. He was tired of being told to stop in the middle of his speech everywhere he went, so he began by saying that this speech would be no different from a university lecture; immediately the police ordered him to stop. Hasegawa concluded it was better to beat a drum than try to make a campaign speech.[9] This kind of suppression was, of course, directed far more against the Labor Farmer Party than against its rivals.

Not only was the vote of the Labor Farmer Party almost equal to the combined total of its two closest rivals, but it also achieved the most balanced and far-flung distribution of all the proletarian parties. Of its total vote 30 per cent came from the big metropolitan areas: Tōkyō–Kanagawa, Ōsaka–Hyōgo, and Kyōto. In the agricultural regions of Kagawa and Niigata alone it received 28,466 votes, 14.7 per cent of its total vote. Other areas in which it received more than 10,000 votes were Hokkaidō and Fukuoka, both mining centers.

The 1928 election results indicated that about 75 per cent of the Social Democratic Party's strength was concentrated in the two largest industrial and commercial cities and their satellites: Tōkyō, with its outlying areas in Kanagawa Prefecture; and Ōsaka, together with Kōbe in Hyōgo Prefecture.[10] The next largest vote was obtained in the coal mining and steel producing centers in Fukuoka. These three areas together accounted for about 90 per cent of the party's votes. That party strength outside these areas was negligible was probably due to the weakness of its supporting farmer organization. Indications are that much of its active support came from urban and industrial workers, although even many of them were politically apathetic and did not vote. Therefore, it is reasonable to postulate that the additional support accrued from intelligentsia, white-collar workers, small businessmen, and other members of the middle class.

In contrast, the Japan Labor-Farmer Party vote was somewhat more widely distributed. About 62 per cent, it is true, was also concentrated in the Tōkyō and Ōsaka–Hyōgo districts; but 16 per cent came from Yamagata and Tochigi prefectures, and 19 per cent from

9. Hakuyōsha, pp. 550–51.
10. For a breakdown of proletarian party vote by prefecture in the 1928 Diet election, see Totten, *JSD*, pp. 192–93.

the agricultural areas of Gumma, Niigata, Shimane, and Kagawa. A considerable agrarian vote thus existed but predominant strength came from the industrial areas. In addition, there was some support from the middle classes to whom the party had appealed on a more radical basis than had the Social Democrats, but in view of the lack of statistics on this point any estimate of the amount of such support would be extremely unreliable.

The smallest of the national proletarian parties in 1928, the Japan Farmers' Party, had less than one fifth of the vote of the Labor Farmer Party. Though it claimed to be a national organization with members in most of the prefectures, voting results would seem to indicate that it padded its membership lists more than any of the other parties.[11] However, in spite of the small vote it received, it did have the aspects of a national party in that it ran candidates and received votes from a number of widely separated areas. It also had the characteristics of a local party in the sense that it did not get even as many as 10,000 votes in any one prefecture, nor did it succeed in electing a single Diet candidate.

This breakdown of the election returns of the proletarian parties in their national debut in 1928 provides a basis for noting the important subsequent changes in the votes they or their successors received in later elections.

Two years later the proletarian parties were given their second opportunity to appeal to the electorate in a national Diet election. Their total vote was almost the same, rising only 34,266 (from 489,753 in 1928 to 524,019 in 1930). The marked differences lay first in the distribution of votes among the parties and secondly in the geographical shifts in their electoral support.[12]

The disappearance of the Labor Farmer Party which had been banned shortly after the 1928 election caused the most marked redistribution of votes among the parties (Table 5). Its successor, the New Labor Farmer Party, purged of most of its Communist leaders, was not only less militant but was organizationally greatly weakened. Consequently in the 1930 election it obtained less than half the number of votes won by its predecessor in 1928. A comparison of the

11. It reported over 70,000, compared to some 15,000 reported by the Labor Farmer, 17,000 by the Japan Labor-Farmer, and 27,000 by the Social Democratic Party. For reported membership figures by prefecture in 1928, see ibid., pp. 186–88.

12. For a breakdown of proletarian party vote by prefecture in the 1930 Diet election, see ibid., pp. 196–98.

TABLE 5. COMPARATIVE PROLETARIAN PARTY ACHIEVEMENTS IN
THE NATIONAL DIET ELECTION OF FEBRUARY 1930 *

PARTY OR GROUP (FACTION OR CLIQUE)	CANDIDATES ENTERED	CANDIDATES ELECTED	VOTES OBTAINED	COMPARATIVE PERCENTAGES
Social Democratic Party (Socio-Democratic clique)	33	2	176,334	33.6
Japan Masses' Party (Japan-Labor clique)	23	2	166,147	31.7
New Labor Farmer Party (Ex-legal left)	14	1	82,678	15.8
National Democratic Party (Ex-Socio-Democrats)	4	0	19,695	3.8
Local proletarian parties	24	0	79,165	15.1
Totals	98	5	524,019	100

* Statistics from *Nihon Rōdō Nenkan, 19* (1938), 280–81. Number of candidates corrected on basis of study of lists where slightly different figures are found in ibid., *12* (1931), 373–78.

prefectural breakdown of the 1930 vote with that of 1928 reveals that areas such as Aomori, Fukui, and Kanagawa, which gave a combined total of some 100,000 votes to the Labor Farmer Party, now were casting them for the other proletarian parties and not for the New Labor Farmer Party. For instance, the Japan Masses' Party received some 5,000 votes in Akita where its predecessor had received none but where the Labor Farmer Party had obtained almost 9,000. Thus it would seem safe to assume that the Japan Masses' Party in this case was absorbing old Labor Farmer Party votes. Nevertheless, the New Labor Farmer Party appeared to inherit its successor's votes notably in two areas: Tōkyō and Kyōto. In Tōkyō its vote of 21,267 was actually some 7,000 votes above its predecessor's, but in Kyōto its vote of 17,108 was some 6,000 less, due largely to Mizutani's defection and opposition.

Another shift in support was caused by the appearance of the National Democratic Party (Zenkoku Minshūtō), formed shortly before the election by a group led by Shōzō Ōya, who had split off from the Social Democratic Party. Though it had the title and aspirations of a national party, its only stronghold was in Ōsaka, where it was apparently successful in diverting over 14,000 votes from its parent body. As a result, the Social Democratic Party's vote in Ōsaka was less than half what it had been in 1928.[13]

Otherwise, the vote of the Social Democratic Party rose some 50,000 to a total of 176,334 in the 1930 election. A notable 8,000 vote gain was made in Fukuoka, giving it a total there of 25,253. With too many candidates in the field, however, it did not concentrate its strength and thus its Diet representation decreased from four to two. A shift in the geographical distribution of the vote was noticeable in the greater support received from agricultural prefectures.

The Japan Masses' Party (successor to the Japan Labor-Farmer Party and thus led by the Japan-Labor clique) almost doubled the vote of its predecessor; it garnered a total of 166,147 votes. It also had a wider geographical distribution, taking in more agrarian areas. In Fukuoka, it made a remarkable gain: 18,726 votes where its predecessor had had none. As a result its Diet representation rose from one to two.

The same trends noted in this Diet election were reflected in the prefectural elections, held at various times from September to October 1931. The organizational difference was that by then all the important factions except the Social Democratic Party had merged to form the National Labor-Farmer Masses' Party and this unity won them thirteen prefectural assembly seats as compared with three for the Social Democratic Party.[14]

The Diet election of 1932 in which the national socialists made their first appearance was the first election after the Manchurian incident (see Table 6). While together holding on to five Diet seats, the National Labor-Farmer Masses' Party and the Social Democratic Party, the only two national proletarian parties running in this election, suffered drastic reverses in terms of electoral support. Though the average number of votes received by each candidate increased and the percentage of candidates elected also rose, the total proletarian vote fell to about half of what it had been in the 1930 election. The Social Democrats, however, lost only 34,072 votes, in contrast to

13. Besides being split just before the election, the "ultraconservatism" of the Social Democratic Party in 1930 was an important reason for its not making a better showing in the election, according to the *Nihon Rōdō Nenkan, 12* (1931), 367.

14. For these 1931 prefectural election figures, see Totten, *JSD,* p. 199.

the 134,156 fewer votes the National Labor-Farmer Masses' Party garnered compared to the aggregate of its predecessors in 1930. The reduced vote reflected the internal factionalism and the general political confusion engendered by the Manchurian incident. Some of the leaders of the amalgamated party believed that their opposition to the take-over in Manchuria had cost them heavily in popular votes. In Ōsaka, the Social Democratic vote fell from 15,526 in 1930 to 6,522, whereas the National Labor-Farmer Masses' Party ob-

TABLE 6. COMPARATIVE PROLETARIAN PARTY ACHIEVEMENTS IN THE NATIONAL DIET ELECTION OF FEBRUARY 1932 *

PARTY OR GROUP (FACTION OR CLIQUE)	CANDIDATES ENTERED	CANDIDATES ELECTED	VOTES OBTAINED	COMPARATIVE PERCENTAGES
Social Democratic Party (Socio-Democratic clique)	15	3	122,262	42.5
National Labor-Farmer Masses' Party (Japan-Labor clique plus Labor-Farmer faction and other similar groupings)	13	2	134,364	46.7
Preparatory Committee for the National Socialist Party (Ex-Socio-Democrats plus ex-Japan-Laborites and other national socialists)	2	0	12,351	4.3
Local proletarian parties	5	0	18,876	6.5
Totals	35	5	287,853	100

* Statistics from *Nihon Rōdō Nenkan*, *19* (1938), 280–81.

tained 35,319 in comparison to its predecessor's 22,140; in Hyōgo the Social Democratic Party received no support, but the National Labor-Farmer Masses' Party managed to win 13,564 votes, though this was almost 7,000 less than received by its predecessor in 1930. The heaviest urban voting was in Tōkyō, of course, where the National Labor-Farmer Masses' Party received only 39,564 votes in contrast to the 71,302 its now component parts, the former New Labor Farmer and Japan Masses' Parties, had received in 1930, while the Social Democrats' vote rose slightly from 38,823 to 43,655.

It was in the agricultural areas, however, that the proletarian parties suffered their greatest losses.[15] For example, 86 per cent of Social Democratic Party votes came from the nonagricultural areas of Fukuoka, Tōkyō, and Ōsaka as did 87 per cent of the National Labor-Farmer Masses' Party's votes. Both parties also lost strength in Kyōto where their support came from radical intelligentsia rather than farmers or workers. The poor election showing plus the fact that various national and local leaders and their labor support were deserting to the national socialist camp convinced many of the social democrats of the need for a united front. Since the government had suppressed the radical left, including the Communists, the remaining weakened left-wing socialists had merged to form one party which was more moderate. Furthermore, the election revealed that it was approximately equal in strength to the Social Democrats. This made negotiations for merger easier. The Socialist Masses' Party was born four months after the election, superseding for good the Social Democratic and National Labor-Farmer Masses' Parties.

The February 1936 Diet election was preceded by prefectural elections in September and October 1935. Since almost all the social democratic leaders were now united into one party, no open struggles broke out among them. However, their vote in these prefectural elections decreased by 54,778 (from the previous 270,376 to 215,598), largely due to losses to the new contenders—the national socialist parties. Nevertheless, as a result of better election strategy, the number of social democratic seats in the prefectural assemblies increased from 17 to 38 if the six successful local party and union candidates are added to the 32 from the Socialist Masses' Party.[16]

In contrast, the national Diet election of 1936 (Table 7) saw a remarkable increase in the proletarian vote—389,905 or almost two and a half times over 1932—although because of the rise in the total vote the percentage was only doubled. Almost five times the former number of Diet seats were won. Of the 23 Diet representatives elected, 12 received the highest vote in their electoral districts. Such conditions as increased commitments in Manchuria, the rise of militarist influence within Japan, the decline in real wages, further suppression of civil liberties, and the corruption of the established parties all probably combined to produce this sizable protest vote.

15. For a breakdown of the proletarian party vote by prefecture in the 1932 Diet election, see ibid., pp. 202–03.

16. For these 1935 prefectural election figures, see ibid., p. 205.

The 1936 results do not show any appreciable change from 1932 in the geographical distribution of votes with its implications concerning the extent of agrarian support. Of the total social democratic vote, 67 per cent came from Tōkyō and Ōsaka and an additional 12 per cent from Fukuoka, which meant that only some 21 per cent of the ballots were cast in predominantly agricultural regions.[17]

Social democratic unity was not destined to last long. It will be remembered that, though originally from the Japan-Labor clique, Katō ran as an independent labor candidate in 1936 in the same dis-

TABLE 7. COMPARATIVE PROLETARIAN PARTY ACHIEVEMENTS IN THE NATIONAL DIET ELECTION OF FEBRUARY 1936 *

PARTY OR GROUP (FACTION OR CLIQUE)	CANDIDATES ENTERED	CANDIDATES ELECTED	VOTES OBTAINED	COMPARATIVE PERCENTAGES
Socialist Masses' Party (Socio-Democratic and Japan-Labor cliques)	30	18	518,844	58.2
All other groups (including Labor-Farmer faction and Katō)	11	5	146,563	16.4
National socialist parties	29	5	226,302	25.4
Totals	70	28	891,709	100

* Statistics from *Nihon Rōdō Nenkan, 19* (1938), 280–81, corrected. Slightly different figures are found in *Rōdō Nenkan* (1936), pp. 82–90.

trict as Asō, the Socialist Masses' nominee, and that the breech was widened the following year when Katō took a leading part in organizing the Japan Proletarian Party in order to press for the popular front idea.

Though the social democratic forces were again divided, they re-

17. For a breakdown of the proletarian party vote by prefecture in the 1936 Diet election, see ibid., pp. 206–07. Shortly after the Diet election, Assembly elections were held for Tōkyō Fu in which of 23 Socialist Masses' Party candidates, 18 were elected, and of 6 candidates put up by Katō's Labor-Farmer Proletarian Conference, 4 were successful. Simultaneously in the Kanakawa Prefectural Assembly 6 of the 7 Socialist Masses' Party candidates got in.

ceived nearly a million and a half votes in the April 1937 Diet election (see Table 8). The upward trend of 1936 was intensified. The total proletarian vote rose 344,894—another third; the percentage, one half; and the number of Diet seats, from 23 to 38. Of the latter, 19 received the highest vote in their election districts.

Aside from the factors previously mentioned which contributed to this large vote during both the 1936 and 1937 elections, there was "the clean election movement," which a "liberal" segment within

TABLE 8. COMPARATIVE PROLETARIAN PARTY ACHIEVEMENTS IN
THE NATIONAL DIET ELECTION OF APRIL 1937 *

PARTY OR GROUP (FACTION OR CLIQUE)	CANDIDATES ENTERED	CANDIDATES ELECTED	VOTES OBTAINED	COMPARATIVE PERCENTAGES
Socialist Masses' Party (Socio-Democratic and Japan-Labor cliques)	66	37	928,934	66.8
Japan Proletarian Party (Kanjū Katō and Labor– Farmer faction)	5	1	75,820	5.5
Local Proletarian Party	1	0	5,547	0.4
National socialists	64	11	379,673	27.3
Totals	136	49	1,389,974	100

* Statistics from *Nihon Rōdō Nenkan*, 19 (1938), 280–81. Slightly different figures are found in *Rōdō Nenkan* (1938), p. 169.

the bureaucracy, led by Fumio Gotō of the Home Ministry, appalled by election scandals, had started. This helped the proletarian parties at the expense of the established forces. Premier Okada had dissolved the Diet in January 1936 to test out this new movement. The dissolution of the Diet on March 31, 1937, by the militaristic Premier General Hayashi was motivated by his desire to disrupt the political parties by subjecting them to campaign exertions after only a year in office. But the results were a repudiation of the Premier in support of the parties.

As a result of the 1937 election, the Socialist Masses' Party became the third largest party in the Diet. In this election only 59 per cent of the vote came from the urban and industrial centers of Tōkyō, Ōsaka, and Fukuoka prefectures, indicating increased agrarian support.[18]

18. For a breakdown of the proletarian party vote by prefecture in the 1937 Diet election, see ibid., pp. 209–10.

The National Farmers' Union, which had sometimes run independent candidates in the past, in 1937 lent its full and effective support to the Socialist Masses' Party.

Following the April 1937 Diet election, the proletarian party movement had to adjust to or succumb to the difficulties of the China war starting in July, and in December and January of the following year the popular front arrests wiping out the Japan Proletarian Party.

The prefectural elections of 1939 reflected these events. Although the Socialist Masses' Party's votes increased from 173,791 in 1935 to 218,482 in 1939, its number of seats remained at 32. Votes for independent proletarian candidates declined and their seats fell from six to two. National socialist representatives, however, leapt from 12 to 29.[19]

In the following year, all political parties were disbanded and in their stead the Imperial Rule Assistance Association was inaugurated by the Konoe government, ostensibly to concentrate all the energies of the nation on the one object of national expansion.

One more election was held before Japan's defeat. The 1942 national Diet election was utilized by the Tōjō government as a plebiscite for approval of its war policies. All the totalitarian organizations of the time were mobilized to convince the people it was their patriotic duty in support of the war effort to cast their ballots for the candidates "recommended" by the government. A total of 471 candidates were recommended for the 466 Diet seats and given special financial assistance.[20] As a result, 381 of those recommended were elected, while only 85 of the 613 candidates not recommended won seats anyway.

A number of former proletarian party leaders ran as independents in this election. According to the author's calculations (see Table 9), only 10 out of the 52 former proletarian candidates were recommended. Eight not recommended were elected in addition to the 10 who were, making a total of 18, less than one half of the total successful in the 1937 election. A breakdown of the vote they received reveals that their total vote was also considerably less than half that of

19. For these 1939 prefectural election figures, see ibid., p. 210.
20. The financial assistance ranged from ¥2,000 to ¥10,000 and was supplied from Emergency Military Funds (*Rinji Gunji Hi*). See Masayuki Shiroki, *Nihon Seitō Shi: Shōwa Hen* (A History of Japanese Political Parties: Shōwa Period) (Tōkyō, Chūō Kōronsha, 1949), pp. 317–19.

the 1937 election.[21] The meaning of this vote is difficult to assess, since only half of it could be considered in any way a protest against Tōjō and even the nonrecommended candidates gave full public support to the war effort.

PARTY ORGANIZATION AND LINKS TO LABOR AND FARMER SUPPORT

In all but this last election, the organized proletarian parties served as the focal points for rallying support to the various candi-

TABLE 9. NATIONAL DIET ELECTION OF APRIL 1942, ACHIEVEMENTS
OF FORMER SOCIAL DEMOCRATS *

FORMER AFFILIATION	CANDIDATES ENTERED	CANDIDATES ELECTED	VOTES OBTAINED	COMPARATIVE PERCENTAGES
Socio-Democratic clique:				
Recommended	1	1	26,401	
Not recommended	14	1	134,929	
			161,330	21.5
Japan-Labor clique:				
Recommended	3	3	84,410	
Not recommended	10	3	107,818	
			192,228	26.5
Other former social democrats:				
Recommended	4	4	79,257	
Not recommended	28	3	177,345	
			256,602	34.2
National socialists:				
Recommended	0	0		
Not recommended	15	4	140,816	18.8
Totals	75	19	750,976	100

* Statistics calculated by author from lists and figures in the Tōkyō *Asahi Shimbun* (May 3, 1942).

dates. Before proceeding to the subject of organized labor and farmer support, it is natural to ask how the parties themselves were organized for their function of vote-getting.

21. For a breakdown by prefecture of the vote received by former social democrats in the 1942 Diet elections, see Totten, *JSD*, pp. 213–14, though it must be pointed out that the criteria for choosing those statistics were reevaluated and revised by the author for the present volume. For candidates' names and groupings, see below pp. 419–21.

On the assumption that party members would be the first to vote for a party, membership statistics should be important in determining party strength. Unfortunately, reported party membership has proved almost totally unreliable. For example, the Japan Farmers' Party reported its membership in 1928 as 70,138 and yet its total vote in the general election that year was only 37,897![22] In contrast to this, the Labor Farmer Party which reported only 15,374 members, garnered 193,027 votes. Throughout the 1930s the reported Socialist Masses' Party membership amounted to somewhere around ten times its actual membership.[23] The parties themselves often had no sure idea of the number of party members, since the local party boss would often pay up the very nominal membership dues for a large number of people in order to secure more seats from his locality at national party conventions. Since party coffers were always low, this practice was often winked at. Nor was it easy to detect.

Theoretically, the highest organ of almost all the parties was the party convention *(taikai)* which usually met once annually. It elected members to the central committee *(chūō iinkai)* which was supposed to meet approximately once a month, but actually met more often in crises and less frequently usually. Members of the smaller central executive committee *(chūō shikkō iinkai)* which met weekly or more often were also elected at the convention. It was usually in charge of the party headquarters *(tō hombu)* which consisted of a permanent office and possibly a meeting hall of moderate size. Clerical help took care of the party files and propaganda. The most important officers elected at the conventions were the chairman of the central executive committee *(chūō shikkō iinchō)* who was the official head of the party, the secretary-general *(shokichō)*, who was often the "power behind the throne," and the treasurer *(kaikei)*.

This type of structure characterized all the proletarian parties. Variations appeared more in the operations of the parties than in their form. Surprisingly, the Social Democratic as well as the Labor Farmer Party supported the principle of "democratic centralism," which is invariably adopted by Communists, but all resorted to expulsions in order to enforce discipline.

Perhaps the most representative in party structure was the Socialist Masses' Party, since it was built on eight years of proletarian party experience. Like so many of its predecessors it was created by merger,

22. For reported party membership figures in 1928, see ibid., pp. 186–87.
23. Information from an interview with Mitsu Kōno on June 2, 1953.

and the joint statement preceding the union outlined the agreed-upon character and structure of the party to be.[24]

The basic function of the party was theoretically to represent workers and farmers and the propertyless masses in general. The "principle of mobilization" (dōinshugi) was to characterize party organization. This was a military term meaning to call up soldiers from peacetime dispersion into military formation. Applied to political parties, it meant to rally the people for political campaigns. Thus, not as much emphasis was placed on permanent organization as, for instance, in the illegal Communist Party, which was less concerned simply with election campaigns.

Party branches (shibu) were organized on a geographical basis. Anywhere from two to some 40 branches would be organized into a regional federation (rengōkai), usually located in the largest city of the region or a central ward of a metropolitan prefecture. Under a branch various types of quasi-occupational units might be set up: (1) factory squads (kōba han); (2) enterprise squads (keiei han) —here "enterprise" is used in the sense of a small business, store, or a small manufacturing establishment; (3) hamlet squads (buraku han)—meaning local community, particularly farming, or semi-farming, or fishing communities; or (4) city resident squads (shimin han). Only the factory squads had subcommittees; these were organized along industrial lines in order to bring together workers with similar problems.

Continuous difficulties were encountered in relations with supporting labor and farmer unions. Union members were supposed to join the party as individuals, but in practice if a top union leader joined a party it meant a "mass conversion," and union money and organization would be made available for political purposes. According to party regulations (Art. 5), an organization could affiliate with the party if it supported the party program and if over half of its executive committee became party members; those organizations with over 1,000 members would be attached to party headquarters; those with less to regional associations or branches. The relationship was actually rather informal and slipshod. There were continuous at-

24. See "Sengen" (Statement), issued by the Council for the Amalgamation of the Proletarian Parties—The Social Democratic and the National Labor-Farmer Masses' Parties—published in the Nihon Minshū Shimbun (June 15, 1932). This was used as the basis for the following discussion, since it outlined, among other things, hoped-for goals in party organization.

tempts to "rationalize" and tighten organization. Yet in political campaigns the personal element was so strong that formalized relationships meant little. Union leaders would use their own union subordinates for legwork. The party tended more to be the net that held together various "bigwigs" who in turn exercised power in behalf of the party through their position within their own organization of basic affiliation—which might be a labor or farmer union, a cultural organization, or a group that published a journal or newspaper.

As might be expected, finances posed a problem, and it was difficult to try to make the process of meeting expenditures with income "automatic." So large a part of the financing of political campaigns remained hidden from the public and even secret from many of the party leaders and functionaries that only the more routine income and expenditures went through party channels. Nevertheless, sympathizers were approached in the name of the party for contributions, especially at election time.

A study of the published figures of the Socialist Masses' Party's finances from 1932 to 1940 [25] reveals that "contributions from supporting organizations" were surprisingly small, gradually descending from a high of 2.8 per cent in 1934 down to 0.2 in 1938. Most income came from the pockets of party functionaries, who in turn had their own sources. Assessments on party officers accounted for about 24 per cent of income in 1933–34 and 6.3 per cent in 1939. The slack here was taken up by the assessments that could be levied on the increasing number of party Diet members, who were expected to turn over to the party a certain amount of their salaries and expense funds derived from membership in the Diet. The percentage of party income from this source rose from 10.9 per cent in 1933 to 44.9 per cent in 1937, which meant that the Japanese government was indirectly underwriting almost half of the expenses of the main proletarian opposition! Beyond that, dues that accrued to party headquarters averaged roughly around 15 per cent. Throughout this period, the item labeled "loans" provided about 30 per cent of income, going up to 50 per cent for the one year 1936. These were probably donations from individuals and organizations, though in some years donations were listed as combined items. Income from renting out the facilities of the party headquarters naturally did not begin until the

25. The following two tables on the annual income and expenditures of the Socialist Masses' Party (1932–39) are based on figures reported in the *Nihon Rōdō Nenkan*

(1933–40); the percentages were calculated by the author. No figures were reported for the years 1935 or 1940; and for 1932 no expenditures, only an income of ¥1,988.95 (68 per cent of this from donations and 32 per cent from loans).

TABLE 1. SOCIALIST MASSES' PARTY ANNUAL BUDGET INCOME (ITEMS EXPRESSED IN PERCENTAGES)

	1933	1934	1936	1937	1938	1939
Brought forward	—	0.7	0.6	—	0.3	0.4
Headquarters dues	14.2 [a]	18.9 [a]	9.8	12.8	15.4	18.0
Contributions from supporting organizations	2.1	2.8	1.3	0.6	0.2	0.5
Annual assessments from Diet members	10.9	11.8	19.8	44.9	34.1	38.7
Officers' assessments	23.8	32.1 [b]	11.3	6.9	6.4	6.3 [c]
Profits from activities	1.1 [d]	—	3.0	—	—	—
Convention delegates' fees	—	2.2	—	—	—	—
Donations	—	*	—	*	*	*
Annual assessments from occupational earnings	—	—	—	—	3.0	1.4
Profits from headquarters building	—	—	—	—	2.0	1.1
Loans	41.7	28.8 *	50.1	30.6	30.7	24.7
Miscellaneous	6.2	2.7	2.0	4.2 *[e]	7.9 *	8.9 *
Totals in per cent	100.0	100.0	100.0	100.0	100.0	100.0
Totals in yen	6,525.44	5,919.39	11,164.40	20,206.51	22,037.57	25,224.10

* Combined items
a. Party member dues
b. Includes special assessment
    (8.1 per cent of budget)
c. Individual assessment

d. Sale of the party organ
e. Includes special annual contribution
    (0.8 per cent of budget)

TABLE 2. SOCIALIST MASSES' PARTY ANNUAL BUDGET EXPENDITURES (ITEMS EXPRESSED IN PERCENTAGES)

	1933	1934	1936	1937	1938	1939
Fund raising costs	2.0	4.9	0.3	—	*	—
Party organ expenses	13.1	11.7	7.1	9.7	17.6	17.1
Special activities expenditures	4.8	6.6	5.6	—	—	—
Office rent and utilities	5.4	5.4 [a]	7.6	—	9.9 [a&b]	6.6 [b]
Communications expenses	14.8 [c]	13.1 [d]	3.4 [e]	3.1	4.9	—
Staff salaries	38.4	31.4	41.9	30.5	32.8	41.4
Money repaid and interest	2.8	5.4	12.0	35.5 [f]	21.3	—

party secured its own building in 1938. The reported total budgets rose steadily from about ¥6,500 in 1933 (the first normal year) to over ¥25,000 in 1939 (the last).

Less can be learned from published party expenditures, because election campaign spending was not included. The largest individual item was always staff salaries, mainly for the young male secretaries working at headquarters. They received from 30 to 42 per cent of outlay annually.

Official policy was always to encourage "new blood" in nominations for party officers, but this conflicted with the desire of those in power to remain there. (Due to the slow growth of the prewar parties, on the one hand, and the cliquishness of the leadership, on the other, an adequate supply of leaders was to become one of the most troublesome problems that faced the social democrats in postwar Japan.)

Party rules stipulated that officers be elected by absolute majority vote. At conventions votes were distributed proportionally among branches on the basis of the number of paid-up members in each territorial branch. The permanent party staff received salaries which were not only meager but often erratically paid, if at all.

Party structures were usually marked by anomalies arising from mergers. Partly consolidation after a merger often took half a year or more and even then, especially on the lower levels, was marred by

	1933	1934	1936	1937	1938	1939
Emergency expenses	—	—	—	8.8	**	32.2
Convention expenses	0.7 g	10.1 g	—	—	4.2 g	2.7
Printing	2.5	2.0	—	—	*	—
Travel	5.3	2.8	—	—	*	—
Miscellaneous	5.8	2.8	2.3	—	4.8 **	—
Other expenditures	4.4 h	3.8 h	19.8	12.4	4.5 h*	—
Totals in per cent	100.0	100.0	100.0	100.0	100.0	100.0
Totals in yen	6,525.44	5,919.39	11,164.40	20,206.51	22,037.57	25,224.10

* and ** Combined items

a. Includes fixtures
b. Includes headquarters building maintenance
c. Includes 5.7 per cent for telephone bills
d. Includes 5.2 per cent for telephone bills
e. Telephone bills only

f. Repayment of previous year's loan was 13.7 per cent and 21.8 for this year's loans
g. Includes meeting hall rent
h. Office supplies included

compromises involving local balances of power rather than hierarchical party control. As throughout the rest of Japanese society, party positions were often misleading indicators of the real leadership.

In fact, the roots of power often lay outside the party, in the supporting labor or farmer organizations. Without an examination of these sources of organized support, the relative strengths not only of the various proletarian parties but also of the factions within them cannot be fully understood. In addition, the party would either organize, or affiliate with, a youth group, a women's federation, a minority organization, salarymen's [26] units, city tenant's groups, a socialist lawyers' association, or any sympathetic or potentially active group. By far the most important of these, however, were the trade unions.

26. By *sarari man* is meant white-collar workers in the large metropolitan bureaucratic organizations who receive regular salaries. See Ezra F. Vogel, *Japan's New Middle Class: The Salary Man and His Family in a Tokyo Suburb* (Berkeley and Los Angeles, University of California Press, 1963), pp. 4–5 and passim.

12: Organized Labor

Struggle, rivalry, and cooperation among organized labor groups crucially affected the proletarian parties. Did not, in fact, the division of the socialist movement into the Communist and social democratic camps first take concrete form in the internal struggle of the General Federation which split it down the middle and resulted in the creation of the rival Council of Japanese Labor Unions in May 1925? The immediate effect of this split, by destroying the unity of the organized labor movement, was to render easier the government's quick decision to order the disbanding of the first proletarian party on December 1, 1925, the day it was born. All subsequent power struggles and antipathies within the labor movement had their repercussions in the proletarian parties and, as the parties became forces in their own right, reverse effects were also generated.

By organized labor support to a proletarian political party we mean contributions of funds from union coffers and mobilization of union members for such tasks as marching in demonstrations with placards, preparing and distributing party literature, and persuading eligible voters through all the means at the disposal of Japanese etiquette as well as any suggested by reading about foreign techniques. In addition we mean by labor support a complex set of relations that

can only be touched on here. For instance, union demands would influence party slogans and vice versa. The parties helped to publicize
the generalized demands of their affiliated unions. When a large-scale
labor dispute broke out, the union officials who were also party functionaries would ask the party to help air the issues of the situation in
the local assembly or national Diet in order to win over public opinion or gain consideration from the police or higher governmental
agencies. The proletarian parties were only too willing to do this. In
fact, if, in a large-scale dispute, violence occurred with resultant
newspaper publicity, even those proletarian parties who opposed the
union leaders on political grounds—such as the Communist issue—
would give unsolicited support to the strike in the form of public
statements. Sometimes they even made donations to union strike
funds in the hope of drawing attention to the party and winning
over rank-and-file sympathy toward the party and its affiliated unions
in the future. Though unions could not legally become constituent
parts of political parties, this situation was in fact achieved by close
coordination and interlocking leadership posts. Farmers and other
groups had similar relationships.

In the light of these interactions and based on the preceding discussion of electoral support for the proletarian parties as a whole, this
chapter attempts to evaluate in greater detail the segment of support
afforded by organized labor. After examining the labor organizations
aligned with each of the social democratic parties at the time of the
1928 election, subsequemt changes will be noted which resulted from
realignments of union forces and shifts in party allegiances due to
changes in socioeconomic and political conditions. Chart 2 of the
Appendix, "Lineages of Japanese Labor Unions," may be referred to
here to clarify both temporal and factional relationships.

LABOR ALIGNMENTS IN THE 1928 ELECTION

In the 1928 election the proletarian parties reflected the cleavages
and comparative strengths of organized labor. The Japan General
Federation of Labor provided the main support for the Social Democratic Party; the Federation of Japanese Labor Unions, which had
broken with the General Federation, supported the Japan Labor-
Farmer Party; and the Council of Japanese Labor Unions, itself the
first major split-off from the General Federation, worked whole-

heartedly to promote the Labor Farmer Party. Not only did organized labor supply the bulk of party campaign workers and funds but actually the majority of party leaders were union officials. A comparison of the labor and party lineage charts in the Appendix will show the party affiliations of the union federations at any given time, for shadings indicate leadership factional allegiance. These charts are not exhaustive and portray only the union federations with the most direct linkages. For instance, in the 1928 Diet election, a number of small unions listed their political affiliation as Social Democratic. But they were too small to be significant. Closely associated with the General Federation, however, were four independent labor organizations which went along with it politically. They will be considered below in relation to the Socio-Democratic clique.

Organizationally, the General Federation was divided into two regional federations, the Kantō and Kansai Labor Federations (Rōdō Dōmeikai), which in turn were composed of local associations of unions (rengōkai) based on region. The trade unions under them were organized along industrial, craft, or enterprise lines. In the Tōkyō Association of Unions, the largest single union was made up of some six thousand textile (muslin) workers, most of whom were women. Three thousand metal workers in zinc and other electroplating companies comprised the next largest group, followed by postmen, a thousand strong. In addition, there were horsewagon drivers as well as leather, sewer-maintenance, and print-shop workers. The Kanagawa Association of Unions was smaller, its largest contingent of over one thousand being metal workers in a variety of industries, followed by cement, electrical, and kerosene workers. Soy sauce brewers, silk spinners, and steel mill workers had separate unions. The Kansai Labor Federation, with a larger number of associations of unions, was composed of a similar variety but a smaller total number. The reported membership of the whole General Federation in 1928 was 39,315, probably a gross exaggeration.[1]

The General Federation's leadership constituted the core of the Socio-Democratic clique with Bunji Suzuki President of the General Federation, and Matsuoka and Nishio, Secretaries-General of the General Federation and the ranking leaders of the Kantō and Kansai Labor Federations respectively. At this time Shōzō Ōya was still head

---

1. For a table of General Federation membership broken down by occupation in organizational units, see Totten, *JSD*, pp. 217–18.

of the strong Ōsaka Association of Unions, but he soon bolted the General Federation and the Social Democratic Party. Through its various splits, the General Federation lost its most militant leadership and most active rank and file.

The conservative attitude of the General Federation was enhanced by the large percentage of women workers in its fold. In 1928 organized women workers, 11,848 in all, represented only 3.9 per cent of organized labor. Of these, 6,884, or 58.1 per cent, most of whom were engaged in the textile industry, belonged to the General Federation and accounted for about one fourth of its membership.[2] They formed such an important segment that the General Federation published a newspaper called *The Working Woman (Rōdō Fujin)*. Yet they considered themselves as only working away from home temporarily (that is, *dekasegi*-type laborers, as described above, page 9, note 6) and were apathetic to social problems, politics, and economic struggle. The fact that most of them were employed in the textile industry, subject to strict hierarchical control, only reinforced an attitude of indifference toward union activities. This type of membership created favorable conditions for control of the unions by labor bosses who were often inclined to act in their own and management's interests. Many of these unions were actually encouraged by employers who felt that unionization under conservative leadership was an effective way of controlling their employees and preventing radicalism.

Four large unions cooperated closely with the General Federation and shared its political sympathies: [3]

1. The Naval Labor League (Kaigun Rōdō Remmei) with a membership of 42,896 was composed of various types of workers in munition factories that were directly under navy management. Despite its large membership, it was a "company union" in character and the most conservative of the four.

2. The General Federation of Labor in Government Enterprises (Kangyō Rōdō Sōdōmei) with a membership of 14,042 included unions mainly in army arsenals, steel mills, the tobacco monopoly, and other government-managed enterprises.

2. *Nihon Rōdō Nenkan, 10* (1929), 285.

3. The listing and characterizations of these unions were suggested by Suehiro, *Nihon Rōdō Kumiai Undō Shi,* pp. 66–68, but since Suehiro lists no authoritative source for his figures (nor any dates), I have used membership figures from *Nihon Rōdō Nenkan, 10* (1929), 285–306, which represent the year 1928.

3. The Japan Seamen's Union (Nihon Kaiin Kumiai) with a membership of 81,534 was an industrial union of seamen. It had the largest membership of any union in prewar Japan. Control within it was very strict, but its welfare activities were extensive. Of all Japanese unions it was the closest in character to the Western model. As a member of the International Federation of Transport Workers' Unions, it affiliated, as we have noted, with the Amsterdam International.

4. The Japan Maritime Officers' Association (Nihon Kaiin Kyōkai) with a membership of 11,124 was a union of ships' officers, closely associated with the Japan Seamen's Union.

Composed of workers in military, naval, merchant marine, and governmental enterprises, these unions were organized in a hierarchical fashion along military lines. Most of them were "closed-shop" unions found in sections of industry which had a comparatively high rate of labor organization. For example, in transportation and communications, 29.8 per cent of the workers were organized in 1931 which was the highest rate of all types of Japanese labor at the time. Of these, approximately 73 per cent were in the Japan Seamen's Union.[4]

These closed-shop unions had been formed not so much for the purpose of forcing the employer to accept union demands (especially when the employer was the government) as to assure the employer a stabilized labor force. This was usually done through labor–management contracts in which the employer agreed to a closed shop, by which he could both keep the union from going leftist and compensate it for its pledge not to strike.[5] Nevertheless, working conditions of laborers in these unions were somewhat better than those of workers in small civilian factories. Civilian industry was often hit by the ups and downs of business cycles, but military industry was usually not affected to an equal extent. The merchant marine, which was monopolized by the giant Mitsui, Mitsubishi, and a few other concerns, was also relatively stable.

Occupying a preferred position in the Japanese labor force, work-

---

4. Specifically, 151,064 of the total of 506,611 workers in transportation and communications were organized, and some 110,000 of the former were members of the Seamen's Union. Suehiro, p. 81.

5. See George O. Totten, "Collective Bargaining and Works Councils as Innovations in Industrial Relations in Japan of the 1920s," in R. P. Dore, ed., *Social Change in Modern Japan* (Princeton, Princeton University Press, 1966).

ers in these industries tended to be relatively conservative and stable in their political attitudes. Their unions usually maintained close connections with the Japan General Federation of Labor. Although the majority of the leaders of the Socio-Democratic clique were from the General Federation, a significant minority came from these associated unions. Such, for example, were Yonekubo—whom we have listed among the "agitator element" in the Socio-Democratic clique —and Chōei Horiuchi, both of whom were simultaneously party and Seamen's Union leaders. Another active party man was Yasutarō Kawamura, head of the General Federation of Labor in Government Enterprises; like Horiuchi and Yonekubo, he was a member of the Central Executive Committee of the Social Democratic Party; he was elected to the Diet in 1936 and 1937 as a representative of the Socialist Masses' Party.

During this same period, 1927–28, the major trade union support for the Japan-Labor clique leaders came from the Federation of Japanese Labor Unions formed at the same time as the Japan Labor-Farmer Party in December 1926. The Federation, as we have seen, consisted of the followers of the union leaders within the General Federation who were dissatisfied with its conservatism.

Because these unions were more aggressive than the average General Federation union, they did not make closed-shop agreements with employers. Their labor–management relationships were far less stabilized. Frequent losers in labor disputes, these unions were often destroyed or else they succumbed to pressures forcing them to withdraw from the Federation. Therefore, they afforded the Japan-Labor clique weaker and less reliable support than the General Federation and its associated unions provided for the Socio-Democrats. In 1928 the Federation reported a membership of only 24,420.[6]

A more limited occupational differentiation among workers characterized the Federation in comparison with the General Federation. In the Tōkyō area, where approximately half of the Federation's unions were located, the overwhelming majority were textile workers (mainly women), followed by metal, machine tool, fertilizer, sugar refining, furniture, and cloth-dying workers. In Kōbe, membership included shipbuilding, paper manufacturing, and button workers;

6. For a table of the Federation of Japanese Labor Union membership in 1927 broken down by occupation in organizational units, see Totten, *JSD,* p. 224.

and in Kyūshū, iron, lumber, coal, and shipbuilding workers. Out-side of the textile industry, no matter where located, and outside of the sugar refining, dyeing, and fertilizer industries located in Tōkyō, each union had only from 200 to 500 members. Not only were its in-dividual unions smaller than those in the General Federation, but they were less widespread. Like the General Federation, the Federa-tion contained a high proportion of women members whose conser-vatism somewhat counterbalanced the more militant attitudes of the majority.

The President of the Federation was Kotora Tanahashi, who, as a student at Tōkyō Imperial University, had been a member of the New Men's Society. He had early come in contact with others who were now Federation union leaders, such as Asō, Sakaru Aki, Bun-roku Fujioka, Matsuta Hosoya, Hitoshi Imamura, Kanjū Katō, and Genji Mochizuki, all whom became original members of the Japan-Labor clique.

Like the General Federation, the Federation had close ties with other unions which supported the Japan Labor-Farmer Party at this time. Three were important: [7]

1. The General Alliance of Japanese Labor Unions (Nihon Rōdō Kumiai Sōrengō) with a membership of 14,155 was originally anarcho-syndicalist and advocated a loose general alliance in opposi-tion to the centralization of the General Federation in the crucial fall of 1922. Even in 1928 various unions belonging to the alliance were publishing newspapers with anarchist names, such as *Black Youth* (*Kokushoku Seinen*). We have already noted that Kōsaburō Saka-moto, head of the General Alliance, was one of the first labor leaders to go over to national socialism.

2. The Japan Stewards' Federation (Nihon Shichū Dōmei) with a membership of 5,600, composed of ship stewards, was more radical than the Seamen's Union; its main strength lay in the Kansai area with its headquarters in Kyōto.

3. The Japan Miners' Union (Nihon Kōfu Kumiai) with a mem-bership of 910 had its greatest concentration of strength in Kyūshū. Of all industrial workers, miners were perhaps the most oppressed and politically and educationally backward. It was through the philanthropy of Baron Ishimoto that this union was originally

7. Note 3 above applies here as well.

formed in the early 1920s.[8] Asō soon became its most powerful leader. But Katō won the struggle that developed between them in 1930 when the union's membership had climbed to 1,805 and withdrew some of its support from the Japan-Labor clique. It was partly utilization of this strength that enabled Katō to form the Japan Proletarian Party in 1937.

The Council of Japanese Labor Unions, mainstay of the Labor Farmer Party in the 1928 election, had a reported membership of 36,000 at the time.[9] Organized on the dual principles of regional and industrial unionism, the Council was a national federation of unions with a wide coverage of localities. It even had branches in Hokkaidō, Shikoku, and the Tōhoku region, areas where no other federations had succeeded in establishing themselves, though its greatest strength lay in the Kantō and Kansai areas. In contrast to the General Federation, its percentage of women members was small. It contained several minor textile unions, but its largest concentrations were among the more "modern" machine tool, metal, electrical, iron, paper, and chemical workers, and among printers.

Most of the Council's leadership came from the working class. More specifically, they had training and experience as skilled workers. This was true of Ritsuta Noda, Chairman of the Central Committee, and such other important leaders as Masanosuke Watanabe, Zentarō Taniguchi, Goichirō Kokuryō, Keiichi Sugiura, Yoshiaki Nakamura, Hiroshi Ōta, and Zenichirō Aogaki.[10] In this respect they were like a section of the Socio-Democratic clique, but politically they were at the other extreme, since many were secretly members of the illegal Communist Party.

The almost simultaneous suppression of the Council and the Labor Farmer Party in May 1928 was a telling blow to Communist influence in the proletarian party movement. Although the Council left some successors, they split between those groups which went underground and those which reconciled themselves to the require-

8. Baron Keikichi Ishimoto's wife, Shizue, described their married life at the Kyūshū coal mines and her husband's radical activities in her autobiography, *Facing Two Ways: The Story of My Life* (London, Cassell and Co., 1935). During the war she divorced Baron Ishimoto and married Kanjū Katō, when he was no longer leader of the miners' union. After the war, she became an active leader of the Social Democratic Party of Japan.

9. For a table of the membership of the Council of Japanese Labor Unions in 1928 broken down by occupation in organizational units, see Totten, *JSD*, pp. 228–30.

10. For a list showing what skills these Council leaders had been trained in, see Eitarō Kishimoto, *Nihon Rōdō Undō Shi*, pp. 180–81.

ments of legal activity. The former were left without any means of expression in the proletarian parties, whereas the latter formed some legal unions which will be described below.

SUBSEQUENT LABOR ALIGNMENTS

This survey of labor support for the various proletarian parties at the time of the 1928 Diet election provides a bench mark from which only the more significant subsequent changes will be noted. To simplify the process, the survey will be divided into three periods: (1) from the 1928 through the 1930 and 1932 Diet elections, (2) from the 1932 through the 1936 and 1937 Diet elections, and (3) from the 1937 election until the dissolution of the organized labor movement.

From the standpoint of labor support, the two important facts concerning the first period (1930–32) were (a) that the Council was dissolved and (b) that the General Federation lost strength to the Federation of Japanese Labor Unions. In spite of its success in the 1928 election (or perhaps because of it), the Council was ordered disbanded on April 10, 1928, less than a month after most of its leaders had been arrested in the March 15th Communist roundup. Though the remnants of the constituent unions of the Council were at first scattered, they soon regrouped into two new organizations: the National Conference of Japanese Labor Unions or "National Conference" (Zenkyō) and the General Council of Japanese Labor Unions or "General Council" (Sōhyō).

The National Conference was organized in December 1928 with about 5,600 members, but its activities were soon severely hampered by police interference, and many of its members were lost in the mass roundup of Communists and other leftists on April 16, 1929. Due to such severe restrictions and to the fact that it came under the control of the illegal Japanese Communist Party, it attempted to gain greater freedom of action by ceasing to exist as a legal organization. It continued underground activities until possibly as late as 1937, but by 1934 had lost most of its effectiveness. Because it had shifted so far from the social democratic movement, it need not be considered further here.[11]

11. For a sympathetic, detailed history of this organization, see Tōru Watanabe, *Nihon Rōdō Kumiai Undō Shi: Nihon Rōdō Kumiai Zenkoku Kyōgikai o Chūshin to Shite* (A History of the Japanese Labor Union Movement: Focusing on the National Conference of Japanese Labor Unions) (Tōkyō, Aoki Shoten, 1954).

Those remnants of the once-powerful Council which did not join
this National Conference were still scattered when the New Labor
Farmer Party was established on November 1, 1929, less than four
months before the Diet election of February 20, 1930. At the time of
the election, the National Conference and most of the smaller unions
which had supported the Labor Farmer Party in 1928 refused to support the new party, making it far weaker than was expected; it received less than half as many votes as its predecessor. However, several remnants of the former Council, located mainly in Tōkyō, Kyōto,
Ōsaka, and their environs, did support the New Labor Farmer Party.
In Tōkyō the most important of them were the Tōkyō Transport
Workers' Union and the Tōkyō Municipal Workers' Union; in
Kyōto, the Dyers' Union and the Ceramic Workers' Union; and in
Ōsaka, the Ōsaka Metal Workers' Union, the All-Ōsaka Lumber
Mill Labor Union, and the Kansai Electrical Workers' Union.

After its poor showing in the February 1930 Diet election, the
New Labor Farmer Party decided that, in order to increase its
strength, it would have to reinforce its bases in the labor and agrarian movements. It was thus at the fourth enlarged meeting of the
Central Committee of the Party that the decision was made to establish the General Council. The formal launching took place on April
18, 1931. According to its founding statement, the General Council
proposed to carry on the spirit of the old Council and to be the
"most leftist" of the legal labor union federations.[12]

Naturally, the question of its relationship with the National Conference arose. Criticizing the latter's assertion that all legal unions
under the conditions then prevailing in Japan were "yellow" (company) unions, the General Council claimed that, though not a "red"
union, it was still definitely not "yellow." The General Council appealed to the National Conference to expel its ultraleftist elements
and join with it in the pressing task of organizing a large leftist front
to oppose the growing strength of the right-wing social democratic
unions; but to no avail.[13]

With a total reported membership in 1932 of 11,400,[14] the Gen-

12. This statement is quoted in the *Nihon Rōdō Nenkan, 13* (1932), 282–83.

13. For an extended statement of this position, see Hakuyōsha, ed., *Nihon Musan
Seitō Shi,* pp. 701–04.

14. For a table of the 1932 membership of the General Council of Japanese Labor
Unions broken down by occupation in organizational units, see Totten, *JSD,* pp.
234–35.

eral Council was actually only a small remnant of the original Council. It was composed of only three regional councils, compared to the eleven of its predecessor. Metal workers made up the largest single labor group, but more interesting were some thousand construction workers in the Chūbu region, since they were mostly Koreans. (The significance of the Korean minority will be discussed in Chapter 14.) The General Council's Chairman, Jōkichi Kimura, and such other important leaders as Kenji Tabei and Tsunekichi Yamazaki as well as Hideo Yamahana—listed above in leadership Grouping IV—were simultaneously leaders of the New Labor Farmer Party. They had organized the General Council after the more radical Professor Hajime Kawakami and Hososako had left the party.

Though less militant than the old Council, leftist discontent within the General Council grew when the New Labor Farmer Party merged with the Japan-Labor clique and the Labor-Farmer faction groups to form the National Labor-Farmer Masses' Party on July 5, 1931. Consequently, in the Diet election of February 1932, the General Council supported only those candidates of that party who were former members of the New Labor Farmer Party. When this already swollen and diluted party merged with the Social Democrats in July, the General Council refused to give any support to the resultant Socialist Masses' Party.[15]

The other important development at the time of the Diet elections of 1930 and 1932 was that the General Federation, which supported the Social Democratic Party, lost strength to the Federation of Japanese Labor Unions which backed the parties led by the Japan-Labor clique. As a result of deteriorating economic conditions during the world depression which began in 1929, groups of laborers in the General Federation, particularly those in the Ōsaka–Hyōgo region, grew more dissatisfied with the conservatism of the General Federation's higher officials. This trend erupted in a revolt at the spring convention of the Kansai Federation when Nishio, representing the conservative leadership, was voted out of office in favor of Ōya. In-

15. Being a leftist federation, the General Council protested the merger which constituted a move to the right. However, it is interesting to note that the General Council itself was not unaffected by the lure of the extreme right; at the time (1932) when Akamatsu and Ōya were withdrawing from the Socio-Democratic and Japan-Labor cliques, respectively, in order to help launch the national socialist movement, supporters of the right appeared within the General Council. They were expelled about the same time. *Nihon Rōdō Nenkan, 14* (1933), 308.

stead of modifying its policies to deal with this situation, the central leadership in Tōkyō took measures to quell the revolt by mass expulsions that affected the large majority of member unions of the Ōsaka Association of Unions as well as their leaders, including Ōya. The expelled leaders and their unions organized the National Federation of Labor Unions (Rōdō Kumiai Zenkoku Dōmei) in September 1929. In the next few months, the same kind of conflict spread to other areas—Hyōgo, Kyōto, the Chūgoku region, and even Hokkaidō—and the newly expelled leaders joined Ōya's new National Federation.

This chain reaction constituted the third major split in the General Federation, skimming off another layer of its more militant elements. The loss of votes by the Social Democrats in Ōsaka and Hyōgo Prefectures in the 1930 election may have been in large measure due to this rupture. It had some 39,000 members as of September 1920. Nevertheless, if all the more politically apathetic "right-wing" unions and federations are classified with the General Federation, they did constitute the majority of all organized labor—perhaps as much as 70 per cent by 1932.

On June 1, 1930, four months after the election, the National Federation merged with the Federation of Japanese Labor Unions (led by the Japan-Labor clique) to form the fairly long-lived National Labor Union Federation, called "National Labor" (Zenrō), which lasted until January 1936. (See Chart 3 in Appendix).

The newly created National Labor reported a membership of some 45,000 with the majority of its members located in the Ōsaka–Hyōgo region. Its next largest concentration of some 10,000 was found in the greater Tōkyō area. Smaller affiliated unions were scattered in Hokkaidō, Tochigi, Kyōto, Kōchi, and Kyūshū. Not only in numbers but also in variety of workers organized, National Labor showed the results of the organizing successes of its predecessors since 1927. The greatest increase was in the category of the more "modern" metal workers. The percentage of "backward" women workers was less than fifteen per cent compared to twenty-five per cent in the General Federation before it split.[16] Ōya became Chairman of National Labor, Aiichi Kamijō, Secretary-General, while Fujioka was probably next in power.

The success and permanence of this defection from the General

16. For a table of the National Labor Union Federation membership in 1930 broken down by occupation in organizational units, see Totten, *JSD*, pp. 237–39.

Federation weakened the Social Democratic Party in the 1932 election, when it obtained no votes in Hyōgo and only 6,552 in Ōsaka; whereas its rival, the National Labor-Farmer Masses' Party with the help of National Labor, won 13,043 votes in Hyōgo and 35,319 in Ōsaka. This weakening of the Social Democrats, along with the rightward drift of the Japan-Labor clique since the Manchurian incident, probably constituted the two strongest reasons for unification of the two cliques in the Socialist Masses' Party four months after the 1932 election.

Unification among the labor federations, however, did not take place until four years later. The first concrete evidence of substantial labor unity can be traced back to June 25, 1931, when leaders from both federations set up in Tōkyō the Japan Labor Club, encompassing nine center-to-right-wing federations, to increase mutual cooperation looking toward the time when greater unification might be achieved.

In the second period—following the 1932 election until just after the last normal prewar election of 1937—labor unity of the moderate and right-wing elements was achieved after the defection of the national socialists but at the expense of the rise on the left of Katō and others demanding solidarity on more leftist terms.

The tentative move toward unification, first evinced in the creation of the Japan Labor Club, developed, after the formation of the Socialist Masses' Party, into a strengthening of the organization and the change of its name to the Congress of Japanese Labor Unions on September 25, 1932. We have already noted the Socio-Democratic influence in its founding statement, advocating anticapitalism, antiCommunism, antifascism, as well as pro-sound-trade-unionism. The Congress was to be a liaison organization to coordinate the activities of the Japan-Labor and Socio-Democratic clique representatives in the Diet and to handle matters of political labor policy, such as petitions to the government concerning proposed labor legislation or regulation. At the time of its formation the Congress was composed of eleven organizations, including, of course, the General Federation and National Labor, with claimed memberships totaling around 280,000.[17]

Protest against even the forerunner of this Congress, the Japan

17. For a list of member unions and membership, see *Nihon Rōdō Nenkan, 14* (1933), 276.

Labor Club, however, had developed in both the Social Democratic
and National Labor-Farmer Masses' Parties, and as we have seen, in
both their left and right wings. The right wing, protesting that the
"three antis" plank was not nationalistic enough, proposed instead
that both the Social Democratic and the National Labor-Farmer
Masses' Parties dissolve and merge to form a new party devoted to national socialism. When Akamatsu and Ōya were defeated with regard
to their proposals, they and their followers seceded from their respective parties and jointly formed the Japan State Socialist Party on May
29, 1932. The next day they consolidated their trade union support
by forming the Japan State Socialist Labor Federation, which on November 20 changed its name to Japan Labor Federation. Only some
3,000 members (the Postmen's Brotherhood led by Akamatsu and
an icemen's union) left the General Federation to join this group,
whereas over 13,000 (the Kyūshū Association of Unions, the larger
part of the Kantō Amalgamated Labor Union, and a section of the
Ōsaka Association of Unions) left National Labor to join it. This was
the first substantial section of the labor movement to embrace national socialism and reject even the nominal label of "social democracy."

This weakening of the ranks of both National Labor and the General Federation strengthened arguments in favor of their eventual
unification. When this came finally in January 1936, there was just
one month to go before the expected Diet election planned for February 20. The new united organization, called the All-Japan General
Federation of Labor (Zen Nihon Rōdō Sōdōmei), had a total
strength of 85,308 members at its founding—16,894 (less than 20 per
cent) of whom were women.[18] Its structure was inherited practically intact from the former General Federation.[19] Its top posts were
divided between the Socio-Democratic and Japan-Labor cliques. Of
the former, Matsuoka was President, Nishio a Vice-President, and
Toraichi Hara, Assistant Secretary; and from the latter were Mitsu
Kōno, a Vice-President and Tadao Kikukawa, Secretary.

The unification of the Socialist Masses' labor support, finally

18. While most sources date the founding of the All-Japan General Federation of
Labor from January 15, 1936, one otherwise accurate source gives it as November 17,
1935: Yoshimichi Watanabe and Shōbei Shioda, *Nihon Shakai Undō Shi Nempyō* (A
Chronology of the History of the Japanese Social Movement), Kokumin Bunko (National People's Library) 434 (Tōkyō, Ōtsuki Shoten, 1956), p. 139.

19. For particulars on this federation, see *Nihon Rōdō Nenkan, 18* (1937), 251–58.

achieved four years later than the political merger that created the party, obviously helped the party at the polls considerably. But no sooner had this unity been achieved than part of the organized support began to crumble under attacks from the army. On September 10, the Ministry of War adopted the policy of forbidding union membership among employees at military arsenals. The heads of the arsenals at Ōsaka, Nagoya, and Ogura were ordered to have those employees who were union members sign a statement swearing that they had withdrawn from the union. This was a severe blow to the 20-year-old General Federation of Labor in Government Enterprises. The party lodged objections with the Ministries of War and Home Affairs and called protest meetings, asking what meaning "national defense in the larger sense" had if defense workers, who were part of the working classes which paid taxes to support the military, were deprived of their independent, previously recognized rights to organize. Because of such party protests, organized labor was all the more willing to work for the election of proletarian candidates in the 1937 election, when the established parties were in greater disarray than ever before.

But, of course, labor was still far from united, for outside of the illegal leftists, a significant section of labor found the Socialist Masses' Party not antimilitarist enough. This was what gave the Japan Proletarian Party what strength it gained in the 1937 election. The origin of these forces can be traced back to November 1, 1931, when 22 unions, affiliated with National Labor but protesting its "fascistic" tendencies as evidenced in the decision to join the Japan Labor Club, decided to form the National Labor [Union Federation] Struggle Combination to Boycott the [Japan Labor] Club (Zenrō Kurabu Haigeki Tōsō Dōmei) usually shortened to "Boycott Combination" (Haidō).

Although National Labor officially expelled the four leading unions in the Boycott Combination on November 27, the organization continued to regard itself as part of National Labor. Gradually its policy became more positive and in March 1933 the group decided to change its name to the National Congress for the Unification of [the] National Labor [Union Federation] (Zenrō Tōitsu Zenkoku Kaigi). At the same time closer relations with other leftist unions were sought. Based on a resolution adopted at the May Day rally in 1933, which was observed separately at the time by the left-

and right-wing unions, this National Congress took the first step toward uniting various leftist unions by forming the Kantō Congress of Labor Unions (Kantō Rōdō Kumiai Kaigi), a regional consultative body in which the following unions were represented: the General Council of Japanese Labor Unions, the Tōkyō Transport Workers' Union, the Tōkyō Municipal Workers' Union, and the Free Alliance of National Labor Unions, as well as the National Congress for Unification of National Labor itself.

After a year's experience in cooperation through this regional consultative body, the National Congress succeeded in persuading the General Council and twelve other labor organizations to merge with it on November 20, 1934, to form the National Council of Japanese Labor Unions (Nihon Rōdō Kumiai Zenkoku Hyōgikai), abbreviated to "National Council" (Zempyō). In comparison with the consultative body that preceded it, the National Council was both smaller and more leftist. Its main slogans were opposition to the Congress of Japanese Labor Unions (the successor to the Japan Labor Club) and opposition to "imperialist war." Its leading personality was Katō, and its Secretary-General was Yamahana, both of whom had by now definitely parted company with the Japan-Labor clique. Two noteworthy characteristics of the National Council were (1) its large proportion of workers classified as miscellaneous—roughly one third—and (2) its relatively small membership, reported to be 12,053.[20]

Although the National Council made a definite attempt to organize all its members into industrial unions, the large proportion classified as miscellaneous indicates how unsuccessful it was. That classification embraced workers in a variety of small factories (*machi kōba*), employing about five laborers on an average. They were too few and too diversified to be organized industrially. Workers in such small factories, usually under the employers' strong paternalistic influence, were often ignorant of union and political matters. A number of them had been organized and brought into the National Council by militant workers who had been fired and blacklisted by larger companies, and thus were forced to find jobs in the smaller, more backward enterprises. There they were in a position to influence and organize their fellow employees.

20. For a table of the National Council of Japanese Labor Unions membership in 1934 broken down by occupation in organizational units, see Totten, *JSD*, pp. 246–47.

Due to its small size the National Council was unable to give effective support to the Japan Proletarian Party in the 1937 election. Of the five candidates put up by the party, only Katō, Chairman of the Central Committee of the National Council, was elected. When the Socialist Masses' Party had earlier rejected the Japan Proletarian Party's overtures to form a popular front, the National Council's relations with other unions had become more strained. It was subsequently unsuccessful in gaining support for its aims through cooperation on the grass-roots level with other unions.

Although there were no further Diet elections in which the proletarian parties as such took part, it is useful to recall a few more developments in connection with labor support for the social democratic movement: (1) the dissolution of the National Council along with the Japan Proletarian Party in December 1937; (2) the withdrawal of the unions led by the Japan-Labor clique from the All-Japan General Federation of Labor in July 1939 for the purpose of shifting their support to the Industrial Patriotic Movement; (3) the General Federation's support of the attempt by the Socio-Democratic clique to form a new proletarian party in 1940; and (4) the total disappearance of the organized labor movement.

The China incident, breaking out on July 7, only a few months after the 1937 Diet election and committing Japan to a long and costly war, quickly stifled the remaining independent labor movement. The activities of the Japan Proletarian Party and its backer, the National Council, barely continued until ordered disbanded on December 22, 1937; they had limited themselves to aiding working-class families whose sons and fathers had been drafted and sent overseas.

Despite being increasingly called upon to suspend any activities (such as political ones) not directly aiding the prosecution of the war, the labor organizations supporting the Socialist Masses' Party continued to be affiliated mainly with the All-Japan General Federation of Labor until it split in July 1939. That split occurred when tension between the Socio-Democratic and Japan-Labor cliques within the leadership of the General Federation reached the breaking point. The immediate issue at stake was how to collaborate with the Industrial Patriotic Movement, whether on the basis of independent union activity or by dissolving the unions and joining the movement en bloc. At the Central Committee meeting held on July

24, 1939, both cliques issued opposing statements on their respective stands, Matsuoka representing the Socio-Democrats and Kōno, Kikukawa, and Kazuo Nagae together representing the Japan-Laborites.[21] This act split the organization. The next day the Socio-Democrats announced that the organization had reverted to its former name, the Japan General Federation of Labor, and that it was dedicating itself to purely patriotic activities. In reverting to its former name, however, it was not resuming its former activities. On November 3, the anniversary of the Meiji Emperor's birthday, the Japan-Laborite leaders organized the Industrial Patriotic Club (Sangyō Hōkoku Kurabu) and took a solemn, religious oath to the Sun Goddess, Amaterasu Ōmikami, to devote the organization to the spread of the Emperor's benevolent rule throughout the world.[22]

In the sense that the Socio-Democrats retained their grip on the large majority of the General Federation's unions, the Japan-Labor clique was weaker in labor support. However, in the Socialist Masses' Party organization, the Japan-Labor clique was the stronger of the two. When the friction between them mounted within the party, the Japan-Laborites succeeded in ousting the Socio-Democratic leaders in March 1940. When the latter decided on a new departure, organizing the Preparatory Committee for the Nationalist Labor Party on April 26, the General Federation withdrew from the Socialist Masses' Party and pledged its full support to the formation of the new party. This action was in vain, as we have noted, because the proposed Nationalist Labor Party was prohibited by the government on May 7, five days before it was to have been launched.

In the absence of a political party to support, the General Federation placed fifteen candidates of its own in the Tōkyō prefectural election of June 1940; but all failed. This was the last blow to the Socio-Democratic clique: its labor support had lost its effectiveness. On July 8, the General Federation disbanded voluntarily and issued a statement promising continued support from its former members on an individual basis for the new totalitarian structure.[23] With the demise of the General Federation, the strongest constituent group in the Congress of Japanese Labor Unions was gone. Therefore, on July 19, 1940, it too disbanded, bringing to an end all independent labor movement activity of any significance in prewar Japan.

21. These statements may be found in *Rōdō Nenkan* (1940), p. 177.

22. This oath is reprinted in ibid. (1940), p. 178. Watanabe and Shioda date the Club from August 19, 1939, p. 153.

23. For the statement, see ibid. (1941), pp. 246–47.

In reviewing the period from 1925 to 1940 as a whole, one can see how closely the fortunes of the proletarian parties were tied to sections of organized labor. The singular success of the Labor Farmer Party in the elections of 1927 and 1928 was in large part due to the impressive organizational activity of the Council of Japanese Labor Unions, which in turn was inspired by the secret and semisecret Communist Party leaders, who proved to be both tough and able. With their arrests and the breaking up of the Council—the one labor federation where they had been strongest—the successors to the Labor Farmer Party suffered increasingly, and only the smallest remnants, which had compromised or changed with the times sufficiently, found their way into the Socialist Masses' Party when it was formed in 1932.

In contrast the Socio-Democrats, based mainly on the stable General Federation, were able to weather the political storms on the party front. They maintained their own party from 1926 to 1932, longer than any other proletarian party to that time (except for the Communists who were continuously reorganizing). In the united Socialist Masses' Party, they maintained a position of factional leadership for the next eight years. Four years in the unified party were to pass, however, before unity was achieved on the labor federation level, so confident and jealous were the Socio-Democrats of their organizational strength in the General Federation. The split in the General Federation in July 1939, when the Japan-Laborites (who were weaker in labor) broke away, heralded the split in the Socialist Masses' Party in March 1940, when the Socio-Democrats (who were weaker on the party level) were expelled.

While increasingly successful in party politics, the Japan-Laborites tended to fall between the two stools of militancy and conservatism in labor organization. They would not go along with the Council in 1925, but they did exploit dissatisfactions with the conservatism of the General Federation leadership to split it and create a basis for their (at the time) "centrist" political party. But they in turn became the victims of national socialist and left-wing splits.

Without trade union support the proletarian parties could probably not have come into existence in the 1920s in Japan, but by the same token the limited size of the organized labor movement restricted party growth in a way analogous to dwarfing a tree by confining its roots in a small amount of soil.

13: Organized Tenant Farmers

Due to the limited size of the nonagricultural sector of the economy, social democracy in prewar Japan could have been successful as a major party movement only if it had, among other things, recruited mass support from the rural population. Yet here it failed; and its failure is highlighted by two experiences in its own history that revealed potential agrarian support. The first was the impetus the agrarian movement gave to launching the proletarian political parties, indicating that farm leaders could act politically. The other was the large rural vote the Socialist Masses' Party received in 1937, which showed that farmers' support could expand. These points will be developed in their proper places in the following analysis. First, however, some comment on the relationship between the labor and agrarian movements will be helpful in discussing the farmers' political role in so far as it relates to what we mean by agrarian support. The analysis can then center on the crucial Diet election of 1928. Subsequent elections will be treated by noting the organizational and affiliational changes that took place.

That industrialization was indirectly responsible for the rise of the agrarian movement has already been argued.[1] It was shown that dur-

1. Chap. 2, above pp. 34–36.

ing the Meiji period forced capital accumulation in the countryside brought into being a large tenant-farmer class. At first its relations with the landlords carried forward into post-Restoration Japan feudalistic traditional modes of behavior. These included provisions for adjusting rents in times of poor harvests. However, as industrialization expanded and the agricultural market became more commercialized and complex, prices for agricultural products became less directly dependent on climate, weather, and agricultural techniques and more influenced by fluctuations in the industrial sector and even by foreign economic conditions. Increasingly, traditional behavior patterns proved inadequate to cope with the new situations.

The great urban centers sucked in the surrounding agricultural produce and sent industrial products and with them new "modernized" modes of behavior into the village communities. Tenant farmers learned tactics of union organization from leaders who had previously had experience in the labor movement. An examination of the chronology and ecology of labor and agrarian disputes reveals that both types were prevalent in the most industrialized areas and progressively least frequent in the more rural, remote prefectures.[2]

At first it took some time for the tenant farmers to learn from their urban cousins, the workers. In the seminal period, the number of labor disputes rose rapidly to a peak of 497 in 1919 which was about ten times that for 1914. The first big peak in tenant-farmer disputes did not come until 1923 when it was 1,917—23 times the figure for 1917.[3] Tenant-farmer organization also trailed labor. By 1919, the Friendly Society, formed in 1912 as a mere mutual aid society, had become a real trade union federation, but it was only after the Rice Riots of 1918 that any large-scale organizational attempts were made by tenant farmers, eventuating, as we have noted, in the significant launching of the Japan Farmers' Union (abbreviated as Nichinō) on April 9, 1922. (When agrarian organization names are mentioned in this chapter it is suggested that the reader refer to the Appendix, Chart 3, "Lineages of Japanese Farmers' Unions," for relationships.)

2. For a statistical study worked out by Koya Azumi and Totten, see George O. Totten, "Labor and Agrarian Disputes . . . ," pp. 187–212, especially 208–11.

3. For statistical tables on the frequency of and number of persons involved in labor and agrarian disputes, as well as the numbers of unions and their memberships, see ibid., pp. 202–03. An extension of the Table on Dispute Rates to include the years 1920–24 is available in mimeographed form from the author.

Some 66 persons attended the inaugural convention at the Christian Youth Hall in Kōbe, representing mainly farmers from the Kansai area. A number of labor people read messages of encouragement, such as the General Federation's Suzuki. By 1926 the union, which was organized on the basis of local branches, grouped in associations of branches, boasted a dues-paying membership of almost 68,000, before it split. While its main economic aim was to reduce tenants' rents and while much of its energy went into cultural uplift, it also entertained political objectives including agitation in favor of better farm legislation.

With the enactment of universal suffrage, the leaders of the union, Sugiyama and Yukimasa, circulated a request to the 28 labor federations which had nationally over a thousand members each to join with them in launching a united proletarian party. It was this move that led to the formation of the Farmer Labor Party on December 1, 1925. Because of Communist influence in the labor movement and the infighting between the General Federation and the Council of Japanese Labor Unions, agrarian leaders had had to take the initiative. Yet despite the last-minute withdrawal of these two labor rivals, the party was immediately disbanded. Again the Farmers' Union had to take the initiative, this time with the one-sided support of the General Federation, in successfully launching the Labor Farmer Party on March 5, 1926.

At first the whole strength of the Japan Farmers' Union was thrown behind the Labor Farmer Party. Although it remained the main agrarian support for that party during the 1928 Diet election, the political squabbles that immediately appeared within the Union whittled away its strength and redistributed factions to other parties. Obviously the agrarian leaders were as much involved in political activity as the labor leaders. The strength of each proletarian faction could be affected by increases or losses of organized groups of tenant farmers.

It will be remembered that the first split in the Japan Farmers' Union occurred at the time of the stormy withdrawal of the General Federation from the Labor Farmer Party, because the party had decided to open its doors to all leftists, including Communists. Hirano took this occasion to pull out from the Union. His following consisted of only a part of the Yamanashi and Fukuoka Prefectural Associations of Unions. With these he formed the All-Japan Farmers'

Union Federation (Zen Nihon Nōmin Kumiai Dōmei), which he used as a basis for setting up the Japan Farmers' Party.

The second split was, of course, a delayed consequence of the formation of the Japan Labor-Farmer Party. When that party was formed by the mutual efforts of leaders from the left wing of the General Federation and the right wing of the Japan Farmers' Union, the centrist leaders of the Japan Farmers' Union were under the impression that this was a tactic to split off General Federation support from the newly formed Social Democratic Party in order to concentrate it behind the Japan Labor-Farmer Party which would eventually merge with the Labor Farmer Party. Under this impression, the Japan Farmers' Union leaders officially pledged their cooperation with the Japan Labor-Farmer Party; this specifically involved the expulsion of six of the Union's leaders who had opposed the formation of the party. However, when the party's leaders went further and demanded the expulsion of fifteen more, the centrists in the Farmers' Union decided that the Japan Labor-Farmer party had no intention of eventually merging with the Labor Farmer Party and in fact was trying to secure all the Farmers' Union support for itself. The Farmers' Union, therefore, reversed itself and, on February 4, 1927, expelled those leaders who had been most active in setting up the Japan Labor-Farmer Party: Asanuma, Sunaga, Miyake, Kawamata, Miwa (all of whom were thereafter considered to be members of the Japan-Labor clique), and seven others.[4] These men, together with some followers, then organized the All-Japan Farmers' Union (Zen Nihon Nōmin Kumiai) on March 1, which immediately pledged its support to the Japan Labor-Farmer Party.

Following these splits in the Japan Farmers' Union there remained no agrarian support for the Social Democratic Party, whose only alternative was to develop its own farmers' organization. It so happened that among the General Federation's unions was the Kantō Brewery Labor Union (Kantō Jōzō Rōdō Kumiai). It was made up of seasonal laborers, working at the Noda Soy Sauce Plant in Chiba Prefecture, who were semiagricultural factory workers, and whose local leadership had produced a model union. Since they had already been organized as workers, it was not too difficult to organize

4. Among the other seven leaders were Chōzō Yukimasa (who had worked with Kagawa in the Kōbe Kawasaki Dockyard strike) and Michio Hosono (who is among those listed in the Japan-Labor clique).

them again in their capacity as tenant or part-time farmers, thereby creating the nucleus for a farmers' union federation. Such an organization was officially launched on March 7, 1927, under the deceptively grand title of the General Federation of Japanese Farmers' Unions (Nihon Nōmin Kumiai Sōdōmei). Led by the leaders of the Japan General Federation of Labor (the Socio-Democratic clique) who were only known in the cities, it had few contacts in the countryside. It succeeded in recruiting no more than three or four hundred farmers, scattered about in the Kantō area.[5] This meager showing emphasized the dominance of the Japan Farmers' Union and its offshoots in the agrarian movement and how essential its participation was to the proletarian parties.

Although at first glance it would seem that the Japan Farmers' Union had nothing to do with the formation of the Social Democratic Party, it must be remembered that the intense antagonism that developed between the right wing of the General Federation and the whole Japan Farmers' Union leadership over the issue of the open door policy in the Labor Farmer Party was the decisive factor in the General Federation's withdrawal and the founding of the Social Democratic Party.

AGRARIAN SUPPORT IN THE 1928 ELECTION

These disputes and splits determined the distribution of organized agrarian support for the proletarian parties in the Diet election of 1928 as follows:

POLITICAL PARTY (LEADERSHIP)	ORGANIZED AGRARIAN SUPPORT
1. Labor Farmer Party (Ōyama and the legal left)	Japan Farmers' Union
2. Japan Farmer's Party (Hirano)	All-Japan Farmers' Union Federation
3. Japan Labor-Farmer Party (Japan-Labor clique)	All-Japan Farmers' Union
4. Social Democratic Party (Socio-Democratic clique)	Federation of Japanese Farmers' Unions

5. This lack of success was due in large part to the failure of the 1927–28 strike at the Noda Soy Sauce Plant—one of the longest and most important in prewar Japan. See George O. Totten, "Worker Protest in Prewar Japan: The Great Noda Strike of 1927–28" (paper presented at the Association for Asian Studies meeting, March 27, 1961).

The farmers' organizations supporting each party were far from equal in size and character, thus affecting the parties differently. The Japan Farmers' Union had by far the largest and most active membership and helped give the Labor Farmer Party the largest vote of any proletarian party. And the majority of that party's votes came from agricultural areas. Therefore, the Japan Farmers' Union will be discussed first and most fully.

The Japan Farmers' Union made clear its all-out support for the Labor Farmer Party at its Sixth Convention (March 1927), after the expulsion of the Japan Labor-Farmer Party supporters. Its Central Committee then decided on the following concrete measures: (1) urge both the Japan Farmers' Union members and as yet unorganized farmers to join the party, (2) attack the "spurious proletarian parties" but cooperate on common issues with their followers, and (3) make the Union "the active campaign troops on the village level." More specifically, Farmers' Union members were to buy and read the party organ, *The Proletarians' Newspaper (Mushansha Shimbun),* understand its directives and the necessity for supporting it, help it financially, take part in its campaigns when needed, and send in active union members to help set up party branches.[6] This kind of support paid off in the 1928 election when, it will be recalled, the party won almost 200,000 votes, only 30 per cent of which were from municipal and industrial areas.

In spite of the role of the Japan Farmers' Union in founding political parties and providing agrarian support, it must not be thought that the farmers themselves were the dynamic force in the proletarian movement. Active members of the Council of Japanese Labor Unions, that is, workers who had had experience in strike activity, usually led the tenant farmers "by the hand," so to speak, and helped them organize. The fact that workers who were members of the most radical labor organization gave the tenant farmers the needed push and know-how goes a long way in explaining why the Japan Farmers' Union was so radical. Added to this was the fact that a number of university graduates, mainly from Waseda and Tōkyō Imperial Universities, having become leftist through participation in the student movement, had taken practically unpaid jobs as secretaries in the Union's branches with the thought that they were selflessly devoting themselves to the "emancipation" of the tenant farmers.[7] The work-

6. These measures are cited in Aoki, *Nihon Nōmin Undō Shi,* p. 202.
7. This and other information of a similar nature was obtained from interviews with

ers and students, however, were only the catalysts in temporarily changing the character of the tenant farmers from conservative to radical.

The character of these farmers included two opposing aspects—what has been called the "Janus head of the Japanese peasant." [8] The peasant farmer appeared to be the picture of feudal subservience to authority and privilege; he was religious and/or superstitious, sure of himself only in traditionally sanctioned behavior. Yet he had another aspect, that of angry, indignant revolt, sometimes phrased in jarring accents—religious heterodoxy in Tokugawa times, natural rights in the old liberal movement, and class emancipation in the 1920s. This vacillation in political attitude derived in turn from his dual social nature of capitalist-tenant (being forced to absorb the risks of the entrepreneur) and agricultural proletarian (inasmuch as the landlord, by reason of the high rent, took a large part of the profits of the enterprise). The fact that the Japanese tenant farmer could find no real security as long as he retained that status meant that his fundamental grievance was against the whole system of tenantry. This accounted for the tendency of farmers in this stratum to be either passive or "rebellious." More specifically it helps explain their widespread support of the radical Labor Farmer Party and of radical ultraright groups, on the one hand, and their comparative apathy toward the milder reformist parties—until the postwar Occupation-sponsored land reform.

This radical response, however, had to be sparked by initiative from the outside, because the tenant farmers were bound to their land, traveled little, and were inexperienced with the newer types of collective action. The Japan Farmers' Union needed to learn techniques and to absorb excitement and self-confidence from the Council. Consciousness of the backwardness of the tenant farmers impelled the leaders of the Farmers' Union to take the initiative in approaching labor groups in order to provide the framework for labor–farmer cooperation in the form of the first proletarian party. The tenant farmers could provide numbers, if the workers provided leadership. At the time of the 1928 election, the Japan Farmers' Union had over

Hanji Kinoshita, Professor of Political Science, Tōkyō University of Education, June 1953. He had an amazing fund of information and gossip about people in the social movements from the ultraleft to the ultraright. In this connection, see his *Gendai Nashonarizumu Jiten,* which contains biographies of leading social democrats who became national socialists.

8. Norman, *Japan's Emergence as a Modern State,* p. 156.

62,000 members to the Council's 36,000. The Labor Farmer Party served both as a political channel and as a liaison agency for struggle tactics and techniques between organized workers and farmers.

The Japan Farmers' Union was not only numerically the largest farmer organization, it was also the most national, in the sense of distribution of its membership throughout Japan. It had branches in 36 prefectures, with memberships ranging up to 12,263 (in Kagawa).[9] Comparing this with election returns by prefecture shows a correlation between Labor Farmer Party votes and the reported size of the prefectural associations of unions (rengōkai) of the Japan Farmers' Union. For instance, the Labor Farmer Party's largest non-municipal vote (16,827) came from Kagawa Prefecture, where the Japan Farmers' Union had its largest memberhsip. Then, if rural Hokkaidō is excepted due to the special case of the mining vote there, the next highest vote area for the party (11,629) was Niigata which had the second largest Farmers' Union branch (6,891); if Fukuoka is excepted for the same reason, the next was Okayama (9,616) where the Union had some 4,500 members; Nara, and other areas showed similar correlations.[10] If the Union had not split, this vote would have been even larger and more widely distributed. For example, the first split, which led to the formation of the Japan Labor-Farmer Party, conceivably deprived the Labor Farmer Party of some 38,000 votes.

The Japan Farmers' Party was the only proletarian party entirely dependent on agrarian votes. Its supporting agrarian organization, the All-Japan Farmers' Union Federation, reported some 25,902 members,[11] but it is doubtful if it had more than a fraction of this

9. For the membership of the Japan Farmers' Union in December 1927 by organizational breakdown, see Totten, *JSD*, pp. 264–65. Total membership was reported as 62,020 in 1,095 branches organized in 30 associations of unions, plus six areas whose branches were directly attached to headquarters. The following prefectures reported over 1,000 members: Hokkaidō, Kyōto, Ōsaka, Hyōgo, Niigata, Nara, Okayama, Yamaguchi, Kagawa, Mie, Akita, Tottori, Ehime, and Fukuoka. The most important Farmers' Union functionaries were simultaneously Labor Farmer Party leaders: Ryūichi Inamura (a writer and Waseda graduate), Tamotsu Nagao (a secret Communist and Labor Farmer Party Diet candidate in 1928), Takeo Yamagami (a Christian and founder of the Union), Shōichi Maekawa, and Hideo Kawai.

10. The proletarian party vote by prefecture for the 1928 Diet election may be found in ibid., pp. 192–93.

11. For the organizational breakdown of the membership of the All-Japan Farmers' Union Federation in December 1927, see ibid., p. 267. This federation reported membership only in Niigata, Yamanashi, Fukuoka, Gifu, Gumma, Hokkaidō, and Shizuoka in that order of importance. Its only important leader was Rikizō Hirano.

amount; it will be recalled that the Japan Farmers' Party membership rolls also were padded. The Federation, for instance, claimed as many as 13,514 members in largely agricultural Niigata Prefecture, but the Japan Farmers' Party received only 9,562 votes there; whereas the Japan Farmers' Union claimed only 6,891 members there, but the Labor Farmer Party which it supported obtained 11,639 votes. Because of the conservative policies of this Federation, as well as its connection with the Seiyūkai,[12] it may be surmised that there was a strong element of landowner support for the purpose of weaning tenant farmers away from the "class-struggle" influence of the Japan Farmers' Union.

In contrast to these two parties, agrarian support was not a major vote-getter for either the Japan Labor-Farmer or the Social Democratic Party. Nevertheless, there was a difference between the two. The Japan Labor-Farmer Party had inherited some important leaders and a definite following from the agrarian movement, whereas the Social Democratic Party got almost nothing from it. For instance, a comparison between the distribution of reported membership and the results of the 1928 election suggests that it was largely due to support from the All-Japan Farmers' Union that the Japan Labor-Farmer Party received the votes it did in Gumma, Niigata, Shimane, Kagawa, and Yamagata.[13] In none of these agricultural prefectures did the Social Democrats obtain votes. Only in Akita, where the Union claimed a large following but where the local organization was not integrated into a *rengōkai* form, was the Union of no apparent electoral aid to the party. Because the Union's largest concentrated membership was found in Ōsaka and Hyōgo, where the party got its second and third highest vote, following industrial Kanagawa, it is probably correct to assume that the Union's support was of importance in these centers where industry and agriculture mingle.

Although its leaders set up the General Federation of Japanese

12. Kaiten Sugai from Niigata was one of the four Japan Farmers' Party candidates to be elected in the September 1927 elections; he was Hirano's and the Federation's main connecting link with the Seiyūkai. Incidentally, another official of the Federation was Benjirō Nakazawa, who was also an advisor to the Japan General Federation of Labor and thus acted as liaison with the Social Democrats.

13. For the organizational breakdown of the membership of the All-Japan Farmers' Union in December 1927, see Totten, *JSD*, p. 268. Sugiyama and Asanuma shared leadership of the Union with one Michita Sō, who was to be active in the agrarian movement only for another year or so.

Farmers' Unions, the Social Democratic Party received almost no agrarian support.[14] It is true that in September 1927, at the time of the prefectural elections, Jirō Usui led a group of about 1,200 members out of the Yamanashi Prefectural Association of Unions (which was affiliated with Hirano's All-Japan Farmers' Union Federation) and into the General Federation. He then won a seat in the Yamanashi Prefectural Assembly on the Social Democratic ticket. Perhaps the party did not want to try its luck further, for it did not put up a Diet candidate in Yamanashi in the 1928 election. (Usui became a Central Committee member.) But, probably due in part to Usui's success, the local Yamanshi Federation of the General Federation was augmented to about 2,000, after a further defection from Hirano's Federation by one Kisuke Ōtaka and his supporters, making it the largest constituent federation; but even this could not be considered significant agrarian support.

SUBSEQUENT AGRARIAN ALIGNMENTS

It is possible in general terms to gauge agrarian support in the later elections by noting what organizational and affiliational changes had taken place in the agrarian movement by the time of each subsequent election. Obviously, the most important organizational change prior to the 1930 Diet election was the mass arrest of Communists and other leftists the month following the 1928 election, which deprived the Japan Farmers' Union of part of its leadership and, in fact, destroyed a number of its branches. The government's order disbanding the Labor Farmer Party and its allied Council of Japanese Labor Unions did not, however, extend to the party's agrarian support, the Japan Farmers' Union.

Perhaps as a protective reaction, these arrests hastened the reunification of the divided Farmers' Union. Even earlier, following the 1928 election, in which the agrarian vote had been split among four proletarian parties, the Japan Farmers' Union had redoubled its efforts to reunite all the agrarian organizations into one so that agrar-

14. For the organizational breakdown of the membership of the General Federation of Japanese Farmers' Unions in December 1928, see ibid., p. 270. The top leaders of this General Federation were not really agricultural leaders; they included Bunji Suzuki, Tetsu Katayama, Katsumaro Akamatsu, and Ryūsuke Miyazaki. Outside of Yamanashi, there were only about 500 members in Tokushima and less than 200 in Kanagawa, Saitama, and Ibaraki.

ian strength would be more concentrated and effective. It had approached, among others, Hirano's Federation and the Socio-Democrat-led General Federation of Japanese Farmers' Unions, as well as the more important All-Japan Farmers' Union, led by the Japan-Labor clique. At first, the response of all of these had been that unity would only be possible if certain radicals, "Fukumoto-ists" (i.e. Communists), were expelled from the Japan Farmers' Union. The mass arrests took the place of expulsions and removed the main objection. Hirano, however, demanded further that any new organization support only a purely agrarian party, but, getting little backing, except from the General Federation, he broke off negotiations. Satisfied that the police had removed the only important obstacle, the All-Japan Farmers' Union was able to reach agreement with the Japan Farmers' Union, and the two formally amalgamated on May 27, 1928, forming the National Farmers' Union (Zenkoku Nōmin Kumiai), known by its abbreviation, "National Farmer" (Zennō) (see the Appendix, Chart 3).

Organizational unity, nevertheless, was not followed by affiliational unity. In fact, there was such division of opinion as to which party to support that National Farmer officially took a position of neutrality, although the various leaders continued their former affiliations on a personal or clique basis. Since some of the strongest Japan Farmers' Union leaders had been arrested, the leadership positions of the new organization were generally taken over by former All-Japan Farmers' Union (i.e. Japan-Labor clique) leaders, such as Sugiyama and Asanuma. They set the tone of National Farmer and decentralized what had been the highly coordinated organization of the Japan Farmers' Union. It was natural that they should try to swing National Farmer to support the Japan Masses' Party during the Diet election of 1930, since they were simultaneously leaders in that party, but they were unsuccessful in the effort.

Although unwilling to go along with the Japan-Labor clique leadership politically, the former Japan Farmers' Union members were themselves divided over their allegiances. A sizable number began protesting against the gradual conservative or rightist drift of National Farmer, and after its second annual convention in March 1929, they coalesced into the Farmer Strugglers' Society (Nōmin Tōsōsha), a faction within National Farmer. Despite the arrest of some 30 of its leaders on April 16, 1929, and spurred on by the deepening world depression, they gathered strength and regrouped into the National Farmers' Union Reform Faction (Zennō Sasshinha) in October. Although united against the trend to the right, some supported the formation of the New Labor Farmer Party on November 1, whereas others attacked its formation, implying that no legal party was worth supporting any more, i.e. only the illegal Communists should be given aid.

Partly due to this division of allegiances, but mainly because of more intense police interference in agrarian local organization and activity, the New Labor Farmer Party in the 1930 Diet election drew considerably fewer votes in Chiba, Kanagawa, Niigata, and Fukui, where it inherited the support of the old Labor Farmer Party, and received none in Hokkaidō, Iwate, Akita, Yamanashi, Nagano, Shizuoka, Aichi, Mie, Nara, Tottori, Okayama, Kagawa, Ehime, Fukuoka, Kagoshima and Okinawa, all of which had been sources of votes for the former party. More specifically, the intense police harassment following the March 15, 1928, raids had brought about the utter destruction of the Japan Farmers' Union branches in Kagawa and Ehime, which had previously helped the Labor Farmer Party capture 16,827 and 8,430 votes respectively.[15] A year later, as a result of the April 16 roundup and its aftermath, the following prefectural associations of unions of National Farmer were either destroyed permanently or forced to cease activity temporarily: Ōsaka, Fukui, Yamagata, Akita, Aomori, Miyazaki, Chiba, Ibaraki Nagano, Okayama, Niigata, Fukushima, Mie, and Kyōto.[16] Thus, it would appear that the destructions, divisions, and realignments in the agrarian movement cost the New Labor Farmer Party proportionally more votes than had the disbanding of the Council of Japanese Labor Unions. That party's total vote in 1930, it will be remembered, was less than half that of the former Labor Farmer Party in 1928.

Conversely, the creation of National Farmer (i.e. the National Farmers' Union) was a definite advantage to the Japan Masses' Party, in which the Japan-Labor clique was dominant. Although the former Japan Farmers' Union leaders who became part of the Japan-Labor clique were not able to secure the official endorsement of National Farmer, as a whole, for the Japan Masses' Party, they did win over large sections which previously had supported the old Labor

15. Aoki, p. 256.
16. Kuroda and Ikeda, *Nihon Nōmin Kumiai Undō Shi*, pp. 126–27.

Farmer Party and which apparently accounted for the Japan Masses' Party vote in Aomori, Akita, Chiba, Aichi, Tottori, Kagoshima, and possibly part of Hokkaidō. As a result, the party received double the vote of its predecessor, the Japan Labor-Farmer Party.

Although the agrarian vote of the Social Democratic Party increased, this was hardly due to the support of the General Federation of Japanese Farmers' Unions, since that organization had not shown any particular record of activity nor had its strength increased. The electoral growth was probably due to the support of independent farmers and small landlords who had been adversely affected by the depression during the last year and who vented their disquiet through the channel of the most moderate of the social democratic parties. Not being part of the organized agrarian movement, theirs may be considered a floating vote. Such a hypothesis is supported by the fact that it did not reappear in the following election, when small landowners benefited from the temporary agricultural and industrial demands arising from the Manchurian incident.

The party that fared worst in the election of 1930 was Hirano's successor to the Japan Farmers' Party which had dropped its pretensions of being a national party and had become the Yamanashi Farmer Labor Party (Yamanashi Nōmin Rōdōtō). Its supporting organization deleted the word "Federation" from its name on July 5, 1928, and thus became the All-Japan Farmers' Union (Zen Nihon Nōmin Kumiai), which, incidentally (as may be seen in Appendix Chart 3), was the name just abandoned by the Japan-Labor clique-led union, when it reunited with the Japan Farmers' Union to become National Farmer on May 27, 1928. Hirano, now leader of both the Yamanashi Labor Farmer Party and the All-Japan Farmers' Union, had earlier joined the Japan Masses' Party but found it expedient to withdraw after being accused of implication in a scandal.[17] Wishing to continue in politics he was forced to form his own party, but his Yamanashi Farmer Labor Party secured less than 10,000 votes, only about one fourth of the vote of its predecessor.

In summarizing organized agrarian support in the 1930 Diet election, it may be helpful to recapitulate as follows:

17. Hirano, along with Asō, was accused by the Labor-Farmer faction of accepting 11,000 yen from Premier Tanaka. The outcome of the affair was that Asō, head of the party, engineered the expulsion of the accusers, but Hirano nevertheless found it expedient to withdraw. Hakuyōsha, ed., *Nihon Musan Seitō Shi*, pp. 122–31.

POLITICAL PARTY (LEADERSHIP)	ORGANIZED AGRARIAN SUPPORT
1. New Labor Farmer Party (Ōyama and the ex-legal left)	The following elements of the National Farmers' Union: (a) Those of the National Farmers' Union Reform Faction who did not follow the Communist line of boycotting the election (b) Other former Japan Farmers' Union elements
2. Japan Masses' Party (Japan-Labor clique)	Former All-Japan Farmers' Union elements of National Farmer
3. Social Democratic Party (Socio-Democratic clique)	The General Federation of Japanese Farmers' Unions
4. Yamanashi Farmer Labor Party (Hirano)	The *new* All-Japan Farmers' Union

The next Diet election, which came in 1932, presented a simpler picture, since there were only two proletarian parties of approximately equal size. The newly formed National Labor-Farmer Masses' Party incorporated all factions (the Japan-Labor clique, the Labor-Farmer faction, and former New Labor Farmer Party elements) except the Socio-Democratic clique which continued to maintain its independence in the Social Democratic Party.

For the National Labor-Farmer Masses' Party (as for the other proletarian parties), the Diet election of 1932 was a severe defeat, and its most telling losses were in the agrarian vote, although what it retained was decisive in getting it one new Diet seat (Matsutani retained his Tōkyō seat as the only other successful party candidate). The fact that certain former New Labor Farmer Party leaders had joined in the formation of this party was evidently not enough to save agrarian support in Aomori, Chiba, Fukui, and Saga, which had gone to the New Labor Farmer Party before. The only predominantly agricultural prefectures where it dared to put up candidates were Niigata and Iwate. National Farmer did not officially endorse this party, but its central clique of leaders were party leaders as well. Out of the twelve candidates the party put up, four were National Farmer leaders. Of these, only Sugiyama, Chairman of the Central Committee of National Farmer, was elected.[18] He ran in Ōsaka, where he received 1,850 votes. While this was an urban area, it con-

18. The other three were Chōzaburō Mizutani, Kunisaburō Izumi, and Shōichi Miyake.

tained many tenant farmers within its boundaries; their support may have proved decisive, for Ōya, also a party candidate but mainly a labor leader, lost.

This party was too far to the right for the leftist faction of National Farmer which, since the 1930 election, had undergone two more transformations (see Appendix, Chart 3). Originally called the Farmer Strugglers' Society, it became the National Farmers' Union Reform Faction and then the Conference to Make the National Farmers' Union More Militant (Zennō Sentōka Kyōgikai), before it adopted the name National Farmers' Union National Congress Faction (Zennō Zenkoku Kaigiha, abbreviated as Zenkaiha) on July 7, 1931. This faction, whose stronghold was in Nagano Prefecture, should be considered more a part of the Communist than the social democratic movement, except that at times the distinction was too fine to be made. As we noted, there had been disagreement within the faction over whether to support the New Labor Farmer Party or boycott the 1930 Diet election.

In the 1932 Diet election it apparently gave no political support except to a local party in Niigata Prefecture which put up as a candidate Susumu Kamimura, who had been attacked by the Communists for his part in forming the New Labor Farmer Party. Although not elected, he drew—largely through this support—2,437 votes, more than obtained by many of the candidates who were elected.[19] Already this faction's connection with National Farmer was slight and hardly continued beyond the year. Constantly harassed by the police, it went more and more underground until its virtual disappearance in March 1934 when its local branches in Ōsaka and Nara returned to National Farmer.

In the right wing of the agrarian movement, an unsuccessful merger had taken place to increase the vote of the Social Democratic Party in the Diet election of 1932. It was unsuccessful because it did not bring votes and broke up soon after the election. Hirano's All-Japan Farmers' Union amalgamated with the General Federation of Japanese Farmers' Unions on January 26, 1931, to form a new Japan Farmers' Union, thus "stealing" the name of what had been the most prominent organization in the agrarian movement.[20] In spite of this,

19. *Rōdō Nenkan* (1933), p. 155. The formal inauguration of the Congress without the "Faction" suffix is given as August 15 (1931) in Watanabe and Shioda, p. 118.

20. Hirano had already taken over the program of the former Japan Farmers' Union almost word for word when he formed the All-Japan Farmers' Union Federation on

however, the Social Democratic Party received no votes in Yamanashi Prefecture, which was the supposed stronghold of Hirano, and in fact lost a number of predominantly agricultural prefectures, such as Miyagi, Tochigi, Gumma, Toyama, Mie, Nara, Yamaguchi, and Kōchi where it had previously received at least a floating vote.

The organized agrarian support for each of the parties in the Diet election of 1932 may be summarized as follows:

POLITICAL PARTY (LEADERSHIP)	ORGANIZED AGRARIAN SUPPORT
1. National Labor-Farmer Masses' Party (Japan-Labor clique, the Labor-Farmer faction and some former New Labor Farmer Party elements)	The following elements of the National Farmers' Union: (a) Former All-Japan Farmers' Union elements of National Farmer (b) Those former Japan Farmers' Union elements who supported the New Labor Farmer Party to the end
2. Social Democratic Party (Socio-Democratic clique)	The *new* Japan Farmers' Union composed of: (a) Former members of the Hirano-led All-Japan Farmers' Union (b) Former members of the General Federation of Japanese Farmers' Unions
3. A local party in Niigata (which put up as candidate Susumu Kamimura, a founder of the New Labor Farmer Party)	The National Farmers' Union National Congress Faction

By the 1936 Diet election, the picture was even simpler than in 1932, since the Socialist Masses' Party had no national proletarian party rivals. It received little significant organized agrarian support. Instead, some farm unions ran their own candidates. In the 1937 Diet election, however, most of the farmers' unions supported it despite the appearance of the newly created Japan Proletarian Party, calling for a broad front of farmers and labor to oppose fascism. A

April 11, 1926, although he claimed to be setting out on a new departure. See Tōru Sōhara, "Nihon Nōmin Kumiai Funjō no Shinsō" (The Truth about the Trouble in the Japan Farmer's Union), *Shakai Mondai Kōza, Kagai Kōwa* (Monographs on Social Problems, Supplementary Volume), Sōichi Ōya, ed. (Tōkyō, Shinchōsha, 1926), p. 18. It will be remembered that Hirano had also taken over the name of the All-Japan Farmers' Union on July 5, 1928, soon after its amalgamation and change of name!

clue to this behavior may be found in the changing character of National Farmer.

Since the election of 1932, National Farmer had grown considerably weaker. The drive for national unity, which followed in the wake of the Manchurian incident, affected the agrarian movement in the same way it did the labor movement. First there were split-offs to the newly risen national socialist or fascist movements and then the organizations themselves became less and less active. Led by Kenichi Yoshida (originally a Japan Farmers' Union leader of the Japan-Labor clique), the right wing of National Farmer attempted to reorient the union to aid the war by putting an end to tenant–landlord disputes and encouraging mutual cooperation in the villages in the spirit of the "Imperial Way." Unable to get National Farmer to move to the right as fast as they wished, the leaders of this faction seceded, taking with them much of National Farmers' membership in Hyōgo, Ōsaka, Wakayama, and Nara, and set up the Imperial Farmers' Federation (Kōkoku Nōmin Dōmei) on December 1, 1933.

National Farmer was also weakened by fear and inertia, rendering it incapable of taking advantage of the rising agrarian unrest. After the Manchurian incident, intimidation by superpatriotic organizations, inspired by the increasing violence of fascism abroad, was added to police repression. Such organizations, for example, were branches of the Local Pride Society (Aikyōkai) and the Agrarian Society for Self-Government (Jichi Nōmin Kyōkai).[21] In the background of this trend was the gradual changeover to a wartime economy that affected adversely the livelihood of the tenant farmers. The number of tenant–landlord disputes stood still for a year after the Manchurian incident, but soon began to climb, breaking new records yearly until 1936. National Farmer, however, did little in leading and organizing these disputes. Its main activity consisted in representing the farmers' interests in court cases by *amicus curiae* briefs. Most of the disputes were carried on by individuals or local community (*buraku*) negotiations directly with landlords or by pleading with officials for governmental arbitration. Consequently, by 1936 National Farmer had declined to only some 32,000 members, about half the size of the Japan Farmers' Union in 1928.

21. Both organizations were founded between 1930 and 1932 by Kōsaburō Tachibana, who was implicated in the assassination of May 15, 1932. See Storry, *The Double Patriots*, pp. 99–100.

This rising agrarian unrest had two results that were apparent by the 1936 election. One was that certain sections of National Farmer demanded more positive agrarian policies than the Socialist Masses' Party offered. A number of local branches asserted their right of freedom of choice in politics, and several actually ran candidates under the National Farmer label in the prefectural elections of 1935 and again in the Diet election of 1936.

The other result of the unrest was that, in spite of its passivity, the Socialist Masses' Party had begun to attract a wider range of unorganized agrarian support by 1936. This could not be explained by the endorsement of the General Federation of Japanese Farmers' Unions (which continued to support the Socio-Democratic clique leaders in the Socialist Masses' Party), since it had shown no particular growth or activity in the intervening years. However, it was now four years since the last Diet election and eleven years since universal manhood suffrage had been enacted. The passage of time itself had helped to give familiarity to the idea of a "proletarian party" as a labor–farmer alliance. For example, the Socialist Masses' Party in 1936 received votes in the agricultural prefecture of Fukushima where none of its predecessors had obtained any. It also drew support in Akita, Tochigi, Gumma, Niigata, Shizuoka, Hyōgo, Kōchi, and Kumamoto. But it was supported by fewer agricultural areas than were the proletarian parties in the first two Diet elections, when campaigning among tenant farmers had been more intense and before radical ultrarightist agrarian organizations had become so numerous.

The returns of the 1936 Diet election, which gave the Socialist Masses' Party the unprecedented total of over half a million votes, helped to convince a great variety of elements within National Farmer, as well as in other agrarian organizations, that this party had some chance of becoming an effective voice of protest to the apparent drift toward war and totalitarianism in Japan. In spite of itself, the Social Masses' Party was taking on the character of a popular front, as was borne out in the Diet election of April 1937 when it received almost a million votes, distributed throughout 32 of the 47 prefectures in Japan.

Although the Japan Proletarian Party did much less well with its popular front in the 1937 election than expected, it did get the support of some agrarian as well as labor elements. Organized out of the

Labor-Farmer Proletarian Conference (Rōnō Musan Kyōgikai) which had run Katō in the 1936 Diet election, this party was officially supported by the North-Japan Farmers' Union (Kita Nihon Nōmin Kumiai), the largest single local agrarian union in Japan, with some 3,000 members. Led by Chōzaburō Koyama, this union had a militant past which could be traced back to 1925 through various transformations and realignments. In the 1932 Diet election, as part of the large Niigata Prefectural Association of Unions (Niigata Ken Rengō-kai) under the influence of the National Congress Faction, it had supported Susumu Kamimura, but in 1934 it reassumed its original name of North-Japan Farmers' Union. In the following year it put up Junji Tamai as a candidate in the Niigata prefectural election, which he won. In 1937, however, when he ran for election to the Diet under the Japan Proletarian Party label, he failed, partly because he was relatively unknown. Outside of the 9,000 votes from Niigata, the Japan Proletarian Party obtained support from no predominantly agricultural areas.

Hirano's unions under various names have been mentioned in connection with the preceding national elections. In 1933, however, he had gone over to ultranationalism and, together with several army generals, had organized the Imperial Way Association (Kōdōkai), a political party under whose label he was finally elected to the Diet in 1936. He held onto Japan Farmers' Union support, however.

Organized agrarian support for the social democratic parties in the Diet elections of 1936 and 1937 may thus be summarized as follows:

POLITICAL PARTY (LEADERSHIP)	ORGANIZED AGRARIAN SUPPORT
I. The Diet Election of 1936	
1. Socialist Masses' Party (Japan-Labor and Socio-Democratic cliques)	a. Those sections of the National Farmers' Union which supported the Japan-Labor clique leaders
	b. General Federation of Japanese Farmers' Unions
II. The Diet Election of 1937	
1. Socialist Masses' Party (Japan-Labor and Socio-Democratic cliques)	a. Many more sections of National Farmer than in 1936
	b. General Federation of Japanese Farmers' Unions
2. Japan Proletarian Party (Katō and the Labor-Farmer faction)	a. Sections of National Farmer under Labor-Farmer faction influence
	b. North-Japan Farmers' Union

Three months after the election, the Japanese armies began in earnest their invasion of China. Within the agrarian movement, as within labor and the Socialist Masses' Party, the tendency toward ultranationalism was sharpened. Paralleling the situation after the Manchurian incident, there were a few who moved rightward too fast to be able to carry much following with them. The bulk of the agrarian organizations consolidated behind the Socialist Masses' Party, achieving a greater unity than ever before, which, however, was devoid of meaning since the party had only the vaguest program, one which the government was already planning to carry out, and also because the party dissolved itself before another Diet election took place.

The first reaction within the agrarian movement to the China incident came in July, two weeks after its outbreak. The Conference of Patriotic Farmers' Organizations (Aikoku Nōmin Dantai Kyōgikai) was formed by the two most rightist agrarian unions, Hirano's Japan Farmers' Union and Kenichi Yoshida's Imperial Farmers' Federation, which at the same time retained their own identity. Both were already supporting the Imperial Way Association. They formed the Conference hoping that the rest of the agrarian organizations would join and swing behind the Imperial Way Association. Although unsuccessful in this, they set the pattern among agrarian unions for conversions to support for the "holy war," pledges to cease internal strife, and endeavors to promote home front agricultural production. They also set the pace for name changes, such as adding "patriotic," "Imperial," or "Greater Japan" to the union names. But no other unions were attracted to this organization and it was dissolved the following year, in November 1938.

The mass arrests of supporters of the popular front idea, which began on December 15, 1937, included Junji Tamai of the North-Japan Farmers' Union, but the organization itself was not ordered to disband. Fearing such an eventuality, however, the union drastically revised its program and pledged to help encourage the agricultural population to support the state under the principle of the congruity of interest between the soldier and the farmer *(heinō itchi)*.[22]

The arrests also included the National Farmer leaders, Hisao Kuroda and Toshio Ōnishi, who as members of the Socialist Masses'

22. See *Nihon Rōdō Nenkan*, 20 (1939), 229–30.

Party had tried to persuade that party to amalgamate with the Japan Proletarian Party. When arrested, they were immediately expelled from the Socialist Masses' Party to show that the party wished to disassociate itself completely from the idea of a popular front. Then National Farmer, the only agrarian organization with a national following, felt it necessary to revise its guiding principle a few days later, on December 29, 1937, from one of fighting for the interests of the agrarian population to one of promoting agricultural production.[23] For the first time it officially endorsed the Socialist Masses' Party and also pledged its cooperation with such semigovernmental organizations as the Industrial Guilds (Sangyō Kumiai) and the Agricultural Associations (Nōkai). Actually, however, it was already in the process of disintegration.

Dissatisfied that National Farmer was pledged to the Socialist Masses' Party and that the Japan-Labor clique leaders were considering amalgamation with the General Federation of Japanese Farmers' Unions, elements under the leadership of Ryūichi Inamura, including remnants of the formerly leftist National Congress Faction, withdrew from National Farmer. On February 13, 1938, they formed the Japan Farmers' League (Nihon Nōmin Remmei) and pledged support to Seigō Nakano's, Eastern Association (Tōhōkai).[24] Inamura had actually supported this party in the last election. He was attracted by the ideas of its leader, a veteran politician who had recently begun to buttress his ultranationalist position with borrowings from Marxism, while vehemently denying accusations of fascism. The membership of the League was reported as 71,900 but in reality was probably less than 5,000.[25]

The remaining majority of leaders in National Farmer felt that more than just a change of principles was needed. After negotiations leading to close working relations with the General Federation of Japanese Farmers' Unions, they formed a new organization on February 6, 1938, called the Greater Japan Farmers' Union (Dai Nihon Nōmin Kumiai). It gained the adherence of the Yamagata Prefectu-

23. This statement may be found in ibid., 20 (1939), 220.

24. This affiliation caused Inamura and others who had previously been the left wing of National Farmer to be purged by the Occupation after the war as ultranationalists. Consequently, when the farmers' union was reorganized after the war, the former leftists could not take the initiative.

25. See *Nihon Rōdō Nenkan*, 20 (1939), 220–21.

ral Farmers' Union (Yamagata Ken Nōmin Kumiai), the Toyama
Prefectural Association of Farmers' Unions (Toyama Ken Nōmin
Kumiai Rengōkai), and the Hyōgo Prefectural Farmers' Union
(Hyōgo Ken Nōmin Kumiai). Bunji Suzuki, Toyohiko Kagawa, and
Isoo Abe from the Socio-Democratic clique acted as Advisors. The
other leaders also came from the various cliques and factions of the
Socialist Masses' Party, such as Sugiyama, Asō (who became the
fourth official Advisor), Shōichi Miyake, Jusō Miwa, Masaru Nomizo,
Michio Hosono, and Seion Kawamata from the Japan-Labor clique,
and Kenji Yamazaki, Takaichi Nakamura, and Shōichi Maekawa,
who were originally in the New Labor Farmer Party. Although it
claimed 70,000 members in 23 prefectures, this union probably had
only some 15,000 members. It was nevertheless regarded as the
largest agrarian union in Japan at the time.[26]

This reorganization, however, was apparently not enough for the
growing totalitarian temper. The Greater Japan Farmers' Union itself drew government disapproval. In the summer of the following
year, negotiations began with Tetsu Katayama and Yoshio Matsunaga of the General Federation of Japanese Farmers' Unions and
Hirano, still heading the Japan Farmers' Union. They eventuated
in the amalgamation of the three organizations, setting up the Federation for Reform of the Land System (Nōchi Seido Kaikaku
Dōmei) on November 29, 1939. Unity was reached on the one point
that all tillers of the soil should be converted into independent
farmers on a hereditary basis. Full support was pledged to the war
effort. Although this organization did not officially endorse any polit-
cal party, the majority of its leaders were from the various leadership factions in the Socialist Masses' Party. In addition, Hirano remained a member of the Imperial Way Association, while Inamura's
group continued to support the Eastern Association. The issue of
party affiliation, however, became academic, as these parties were
dissolved in 1940.

No matter how rightist or ultranationalist any agrarian organization became, it could not survive as an independent organization
within the Japanese wartime structure which attempted to be totalitarian. The Japan Farmers' League was dissolved in July 1940. The
Federation for Reform of the Land System, however, continued in

26. Ibid.

existence for two years after the political parties had been disbanded and after the labor unions had been forced into the Patriotic Industrial Association. It was finally ordered to break up by the Tōjō Government in 1942, bringing to an end the last traces of the organized agrarian movement in Japan, until the "liberation of defeat."

14: Organized Women and Minority Groups

Political support by women, by former social outcastes, and by the Korean minority proved to be of various degrees of significance to the social democratic movement in prewar Japan. Though made up of laborers, farmers, and other social strata, each of these three groups had characteristics of its own which determined the nature of its support for Japanese social democracy. A number of the former social outcastes or "untouchables,"—what the Japanese call the "special community people"—became ardent activists. But even suspicious Koreans were attracted to the proletarian movement. Women were recognized as potentially important, though conditions for realizing their potentialities in politics did not come into existence until after Japan's defeat.

UNENFRANCHISED WOMEN

Not only did tradition place women in an inferior social position but legal barriers specifically prohibited them from playing any significant political role. In 1889, just as the Meiji Constitution was promulgated, providing for a Diet with limited manhood suffrage, a

decree was issued forbidding women any political rights.[1] Women
were not even allowed to attend meetings where political subjects
would be discussed. The severity of this prohibition was only slightly
reduced in 1922 when the law was revised to allow women to attend
and hold political meetings, but not until after the surrender was the
ban on women's joining or forming political parties lifted.

In the 1890s, at the very outset of the socialist movement itself,
some women were converted to a socialist persuasion and subsequently became the most active element in the feminist movement
for equality, a primary aim of which was the abolition of restrictions
against political participation.[2] The first important feminist organization was the Blue Stocking Society (Seitōsha), started in 1911,
composed of middle-class ladies who had attended the new women's
institutions of higher learning. This society included some of the
most radical women of the time, such as Noe Itō, who later married
the famous anarchist Sakae Ōsugi.[3]

In consonance with the socialist movement as a whole, socialist
women turned their attention to the labor movement in the immediate post-World War I peroid.[4] Some aided in the organization of a
women's section in the Friendly Society in 1916 and helped bring the

1. This was the Law on Assembly and Political Associations (*Shūkai Seisha Hō*) promulgated in October 1889. After several revisions, the strict prohibitions against political activities by women were incorporated into Article 5 of the Peace Police Law
(*Chian Keisatsu Hō*) of 1900. Thereafter, feminist agitation was directed specifically
toward the abolition of this article. Itsue Takamure, *Nihon Josei Shakai Shi* (A Social
History of Japanese Women) (Ōsaka, Shin Nihonsha, 1943), p. 227.

2. One of the earliest women socialists was Eiko (Fukuda) Kageyama who had been
active in the liberal movement with such leaders as Kentarō Ōi. Other socialist women
included Tameko Sakai, Fumiko Nishikawa, Kiyoko Endō, Utako Imai, and Suga Kanno.
Kanno was executed with Shūsui Kōtoku in the Great Treason Trial of 1911. For an
account of socialist women's activities during this period, see Kiyoshi Inoue, *Nihon
Josei Shi* (A History of Japanese Women) (Tōkyō, Sanichi Shobō, 1949), pp. 285–98.

3. At that time Noe Itō was still married to Jun Tsuji. Besides Noe Itō, the Society
attracted such leading feminists as Akiko (Raichō) Hiratsuka, Hatsuko Nakano, Suga
Kanno, and the poetess Akiko Yosano. The Society was inspired by the British Blue-
stockings of the 1750s, which indicates how far behind their British sisters the Japanese
felt themselves to be. There exists an extended account of this Society (which lasted
till 1915) in Kazuo Nakagawa, *Nihon Josei Shiron* (On the History of Japanese Women)
(Tōkyō, Nihon Tosho K. K., 1925).

4. In the labor movement they found that male workers not only looked down on
women in the traditional Japanese manner but also feared their advance into jobs
hitherto held by men. This is, of course, a phenomenon encountered everywhere in an
early stage of industrialization. For Japanese examples, see Takamure, p. 247.

plight of Japanese working women to the attention of the world.[5] In 1919, for instance, this women's section sponsored a rally of about a thousand men and women textile workers to ratify a statement addressed to the International Labor Organization on the situation of Japanese women workers. In 1921 women socialists formed the Red Wave Society (Sekirankai) and attempted to observe International Women's Day in Japan.[6]

The most immediate objective, however, was to secure the suffrage. For this purpose the New Women's Society (Shin Fujin Kyōkai) was organized in 1919. It was partially successful in March 1922 when the Seiyūkai majority party in the Diet modified the prohibition against women's participation in politics to the extent of allowing them to attend and hold political meetings. This success spurred the organization of a larger women's federation in 1923 to agitate not only for the ballot for women but for the right to join political parties and for other civil liberties as well.[7] After several organizational changes this group came to be known as the Federation to Secure Women's Suffrage (Fusen Kakutoku Dōmei).[8] By 1930 it became the central rallying point of the feminist movement. However, in 1924, while the possibility still existed that women might be included in the impending bill for universal suffrage, socialist women shifted their attention to the Society for the Study of Politics (Seiji Kenkyūkai) whose real purpose was to prepare for the formation of a proletarian political party. As a result, a women's section was set up in the Association.[9] Encompassing various brands of

5. They began publishing a journal called *The Friendly Woman* (*Yūai Fujin*) in July 1916 but could only carry it to March 1917 for lack of support.

6. Although the Red Wave Society was quickly suppressed, it was revived the following year, in 1922, as the Society of the Eighth (Yōkakai), to prepare for celebrating International Women's Day, March 8th. Its leaders included Kikue Yamakawa (wife of Hitoshi Yamakawa), Mae Sakai, Hisako Kutsumi, and Sadayo Nakasone. Inoue, p. 326.

7. For a discussion of the important civil rights denied to women (regarding divorce, occupations, ownership of property, etc.) and for which they had to agitate, see Takamure, pp. 213–22.

8. Composed mainly of middle-class ladies, the Federation to Secure Women's Suffrage included some who again became active in postwar Japan, such as Akiko (Raichō) Hiratsuka, Mumeo Oku, and Fusae Ichikawa. For an account of women active in the postwar as well as the prewar feminist movement, see Abe, *Gendai Nihon Jimbutsu Ron,* pp. 243–52.

9. Such women as Mumeo Oku, Kikue Yamakawa, and Izuko Niizuma were in the women's section of the Society for the Study of Politics. Most of its members were living in Tōkyō and a few in Ōsaka and Kōbe. They were all middle-class housewives or career women; none was a worker or farmer. Takamure, p. 247.

socialists, however, the Association soon split up, and rifts affected the women's section as well.

Although sorely disappointed because the Universal Suffrage Act of 1925 did not extend the vote to women, socialist women were determined to take part in the proletarian party movement to the extent that this law allowed. Since they were not permitted to become party members, they could only form auxiliary organizations to support the proletarian parties. After several unsuccessful attempts to organize a united group, the Kantō Women's Federation (Kantō Fujin Dōmei) was formed on July 2, 1927, and soon announced its support for the Labor Farmer Party, even though some of that party's leadership considered the women's group unnecessary and possibly fostering sectarian issues. This was the first women's group attached to a political party and, compared to the others, the strongest and most militant. It included the women's sections of the Japan Farmer's Union and the Council of Japanese Labor Unions as well as young intellectuals among whom were relatives of the party's leaders.[10] Though militant, it was short-lived and was dissolved along with the Labor Farmer Party after the mass arrests of March 15, 1928.[11]

The Social Democratic Women's Federation (Shakai Minshū Fujin Dōmei), as its name implies, was set up in November 1927 to support the Social Democratic Party. Composed mainly of wives and relatives of the party's leaders, it also included the women's section of the General Federation.[12] Inclined more toward social work than politics, it gradually died of inactivity. Another fragmentation, the National Women's Federation (Zenkoku Fujin Dōmei) was formed on October 2, 1927, to support the Japan Labor-Farmer Party. Made up of working women from the women's section of the Federation of Japanese Labor Unions, it also included family members of the

10. Leaders of the Kantō Women's Federation included Ryō Nozaka (wife of Sanzō Nozaka, a Communist leader), Hideko Tajima, Mina Yamauchi, and Tsuru Yanagi; the latter three were also union leaders. Kyōchōkai, *Saikin no Shakai Undō*, p. 651.

11. In this and the mass arrests of April 16, 1929, some 3,000 people were arrested, 825 of whom were brought to trial. Of these, 18 were women. Inoue, p. 344.

12. Leaders of the Social Democratic Women's Federation included Akiko Akamatsu (wife of Katsumaro Akamatsu), Tsuneko Akamatsu (his sister, a union leader), and Yasuko Yamada. There was also another group, the Working Women's League (Rōdō Fujin Remmei), set up on July 10, 1927, but its members soon transferred what little political work they did to the Federation. *Saikin no Shakai Undō*, p. 651.

party's leaders, a few nurses, and a few teachers.[13] Its name was changed to the Proletarian Women's Federation (Musan Fujin Dōmei) when the party reorganized in the following year, but due to party splits thereafter it, too, soon became inactive.[14]

At their height, these women's auxiliary organizations claimed anywhere from 400 to 1,000 members each, but in reality, although exact statistics are not available, their numbers were far less.[15] Not only were these groups divided, reflecting the schisms in the social democratic movement, but they were also ineffective. They did, however, encourage some women to aid in party propaganda work and to campaign for party candidates at election time, but such activities took them away from organizational work in the unions where they might have been more effective in concretely helping women to better their lot. Their effectiveness was reduced further because they had to fight against a lack of understanding of women's problems on the part of proletarian party leaders themselves.

After the disappointing Diet election of 1928, socialist women again turned their attention to the Federation to Secure Women's Suffrage, mentioned above. As a result, the Federation formed a special committee to press for recognition and support of their demands by the Minseitō, the Seiyūkai, and the proletarian party representatives in the Diet. Thus, both bourgeois- and proletarian-oriented women cooperated and, after the 1930 election, even formed a united front on this issue. They held mass meetings and distributed literature, but just as they were gathering strength the Manchurian incident occurred, starting the chain of events that led to the totalitarian wartime structure. After the China incident, the Federation

13. Leaders of the National Women's Federation included Shizuko Kikukawa, Sadayo Orimoto, and Tomie Iwauchi. Ibid., p. 652.

14. The name Proletarian Women's Federation was adopted when the Proletarian Women's League (Musan Fujin Remmei) merged with the National Women's Federation. Led by Nae Sakai and Taiko Hirabayshi of the Labor-Farmer faction, the League had been attached to the Proletarian Masses' Party. When this party merged with the Japan Labor-Farmer Party to form the Japan Masses' Party in December 1928, it was natural for the League to amalgamate with the Federation. When the merger proved unsuccessful and split in June 1929, the women's group divided again and soon became defunct.

15. The Harmonization Society estimated that only 10,000 women were involved in reform organizations. At the same time (1929) there were about four million women organized in the type of organization oriented toward keeping women in their traditional place. *Saikin no Shakai Undō,* pp. 655, 717.

joined the government-sponsored League of Women's Organizations (Fujin Dantai Remmei) which absorbed all women's groups and diverted their work to mobilizing the war spirit among women.

Among the victims of the mobilization of the war spirit was the agitation for birth control which was led by Baroness Shizue Ishimoto. She had been active from before March 1922 when she and others had boldly gone to the boat to welcome Margaret Sanger to Japan. At the time, the Ministry of Home Affairs almost refused to permit that famous American advocate of birth control to land. The Baroness' brother, Yūsuke Tsurumi, had done some writing on behalf of equality for women; and in the proletarian camp, Isoo Abe and Tetsu Katayama had for years supported family planning. Her political position was of the most moderate social democratic variety; but the idea of birth control was anathema to the military. Therefore, her high family connections did not prevent her arrest in the roundup of December 1937, even though it was directed mainly at the popular front leaders. She had married into the nobility; her former husband's father had been a Minister of War in the second Saionji Cabinet; and her brother was then a Minseitō Diet member. Her arrest shows how broad the supression of even the women's movement had become.[16]

THE SPECIAL COMMUNITIES: A SOCIAL MINORITY

More important than the participation of women in the social democratic movement was that of the so-called "special community" people (tokushu burakumin). They were not a religious, ethnic, or racial minority, though many outsiders maintained they could always spot them by features and mannerisms.[17] They were a social minor-

16. We have earlier noted that Baroness Ishimoto's arrest eventually led to her marriage to Kanjū Katō and to her becoming the most prominent and powerful woman in the postwar Social Democratic Party. See the interesting account of her arrest and her postwar war activities in Mary Beard, *The Force of Women in Japanese History* (Washington, D.C., Public Affairs Press, 1953), pp. 167–78.

17. Surprisingly enough, Toyohiko Kagawa in his early books voiced prevalent attitudes of prejudice toward the *tokushu burakumin* and erroneous notions as to their origins. "Nobody," he wrote, "can deny that the special community people are a criminal race in the Japanese Empire . . . a degenerate or slave or worn-out indigenous race" of diverse origins. He thought he detected remnants of Chinese words in the speech of some communities and of Korean in others. From their skin pigmentation he came to think of some as descendants of Caucasians and some, of Negroes. See his *Himmin Shinri no Kenkyū* (A Study of the Psychology of the Poor) (Tōkyō, Keiseisha,

ity, insultingly referred to by a four-finger hand gesture signifying "animal-like." The prejudiced avoided even eating with them, much less contemplating intermarriage with them. Descendants of what was a pariah caste during the Tokugawa Shogunate, they continued to be the most discriminated-against minority group in post-Restoration Japanese society. During the Tokugawa period they were generally referred to as the *"Eta,"* which means "defilement abundant."[18] This term has gained some circulation among English-speaking scholars on Japan, but, as can be surmised by its translation, it is an opprobrious epithet carrying connotations possibly more disagreeable to those it designates than the term "nigger" to American Negroes. Also Eta is only one of many such derogatory names for this group.[19] The term accepted by unprejudiced people today, including the persons designated, is "special community" people, or better still, simply "community" people *(burakumin).*[20]

Prejudice against them stems from a long history of segregation. There are several theories regarding the origin of the Eta, but the one accepted on a scholarly level in prewar Japan was that of Professor Teikichi Kida who traced them to the *Etori* or food catchers of the pre-Heian period.[21] At some points in history their ancestors held high social position, but during the Tokugawa Shogunate they were assigned to the lowest social category, even below a migrant

1916), pp. 98–101, and his *Seishin Undō to Shakai Undō* (A Movement, Spiritual and Social) (Tōkyō, Keiseisha, 1919), passim. I am indebted to Mr. Hiroshi Wagatsuma for these citations. Actually, objective study finds the special community people no different racially from the rest of the Japanese (who have, of course, an ancestry of many racial strains).

18. This translation is Basil H. Chamberlain's in his *Things Japanese* (6th ed. rev. London, K. Paul, Trench, Trubner, and Co., 1939), p. 150. This book was first published in 1899.

19. A list of such derogatory names, arranged according to locality where used and with translations where possible, has been compiled by Shigeaki Ninomiya, in his "An Inquiry Concerning the Origin, Development, and Present Situation of the Eta in Relation to the History of Social Classes in Japan," *The Transactions of the Asiatic Society in Japan,* 2nd Series, *10* (December 1933), 137–39. See also Hugh H. Smythe, "The Eta: A Marginal Japanese Caste," *American Journal of Sociology,* 58 (September 1952), 194–96.

20. The most comprehensive work on the *burakumin* is George DeVos and Hiroshi Wagatsuma, ed., *The Invisible Race: Studies of the Outcaste Tradition in Japan* (Berkeley and Los Angeles, University of California Press, 1966). Chapter 4, by George O. Totten and Hiroshi Wagatsuma, presents a detailed history of the political movements of the "special communities" from the Meiji period to the end of World War II.

21. Teikichi Kida, "Tokushu Buraku Kenkyū" (A Study of the Special Communities), *Minzoku to Rekishi* (Race and History), 2 (1919).

class known as "nonhumans" (hinin). It was decreed that they alone
were to be employed in certain undesirable social and economic
functions, such as scavenging, disposing of dead animals, slaughter-
ing, tanning, leather goods manufacturing, executing criminals, un-
dertaking, and guarding cemeteries. The Buddhist prohibitions
against killing and meat eating reinforced the popular prejudice
against them. Toward the end of the Tokugawa Regime discrimination against them was further intensified by deteriorating economic
conditions.

In 1871 the first flush of egalitarian sentiment after the Restoration led to the official emancipation of the Eta who were henceforth
declared to be part of the "common people" (heimin).[22] However,
since no economic measures were taken to make the emancipation a
reality, the majority of these "new common people" (shin heimin),
as they were sarcastically called, were left in a worse condition than
before. Those who had money enough or were engaged in migratory
occupations could move away from the ghettos and melt in with the
rest of the people, but the vast majority could not leave the special
communities. They lost the special rights they had been accorded in
feudal society, such as monopolies in the leather-goods and other occupations, and their emancipation came too late for them to get a fair
share in the new redistribution of land. Over half the households
continued to farm on inferior plots. Some, especially those near big
cities, continued to butcher and tan, while others took over jobs no
one else would have. Those who have tried to "pass" and rise up the
social ladder were in constant fear that their ancestry would be discovered. It was only natural that eventually these people would take
collective action to better their lot.

The immediate conditions that inspired the special community
people to organize the National Leveling (or Levelers') Society (or
Association) (Zenkoku Suiheisha) on March 3, 1922, were the same
ones that gave rise to the social democratic movement itself. Without
reviewing all these conditions, it may be pertinent to mention two of
them. One was the postwar economic dislocation exemplified by the
great Rice Riots of 1918. It has been estimated that about 80 per cent
of the 6,000 persons arrested in connection with the riots were special community people.[23] The other was the rising current of demo-

22. The "Eta Emancipation Decree" (Eta Kaihō Rei) was Proclamation No. 61, issued
by the Council of State on August 28, 1871. For a translation, see Ninomiya, p. 109.
23. Nimoniya's footnote mentions four sources for this statement. Ibid., p. 127.

cratic and socialist thought. This was given expression in an article by Manabu (Gaku) Sano, the Waseda University professor who became a Communist, which was distributed at the meeting that launched the movement for self-emancipation. The article explained the groundlessness of discrimination against the special communities, argued that true emancipation was possible only through a socialist revolution, and laid down two fundamental principles: (1) the emancipation of the special community people must begin with their own demands for the abolition of unjust discrimination, and (2) the movement thus begun must be in concert with the proletarian movement as a whole.[24] A similar line of thought was also advocated by some socialist but non-Communist members of the Buddhist clergy, such as Sangendō Miura [25] and Abbot Akamatsu,[26] who actually helped inspire organization among the special communities. In spite of the fact that the Buddhist clergy had traditionally carried on charity work among the burakumin, these former outcasts, in attempting to stand on their own feet, began to refuse the charity of the temples and instead seek emancipation through political channels.

Previous experience had taught them that they could be politically effective. As early as 1890 their support had been instrumental in electing to the Diet Chōmin (or Tokusuke) Nakae, the most democratic of the old "liberal movement" theoreticians.[27] Later they had even succeeded in electing to the Diet members of their own class. Their poverty, however, minimized their effectiveness. Though they claimed that some 6,000 special communities containing about three

24. This article first appeared in the July 1921 issue of the journal *Kaihō* (Emancipation) and was entitled, "Tokushu Buraku Kaihō Ron" (On the Emancipation of the Special Communities). Upon reading the article, three special community youths from Nara Prefecture, who had been thinking along similar lines (under the influence of a socialist Buddhist, Miura, mentioned below) determined to help get a national organization of special community people started. They immediately went to Tōkyō to visit Sano, who was then a professor at Waseda University, and got his permission to use the article in revised form as a prospectus for the new organization—which became the National Leveling Society—and to change the title to read, "Yoki Hi no Tame ni" (For a Better Day). *Saikin no Shakai Undō*, p. 471.

25. Miura was one of the small group of Buddhist clergy interested in socialism. See Totten, "Buddhism and Socialism . . . ," p. 298.

26. The Abbot was the father of Katsumaro Akamatsu. His daughter, Tsuneko, lived with him for a time in a special community. Beard, p. 186.

27. Shin Nihon Rekishi Gakkai (New Japan Historical Institute), ed., *Shin Nihon Rekishi: Kindai Shakai* (New Japanese History: Modern Society) (Tōkyō, Fukumura Shoten, 1953), p. 134. For an account of Nakae's political orientation, see Ike, *The Beginnings of Political Democracy in Japan*, pp. 124–29.

million inhabitants existed throughout Japan, their full strength could not be utilized as long as economic qualifications barred so many of them from voting. Although there is no reliable information, the figure of a million and a half special community persons is considered more accurate but even this figure was of no small political significance.[28]

In its attempt to raise living standards in the special communities, the Leveling Society at first concentrated on getting individual or group apologies for overt acts of prejudice. The struggle to obtain apologies sometimes pitted the majority society more openly against the special community and even resulted in some bloodshed.[29] The ensuing arrests and trials revealed how prejudiced the courts were against the people of the special communities. It seemed to the members of the Society that the only way to raise their social position was to lower the people at the top of the hierarchy, i.e. all those who held titles of nobility (*kazoku, kizoku,* and by implication the *kōzoku* or imperial family). They decided to start by requesting Prince Iesato Tokugawa to renounce his title, since his ancestors, in the eyes of the Levelers, were mainly responsible for holding down the Eta during the Tokugawa regime.[30] The failure of this attempt was a factor in convincing the members of the need for allying themselves with labor and agrarian organizations and with the proletarian parties. Since the "Bolshevik faction" (to use the terminology of the day) monopolized the cry for political action, it gained the upper hand in the organization as a whole. The "Bolsheviks" (pro-Communists) were opposed by an anarchist and a conservative faction. The anarchists were militant against political action; the conservatives, uninterested in it.[31]

28. For a discussion of this figure, see Ninomiya, p. 113. As late as 1948 the best available figures were considered to be those published by the Welfare Ministry in 1935. See Buraku Kaihō Zenkoku Iinkai (National Committee for Community Emancipation), ed., *Buraku Kaihō e no Sanjū Nen* (Thirty Years Toward Community Emancipation) (Tōkyō, Kindai Shisōsha, 1948), pp. 224–25. Recent government figures put the total number of special communities at 4,133 with an aggregate population of 1,220,157 distributed throughout 29 prefectures. Chūō Seishōnen Mondai Kyōgikai (Central Conference for Youth Problems), eds., *Seishōnen Hakusho* (White Paper on Youth) (Tōkyō, 1962), but DeVos and Wagatsuma believe these are serious underestimates.

29. Well-known incidents of this nature were the fight between the National Essence Society (Kokusuikai) and the Levelers in March 1923, and the Serada Massacre in January 1925. These are described in detail in Buraku Kaihō Zenkoku Iinkai, pp. 48–62.

30. This decision and its aftermath are described in ibid., pp. 63–77.

31. Since these factions opposed political action and were not involved in the social

To aid in the formation of the first proletarian party, the members of the Bolshevik faction organized themselves into the Proletarian Federation of the National Leveling Society (Zenkoku Suiheisha Musansha Dōmei) in October 1925 and on December 1 took part in the abortive formation of the Farmer Labor Party. The right-wing General Federation had considered this Proletarian Federation Communist-dominated and demanded that it, too, be kept out of the formation of the Labor Farmer Party in March, along with the leftist Council and another group. This exclusion was reaffirmed at the party's third Central Executive Committee meeting in July. But the leftists continued fighting. The Proletarian Federation had good leverage in influencing the Japan Farmers' Union to fight against the continued exclusion, because so many Levelers and other special community people were active in it.

In August the Proletarian Federation sponsored a rally to keep the issue alive. The "open door" policy finally won the day and the party's first move was to invite support from the Leveling Society. This victory, however, temporarily cost the party most of its organized support, when the General Federation and other groups pulled out, leaving it reeling from the blow, with only the Japan Farmers' Union and the rather unimportant Ceramics Federation remaining. Two days before the big split, the Proletarian Federation had responded by formally organizing the National Leveling Society's League to Support the Labor Farmer Party (Zenkoku Suiheisha Rōdō Nōmintō Shiji Remmei) on October 22. Later the party gave four seats on the Central Executive Committee to its leaders and agreed to adopt a plank opposing "feudalistic prejudices and discrimination." In the 1928 Diet election three Levelers became Labor Farmer Party candidates, though none was elected.[32]

One of these three can serve as the most outstanding example of the political activities of the Leveling Society in relation to the proletarian parties. Jiichirō Matsumoto became Chairman of the Society's Central Committee in 1925 and remained in that position into the postwar period. A building contractor of some means, Matsu-

democratic movement, they will not be discussed here, but for their viewpoints see Kyōchōkai, *Saikain no Shakai Undō*, pp. 471–82.

32. The three candidates were Jiichirō Matsumoto (Fukuoka), Seijirō Miki (Okayama), and Kazutaka Kiyohara, alias Mankichi Nishimitsu (Nara). Where there were no Leveler candidates, the special communities were called upon to support other Labor Farmer Party candidates, such as Chōzaburō Mitzutani and Senji Yamamoto. Ibid., pp. 484–85.

moto nevertheless obtained only a middle-school education, because he was expelled for expressing opposition to discrimination.[33] In 1926 he led a dramatic campaign against discrimination in the Fukuoka Regiment in Kyūshū.[34] Its most vigorous supporters were the Miners' Union, the Japan Farmers' Union, and other organizations supporting the Labor Farmer Party; their cooperation cemented relations between the party and the Society. Unfortunately for the leaders of the campaign, however, the police built up a case against them, charging that they had conspired to use violence against the regiment. The case became a cause célèbre in the courts and dragged on for three years, eventually reaching the Supreme Court. The final verdict was three years of hard labor for nine men, six of whom died in prison. Matsumoto was one who survived. During the trial several hundred members of the Leveling Society were caught in the mass arrests of March 15, 1928, and April 16, 1929.

After the dissolution of the Labor Farmer Party, the Society followed Ōyama's lead and supported the formation of the New Labor Farmer Party, preferring restricted parliamentarianism to the illegal activities advocated by the Communists. As the new party moved to the right, a controversy developed in the Leveling Society over its own organization and strategy. The more radical faction proposed dissolving the Society completely and encouraging the members to join labor and farmer unions individually, arguing that liberation of the special communities could only be attained through the emancipation of the working class as a whole. The more conservative faction insisted that the Society remain intact. A compromise was eventually reached by which the Leveling Society would be retained as a national organization but activity would be concentrated in Community Committees (Buraku Iinkai) which would join

33. It was said that much of the financing of the Leveling Society came from Matsumoto's own pocket. See Akasaka, *Musantō o Ugokasu Hitobito: "Jimmin Sensen" to wa Uani ka?*, pp. 56–61. For an account of Matsumoto's life, see Nuisaburō Inoue, *Gendai Seijika Retsuden* (Biographies of Contemporary Politicians) (Tōkyō, Kaname Shobō, 1953), pp. 168–74.

34. In its campaign the Leveling Society emphasized that its members in the armed forces and its other supporters were fighting for the preservation of "human rights" for all soldiers and sailors, and that as long as the army was a "class" army, it would be used in the interests of the ruling class and not for the working people. The campaign is described with relevant documents in Buraku Kaihō Zenkoku Iinkai, pp. 77–100. Also see Buraku Mondai Kenkyūjo ("Community" Problems Research Institute), ed., *Buraku no Rekishi to Kaihō Undō* ("Community" History and Emancipation Movements) (Kyōto, Buraku Mondai Kenkyūjo, 1955), pp. 251–52.

in all movements for raising the living standards of the people in the special communities.[35]

The new organizational strategy was tested and proved successful in a mass campaign in 1933, which revealed the strength of the revived Leveling Society and demonstrated that it could be a political asset to the newly formed Socialist Masses' Party in which all the social democratic factions had united in 1932. The object of the campaign was to reverse a discriminatory decision in the Takamatsu Local Court in Kagawa Prefecture which in effect had found a man guilty of hiding the fact that he was from a special community when he proposed marriage to a noncommunity girl. Since such a decision negated the Emancipation Decree of 1871, a campaign to reverse it was bound to receive the overwhelming support of the inhabitants of special communities.

A troop was organized to proceed from Kyūshū northward to Tōkyō in October 1933, visiting all important concentrations of special communities on the way, making speeches, and gathering signatures on a petition. In spite of constant police interference, the troop of 50, led by Matsumoto, was welcomed by almost 200,000 people along the way; its members made speeches at 47 places to an aggregate audience of some 163,000. In Tōkyō they met with various government officials. Two large receptions were held for them by the Socialist Masses' Party, and others by various labor and consumer unions. The campaign was almost immediately successful, for in the following month the condemned man was released, the judge discharged, and the prosecutor removed.[36]

Subsequently, relations between the Society and the Socialist Masses' Party became closer. Though Matsumoto ran as an independent candidate in the national Diet elections in 1936 and 1937 and was elected both times, he often cooperated closely with the Socialist Masses' Party.[37] Haruji Tahara, also a man of special com-

35. This controversy is covered and the dissolution proposal is quoted in full in Buraku Kaihō Zenkoku Iinkai, pp. 124–42.

36. The trial and campaign are described in full in Keikan Koyama, *Seigantai wa Ikani Tatakatta ka?* (How Did the Petition Troop Fight?) (Hamamatsu, Zenkoku Suiheisha Shizuoka Rengōkai, 1934).

37. Mitsu Kōno reports that Matsumoto joined the Socialist Masses' Party after the 1937 election; see Kōno, *Nihon Shakaiseitō Shi*, p. 143. But the Special Higher Police state that he never became a full-fledged member although he was a member of the party's Diet Members' Association (Shadaitō Daigishikai) from which he was expelled along with the party members involved in the Saitō affair in 1940. See the confidential

munity origin, was elected to the Diet in 1937 on the Socialist Masses' Party slate. Since he took an active part in the party, we included him in the list of Japan-Labor clique members, although he was a latecomer. He was far better educated than Matsumoto, having not only graduated from Waseda but studied in the United States as well. Like many Levelers he was active in the Japan Farmers' Union and other farmer groups. In such men the special communities contributed an element of leadership in the social democratic movement that reached into the Diet itself.

The Leveling Society was the only organization of the "social movement" to survive the war. After the war had begun and even after Seigō Nakano's ultranationalistic Eastern Association had been dissolved, the National Leveling Society still continued in existence. Matsumoto was called to the Ministry of Home Affairs and warned that he would not be recommended in the 1942 election if he did not dissolve the organization, but he refused.[38] Since the government knew that he would be elected anyway, he received a governmental recommendation in the "Tōjō election" and was duly elected.[39] (After the surrender the Leveling Society was one of the first to take part in organizing the new Social Democratic Party of Japan.)

As an element in the Japanese social democratic movement, the National Leveling Society—representing the most depressed minority in Japan—was continually attracted to the left but its leadership was adroit enough to steer it clear of extinction. It was the only element in which progressive Buddhist influence was found, a fact which may evoke comparisons with the importance of religion to the Negroes in America and to the Jews the world over. The poor of the special communities were drawn to the radical social movement by the realization that only through labor or farmer organization were they able

---

journal put out by the Peace Preservation Section of the Ministry of Home Affairs, *Tokkō Geppō* (Special Higher Police Monthly Report) (April 1940), p. 35.

38. For Matsumoto's account of the conversation, see Buraku Kaihō Zenkoku Iinkai, pp. 204–07.

39. Due to these special circumstances, Matsumoto was at first excepted from the Occupation purge of all Diet members who were recommended by the Tōjō government in the 1942 election, but Premier Yoshida purged him in 1949 supposedly for his membership in a prewar ultranationalist organization but actually, it is widely believed, because of his postwar leftist political activities. See Kiyoshi Inoue and Taisaku Kitahara, *Buraku no Rekishi* (A History of the [Special] Communities) (Tōkyō, Rironsha, 1964), pp. 127–39.

to better their living standards and escape being increasingly isolated and discriminated against.

THE KOREANS: A NATIONAL MINORITY

Like the special community people, Koreans formed an oppressed minority in Japan. Though racially almost indistinguishable from the Japanese, the Koreans have their own language, culture, and history. Those in Japan, therefore, could be considered a national minority.[40] During the decade following World War I, when the social democratic movement gained its mass following, about 400,000 Koreans migrated to Japan in spite of the social prejudice they encountered there. The vast majority of these were farmers turned industrial workers who came to sell their unskilled services in the Japanese labor market. They lived in slum conditions inferior to those of most of the worst-off Japanese laborers. They received the lowest pay and were the first discharged from work when economic conditions deteriorated. Not only were they discriminated against, but in one of the most terrible pogroms in recent history thousands of them were massacred at the time of the great 1923 Tōkyō earthquake. During the post-World War I period, there were also several thousand Korean college and university students in Japan, the majority of whom were poor, discontented, and without a secure future. The businessmen among the Koreans were minor tradesmen or very small-scale operators. At first glance, then, it would seem natural for the Koreans residing in Japan to be drawn into the socialist movement, as were the special community people.

Unlike the latter, however, the Koreans did not legally enjoy the rights of Japanese citizenship. Through the Japanese annexation of Korea in 1910 the Koreans received Japanese nationality but not Japanese citizenship. Only after the Korean nationalist uprising in 1919 did the Japanese government proclaim "equality" between Japanese and Koreans, but this equality did not include the right to vote. In 1925, when the Universal Manhood Suffrage Act was passed, some 140,000 Koreans residing in Japan became eligible to vote in

40. A comprehensive study of this subject is Edward W. Wagner, *The Korean Minority in Japan, 1904–1950* (New York, Institute of Pacific Relations, 1951). Interestingly enough, at first Manabu Sano and others also considered the special community people an "oppressed national minority" in Marxist terms.

Japanese elections provided they could meet the regular requirements for voting. All but a tiny minority were unable to take advantage of this, however, for the law required proof of residence for a
period of at least one year as well as proof of nonreliance on relief or
similar governmental support.[41] After the middle 1930s conditions
changed again and Koreans were completely excluded from the Japanese electorate. Having no opportunity to express themselves
through the franchise, they were not drawn to the social democratic
movement which relied heavily on parliamentary means for bringing
about reform.

Although excluded effectively from the ballot, the possibility of
supporting the social democratic movement through participation in
the labor movement was still open to them, but here again they were
unable to make much headway, and where they were active, their
support went to the Communists. They did not make good material
for labor organizations because they were unskilled, frequently working on government relief projects, largely illiterate, struggling with a
foreign tongue, and often migrant. Nevertheless, a group of radical,
anti-Japanese Korean students and intellectuals organized a General
Federation of Korean Laborers in Japan (Zai Nihon Chōsen Rōdō
Sōdōmei) in 1925,[42] which acted as a liaison between five Korean
labor unions, one in each of the five big cities. Its leaders also appeared at Japanese union conventions and tried to win sympathy for
the Korean people. Despite its name, it was most sympathetic to the
pro-Communist Council and later to the National Conference of
Japanese Labor Unions.

Most of the Koreans in Japan had originally been engaged in agriculture in their native villages, but in Japan they could get neither
land nor employment as agricultural workers. Therefore, they
found no place for themselves in the Japanese agrarian movement.

Only in the most extreme sections of the proletarian movement
did Korean students and intellectuals play any role. After the
Japanese suppression of the supposedly nonviolent nationalist demonstrations throughout Korea on March 1, 1919, for a Korean to be
an active nationalist also meant being a revolutionary, because there
seemed to be no possibility of achieving Korean independence by

41. Ibid., p. 20. Some politically moderate Koreans interested in the poletarian movement did make an attempt to take advantage of the ballot but apparently with little
success. Kyōchōkai, Saikin no Shakai Undō, p. 195.

42. Ibid., pp. 195, 233.

nonviolent means. Within this revolutionary framework there were three tendencies: "bourgeois" nationalist, anarchist, and Communist. The middle-class revolutionaries fled abroad and organized a government-in-exile under Syngman Rhee. The anarchists engaged in sporadic violence and the Communists engaged in organized underground activities. The most sensational and extreme of the anarchist activities was the attempted assassination of Crown Prince Hirohito in 1923 by the Korean, Pak Yŏl.[43] Most of the Korean residents in Japan who supported Japanese proletarian organizations were caught in the March 15 and April 16 arrests in 1928–29.[44]

In keeping with the geographical position of Korea between Russia and Japan, Korean leftists fluent in both Russian and Japanese made natural intermediaries between the Comintern and those Japanese considered most likely to form a Japanese Communist Party. Among those contacted by Koreans were Sakae Ōsugi, Toshihiko Sakai, and Hitoshi Yamakawa,[45] but with the advent of the 1930s such a role became almost impossible.[46]

What the three groups discussed in this chapter had in common was the experience of social and legal discrimination. The legal disabilities against the special community people had been removed early, but social discrimination persisted; consequently they became

43. Sometimes transliterated Bak Yul (both of these are in the Korean word order), his name was pronounced Retsu Boku in Japanese, and his alias was Daisuke Naniwa. He was married to a Japanese, Fumiko Kaneko. For his crime he was imprisoned in Japan from 1924 to 1945, after which he chose to go to North Korea.

44. How the nationalist aspirations of Korean intellectuals in Japan were tied up with revolutionary activity is vividly described in such books as: Katsunosuke Yamamoto, *Nihon o Horoboshita Mono: Gumbu to sono Hōkai no Katei* (What Ruined Japan: The Creation of the Military Dictatorship and the Process of Its Destruction) (Tōkyō, Shōkō Shoin, 1949); Younghill Kang, *The Grass Roof* (New York, Charles Scribner's Sons, 1931); and Kim San and Nym Wales, *Song of Ariran* (New York, John Day, 1941).

45. For instance, when Eizō Kondō went to Shanghai from Japan in the spring of 1921 in connection with the arrangements for founding a Japanese Communist Party, he met a group of a dozen Comintern representatives. The head of the group, Pak Chin-sun, and most of the others were Koreans who knew Japanese and were well acquainted with the Japanese socialist movement. They also knew Russian and the situation in the Soviet Union. See Eizō Kondō, *Kominterun no Misshi: Nihon Kyōsantō Sōsei Hiwa* (Secret Messenger of the Comintern: The Secret Story of the Creation of the Japanese Communist Party) (Tōkyō, Bunka Hyōronsha, 1949), pp. 128 ff.

46. The post-World War II Japanese Communist Party, however, boasted several top Korean members with active records of Communist activity dating back to the 1920s: Tenkai Kin, Ontetsu Boku, and Kenichi Itō. Also Koreans were most helpful to the Japanese Communist leaders when they went underground during the Korean War.

the most politically active and best organized of the three categories. Legal disabilities against women were stubbornly upheld by the dominant conservative parties, though hope for their elimination burned brightly for a while in the 1920s. And prejudice against Koreans varied with changes in policy toward Korea and other colonial and occupied areas, but with each new surge of Japanese aggression abroad the Koreans were driven to either greater despair or extremism.

The egalitarian aspect of socialist thought resulted in proletarian party demands for improving the status of each of these groups. As we have seen in Chapter 9, all the parties at first championed not only political but also legal and economic equality for women, and in addition special protection for women workers and youth with regard to night work and hard physical labor. It was during the life of the Socialist Masses' Party that the "blackout" on the feminist question came, although Abe and Katayama of the Socio-Democratic clique continued to speak out on this issue. Since legal disabilities fitted in with the prevalent concept of the social position of women in the "house" (*iye* or *ie*), most women were not conscious of them as unjust. It was undoubtedly only a tiny minority of the potentially powerful female segment of the population who espoused an ideology that supplied them with reasons and remedies for their discontent.

In contrast, both the special community and Korean minorities were acutely conscious of the injustice of their condition. But while the special community people had no alternative other than to seek equality and integration, the Koreans, except for a few, preferred separation, i.e. the liberation of Korea. To be sure, the proletarian parties called for "liberation of the colonies" in the 1920s, as we have seen in Chapter 10, but Korea and Taiwan were not specifically named, except by Communists. Gradually, the slogan came to mean something entirely different: liberation of the British and other European colonies by the Japanese military forces. This shift could only alienate the Koreans further.

In addition to equality, the socialist concept of "emancipation" meant the freeing of the economically depressed classes from the shackles of poverty. Since women were found in all social strata, this tenet would appeal only to women of the laboring and agrarian classes plus a number of progressive-minded intellectuals. It was for this reason that ideas of economic improvement were so often associated with demands for political equality for women. Ideological divisions thus crept into women's organizations that envisioned any altering of the position of women in Japanese society and reduced their organizational impact.

Finally, inasmuch as social discrimination reinforced the economic inferiority of the special communities, they had a double reason to support the proletarian movement. But since they suffered no special legislation directed against them (as, for example, the Negroes in the South in the United States), a political movement which would examine the records of individual assembly and Diet candidates to "reward friends and punish enemies" would be of little help. The solution arrived at was to support Matsumoto and a few other militant candidates of *buraku* background whose presence in the Imperial Diet could give the special communities the satisfaction that "one of our boys made it" and who at the same time expressed a measure of defiance against the upper class by their manners and dress and by cooperating with the labor- and agrarian-backed proletarian parties.

Conclusion

15: Characteristics of Japanese Social Democracy

Social democracy in prewar Japan was at once a part of Japanese political life and a segment of a world phenomenon. Consequently it contained both peculiarly Japanese characteristics and aspects shared universally by social democratic movements elsewhere. Disentangling the two will help relate our findings to both the Japanese scene and to the sociopolitical forces at work in the world at large.

JAPANESE AND UNIVERSAL ASPECTS

Many foreigners are surprised to learn that a social democratic movement even existed in prewar Japan, and they immediately tend to think of it as an "artificial imitation" of something Western, or as something "un-Japanese." Yet from the point of view of its composition, it was entirely Japanese. All of its leaders and its entire support were Japanese. Although this may at first appear to be an obvious remark, it must be remembered that the socialist movement in the United States, for instance, was at the outset largely made up of foreign-born.[1] During the last century much of the socialist writing

1. "The affiliated foreign-language groups provided one of the most dependable and numerically stable elements in the American Socialist Party." See Donald Drew Egbert

in the United States was done in German, and this was certainly one of the factors that inhibited the spread of socialist thought in the American environment.[2] Even today left-wing movements in America are influenced by traditions that have come down only one or two generations from European immigrants. In contrast, leaders of the socialist movement in Japan did not suffer, as did many socialists in the United States, from the fact they spoke with a foreign accent or were culturally set apart from the rest of the nation.

Although Japanese in personnel, it is true that the movement was motivated by ideas imported from abroad. In fact, we have traced the origin of the Japanese labor movement to the Shokkō Giyūkai (Knights of Labor), formed in San Francisco in 1890 by Japanese residing in California. When these organizers returned to Japan and set up the first trade unions, they brought with them both their foreign ideas and their experience with organizational techniques learned in America. The socialist study groups formed in Japan at about the same time were likewise inspired by newly imported Christian, humanitarian, and liberal ideals, and the works they set out to study and translate, such as those by Lassalle, Proudhon, Marx, and others, were all foreign. One of the most difficult tasks facing these early Japanese socialists was the creation of a new vocabulary to make the alien words and concepts understandable in Japanese.

Except for the very temporary organization of the Knights of Labor in San Francisco, however, the Japanese labor movement did not develop as an organized movement on foreign soil. It was never carried on by an elaborate apparatus of fugitives abroad as was, for instance, the movement of the Russian Social Democrats before World War I or the Chinese revolutionists who were led by Sun Yat-sen. This may be a root cause for the subsequent development of a (reformist) social democratic movement in Japan, because when socialists are forced from their own shores they are apt to believe that the only hope for their movements lies in revolutionary overthrow of their government. There was very little latitude (or freedom) for the growth of the early socialist movement in Japan but the little

and Stow Persons, *Socialism and American Life* (2 vols. Princeton, Princeton University Press, 1952), *1*, 554.

2. See, for instance, W. F. Kamman, *Socialism in German American Literature* (Philadelphia, 1917) and United States Government, Office of Strategic Services, ed., *Foreign Nationality Groups in the United States* (Washington, D.C., U.S. Gov't. Printing Office, 1943).

there was made it unnecessary for the socialists to either flee or go underground completely and thus opened the way for social democratic beliefs in the possibility of nonviolent change.

How well the imported socialist ideas were digested in Japan or how true a reflection of Western concepts was embodied in the theoretical and polemical writings of the newly converted Japanese socialists are questions outside the focus of this study. What is relevant here is that regardless of the particular foreign inspiration of their ideas, the Japanese socialists created a movement designed to bring about changes in the Japanese environment.

Considering the Japanese socialist or social democratic movements as segments of an international phenomenon does not necessarily require measuring their accuracy in immitating foreign models of action. It does, however, require awareness of the extent to which certain people in Japan were behaving in the same way as similar people in other countries. The resulting movements then may be considered peculiarly Japanese to the degree that they varied from their counterparts elsewhere. This approach will rescue the analysis from the error of treating Japanese social democracy as merely a Western movement in a Japanese setting.

We may now review those characteristics of the Japanese social democratic movement in which the more universal aspects (those shared with social democracy in general) are primary, while the peculiar (Japanese) aspects are secondary, that is, in terms of its being a *mass* social movement with a *class* composition and employing essentially *evolutionary* tactics.

Although comparatively small in numbers, the Japanese social democratic movement was undeniably a mass social movement. It attempted to utilize the weight of numbers to secure its ends. It employed organized mass action in the form of demonstrations, parades (such as on May Day), rallies to support particular issues, mass collection of signatures on petitions, and the less organized action of support for political candidates at the polls. The leaders, funds, and facilities of mass labor and agrarian organizations gave the political movement its vitality. In fact the very formation of the proletarian parties was dependent on the pledged support of the leaders of such organizations. The large, established, conservative parties in Japan, such as the Seiyūkai and the Minseitō, were not the centers of mass movements in the same sense. To be sure, they rallied large numbers of people to vote during elections, usually many times those mustered by the proletarian parties, and they did during certain crises stir up mass demonstrations, but not to bring pressure from below for fundamental changes in the existing social order. Instead they appealed to the electorate for endorsement of Japanese statesmen or politicians in or out of office who were fundamentally wedded to the status quo and wished only to change policies on certain issues or oust their rivals from the emoluments of office.

The mass character of the movement, shared by other social democratic movements, was the product of certain similar conditions of modernization, i.e. industrialization with its various concomitants of universal education, mass communication, and centralized facilities. The appearance of a class of industrial laborers with common problems of defending themselves against unemployment and poor working conditions as well as of bettering themselves was the sine qua non of socialist movements, though such conditions did not necessarily produce social democratic political parties.

That the Japanese movement remained small in relation to its potential growth, compared to Europe though not perhaps in comparison to other parts of Asia, reveals its peculiar character as a product of the Japanese environment. Of all the limiting environmental factors examined in this study perhaps the single most important was that the great agricultural community served as both the source of workers in Japan and as the support and refuge of the unemployed. The majority of the work force for a long time was made up of women temporarily working away from home and therefore not very amenable to being organized into militant unions. As for the male workers, they could survive periods without work and without wages by returning to their native villages, and thus unions were not such a life-or-death matter to them as to workers in countries with a different agrarian economy. The submerged surplus population in the villages kept industrial wages low and made it easy to break unions. From this central fact flowed a host of others: the temporary nature of large segments of labor, which drove workers frantically to seek permanent attachment to an enterprise; the constant contact with the preindustrial village environment; the paternalism which in the larger factories promoted a paramilitary hierarchy among the workers and which in the textile mills regulated the lives of the factory girls from dawn to dusk, and which again in the small workshops imposed a feudalistic familial relationship between employer and employees, between masters and apprentices. All such factors contributed to form the peculiarities of the Japanese movement.

In its universal social democratic aspects, the Japanese movement was also a *class* movement. What is meant by this is answered in so many ways by social democrats the world over, and is related to so many subsidiary problems, that no precise definition is offered here. It is almost universally true that the theoretical questions connected with the concept of class—questions such as class conflict or class harmony, class interest or national interest, what constitutes a class, which classes are natural allies, and so forth—are constant sources of polemics between the left and right wings of social democratic movements. Nevertheless, one conclusion of this study is that the Japanese social democratic movement was a class movement. Its main core consisted of organized labor; agrarian support was an important element; and it appealed to the unpropertied or proletarian classes in the broadest sense of these terms. Although composition has varied markedly from country to country (especially with regard to the agrarian element), social democracy elsewhere has universally been a class movement in the same sense and has likewise been torn by internal conflict concerning the emphasis that should be given to class in its composition.

An examination of the problem of class emphasis as it existed in the Japanese movement compared to how it has been posited elsewhere will serve to bring out the more peculiarly Japanese characteristics in this regard. In its tersest terms, the question is whether a social democratic party should be a class or a national party. Those who hold to the class party view see the social democratic (or socialist) party as the political organ of the proletarian class or classes standing in opposition to the bourgeois parties. Believing that the real interest of the nation lies in the transformation of the economy from capitalism to socialism, they argue that the only class with the drive and power to effectuate this transformation is the class of modern industrial workers; and therefore a socialist party can be true to its goal only if it is conscious of being a labor party and is predominantly composed of industrial workers. This is, in general, a left-wing position in the social democratic movement the world over.[3]

3. For a discussion of the problem from this point of view, see Hitoshi Yamakawa, *Rōdō Kaikyū no Seitō* (The Working Class Party) (Tōkyō, Rōdō Bunkasha, 1949), and by the same author, *Kaikyū Tōsō no Tsuihō* (Banishing the Class Struggle) (Tōkyō, Kaizōsha, 1949).

In opposition to this view, other social democrats believe the class character of the party should be deemphasized because striving for the amelioration of the lot of the working people contributes to the common good of the whole nation. They therefore hold that a social democratic (or socialist) party should emphasize its character as a national party, reflecting the makeup of the nation as a whole.

Since the right wing universally holds that the party should de-emphasize its class character, it welcomes leaders from any class as long as they support the party's aims. This is the dominant trend in the more conservative social democratic parties of England, France, and Sweden.[4] The left wing, however, which supports the concept of a class-oriented party, is divided on the question of whether leaders who do not come from working-class backgrounds can be trusted to uphold the class aims of the party.

On the international scale, both of the left-wing types are found. For instance, the left wing of the German Social Democratic Party which split off in 1917 to become the Independent Social Democratic Party was led by middle-class intellectuals in contrast to the right wing whose leaders had risen mainly from the working class through trade union activity. Yet the (middle-class) left-wing leaders constantly sought to sharpen the class character of their party, while the right-wing (working-class) leaders emphasized the party's national character. The two wings of the present British Labor Party would appear to be a similar example, since the right wing of the party finds its main support in the phalanx of organized labor, whereas the left wing is supported by the local party branches throughout the country which are composed of a variety of people, many of whom are middle-class intellectuals. Yet in England the left wing tends to distrust socialist leaders who are not of working-class background. They also suspect that leaders, originally from the working class, who have reached positions of power and prestige with the possibility of receiving a title of nobility, will lose sight of the interests of labor as they believed Ramsay MacDonald did in 1931. Thus, typically, Aneurin Bevan, former leader of the left wing, warned against the leadership

4. This trend is brought out in such works as the following: G. D. H. Cole, *A History of the Labour Party from 1914* (London, Routledge and Kegan Paul, 1948); François Goguel, *La Politique des Partis sous la troisieme Republique* (Paris, Édition du Seuil, 1948); and Herbert Tingsten, *Den Svenska socialdemokratiens ideutveckling* (The Ideological Development of Swedish Social Democracy) (2 vols. Stockholm, Tidens Förlag, 1941).

of the party falling into the hands of "unrepresentative types" who do not speak "with the authentic accents of those who elected" them.[5]

In prewar Japan, the social democratic leaders who emphasized the class appeal of the proletarian parties ranged from the pro-communists in the Labor Farmer Party (and its successor, the New Labor Farmer Party) through the leftist but anticommunist Labor-Farmer faction people to members of the centrist Japan-Labor clique (until shortly after the Manchurian incident). Nevertheless, examination of the backgrounds of these leaders revealed that the large majority of them were not from the working class and that their university education further differentiated them from the rank-and-file laborers whom they led in unions and to whom they appealed in political campaigns. Thus they were in no position to advocate the limitation of leadership positions to those who had a "proletarian" origin.

The right-wing Socio-Democratic clique leaders, on the other hand, who were in fact originally more largely drawn from the laboring class, laid less emphasis on the class nature of the proletarian parties they led. They were also proud of the prestige of the older middle-class leaders in their midst, though distrustful of their contemporaries who were university educated and who had come into the movement from the student organizations.

In concluding these observations on the composition of the prewar Japanese social democratic leadership in relation to the left- and right-wing views on the class emphasis of proletarian parties, it may be said that those left-wing leaders who insisted on a class-oriented party could not go so far as to insist that leadership be recruited on the basis of class qualifications, not only because they themselves had come from relatively privileged homes which could afford to give them higher education, but also because some of the leaders who could best qualify as coming from the working class were most positive in their rejection of the doctrines of uncompromising class conflict. But by deemphasizing the class character of their mission, the center and right wings of the movement laid themselves open to the lures of nationalism and appeals to support their own country's aggression abroad.

Besides being a mass social movement with a class composition, another universally social democratic aspect of the Japanese movement was that it employed essentially *evolutionary* tactics. It saw its

5. Aneurin Bevan, *In Place of Fear* (New York, Simon and Schuster 1952), p. 15.

goals of fundamental changes in the social order as far-off ones which could only be achieved through a slow, evolutionary process. More specifically, it championed parliamentary means to achieve reforms. In this it was at one with all social democratic movements after the appearance of Soviet Communism.

This advocacy of evolutionary means and the rejection of non-parliamentary methods perforce gave social demoracy the subsidiary function of counteracting Communism. Modern social democracy came into existence through its competition with Communist elements for the same tradition, for support from the same classes, and with many of the same lesser tactics. Right-wing social democracy the world over contains some of the most anticommunist leaders to be found, although, since the movement is so marked by internal variations, there are cases when the left wing is under strong Communist influence (e.g. the Nenni Socialists for a time in postwar Italy or the prewar Labor Farmer Party in Japan after its adoption of the "open door" policy). Since internationally the right wing has usually been far stronger than the left in social democratic movements, counteracting Communist influence has been a dominant social democratic function.

The Japanese movement has shared this general aspect. If the Japanese government had taken equally suppressive measures against the social democrats as it did against the Communists, the social democratic movement would have lost much of its raison d'être as an evolutionary group and more of its support would have undoubtedly turned to revolutionary leaders. Although the government passed the broadest type of suppressive legislation at the time of the enactment of universal manhood suffrage, it was not applied to the social democrats while the Communist movement was growing. Such legislation—against anyone attempting to alter the national polity (*kokutai*) or disavowing the system of private property—could have been applied to all socialists. But the Japanese government recognized the value of the function of the social democrats in keeping a number of dissatisfied groups from becoming irreconcilably antigovernment. This was a primary function of the Japanese movement because certain prevailing conditions, such as the extremely limited powers of the Diet and the gradually rising tide of ultranationalism, prevented the movement from achieving any real legislative reforms. After the disappearance of the Communist movement, the Japanese social democrats lost much of their devotion to social democracy and became increasingly national socialist or ultranationalistic in character.

In this connection it must be mentioned, however, that the Japanese social democrats, as was characteristic of those who espoused an evolutionary approach, always disavowed the methods of violence. Organized violence did not break out between social democrats and Communists in Japan the way it did, for instance, in pre-Hitler Germany where actual battles were fought in the streets. Even the self-proclaimed fascists in Japan were mild compared to the German Nazis and Italian Fascists when they were struggling for power. An important reason is probably to be found in the fact that the German and Italian governments at the time were weak, whereas the Japanese government was always strong vis-à-vis mass movements whether of the right or the left. Even the actual uprising of military troops in February 1926 in retrospect appears to have been a pathetically ineffective attempt at overthrowing the government.

The Japanese social democrats' rejection of violent methods appears all the more striking in light of the widespread use of assassination and all the lesser forms of physical violence by Japanese ultranationalist rightists both against those in power and against the left. To the list of important statesmen assassinated in Japan may be added such leftists as Sakae Ōsugi (the anarchist) and Senji Yamamoto (the procommunist Labor Farmer Party Diet member). Many social democratic politicians were assaulted by rightist hoodlums. This kind of incident happened more frequently to leftist leaders, such as Ōyama,[6] but is also extended to such right-wing social democrats as Abe and Yoshino. Added to this were violence and torture at the hands of the police and Kempeitai. Of course, within the labor movement clashes with the police and paid strikebreak-

6. The assassinations of Ōsugi and Yamamoto have been alluded to in the text. Here a couple of instances of attempts on Ōyama's life might be mentioned: (1) After the 1923 great earthquake in Tōkyō when Ōsugi was murdered, Ōyama was apprehended by military officers who planned to assassinate him, but such a commotion was caused by neighbors and by newspaper correspondents that they gave up the attempt—see Nihon Kindai Shi Kenkyūkai (Institute of Modern Japanese History), ed., *Kindai Nihon Jimbutsu Seiji Shi* (A Political History of Modern Japanese Personages) (2 vols. Tōkyō, Tōyō Keizai Shimpōsha, 1956), 2, 107–08. (2) When Ōyama fled to the United States a young would-be assassin came along on the same boat but during the voyage became so impressed with the character of Ōyama that he confessed—see Kitazawa et al., *Ōyama Ikuo Den*, pp. 252–53.

ers were frequent, but the social democratic labor leaders, especially the right wing, advocated nonviolent methods (even passive resistance) and tried to reduce the number of strikes to a minimum.

Lest it appear that the Japanese social democrats acted contrary to Japanese mores in advocating nonviolent methods, it must be mentioned that Japanese public opinion reacted sharply against violence except where a higher value was at stake, e.g. patriotism or loyalty to the throne. Political assassins in Japan would often give themselves up readily, knowing that pleas of patriotic motivation would be effective in mitigating any punishment. That course was closed to social democrats who advocated a fundamental change in the social order through parliamentary means.

COMPOSITION OF THE MOVEMENT

In reviewing the universal aspects of social democracy—such as its mass, class, and evolutionary character—the more peculiarly Japanese variations of social democracy have also been noted. In examining in more detail some of the conclusions derived from our analysis of organized support, more can be said about the particular as well as the general aspects of Japanese social democracy.

In outline, the composition of the Japanese socialist movement went through four stages: (1) From its inception to the end of World War I, it was composed mainly of intellectuals. (2) Between the end of the war and the formation of the proletarian parties in 1926 it suddenly became a mass movement of organized laborers and tenant farmers. Its leaders were largely intellectuals but they were working closely with their followers in building the labor and agrarian unions. This was a period of rapid growth which entailed the recruitment of leaders from the rank and file of union members. (3) From the formation of the political parties until the early 1930s after the Manchurian incident, the structure of the movement changed so that the proletarian political parties were superimposed on the trade union and agrarian organizations. When the movement began to center in the new proletarian parties, it had to appeal to the large electorate in the urban centers and in this way came to involve larger groups of students, professional people, all types of salaried employees, and people connected with the small retail and manufacturing establishments. At this time also the leadership broadened to include political leaders who came from outside the labor and agrarian movements, men from universities and the worlds of journalism and law. (4) From the early 1930s to 1940, the movement expanded to the point where it secured the large votes of 1936 and especially of 1937 when the Socialist Masses' Party garnered over a million ballots. During this period, organized support was relatively less important than before. The main agrarian union was less under party influence than in the early days. The leadership of the movement was less involved in labor and other mass organizational work and more occupied with political activity. The gap between leadership and following widened. The leaders were eventually largely absorbed into the government-sponsored organizations while the rank and file were forced into them en masse.

Although in broadest outline these stages—emphasizing in turn (1) intellectuals, (2) trade unions, (3) unions plus electorate, and (4) broader electorate relative to organized support—are somewhat analogous to those in the development of socialist movements elsewhere, a marked feature of the Japanese situation was the relative weakness of trade union support. In Europe the socialist parties had been built on the foundation of old, established trade union movements with years or decades of experience. The Japanese proletarian parties, on the other hand, came into being shortly after the labor unions first became mass organizations. More rapidly developed and consequently less sturdy, unions in Japan were, of course, coefficients of an industrialization compressed into a relatively short time span. This young union movement did not supply solid, substantial membership, financial support, and leadership to the extent that trade unions did for the British Labor Party, for example. Although in Japan the Socio-Democratic clique maintained control over the General Federation, even this did not constitute an impressive trade union basis.

The distinguishing element in the Japanese movement was the tenant farmers. Where strong agrarian support for social democracy exists in Western countries, as, for instance, in Canada, the farmers have been deeply affected by the industrial revolution; they own their own land; and their espousal of socialism derives from their struggles against the monopolies which control the transportation and marketing of farm produce and the production of the necessities for mechanized agriculture.[7] In Japan, however, the problem of land tenantry,

7. See, for instance, S. M. Lipset's study on agrarian support for the Canadian Com-

to which we have devoted some attention, added a complication not usually found in the industrialized societies where social democratic movements have developed.

Agrarian support for social democracy in Japan was necessary because the prospect of achieving a parliamentary majority without votes from the countryside electorate was distinctly unpromising. The extent of farm tenantry and the unrest engendered by its attendant conditions provided potentially militant support, as could be inferred from the great Rice Riots of 1918. From the very beginning the Japan Farmers' Union took an active part in the formation of "labor–farmer" proletarian parties. The tenant and poor independent farmers were considered part of the large unpropertied or proletarian class, and thus the parties at the time were called "proletarian" in the sense of "propertyless" rather than "labor." [8]

The nature of this support, however, was even less stable than that of labor. It tended to be either radically militant, as seen in the agrarian support for the pro-communist Labor Farmer Party in 1928, or extremely conservative and somewhat antilabor, as observed in the support commanded by Hirano and his early attempt to develop a purely farmers' party. The need for long overdue land reform in Japan—somewhat analogous to the contemporaneous situation in China—tended to make agrarian support at times "too hot to handle." The right-wing social democrats, such as the Socio-Democrats who were very firm in accepting only "moderate" support, could make little headway in securing the kind of agrarian constituency they wished. The overwhelming majority of the agricultural community remained unreceptive or hostile to social democracy. Though this can be attributed largely to the landowning gentry's active efforts to keep out "unsettling" influences, it was also a reaction against industrialism which appeared to the peasants to be ultimately responsible for their woes.

The problem of social and national minorities also varies considerably from country to country. Yet, strangely enough, on this point, strikingly universal aspects are noticeable. Minority interests have

---

monwealth Federation in Saskatchewan, *Agrarian Socialism* (Berkeley and Los Angeles, University of California Press, 1950).

8. In postwar Japan the term *"musan"* (proletarian) as an adjective for left-wing political parties has tended to disappear in favor of *"kakushin"* which may be translated as "renovationist," "reformist," or "socialist."

been championed by the majority of socialist parties throughout the world and most vigorously by their leftist elements. For instance, in their hour of trial the Jews were defended by the German Social Democratic Party and by the Communists, even though the Jews in Germany belonged mainly to the middle class. More frequently the victims of discrimination are concentrated in the lowest economic or social strata. Such is the case in India where the Socialist Party has always had an economic program for the further emancipation of the untouchables. Also in the Union South Africa, the Labor Party has fought for the rights of the Coloreds, Indians, and Negroes (or Bantu) although, in numbers, the Negroes can hardly be called a minority. In Belgium and Holland the cultural minority problem is one of the most important for the socialist parties.

Where minority groups have a low potential in terms of numbers, however, their role appears to be insignificant. Such is the case, for instance, with the Lapps in Sweden in relation to the Swedish Social Democratic Party and with the Bushmen in Australia with regard to the Labor Party there.

In prewar Japan both of these generalizations find substantiation. The Ainu aborigines, the "purest" of whom still live on reservations in Northern Japan and who are decreasing numerically, have remained outside the Japanese social democratic movement. Also the Koreans residing in Japan saw little future for themselves within the confines of the Japanese Empire; the Japanese government did not provide sufficient evidence of good faith to raise hopes for equal opportunities; and therefore they found little impetus to support the moderate social democratic movement. On the other hand, the special communities of the former pariah Eta caste did supply a significant and persistent element of support for social democracy, particularly after the suppression of Communist and pro-communist groups to which the Leveling Society of the special communities had first been drawn.

Prewar social democratic leaders likewise exhibited both universal and more particularly Japanese characteristics. When considered as a whole rather than in terms of the various cliques and factions, social democratic leadership was seen to consist of both workers and intellectuals. This accords with social democratic experience universally; it is the proportion of workers to intellectuals that varies from country to country. Again, in Japan (as is generally true in social democratic experience) there was no outstanding leader who was entirely the product of an agrarian background.

The tenant farmers first formed an organized movement under the stimulation and guidance of labor leaders. This again is indicative of how closely the development of social democracy is linked to industrialization. Probably a detailed study of this problem on a comparative basis would reveal that the more rapid the industrialization in a country the more dependent its social democratic movement is on intellectuals for leadership. If the development of industrial capitalism comes about more gradually, the general educational level is likely to be raised quickly enough to render the differences between the intellectual and the worker less obvious. In any case, it must be remarked that the working-class leaders in the Japanese movement (and this is probably universally true) had acquired in their rise to leadership much of the training and skill possessed by the university-educated leaders. In fact, the Ōsaka Labor School was set up by a group of unions in 1921 especially for the purpose of training potential leaders from working-class backgrounds.[9] By the time social democratic leaders entered the Diet, there was little in manner, bearing, public speaking ability, or general knowledge to distinguish those who had had formal higher education from those who had not. This would appear to be generally true in Europe, with the possible exception of England, where class differences in speech and accent are especially marked and difficult to overcome.

If Japanese social democratic leaders are analyzed in terms of "political generations," their more particular aspects are again apparent. If a political generation is composed of "individuals of approximately the same age who have shared, at the same age, certain politically relevant experiences," [10] prewar Japanese social democratic leadership falls into two political generations: (1) those who had

9. For an account of the founding and functioning of this school, see Ōsaka Rōdō Gakkō Jūnen Shi Hensan Iinkai (Committee for the Compilation of the Ten Year History of the Ōsaka Labor School), ed. *Ōsaka Rōdō Gakkō Jūnen Shi: 1921–1931* (The Ten Year History of the Ōsaka Labor School: 1921–1931) (Ōsaka, Ōsaka Rōdō Gakkō Shuppambu, 1931). One of the most ardent of the original promoters of this school was Suehiro Nishio who knew from personal experience how important education was for labor leaders. Ibid., p. 8. Kagawa helped supply money for the school and the Ōhara Institute teachers. (In postwar Japan the need for such labor schools all but vanished, because much about trade unionism could soon be freely learned in the ordinary public schools.)

10. Heberle, *Social Movements*, pp. 119–20.

been active in the socialist movement before the First World War, and (2) those who first became socialists in the five year period immediately following that war.[11] The first generation has been called "veteran socialists" in this study; they shared such formative experiences as the early introduction of socialist ideas from abroad, the antiwar agitation during the Russo-Japanese War of 1904–05, the many short jail sentences for "seditious" or "inflammatory" writings, and the period of enforced "hibernation" for socialists after the Kōtoku Trial of 1910–11. Sharing the same experiences, however, did not mean that they all reacted alike. Some became anarcho-syndicalists, some later became Communists, some Socio-Democrats, and even national socialists, though most eventually became part of the Labor-Farmer faction. Although they argued with one another, they spoke the same language in the sense that they had all helped introduce foreign concepts and together had contributed to making them Japanese. They were familiar with the same "incidents" in the socialist and labor movements, and together they had studied the rapid development of the industrial revolution in Japan. They could all claim the same tradition, reaching back to the first Social Democratic Party of 1901—a thin and recent tradition compared to those in England, France, and Germany.

This tradition, however thin, was inherited by the younger generation which was composed mainly of university students graduating in the period from 1918 to 1923. These young men were stimulated first by events outside Japan. After their interest had been aroused by the European postwar revolutions, they discovered that there was a socialist tradition in their own country. At the same time they saw the labor movement developing haphazardly and realized they could contribute by giving it leadership and organization. Young and untrained as they were, they found that their easy access, through books, to the experiences of other countries enabled them to play important roles. This was the process which drew Asō, Kōno, Katō, and most of what came to be the Japan-Labor clique into the socialist and labor movements.

The Russian Revolution served as the catalyst uniting the older and younger political generations of socialist leadership. Stirred by

11. The present author first published his ideas on Japanese socialist "political generations" in "Problems of Japanese Socialist Leadership," *Pacific Affairs, 28* (June 1955), 160–69. This was translated into Japanese and appeared as "Nihon Shakaitō no Shudō-ken o Meguru Shomondai," *Amerikāna* (Americana), *1* (November 1955), 1–10.

reports of the Revolution, they wanted to learn what was behind it; since what material on socialism existed in Japanese had been either written or translated by the "veteran socialists," the younger men in this way came to know of them and to meet them personally. Inspired now by actual persons, they turned from theory to activity in the labor and agrarian movements. The Russian Revolution was the source of the "Bolshevism" in Japan from 1921–24 that affected the whole socialist movement and was also, of course, the inspiration for the formation of the Japan Communist Party, in July 1922, in which both veteran socialists and some products of the second generation participated.

The fact that many of the later leaders of the social democratic movement in Japan took part in the formation of the early Communist Party marks the Japanese off from most other social democratic movements. Elsewhere the pre-World War II Communist parties were usually founded by the radical wing of the existing social democratic party, often a small splinter movement. In Japan, those who took part in first organizing the Communist Party were among the most active and prominent socialists, such as Sakai, Arahata, and Yamakawa, as well as some of the most promising younger men, such as Akamatsu, Inomata, and perhaps Asanuma. After this "decisive experience," however, the veteran socialists who joined the party gradually withdrew from it and turned to attack it, and subsequent Communist recruits came largely from among people newer to the socialist movement. This later trend approximated more closely experience elsewhere, for many former Communist leaders in other countries have also eventually become important social democrats.

The post-World War I political generation, recruited mainly from the student movement centering in the New Men's Society, the Founders' Federation, and other student groups, was not succeeded by another political generation until after World War II. Following the crystallization of the various cliques and factions in 1926–27, no new blood suddenly surged into the leadership because the important positions were already filled and the movement did not expand sufficiently to offer further opportunities. It may be that this very inability to grow and expand had much to do with the factionalism that continued to plague the movement.

Factionalism is difficult to deal with as a characteristic, because, on the one hand, it is especially marked in leftist movements the world over, and, and, on the other, it is found in all political activity in Japan from the very right to the extreme left.[12] Diagrams or charts of the lineages of the political parties in almost any country picked at random tend to reveal that the parties on the left are the most fragmented. If such charts are drawn to show the factions within the social democratic parties, the fragmentation is even more striking.

In this respect the Japanese movement is no exception, though a thorough comparative study might well show it to be unsurpassed in the number of social democratic parties formed in the given time period. Considering the degree of fragmentation it may be safe to say that the usual leftist feature of factionalism overlays the already divisive tendencies in Japanese society to make the Japanese movement unique in its degree of factional strife.

In Japan the established or "bourgeois" parties were also marked by the most intense and violent factionalism. Many have been the occasions, for instance, when the police have had to intervene to prevent physical violence between two factions of the Seiyūkai barricaded on separate floors of the party headquarters in Tōkyō.[13] Factionalism pervaded every element of national life: the army, the bureaucracy, the aristocracy, as well as the parties. In fact, one observer of the prewar Japanese scene asserted, "Each 'group' is so shot through with schisms that it has been impossible for any single movement to control affairs in Japan completely according to its own program." [14]

It has often been noted that the intense ultranationalism expressed in the totalitarian ideology of the Imperial Way (*Kōdō*) was an inverted expression of the inner conflicts in the nation. Only the most intense emphasis on unity could overcome the internal disunity that would weaken the nation in time of war. Likewise, in the Japanese labor and socialist movements, the cry for unity was constantly

12. That factionalism characterizes both the right and the left and in fact the whole of Japanese society is one of the conclusions of Robert A. Scalapino and Junnosuke Masumi, *Parties and Politics in Contemporary Japan* (Berkeley and Los Angeles, University of California Press, 1962), pp. 57–59, 99–100, and 149. For further hypotheses, see George O. Totten and Tamio Kawakami, "The Functions of Factionalism in Japanese Politics," *Pacific Affairs, 38* (Winter 1965–66).

13. Mentioned, for instance, in Charles B. Fahs, *Government in Japan: Recent Trends in Its Scope and Operations* (New York, Institute of Pacific Relations, 1940), p. 80 n.

14. The observer was Robert Karl Reischauer in his *Japan, Government–Politics* (New York, Thos. Nelson and Sons, 1939), p. 191.

heard. Anyone reading the literature of the movement is struck with the fervor of the cry: "Labor can have strength only through unity." The irony of the situation was that, because of the "conditions" set by each group, such unity was reached only through the rise of a nationalism that divested labor as a whole of its independence and that robbed the social democratic movement of its social democratic character. The demise of the movement in Japan was in part due to an inability to unite its forces during a time when it might have been able to fight effectively for its goals.

Another particularly Japanese feature of the factionalism that plagued the social democratic movement in Japan was the extraordinary continuity and cohesiveness of its cliques or factions. Although there were additions and secessions, the hard core of the Socio-Democratic and Japan-Labor cliques remained intact from 1926 on and well into the postwar period. Just as the existence of factionalism in the Japanese social democratic movement may be far greater in degree than is generally the case, so, too, the persistence of the same personnel within the factions is also probably significantly greater than elsewhere. Here again, a feature that characterizes all of Japanese society may be responsible. In Japan factions are held together by the *oyabun–kobun* (master–follower) or *sensei–deshi* (teacher–pupil) relationship. Asō was openly spoken of as the *"oyabun"* of the Japan-Labor clique: while Abe was called the *"sensei"* of the Socio-Democrats. However, since such relationships in Japan do not require the charisma of a *Fuehrer* in the German sense, the cliques continued in existence even after the deaths of these two men. They were held together through group loyalty of a kind that can be traced back to Japan's recent feudalism. Members of the group honored the bonds of "personal relations," which meant that individual members would often suppress their own differences of opinion in the interests of group solidarity.[15]

Surprisingly, Japanese social democratic leaders often displayed a singular lack of democratic concern in organizational matters in spite of their theoretical espousal of democracy. This was, of course, partly due to the feudalistic element of group loyalty, but much of it was probably the result of the type of organized support from which they derived their power.

15. This point was made clear to the author in an interview with Mitsu Kōno of the Japan-Labor clique.

Many of the right-wing social democratic leaders, especially the Socio-Democratic labor leaders, included under their jurisdiction the largest segment of organized women workers. These submissive factory girls had usually been organized in the large textile mills, but the unions so formed became mere intermediaries between the women and the employer and were not democratically run. In other cases, the union leader was on the employer's payroll as personnel director of a closed shop. The labor union boss was able to discharge from the plant any worker who objected to union policies. The General Federation became more boss-controlled and less democratic as it expelled the various unions that dared to oppose the central committee's dictation. Thus, in the Social Democratic Party for instance, the prestige-element leaders could speak about the value of democracy as opposed to dictatorship, but some of the working-class leaders, such as Nishio, Matsuoka, and Doi, often used undemocratic and dictatorial methods to maintain their positions with the General Federation.

IDEOLOGICAL ROLES

The foregoing review suggests some reflections on the significance of the movement with regard to democracy, communism, socialism, and fascism. Theoretically, we might expect that the development of democracy in Japan would find its strongest impetus in the social democratic movement. However, the composition of the social foundations of the movement is an imporant consideration in whether democracy could have developed in prewar Japan. One of the central reasons why the old liberal movement of the 1870s and 1880s did not eventuate in a victory for democracy in Japan was the weakness of the more modern elements of the Japanese middle classes of the time; that is, the very small proportion of urban merchants and industrialists and the dominance of landlords who opposed land reform. Later, as the merchants and industrialists grew in number, they came to benefit indirectly by the tenantry system and this contributed to their inertia with regard to the struggle to place real power in a parliament responsive to a wide electorate who would demand greater reforms and liberties.

In this situation, Japanese intellectuals such as Abe and Yoshino, who had become impressed with Western democracy, looked to the nonpropertied proletarian masses rather than to the more comfortable middle classes to take up the struggle for democracy in Japan. However, the very weight of the problems of farm tenantry severely hindered efforts of the urban working classes to organize and act effectively. Thus democratic development was restricted even before the rise of ultranationalism.

At the time universal manhood suffrage was instituted and the proletarian parties organized, it appeared as though the Japanese parliamentary system was becoming more democratic. In the post-World War I decade encouraging signs heralded the possiblity of responsible party government (i.e. party-controlled cabinets) developing in Japan as in England during the last century. In such a context the new Japanese proletarian parties, like the European social democratic and even Communist parties, in representing strata of society hitherto unrepresented, in demanding reforms, and in insisting on minority rights, had an important role to play in democratizing the party system.

Nevertheless, just at the time of the appearance of the proletarian representatives in the Diet, a crisis was already shaping up in the Japanese political structure. Parliamentarism which had seemed to be proceeding in a "normal course" had come in conflict with the old orthodox ideology of the Imperial Way as espoused by the militarists. With the coming of the world depression and the increasing involvement of Japan in China, authoritarian, militarist, and ultranationalist currents ran more swiftly.

The newly elected social democrats had to decide how to react to the military as the rising force in Japanese politics. Should they defend the bourgeois parties or should they support the militarists? And was the bureaucracy a friend or foe? The questions, of course, were not quite this clear-cut and the social democrats did not give unequivocal answers. But the Japan-Labor clique in particular came to support the military more and more against the established parties, arguing that in Japan the army was the real agent of reform. In the end, they decided that the Socialist Masses' Party should lead the procession in party dissolutions to make way for the attempted totalitarian wartime structure.

Though the social democratic movement was fundamentally impotent in developing democracy in prewar Japan, it was a force in hindering the growth of Communism. The character of the Japanese socialist movement changed after the formation of the Japan Communist Party. In fact the social democratic movement came into being largely as a reaction to it. Up to that time the goals of the socialist movement had been amorphous; now with the appearance of the Communist Party which was clear in its goals and decisive in its action and linked to an international apparatus, the rest of the socialist movement gradually became more self-aware and thus more social democratic. Even the veteran socialists who had been midwives to its birth turned away from the party in its infancy and did much to prevent its growth and bring about its early (though not permanent) demise. Members of the younger generation stepped into the breach; an older exception was Dr. Kawakami.

The social democratic movement's gradual deemphasis of democracy at the expense of its emphasis on socialism may also have had an effect in hastening the trend toward government control over the Japanese economy. On the question of whether to support the army's adventure in Manchuria in 1931, the Socio-Democrats argued that the army should be supported if it would institute "socialist control" over the economy of Manchuria and keep it out of the hands of the zaibatsu. With this start, the "socialism" of the Japanese social democrats, as a whole gradually, though not without ambivalence, came more and more to coincide with the militarists' cry for tighter government controls on and planning in the economy, a trend which eventuated in the setting up of the Planning Board in 1937 (partly inspired by the example of Soviet Russia). By the end of 1937 the ideology of the social democrats closely approximated that of the national socialists.

National socialist or "fascist" movements in Japan also developed from below. Although small groups of intellectuals earlier espoused national socialism, the first mass support was secured through the conversion in 1932 of social democrats who commanded organized labor support, as earlier seen in the fascist movements in Italy and Germany. The very weakness of the labor and social democratic movements in Japan, however, prevented them from providing large mass followings for the national socialists.

What has been called "military fascism" in Japan, however, did not arise from below as it did in Italy or Germany. Mass movements of protest were unable to generate the power they did in Europe where individualism had already atomized the societies and where many wished to "escape from freedom." Government-sponsored mass movements in Japan arose out of the new drives toward reintegration. Though well on its way in the process of modernization, Japanese society was fragmented but not atomized. Rife with groups and cliques, it needed unity in order to carry on modern warfare. But this unity was achieved mainly from above by a balance of the various segments of the ruling classes with the military in a key position. The masses of the country rallied around the traditional symbol of the Emperor, and the central government's control extended down through various levels of the bureaucracy into the local neighborhood and block associations.

In Germany and Italy, sections of the large socialist movements turned from democratic to nationalistic methods to achieve "socialism." The fascist movements succeeded, because elements of the bureaucracy, the giant financial interests, and the military, frightened in the face of the pressure for change and action, gave aid to that section of the large, divided socialist movement that appeared to them to be able to create order without making fundamental changes in the economic organization of the country: the fascist.

In Japan, however, the analogous forces of government, big business, and the military were never weak in relation to the leftist forces, not only because of their police methods, but also because social and economic factors hindered really mass growth in the leftist movements. Sections of the military certainly aided the Japanese fascist forces and used them, but only for limited purposes, and later suppressed them. It is interesting to note that in the Tōjō election of 1942 many of the fascist or ultranationalist groups (tinged with socialist ideas) were not recommended for election by the government. The radical rightists in Japan relied on actual military units and on small bands of fanatics using terroristic methods to gain their ends, rather than on large-scale mass action in which laborers and other groups would be important. Since it was imposed from the top down, "military fascism" in Japan was never as totalitarian or as "modern" as fascism in Italy and Germany.

Despite the social, economic, and political limitations on the growth of social democracy in prewar Japan, the trials and tribulations it underwent molded the characteristics of the movement that was to reemerge in the freer air of post-surrender Japan, characteristics that are still recognizable in the far more mature, though still frustrated, socialist opposition today.

Appendices

Appendix I

These charts attempt to give a precise chronological listing as well as depict graphically leadership clique or factional continuity throughout the various organizational transformations. Charts in the first five of the following works were studied for suggestions and then checked with the chronology in the sixth.

1. Keiichirō Aoki, *Nihon Nōmin Undō Shi* (A History of the Japanese Agrarian Movement), Tōkyō, Minshu Hyōronsha, 1947.
2. Yoshinaga Irimajiri, *Seiji Gojū Nen Shi* (Fifty Years of Political History), Tōkyō, Jiji Tsūshinsha, 1951.
3. Shakai Keizai Rōdō Kenkyūjo, *Kindai Nihon Rōdōsha Undō Shi* (A History of the Modern Japanese Laborers' Movements), Niigata, Hakurinsha, 1947.
4. Mosaburō Suzuki, *Ai to Tōsō* (Love and Struggle), Rōdō Bunkasha, 1949.
5. Kōki Yanada, *Nihon Shakaitō* (The Social Democratic Party of Japan), Tōkyō, Hōbunsha, 1956.
6. Yoshimichi Watanabe and Shōbei Shioda, *Nihon Shakai Undō Shi Nempyō* (A Chronology of the History of the Japanese Social Movement), Kokumin Bunko (National People's Library) 434, Tōkyō, Ōtsuki Shoten, 1956.

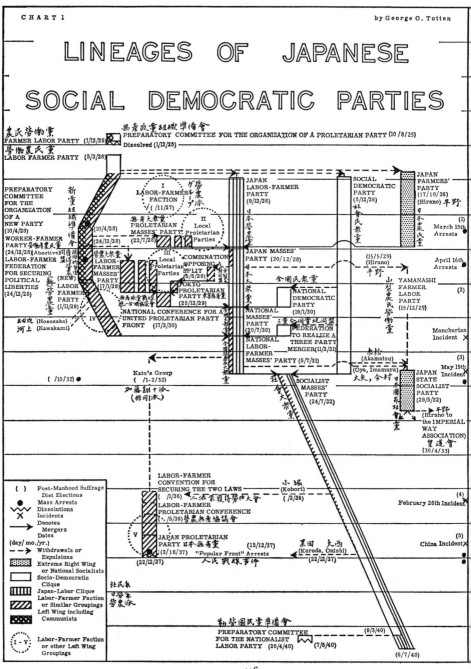

Lineages of Japanese Labor Unions

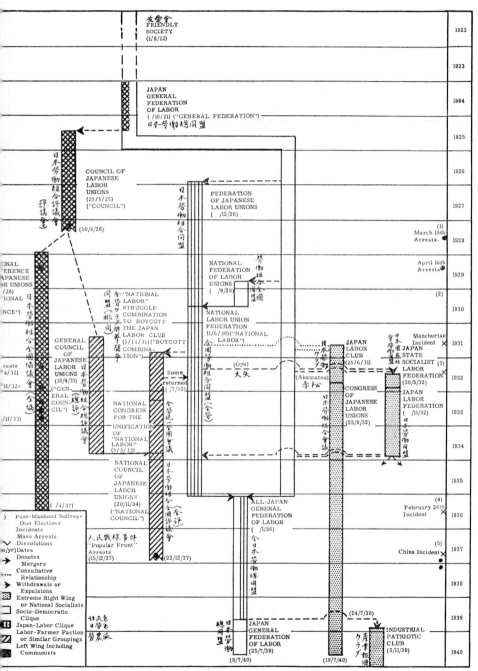

Lineages of Japanese Farmers' Unions

日本農民組合 JAPAN FARMERS' UNION (日農) (9/4/22)

ALL-JAPAN FARMERS' UNION 全日本農民組合 (1/3/27)

ALL-JAPAN FARMERS' UNION FEDERATION 全日本農民組合同盟 (11/4/26)

(1)

GENERAL FEDERATION OF JAPANESE FARMERS' UNIONS 日本農民組合総同盟 (7/3/27)

ALL-JAPAN FARMERS' UNION 全日本農民組合 (5/7/28)

(2)

● (15/3/28)

● (16/4/29)

FARMER STRUGGLERS' SOCIETY 農民闘争社 (/3/29)

NATIONAL FARMERS' UNION 全国農民組合 (27/5/28) ("NATIONAL FARMER") 全農

NATIONAL FARMERS' UNION REFORM FACTION 全農刷新派 (/10/29)

CONFERENCE TO MAKE THE NATIONAL FARMERS' UNION MORE MILITANT 全農戦闘化協議会 (20/4/30)

NATIONAL FARMERS' UNION NATIONAL CONGRESS FACTION 全国会議派 (7/7/31) (全会派)

JAPAN FARMERS' UNION 日本農民組合 (26/1/31)

(3)

GENERAL FEDERATION OF JAPANESE FARMERS' UNIONS 日本農民組合総同盟 (29/4/32)

(7/3/34)

OSAKA AND NARA ASSOCIATIONS OF UNIONS 大阪連合奈良合会

IMPERIAL FARMERS' FEDERATION 皇国農民同盟 (1/12/33)

NORTH-JAPAN FARMERS' UNION 北日本農民組合 (/10/34)

(4)

Post-Manhood Suffrage Diet Elections { ( ) }

Mass Arrests ●

(day/mo./yr.) Dates

Denotes Mergers

Withdrawals or Expulsions

Consultative Relationship

Extreme Right Wing and National Socialists

Socio-Democratic Clique 社民系

Japan-Labor Clique 日労系

Left Wing, Including Labor-Farmer Faction 労農派

Left Wing, Including Communists

(5)

人民 "Popular" 戦線事件 Front

CONFERENCE OF PATRIOTIC FARMERS' ORGANIZATIONS 全国農民団体協議会 (/11/38)

Kuroda, Onishi, Okada 黒田, 大西, 岡田

GREATER JAPAN FARMERS' UNION 大日本農民組合 (6/2/38) (Sugiyama) (杉山)

JAPAN FARMERS' LEAGUE 日本農民連盟 (13/2/38) (Inamura) 稲村

(/7/40)

Disbanded in 1942

FEDERATION FOR REFORM OF THE LAND SYSTEM 農地制度改革同盟 (29/11/39)

408

Appendix II

PARTY NAME TRANSLATED	PARTY NAME ROMANIZED	CONVENTIONS (DISSOLUTIONS)	DATES
Preparatory Committee for the Organization of a Proletarian Party	Musan Seitō Soshiki Jumbi Iinkai	Founding (Dissolved)	Aug. 10, 1925 (Dec. 1, 1925)
Farmer Labor Party	Nōmin Rōdōtō	Founding (Dissolved)	(Dec. 1, 1925) Dec. 1, 1925)
Labor Farmer Party	Rōdō Nōmintō	Founding First Second (Dissolved)	March 5, 1926 Dec. 12–13, 1926 Dec. 10–12, 1927 (April 10, 1928)
Japan Farmers' Party	Nihon Nōmintō	Founding Second	Oct. 17, 1926 Dec. 1, 1927

* The illegal Communist Party is not included nor are most national socialist parties.

PROLETARIAN PARTY CONVENTION DATES (CONT.)

PARTY NAME TRANSLATED	PARTY NAME ROMANIZED	CONVENTIONS (DISSOLUTIONS)	DATES
		(Dissolved)	(Dec. 20, 1928)
Social Democratic Party	Shakai Minshūtō	Founding	Dec. 5, 1926
		Second	Dec. 4–5, 1927
		Third	Dec. 9–11, 1928
		Fourth	Dec. 8–10, 1929
		Fifth	Dec. 7–9, 1930
		Sixth	Jan. 19–20, 1931
		(Dissolved)	(July 24, 1932)
Japan Labor-Farmer Party	Nihon Rōnōtō	Founding	Dec. 9, 1926
		Second	Nov. 27–29, 1927
		(Dissolved)	Dec. 20, 1928
Japan Masses' Party	Nihon Taishūtō	Founding	(Dec. 20, 1928)
		Second	Dec. 15–16, 1929
		(Dissolved)	(July 20, 1930)
Yamanashi Farmer Labor Party (Local)	Yamanashi Nōmin Rōdōtō	Founding	Dec. 12, 1929
		First	March 17, 1930
		(Dissolved)	(?)
National Democratic Party	Zenkoku Minshūtō	Founding	Jan. 15, 1930
		First	Jan. 18–19, 1930

PARTY NAME TRANSLATED	PARTY NAME ROMANIZED	CONVENTIONS (DISSOLUTIONS)	DATES
		(Dissolved)	(July 20, 1930)
National Masses' Party	Zenkoku Taishūtō	Founding	July 20, 1930
		Second	Dec. 1–3, 1930
		(Dissolved)	(July 5, 1931)
National Labor-Farmer Masses' Party	Zenkoku Rōnō Taishūtō	Founding	July 5, 1931
		Second	Dec. 5–7, 1931
		(Dissolved)	(July 24, 1932)
Proletarian Masses' Party	Musan Taishūtō	Founding	July 22, 1928
		(Dissolved)	(Dec. 20, 1928)
Tōkyō Proletarian Party (Local)	Tōkyō Musantō	Founding	Dec. 25, 1929
		(Dissolved)	(July 20, 1930)
Labor-Farmer Masses' Party (Local)	Rōnō Taishūtō	Founding	Jan. 17, 1929
		(Dissolved)	(March 17, 1930)
National Conference for a United Proletarian Party Front	Musan Seitō Sensen Tōitsu Zenkoku Kyōgikai	Founding	March 17, 1930
		(Dissolved)	(July 20, 1930)
Preparatory Committee for the Organization of a New Party	Shintō Soshiki Jumbikai	Founding	April 10, 1928
		(Dissolved)	(Dec. 22, 1928)
Worker Farmer Party	Rōdōsha Nōmintō	Founding	Dec. 22–24, 1928
		(Dissolved)	(Dec. 24, 1928)

PROLETARIAN PARTY CONVENTION DATES (CONT.)

PARTY NAME TRANSLATED	PARTY NAME ROMANIZED	CONVENTIONS (DISSOLUTIONS)	DATES
Labor-Farmer Federation for Securing Political Liberties	Seijiteki Jiyū Kakutoku Rōnō Dōmei	Founding (Changed name to Rōnō Dōmei) (Dissolved)	Dec. 28, 1928 (Aug. 16, 1929) (Nov. 1, 1929)
(New) Labor Farmer Party	(Shin) Rōnōtō or Rōdō Nōmintō	Founding Second (Dissolved)	Nov. 1–2, 1929 Dec. 19–21, 1930 (July 5, 1931)
Japan State Socialist Party	Nihon Kokka Shakaitō	Founding Second (Dissolved)	May 29, 1932 Jan. 22, 1933 (Dec. 1933)
Socialist Masses' Party	Shakai Taishūtō	Founding Second Third Fourth Fifth Sixth Seventh Eighth (Dissolved)	July 24, 1932 Dec. 8–10, 1933 Jan. 20–22, 1935 Jan. 18, 1936 Dec. 20–22, 1936 Nov. 15, 1937 Nov. 20–21, 1938 Dec. 9–10, 1939 (July 6, 1940)
Labor-Farmer Proletarian Conference	Rōnō Musan Kyōgikai	Founding First	May 4, 1936 Feb. 21,

PARTY NAME TRANSLATED	PARTY NAME ROMANIZED	CONVENTIONS (DISSOLUTIONS)	DATES
		(Decided to change name)	1937 (March 18, 1937)
Japan Proletarian Party	Nihon Musantō	Founding	March 18, 1937
		(Dissolved)	(Dec. 22, 1937)
Preparatory Committee for the Nationalist Labor Party	Kinrō Kokumintō Jumbikai	Founding	April 26, 1940
		(Dissolved)	(May 7, 1940)

Appendix III

PROLETARIAN PARTY CANDIDATES FOR IMPERIAL DIET ELECTIONS, LISTED BY YEAR, AFFILIATION, AND ELECTORAL DISTRICT, INDICATING THOSE ELECTED AND CERTAIN OTHER RELEVANT INFORMATION

Note: Those elected are indicated by an asterisk (*). The electoral district number follows the name of the prefecture when the prefecture is divided into more than one district. The sources used are: *Nihon Rōdō Nenkan* and *Rōdō Nenkan,* and Masao Naka, *Senkusha no Keifu: Shakaitō Zenshi* (fully cited elsewhere); for the 1942 election: *Asahi Shimbun* (May 3, 1942). As these sources sometimes contradict one another, the most reliable data were chosen by further careful checking. In a few cases, alternate readings for names are given. Some people are better known by the *on*-reading of their names than by the proper reading. The names of all those who have been elected to the Diet have been checked in the Shūgiin (House of Representatives), ed., *Gikai Seido Shichijū Nen Shi: Shūgiin Meikan* (Seventy Years' History of the Parliamentary System: House of Representatives Biographical Register) (Tōkyō, Ōkaurashō Insatsukyoku, 1962). "National socialists" are not listed except for the 1942 election.

THE 1928 DIET ELECTION

Labor Farmer Party: (40 candidates; 2 elected)	Electoral District	Labor Farmer Party (cont.)	Electoral District
		Fuse, Tatsuji	Niigata 2
Akiwa, Matsugorō	Tōkyō 5	Hatakeyama, Matsu-	
Amatatsu, Masanori	Kagoshima 2	jirō	Akita 1
Araoka, Shōtarō	Hokkaidō 2	Iguchi, Masao	Okinawa
Chikauchi,		Inoue, Otokichi	Niigata 1
Kanemitsu	Hyōgo 2	Ishiwatari, Haruo	Aomori 2
Fujimori, Seikichi	Nagano 3	Izumi, Kunisaburō	Iwate 1
Furuya, Sadao	Yamanashi	Kamimura, Susumu	Kagawa 1

1928 DIET ELECTION (CONT.)

Labor Farmer Party (cont.)	Electoral District
Karazawa, Kiyohachi	Tōkyō 4
Katō, Kanichi	Hokkaidō 3
Kawai, Hideo	Mie 2
Kida, Shigeharu	Hokkaidō 4
Kiyohara, Kazutaka	Nara
Koiwai, Jō (Kiyoshi)	Ehime 2
Matsumoto, Jiichirō	Fukuoka 1
Matsuo, Eiichi	Kagoshima 1
Miki, Seijirō	Okayama 1
Minami, Kiichi	Tōkyō 6
*Mizutani, Chōzaburō	Kyōto 1
Murakami, Kichizō	Tottori
Namba, Hideo	Okayama 2
Noda, Ritsuta	Ōsaka 1
Ōhashi, Harufusa	Ōsaka 4
Ōyama, Ikuo	Kagawa 2
Sawada, Matsutarō	Akita 2
Shigematsu, Aisaburō	Fukuoka 3
Shindō, Kanji	Kanagawa 1
Sugiura, Keiichi	Shizuoka 1
Takeo, Hajime	Chiba 2
Tamura, Sennosuke	Fukui
Tokuda, Kyūichi	Fukuoka 4
Yamamoto, Kamejirō	Kagoshima 3
Yamamoto, Kenzō	Hokkaidō 1
*Yamamoto, Senji	Kyōto
Yamazaki, Tsunekichi	Aichi 1

Social Democratic Party: (17 candidates; 4 elected)

*Abe, Isoo	Tōkyō 2
Akamatsu, Katsumaro	Miyagi 1
*Kamei, Kanichirō	Fukuoka 2
Katayama, Tetsu	Kanagawa 2

Social Democratic Party (cont.)	Electoral District
Kikuchi, Hiroshi (Kan)	Tōkyō
Koike, Shirō	Fukuoka 4
Miyazaki, Ryūsuke	Tōkyō 3
*Nishio, Suehiro	Ōsaka 3
Ogawa, Kiyotaka	Tōkyō 4
Okazaki, Ken	Kanagawa 1
Shimoda, Kinsuke	Tōkyō 7
*Suzuki, Bunji	Ōsaka 4
Taman, Kiyoomi	Ōsaka 1
Tametō (Tamefuji), Gorō	Tōkyō 6
Tsutsumi, Yoshiaki	Hyōgo 1
Yonekubo, Mitsutsuke (Manryō)	Hyōgo 2
Yoshikawa, Suejirō	Kyōto 1

Japan Labor-Farmer Party: (13 candidates; 1 elected)

Asō, Hisashi	Tochigi 1
Fujimoto, Kinsuke (also endorsed by the Japan Farmers' Party)	Kagawa 2
Fukuda, Kyōji	Shimane 1
Inada, Naomichi	Tottori
Katō, Kanjū	Tōkyō 5
*Kawakami, Jōtarō	Hyōgo 1
Matsutani, Yojirō	Tōkyō 6
Sakamoto, Kōsaburō	Ōsaka 4
Shirahata, Matsunosuke	Yamagata 2
Sugiyama, Motojirō	Ōsaka 5
Sunaga, Kō	Gumma 1
Tsunajima, Seikō	Niigata 3
Yoshida, Kenichi	Hyōgo 3

1928 DIET ELECTION (CONT.)

Japan Farmers' Party: (12 candidates; 0 elected)	Electoral District
Hata, Kōsaku	Gumma 2
Hirahara, Mitsuchika	Kyōto 2
Horii, Hisao	Hokkaidō 2
Katō, Imaichirō	Aichi 2
Ōishi, Sakae	Fukuoka 3
Saeki, Sennosuke	Fukuoka 2
Sakamoto, Toshikazu	Gumma 1
Suga, Shunei	Hokkaidō 4
Sugai, Kaiten	Niigata 2
Takahashi, Kameki-chi	Yamanashi
Yabe, Jingo	Tōkyō 7
Yokota, Tamon	Tōkyō 6

Local Proletarian Parties: (6 candidates; 1 elected)	Electoral District
*Asahara, Kenzō (Kyūshū People's Rights Party)	Fukuoka 2
Imai, Yoshiyuki (Kako)	Ōsaka 3
Kawashima, Fujirō	Kanagawa 2
Nakazawa, Benjirō	Gifu 2
Ōsawa, Ichiroku (also endorsed by both the Japan Labor-Farmer and Japan Farmers' parties)	Tochigi 2
Ōtaguro, Hikohachi	Nagasaki 2
[Takahashi, Seihachirō (sometimes listed among local proletarian candidates)]	[Fukuoka]

THE 1930 DIET ELECTION

New Labor Farmer Party: (14 candidates; 1 elected)	Electoral District
Hososako, Kanemitsu	Kyōto 2
Ishiwatari, Haruo	Aomori 2
Kamimura, Susumu	Niigata 2
Kawakami, Hajime	Kyōto 1
Kinoshita, Genkichi	Hokkaidō 1
Kida, Shigeharu	Hokkaidō 4
Koiwai, Jō (Kiyoshi)	Ōsaka 4
Nakamura, Takaichi	Tōkyō 2
*Ōyama, Ikuo	Tōkyō 5
Shigematsu, Aisaburō	Saga 1
Shindō, Kanji	Kanagawa 1
Tamura, Sennosuke	Fukui
Takeo, Hajime	Chiba 2
Tomiyoshi, Eiji	Kagoshima 2

Japan Masses' Party: (23 candidates; 2 elected)	Electoral District
Aki, Sakaru (Sakan)	Kōchi 1
Araya, Sōji	Aichi 1
*Asahara, Kenzō	Fukuoka 2
Asanuma, Inejirō	Tōkyō 4
Asō, Hisashi	Tochigi 1
Hosono, Michio	Niigata 2
Imamura, Hitoshi	Nagasaki 1
Kanai, Yoshiji	Kanagawa 1
Katō, Kanjū	Tōkyō 5
Kawakami, Jōtarō	Hyōgo 1
Kawamata, Seion	Akita 2
Kojima (Ojima), Koichirō	Yamagata 2
Kojima, (Ojima), Toshio	Aomori 1

THE 1930 DIET ELECTION (CONT.)

Japan Masses' Party (cont.)	Electoral District	Social Democratic Party (cont.)	Electoral District
Kōno, Mitsu	Tōkyō 1	Shimoda, Kinsuke	Tōkyō 7
*Matsutani, Yojirō	Tōkyō 6	Suga, Shunei	Hokkaidō 4
Moriwaki, Isae	Tottori	Suzuki, Bunji	Ōsaka 4
Ōki, Takeo	Saitama 1	Tametō (Tamefuji),	
Sakamoto, Kōsaburō	Ōsaka 4	Gorō	Tōkyō 6
Shirahata, Matsuno-		Tsunetsuka (Kyōzuka),	
suke	Yamagata 2	Shigeichi	Toyama 1
Sugiyama, Motojirō	Ōsaka 5	Usui, Jirō	Yamanashi
Sunaga, Kō	Gumma 1	Yamamoto, Kamejirō	Kagoshima 3
Tanahashi, Kotora	Hyōgo 2	Yamazaki, Kazuo	Nagano 3
Yoshida, Kenichi	Hyōgo 3	Yonekubo, Mitsusuke	
		(Manryō)	Hyōgo 2
Social Democratic Party: (*33* candidates; 2 elected)		Yoshida, Minoru	Tōkyō 1
		Yoshikawa, Suejirō	Kyōto 1
Abe, Isoo	Tōkyō 2	*National Democratic Party:* (*4* candidates; 0 elected)	
Abe, Onchi			
(Yoshitomo)	Tōkyō 3		
Akamatsu, Katsu-		Furuno, Shūzō	Ōsaka 3
maro	Miyagi 1	Miyazaki, Ryūsuke	Tōkyō 4
Fujita, Kisaku	Nagano 2	Ōya, Shōzō	Ōsaka 4
Horigoshi, Kōshirō	Tochigi 2	Taman, Kiyoomi	Ōsaka 1
Horita (Hotta),			
Keiichi	Mie 2	*Local Proletarian Parties:* (*24* candidates; 0 elected)	
Kagawa, Toyohiko	Tōkyō 4		
Kamei, Kanichirō	Fukuoka 2		
*Katayama, Tetsu	Kanagawa 2	Aogaki, Zenichirō	Hyōgo 1
Katsuda, Hosaku	Shizuoka 2	Etō, Genkurō (Nara	
Koike, Shirō	Fukuoka 4	United Front)	Nara
Kurino, Tanizō	Yamaguchi 1	Fukuda, Kyōji (ex-	
Matsunaga, Yoshio	Saitama 1	pelled in 1929	
Matsuoka, Komaki-		from Japan	
chi	Tōkyō 5	Masses' Party)	Shimane 1
*Nishio, Suehiro	Ōsaka 3	Hirano, Rikizō	Yamanashi
Ogasawara, Kanichi	Nagasaki 2	Inomata, Kōzō	Niigata 3
Oka, Seishi	Ōsaka	Ishibashi, Genshirō	
Okazaki, Ken	Kanagawa 1	(Chiba Labor-	
Ōsawa, Ichiroku	Gumma 1	Farmer Party)	Chiba 1
Saitsubara, Seki	Hiroshima 2	Izumi, Kunisaburō	
Satake, Haruki	Kōchi 2	(Iwate Proletarian	
Shimanaka, Yūzō	Nara	Party)	Iwate 2

THE 1930 DIET ELECTION (CONT.)

Local Proletarian Parties (cont.)	Electoral District	Local Proletarian Parties (cont.)	Electoral District
Kaneko, Yōbun (Yoshitarō) (Akita Proletarian Party)	Akita 1	Party) Nishi, Kenichirō	Gifu 2 Niigata 2
Kikuchi, Yōnosuke (Miyagi Masses' Party)	Miyagi 1	Ōhashi, Harufusa Ōishi, Sakae (Fukuoka Devoted Labor	Ōsaka 4
Kurusu, Shichirō (Proletarian Masses' Party)	Ōsaka 2	Party) Sakai, Toshihiko (Tōkyō Proletarian	Fukuoka 3
Miki, Seijirō	Ōkayama 1	Party)	Tōkyō 1
Miyamoto, Kumaki-chi	Saitama	Takatsu, Seidō (Chūgoku Proletar-	
Mizutani, Chōzaburō (Labor-Farmer		ian Party) Takeda, Nobujirō	Hiroshima 1 Fukuoka 1
Masses' Party)	Kyōto 1	Ueda, Otoichi (National Farmers'	
Nakanishi, Inosuke (Tōkyō Proletarian		Union Prefectural Federation)	Mie 2
Party)	Tōkyō 6	Uei, Genji	Gifu
Nakazawa, Benjirō (Chūbu Democratic		Uemura (Kamimura), Tomokiyo	Ōsaka

THE 1932 DIET ELECTION

Social Democratic Party: (15 candidates; 3 elected)	Electoral District	Social Democratic Party (cont.)	Electoral District
		Suzuki, Bunji	Tōkyō 6
*Abe, Isoo	Tōkyō 2	Yamamoto, Kamejirō	Kagoshima 3
Abe, Onchi (Yoshitomo)	Tōkyō 3		
Horiuchi, Chōei	Kanagawa	National Labor-Farmer Masses' Party: (13 candidates; 2 elected)	
*Kamei, Kanichirō	Fukuoka 2		
Katayama, Tetsu	Kanagawa 2		
*Koike, Shirō	Fukuoka 4	Asahara, Kenzō	Fukuoka 2
Koyama, Hisao	Tōkyō	Asanuma, Inejirō	Tōkyō 4
Koyama, Makoto	Nagano 2	Asō, Hisashi	Tōkyō 5
Majima, Kan	Tōkyō	Furuichi, Haruhiko	Fukuoka
Matsunaga, Yoshio	Saitama 1	Izumi, Kunisaburō	Iwate 2
Matsuoka, Komakichi	Tōkyō 5	Kanai, Yoshiji	Kanagawa 1
Nishio, Suehiro	Ōsaka 3	Kawakami, Jōtarō	Hyōgo 1
Sasai, Genjirō	Kyōto	*Matsutani, Yojirō	Tōkyō 6

THE 1932 DIET ELECTION (CONT.)

National Labor-Farmer Masses' Party (cont.)	Electoral District
Miyake, Shōichi	Niigata 3
Mizutani, Chōzaburō	Kyōto 1
Ōya, Shōzō	Ōsaka 4
*Sugiyama, Motojirō	Ōsaka 5
Taman, Kiyoomi	Ōsaka 1

Preparatory Committee for the National Socialist Party: (2 candidates; 0 elected)	
Kuru, Kōzō	Hyōgo
Sakamoto, Kōsaburō	Ōsaka 4

Local Proletarian Parties: (5 candidates; 0 elected)	Electoral District
Akamatsu, Iomaro	Ōsaka
Kamimura, Susumu (National Farmers' Union National Congress Faction)	Niigata 2
Katō, Kanjū (Boycott Combination)	Tōkyō 5
Minami, Kiichi	Tōkyō 6
Yoshida, Yoshiichi (Yuichi) (Tōkyō Communications Workers' Union)	Tōkyō 5

THE 1936 DIET ELECTION

Socialist Masses' Party: (30 candidates; 18 elected)	Electoral District
*Abe, Isoo	Tōkyō 2
*Asanuma, Inejirō	Tōkyō 4
*Asō, Hisashi	Tōkyō 5
Dōmoto, Tamehiro	Fukuoka 4
Ishiyama, Torakichi	Tochigi 1
*Kamei, Kanichirō	Fukuoka 2
*Katayama, Tetsu	Kanagawa 2
Kawai, Giichi	Hyōgo 3
*Kawakami, Jōtarō	Hyōgo 1
*Kawamata, Seion	Akita 2
*Kawamura, Yasutarō	Ōsaka 4
Kikuchi, Yōnosuke	Miyagi 1
*Kōno, Mitsu	Tōkyō 1
Miura, Aiji	Fukuoka 2
*Miyake, Shōichi	Niigata 3
Miyamura, Matahachi	Kumamoto 1
*Mizutani, Chōzaburō	Kyōto 1
Nakamura, Takaichi	Tōkyō 7
Noguchi, Hikoichi	Fukuoka 3
*Okazaki, Ken	Kanagawa 1
Sasaki, Tōgo	Miyagi 2

Socialist Masses' Party (cont.)	Electoral District
*Satake, Haruki	Kōchi 2
*Sugiyama, Motojirō	Ōsaka 5
Sunaga, Kō	Gumma 1
*Suzuki, Bunji	Tōkyō 6
Tahara, Haruji	Fukuoka 4
Takahashi, Takeo	Hiroshima 1
*Taman, Kiyoomi	Ōsaka 1
*Tsukamoto, Jūzō	Ōsaka 3
*Yamasaki, Kenji	Shizuoka 2

Other Proletarian Candidates, Independent or Affiliated with a Local Party or Union: (11 candidates; 5 elected)	
*Katō, Kanjū (National Council; Labor-Farmer Proletarian Conference)	Tōkyō 5
*Koyama, Makoto (close to Socialist Masses' Party)	Nagano 2

THE 1936 DIET ELECTION (CONT.)

Other Proletarian Candidates (cont.)	Electoral District	Other Proletarian Candidates (cont.)	Electoral District
* Kuroda, Hisao (National Farmer; Okayama Proletarian Organizations Conference)	Okayama 1	Mitamura, Takeo (National Farmer)	Gifu 2
Maekawa, Shōichi (close to National Farmer)	Kagawa 1	Nagao, Tamotsu (Yū) (National Farmer)	Hyōgo 2
*Matsumoto, Jiichirō (National Leveling Society)	Fukuoka 1	Takeo, Hajime (Independent)	Chiba 2
Mikami, Joichi (Hiroshima Farmers' Club)	Hiroshima 2	*Tomiyoshi, Eiji (close to National Farmer)	Kagoshima 2
		Umezawa, Jisaku (Shiga Devoted Labor Democratic Federation)	Shiga

THE 1937 DIET ELECTION

Socialist Masses' Party: (66 candidates; 37 elected)	Electoral District	Socialist Masses' Party (cont.)	Electoral District
		*Kawamata, Seion	Akita 2
*Abe, Isoo	Tōkyō 2	*Kawamura, Yasutarō	Ōsaka 4
*Abe, Shigeo	Tōkyō 4	Kikuchi, Takeshi	Oita 1
Aki, Sakaru (Sakan)	Kōchi 1	*Kikuchi, Yōnosuke	Miyagi 1
*Asanuma, Inejirō	Tōkyō 3	Kinoshita, Gengo	Hokkaidō 2
*Asō, Hisashi	Tōkyō 5	Kojima (Ojima), Koichirō	Yamagata 2
Fujii, Shōsei	Nagasaki 2	*Kōno, Mitsu	Tōkyō 1
Furusawa, Hi (Akira)	Akita 1	*Kuroda, Hisao	Okayama 1
Furuya, Sadao	Yamanashi	Maeda, Einosuke	Hiroshima 2
Hayashida, Tetsuo	Ehime 2	*Maekawa, Shōichi	Kagawa 1
Inamura, Ryūichi	Niigata 2	*Matsumoto, Jiichirō (not strictly officially endorsed)	Fukuoka 1
*Inoue, Ryōji	Ōsaka 2	*Matsunaga, Yoshio	Saitama 1
*Ishiyama, Torakichi	Tochigi 1	*Miwa, Jusō	Tōkyō 5
Itō, Ushirō	Fukuoka 2	Miya (Mitani), Buntarō	Hiroshima 3
Iwabuchi, Kenjirō	Aomori 2	*Miyake, Shōichi	Niigata 3
*Kamei, Kanichirō	Fukuoka 2	Miyamura, Matahachi	Kumamoto 1
Kaneko, Kamekichi	Tochigi 2		
*Katayama, Tetsu	Kanagawa 2		
*Katō, Ryōzō	Gifu 3		
*Kawai, Giichi	Hyōgo 3		
*Kawakami, Jōtarō	Hyōgo 2		

THE 1937 DIET ELECTION (CONT.)

Socialist Masses' Party (cont.)	Electoral District
*Mizutani, Chōzaburō	Kyōto 1
*Nagae, Kazuo	Hyōgo 1
*Nakamura, Takaichi	Tōkyō 7
Nishimura, Eiichi	Ōsaka 6
Nishimura, Kikujirō	Aomori 1
*Nishio, Suehiro	Ōsaka 4
*Nomizo, Masaru (Katsu)	Nagano 3
Oda, Sakae (as second highest vote getter, became Diet member in April 1938 when something happened to incumbent)	Okinawa
*Okazaki, Ken	Kanagawa 1
Ōno, Takafuji	Shizuoka 2
Santoku, Iwao	Kagawa 2
Sasaki, Tōgo	Miyagi 2
*Satake, Haruki	Kōchi 2
Satake, Shinichi	Hiroshima 1
Shigei, Shikaji	Okayama 2
*Sugiyama, Motojirō	Ōsaka 5
*Sunaga, Kō	Gumma 1
*Suzuki, Bunji	Tōkyō 6
*Tahara, Haruji	Fukuoka 4
*Taman, Kiyoomi	Ōsaka 1
Tamura, Sadaichi	Yamaguchi 1

Socialist Masses' Party (cont.)	Electoral District
Tanahashi, Kotora	Nagano 4
Tanaka, Yoshio	Kyōto 2
*Tomiyoshi, Eiji	Kagoshima 2
*Tsukamoto, Jūzō	Ōsaka 3
Ueda, Otoichi	Mie 1
Watanabe, Mansaku (not officially endorsed)	Nagano 1
Watanabe, Sen	Wakayama 2
*Yamasaki, Kenji	Shizuoka 2
*Yonekubo, Mitsusuke (Manryō)	Hyōgo 2

Japan Proletarian Party:
(5 candidates; 1 elected)

*Katō, Kanjū	Tōkyō 5
Kuroda, Yasuji	Tōkyō 3
Miura, Aiji	Fukuoka 2
Suzuki, Mosaburō	Tōkyō 6
Tamai, Junji	Niigata 2

Local Proletarian Party
(1 candidate; 0 elected)

Yubara, Hikozō (Tottori Proletarian Organizations Conference)	Tottori

THE 1942 DIET ELECTION

Former Socio-Democrats: (15 candidates; 1 recommended; 2 elected)	Electoral District
Hara, Hyō (Hyōnosuke)	Tōkyō 2
Inoue, Ryōji	Ōsaka 2
Itō, Ushirō	Fukuoka 2
Kamei, Kanichirō	Tōkyō 5

Former Socio-Democrats (cont.)	Electoral District
Kanemasa, Yonekichi	Ōsaka 3
Katayama, Tetsu	Kanagawa 2
Kawamura, Yasutarō	Ōsaka 4
Maeda, Einosuke	Hiroshima 2
Matsunaga, Yoshio	Saitama 1
Matsuoka, Komakichi	Tōkyō 5

THE 1942 DIET ELECTION (CONT.)

Former Socio-Democrats (cont.)	Electoral District
*Nishio, Suehiro	Ōsaka 4
Satake, Haruki	Kōchi 2
*Taman, Kiyoomi (recommended)	Ōsaka 1
Ujihara, Ichirō	Kōchi 2
Yonekubo, Mitsusuke (Manryō)	Hyōgo 2

Former Japan-Laborites: (13 candidates; 3 recommended; 6 elected)

Dōmoto, Tamehiro	Fukuoka 2
Katō, Ryōzō	Gifu 3
*Kawakami, Jōtarō (recommended)	Hyōgo 1
*Kawamata, Seion	Akita 2
*Kōno, Mitsu	Tōkyō 1
*Miyake, Shōichi	Niigata 3
Nagae, Kazuo	Hyōgo 1
*Sakamoto, Masaru (recommended)	Hyōgo 2
*Sugiyama, Motojirō (recommended)	Ōsaka 5
Sunaga, Kō	Gumma 1
Tahara, Haruji	Fukuoka 4
Tsunada, Tsunakichi	Tōkyō 3
Yao, Kisaburō	Shiga

Other former proletarian party leaders: (32 candidates; 4 recommended; 7 elected)

Furusawa, Hi (Akira)	Akita 1
Furuya, Sadao	Yamanashi
Hayashida, Tetsuo	Ehime 2
Ii, Seiichi	Niigata 2
*Imai, Yoshiyuki (Kakō) (recommended)	Hyōgo 1
Inada, Naomichi	Tottori 1

Other former proletarian party leaders (cont.)	Electoral District
Inamura, Ryūichi	Niigata 3
Ishikawa, Kyōichi	Kanagawa 1
Ishihara, Yoshiyuki	Okayama 1
*Izumi, Kunisaburō (recommended)	Iwate 2
Kanai, Yoshiji	Kanagawa 1
Kaneko, Masutarō	Tochigi 1
Kawashima, Kinji	Saitama 1
*Kikuchi, Yōnosuke (recommended)	Miyagi 1
Kinoshita, Gengo	Hokkaidō 2
Kumamoto, Torazō	Tōkyō 6
*Maekawa, Shōichi	Kagawa 1
Makoshi (Umakoshi), Ōsuke	Ehime 2
*Masaki, Kiyoshi	Hokkaidō 1
*Matsumoto, Jiichirō (recommended)	Fukuoka 1
Mizuno, Jitsurō	Aichi 1
*Mizutani, Chōzaburō	Kyōto 1
Nakamura, Takaichi	Tōkyō 7
Nakazawa, Benjirō	Saitama 2
Oda, Sakae	Okinawa
Santoku, Iwao	Kagawa 2
Shōji, Hikoo	Tottori 1
Tanaka, Yoshio	Kyōto 2
Tomiyoshi, Eiji	Kagoshima 2
Tsukamoto, Jūzō	Ōsaka 3
Watanabe, Mansaku	Nagano 1
Yubara, Hikozō	Tottori

Former proletarian leaders who became national socialists: (14 candidates; 0 recommended; 4 elected)

Akamatsu, Katsumaro	Hokkaidō 4
Aki, Sakaru (Sakan) (former Japan-Laborite)	Kōchi 1
Fujiwara, Shigetarō	Nagasaki 2

THE 1942 DIET ELECTION (CONT.)

Former proletarian leaders who became national socialists (cont.)	*Electoral District*	*Former proletarian leaders who became national socialists (cont.)*	*Electoral District*
*Hirano, Rikizō	Yamanashi	Farmer Party)	Hyōgo 2
Inatomi, Takato (Ryōjin) (former Socio-Democrat)	Fukuoka 3	Ōhashi, Harufusa (originally Labor Farmer Party)	Ōsaka 4
Kanda, Hyōzō (originally Labor Farmer Party)	Kyōto 1	Shinoda, Yasohachi (originally New Labor Farmer Party)	Tōkyō 5
Koike, Shirō (former Socio-Democrat)	Fukuoka 4	Yamamoto, Kamejirō (former Socio-Democrat)	Kagoshima 3
*Mitamura, Takeo (Eastern Association)	Gifu 2	*Yamasaki, Tsunekichi (originally Labor Farmer Party	Aichi 1
Miyazaki, Ryūsuke (Eastern Association)	Tōkyō 6	*Yoshida, Kenichi (former Japan-Laborite)	Hyōgo 3
Nagao, Tamotsu (Yū) (originally Labor			

Index

Index includes Romanizations of Japanese names for most organizations and laws mentioned in the text, as well as entries under English names. Author entries include page reference to only the *first* appearance of each work, where full bibliographical citation appears.

Italicized page numbers refer to tabular material.